THE BLACK LAWS IN THE OLD NORTHWEST

Recent Titles in
Contributions in Afro-American and African Studies

From Exclusion to Inclusion: The Long Struggle for African American Political Power
Ralph C. Gomes and Linda Faye Williams, editors

Mental and Social Disorder in Sub-Saharan Africa: The Case of Sierra Leone, 1787-1900
Leland V. Bell

The Racial Problem in the Works of Richard Wright and James Baldwin
Jean-François Gounard; Joseph J. Rodgers, Jr., translator

Renaissance Man from Louisiana: A Biography of Arna Wendell Bontemps
Kirkland C. Jones

A Struggle Worthy of Note: The Engineering and Technological Education of Black Americans
David E. Wharton

African American Soldiers in the National Guard: Recruitment and Deployment During Peacetime and War
Charles Johnson, Jr.

Religion and Suicide in the African-American Community
Kevin E. Early

State Against Development: The Experience of Post-1965 Zaire
Mondonga M. Mokoli

Dusky Maidens: The Odyssey of the Early Black Dramatic Actress
Jo A. Tanner

Language and Literature in the African American Imagination
Carol Aisha Blackshire-Belay, editor

Visible Ellison: A Study of Ralph Ellison's Fiction
Edith Schor

The Early Black Press in America, 1827 to 1860
Frankie Hutton

THE BLACK LAWS IN THE OLD NORTHWEST

A DOCUMENTARY HISTORY

STEPHEN MIDDLETON

FOREWORD BY LINDA McMURRY

Contributions in Afro-American and African Studies,
Number 152

Greenwood Press
Westport, Connecticut • London

Library of Congress Cataloging-in-Publication Data

Middleton, Stephen.
The Black laws in the Old Northwest : a documentary history / Stephen Middleton ; foreword by Linda McMurry.
p. cm.—(Contributions in Afro-American and African studies, ISSN 0069-9624 ; no. 152)
Includes bibliographical references.
ISBN 0-313-28016-9 (alk. paper)
1. Afro-Americans—Legal status, laws, etc.—Northwest, Old—History—19th century. 2. Race discrimination—Law and legislation—Northwest, Old—History—19th century. 3. Slavery—United States—Legal status of slaves in free states. I. Title. II. Series.
KF4757.M48 1993
346.7301'3—dc20
[347.30613] 91-47063

British Library Cataloguing in Publication Data is available.

Library of Congress Catalog Card Number: 91-47063
ISBN: 0-313-28016-9
ISSN: 0069-9624

First published in 1993

Greenwood Press, 88 Post Road West, Westport, CT 06881
An imprint of Greenwood Publishing Group, Inc.

Printed in the United States of America

The paper used in this book complies with the Permanent Paper Standard issued by the National Information Standards Organization (Z39.48-1984).

P

In order to keep this title in print and available to the academic community, this edition was produced using digital reprint technology in a relatively short print run. This would not have been attainable using traditional methods. Although the cover has been changed from its original appearance, the text remains the same and all materials and methods used still conform to the highest book-making standards.

In Memory of my father

Lewis Middleton, Sr.
(1920-1978)

and

my brother

Julius "Buck" Middleton
(1949-1992)

Contents

Foreword

Gunnar Myrdal chose the title An American Dilemma for his classic 1944 study of race relations in the United States. In it he stressed the conflict between American ideals and the nation's treatment of African Americans. He wrote eloquently of the white response:

> To the great majority of white Americans the Negro problem has distinctly negative connotations. It suggests something difficult to settle and equally difficult to leave alone. It is embarrassing. It makes for moral uneasiness. The very presence of the Negro in America; his fate in this country through slavery, Civil War and Reconstruction; his recent career and his present status; his accommodation; his protest and his aspiration; in fact his entire biological, historical and social existence as a participant American represent to the ordinary man in the North as well as in the South an anomaly in the very structure of American society. To many, this takes on the proportion of a menace--biological, economic, social, cultural, and, at times, political. This anxiety may be mingled with a feeling of individual and collective guilt. A few see the problem as a challenge to statesmanship. To all it is trouble.

Later scholars have questioned whether there was a dilemma. Some have claimed that few white Americans have ever been tormented by the contradictions. Historian Nathan Huggins has declared that at the time of America's birth, with its midwife of natural rights, "the dilemma should have been numbing, but it did not trouble the Founding Father's enough to confront it." Huggins does agree that African Americans have been considered anomalies. To him, western expansion merely continued an established pattern of duality regarding African Americans.

Thus, the two paths of American community development regarding race, stemming from the earliest times in the seventeenth century, were to extend themselves throughout the continent. Blacks would be suitable instruments of development for the wealth of white men. Or they would be unwelcome, excluded as far as that might be possible. Either way, blacks would be outside the community.

This compilation of black codes in the five states making up the Old Northwest territory illustrates how the clash of ideals and realities found expression in the law--mainly by defining African Americans as "outside the community." The issue of slavery in the area was apparently settled by law, with the Northwest Ordinance prohibiting it. Yet the law and reality did not always coincide. Territorial Governor Arthur St. Clair effectively subverted the law. Residents in the areas that became Illinois and Indiana actually tried to get the prohibition against slavery legally removed and, failing that, instituted a disguised slavery through a perversion of indentured servitude for African Americans. Only after the failure to make African Americans "suitable instruments of development for the wealth of white men" did those new states follow the path of exclusion favored by white Ohioans.

The clash of ideals is clearly seen in the state constitutions that included declaration's of rights, but then had to reconcile the presence of African Americans, who were clearly perceived as belonging outside the community. Most whites would probably have preferred to ignore the contradictions, but the courts often forced consideration. The black codes that emerged reflected the need to reconcile law and prejudice. The extent of that need varied. In Michigan and Wisconsin small black populations lessened the urgency to define the status of African Americans as outside the community, resulting in fewer openly discriminatory laws.

The documents in this compilation illustrate the complexity of the white response to slavery. Laws against kidnapping coexisted with laws enabling slave owners to recapture runaway slaves. True abolitionist sentiment coexisted with a free-soil mentally aimed primarily at keeping the region "white." People with either motivation united uneasily to pass resolutions against the expansion of slavery in the late antebellum period. The widespread support of colonization indicates that, regardless of motivation, few people could visualize a true community that was both black and white.

The large number of laws and court cases regarding the status of African Americans in these "free" states indicates that Myrdal's "dilemma" was indeed "American" and not merely Southern. Slavery influenced white actions both below and above the Mason-Dixon Line. That the legal end of slavery had profound consequences even where it did not exist is seen in the legal changes that occurred in the Northwest in the wake of the Civil War.

The actions in courtrooms, constitutional conventions, and legislative bodies both mirrored and shaped white Americans' attempts to determine the status of African Americans under changing conditions. This book clearly demonstrates that the law is a valuable prism for refracting the white response to color.

Linda McMurry
North Carolina State University

Preface

It has been more than a century since the emancipation of African Americans from slavery and a few decades since the civil rights revolution in the United States. However, at the publication of this volume, sporadic episodes of violence between black and white Americans are far too common. Misunderstanding between these Americans covers everything from affirmative action to public education. Hostilities between these races are not always expressed violently. According to newspaper accounts, the exclusion of black children from "private" swimming pools and the exclusion of blacks from neighborhood country clubs (even when they live in the community where the club is located) is far too common. Why has racial discrimination persisted in the United States so long after emancipation? I don't know. Compiling documents for this book makes it clear that a "free zone" does not mean the absence of racial prejudice.

The Northwest Territory, under the Ordinance of 1787, was such a free jurisdiction. The ordinance's sixth article declared slavery illegal, and presumably, entitled African Americans to citizenship status. In no way did the ordinance subjugate blacks already living in the Old Northwest. Yet clever white residents found ingenious ways to violate America's first antislavery and civil rights document.

When states formed in the Northwest Territory adopted "black laws," they too abridged the legal rights of black people. This is the subject of this volume, and it is a reminder to Americans of all races that the United States inherited a racial policy that still haunts our country. It is ironic that this racist creed also arose in the Old Northwest, a region supposedly dedicated to "freedom."

The black laws were state statutes, dedicated to a policy of racial discrimination. States in the Old Northwest adopted them to subordinate a racial group solely because of their color. The states organized in the Old Northwest, except Wisconsin, legalized racial oppression. Although Wisconsin did not officially adopt "black laws," its citizens were not humanitarians or racial reformers.

Wisconsin's racial code maintained the policy of white supremacy, especially in intimate contact between the races. These northwestern states had one positive social and legal feature: they prohibited slavery. Their racial policies and statutes, however, closely mirrored legislation adopted by slave states. The black laws, enacted by states in the Old Northwest, which have never been presented in book form, are chronicled in this volume.

Now for a word about the organization of this work. First, let me acknowledge that there is nothing scientific about the arrangement of the documents herein. I have tried to group related documents into what I call document sets. This was not always easy, and, in a few instances, I have stretched subjects in order to place them. I am sure readers will have their own ideas regarding some of my choices.

I have also tried to keep my commentary to a minimum. The documents included here are overwhelming, and speak for themselves. Allowing readers to see and form opinions about the documents they read is one goal in a documentary collection. I have been guided by this consideration in the arrangement of this book.

I have added commentary, however. Each part of the book is preceded by introductory remarks, in which I try to acquaint readers with each state in the Old Northwest. It is hoped that this will enable readers to place the documents in perspective. Second, I have also provided a short introduction to each document set. Once again, I have tried not to summarize the documents; rather, I have emphasized some of the themes they addressed and the problems that confronted African Americans in that area. Finally, I have added an extensive, but select, table of annotated cases and a list of suggested readings. The cases will provide readers with a perspective on the adjudication of race, slavery, and civil rights in the Old Northwest.

Acknowledgments

Writing a book or, as in this case, compiling documents, can sometimes be a lonely undertaking. Encouragement from friends and scholars is vital. I was fortunate enough to have friends and colleagues who inspired me during some lonely times. It is impossible to identify each person by name, but I salute them all here. I especially appreciate my colleagues in the History Department at North Carolina State University who frequently inquired about my progress. They provided helpful suggestions about choosing a publisher for this book. I also appreciate encouragement from Burton F. Beers, a generous scholar, and the comments of Alexander DeGrand and Richard Slatta. The members of the department's occasional seminar on African-American/Southern history--James Crisp, William Harris, Walter Jackson, Linda McMurry, Gail O'Brien, John David Smith, Pamela Tyler, and Joanne Woodard--also read and commented on parts of this manuscript.

I have been aided by the works of many scholars, and inspired by their interest and questions about my pursuits. Paul Finkelman's books have steered me to the Old Northwest and the black laws. Thomas D. Morris answered my query during the early stages of this project and assured me that it was worthwhile: "Such collections are an invaluable source for scholars precisely because much of the documentary information is so deeply buried that it is nearly inaccessible."

Helpful librarians at the Library of Congress, Ohio Historical Society, Western Reserve Historical Society, North Carolina Supreme Court Library, Duke University Law School, and the University of North Carolina Law School in Chapel Hill made my task easier. Consultants in the Humanities Lab at North Carolina State University also provided technical support. They converted my Microsoft Word files to the word processing program used by the History Department. I owe special thanks to Sharon Darden who typed the original draft of this manuscript under less than ideal conditions. She read badly copied pages, small type, and my handwritten notes with no complaints. I am also grateful to Kathy Anderson who upon joining the department temporarily plunged into this project enthusiastically. And I am grateful for the help of June Bowles who prepared the final draft of this monograph. Also, Donna Weeks, who has a special talent for pagination, completed the camera ready copy of the work. The editors at Greenwood Press assigned to me were terrific. Each editor, especially Catherine A. Lyons, rendered services beyond the call of duty. And thanks to everyone else who read the whole or any part of the manuscript. I could not have reached my goal without them.

I also want to thank my family for their patience and support. Earline, my wife, and our children, Stephen, Eric, and Jessica, were superb. I wish I could promise them that this is my last project.

Ordinance of 1787, Article 6

There shall be neither slavery nor involuntary servitude in the said territory, otherwise than in the punishment of crimes, whereof the party shall have been duly convicted: *Provided always*, That any person escaping into the same, from who labor or service is lawfully claimed in any one of the original States, such fugitive may be lawfully reclaimed, and conveyed to the person claiming his or her labor or service as aforesaid.

Be it ordained by the authority aforesaid, That the resolutions of the 23d of April, 1784, relative to the subject of this ordinance, be, and the same are hereby, repealed, and declared null and void.

Done by the United States, in Congress assembled, the 13th day of July in the year of our Lord 1787, and their sovereignty and independence the twelfth.

Introduction

The United States acquired the Northwest Territory in 1781 in a compromise between large states and small states over ratification of the Articles of Confederation. A few of the original colonies had acquired lands in the West after adoption of the Declaration of Independence. Their holdings stimulated debate between small landless states and large landholding states. Small states feared that large states with western lands might lord over them. Landless states--Delaware, Maryland, New Jersey, Pennsylvania, and Rhode Island--wanted the entire territory to become common land. The exigency of the situation--union or disunion--persuaded landholding states to turn their claims over to the federal government by 1781. The United States under the Articles of Confederation soon faced other hurdles in the West: governance, settlement, and uprisings by Native Americans. The United States under the Constitution later faced the problem of African slavery.[1]

For African Americans, life in the United States has been a long journey from slavery to freedom. The year 1619 marked their official arrival in Virginia, the first permanent English colony in North America. Traders from the Dutch Republic, seventeenth-century masters of the high seas, exchanged in Virginia about twenty enslaved Africans for supplies. John Rolfe observed their arrival. "About the latter end of August, a Dutch man of Warr of the burden of a 160 tunes arrived at Point-Comfort . . . . He brought not any thing but [twenty] and odd Negroes, [which] the Governor and Cape Marchant bought for victual."[2] Africans did not become slaves in Virginia immediately, but by 1660 they sank into perpetual slavery.

While the English settled the Atlantic Coast, France penetrated the Northwest Territory. The Old Northwest which lay north and west of the Ohio River included the present-day states of Ohio, Indiana, Illinois, Michigan, and parts of Wisconsin. French traders brought African slavery to the area. Philip Francis Renault established a settlement in 1719 with about 500 enslaved Africans. Hence, the African presence in the Old Northwest predated significant English settlement there. Africans worked in lead and salt mines and at other mineral reserves throughout the region. French occupation of the Old Northwest was negligible, unlike their English neighbors. The French primarily wanted to establish trade networks with the Indians; however, their domination of the Northwest ended in 1763 when the victorious English virtually eliminated France's commercial enterprise in North America.[3]

Historians have debated extensively the enslavement of Africans in America. They have quarreled over whether slavery caused racial discrimination or if racial prejudice precipitated slavery. Carl Degler and Oscar and Mary Handlin advanced the best-known arguments on the origins of slavery. The Handlin thesis argues that slavery developed in a world of unfreedom. Driven by the economic imperatives of the times, European landowners exploited white indentured servants, Native Americans, and Africans. Africans proved to be their most reliable source of labor. After enslaving Africans, the Handlins argue, slave holders created a litany of rationales to justify the practice. Hence, slavery produced race prejudice. In contrast, Degler argues that whites embraced a long-standing color prejudice. Black Africans, he concludes, faced discrimination from whites from the start in colonial America.[4]

Neither the Handlins nor Degler is completely wrong. The English had demonstrated their racism in their treatment of Native Americans, Africans in the West Indies, and by their participation in the African slave trade. Their attitudes regarding Africans went far beyond mere cultural ethnocentrism. Racism undoubtedly influenced the development of slavery in North America, but slavery also took on a life of its own. Whites and blacks, nurtured in a society that approved slavery, acquired by osmosis the cultural mores of the community in which they live. Slavery, once established, probably strengthened the racism of whites. It is unthinkable that slavery and racism were other than companions--twins--in the debasement of Africans.

This debate notwithstanding, by the eighteenth century, each of the thirteen colonies had adopted slavery. A few colonies began haltingly, however. In 1641, lawmakers in colonial Massachusetts passed the Body of Liberties, which had approved slavery. Only persons who were captured in just wars or sold to the settlers could legally be enslaved. Rhode Island adopted its statutory provision in 1652, declaring "that no black mankind or white being forced by covenant, bond or otherwise, [was] to serve any man or his assignees longer than ten years." At first Georgia abolished slavery entirely, although for reasons other than abolitionism. The founders organized

Georgia in order to transform indigent whites into self-supporting citizens. They believed that slavery would foster dependence, not independence and industry. Obviously, settlers in these colonies experienced ambivalence toward slavery. Other colonies, however, adopted slavery without reservations. The proprietors in Carolina, for example, resorted to slavery in order to populate the colony quickly. In its Fundamental Constitution, Carolina provided masters absolute authority over enslaved Africans. The proprietors also provided headrights to planters who brought over servants and slaves. Slavery, therefore, developed in Carolina almost from the inception of the colony.[5] Virginia and Maryland were clearly leaders in the enslavement of Africans, and settlers there approved slavery in their laws by 1663. Their legislatures did not create slavery, however. Community approval preceded statutory law governing slavery.

The American Revolution produced opportunities for freedom. For example, Quakers manumitted their slaves during the seventeenth century and closed their sanctuaries to Friends who practiced slavery. Northern colonies, perhaps because they did not consider slavery vital to their economic survival, provided for the gradual emancipation of enslaved African Americans. Massachusetts led the way and provided protection for abused Africans. In *Commonwealth v. Jennison* (1783) the Supreme Court ruled that Massachusetts did not recognize slavery in its constitution or laws. Other Northern states took similar steps to abolish slavery. By the turn of the century, the North had become a liberated zone. As A. Leon Higginbotham puts it, the gradual abolition policy of the North "was a significant changing of the tide toward ultimate freedom for blacks." For all of its failings, at least for Africans, the American Revolution was still one step toward their liberation.[6]

Developments after the revolution manifested unsettled questions. Congress addressed the status of African Americans in the Old Northwest in 1784. Thomas Jefferson, along with other whites, wanted to close the territory to slavery. Undoubtedly, they had mixed reasons. Some had genuine concerns for the liberation of enslaved African Americans; others had political and economic motives. Jefferson, the leading opponent of slavery in the Old Northwest, embraced the latter perspective. He expressed fears of sectional rivalry as early as 1783. "If a Northern state be first laid off on the [Great] lakes it will add a vote to the Northern scale; if on the Ohio it will add one to the Southern." Others feared that slave labor might discourage immigration from the East. By the mid-1780s, there were strong feelings against slavery in the Old Northwest.[7]

Jefferson headed the 1784 Congressional Committee on western lands to plan a government for the territory. When slavery came up during the debates, Jefferson proposed that Congress open the region to slavery until 1800. He did not give any indication whether he favored complete abolition in 1800 or adoption of a gradual emancipation plan. Jefferson had been familiar with gradual emancipation and favored applying that program in the region. He primarily wanted to stifle sectional rivalry. His proposal to ultimately ban slavery in the region was no more than a strategy to ease sectional rivalry. At any rate, Southern members of the Congressional Committee, except Jefferson, unanimously voted against the proposal.[8]

When the topic of African slavery surfaced at a committee meeting in 1785, Rufus King, delegate from Massachusetts, proposed its outright abolition: "[T]here shall be neither slavery nor voluntary servitude in any of the states, described in the resolve of Congress April, 1784 [*sic*], otherwise than in punishment of crimes."[9] King had been accustomed to gradual emancipation from his experience in Massachusetts. The Congressional Committee was not intrigued, however, and defeated his proposal.

When the committee took up the question again in 1787, there had already been strong sentiments for prohibiting slavery in the Old Northwest. In addition to King, David Howell of Rhode Island and other members of the Congressional Committee who were from the North, favored a gradual abolition policy. It is reasonable to assume that they favored this plan to facilitate emancipation. Slavery in the Southwest territory concerned Southern members on the committee. Squatters from Virginia and the Carolinas had already settled in the Southwest, in the unorganized territory of Kentucky and Tennessee. But Jefferson and King had made no distinction between Northwest and Southwest territories. Their proposal to ban slavery would have applied equally to both regions.

King and his colleagues did not recognize that southern members on their committee were worried about the prospect that a free territory might liberate slaves. They had been familiar with *Somerset v. Stuart* (1772) and the ruling of English judge Lord Mansfield.[10] Mansfield had declared that slavery could only exist in England by positive law. When a master carried a slave into a free jurisdiction, therefore, the enslaved person would become free automatically. Southerners feared that a free territory might adopt this creed and liberate runaway slaves or those visiting with slave holders could be freed by this doctrine. Consequently, they wanted greater security for slavery. In a compromise, they limited their quest for expansion to the Southwest, a decision they later regretted during the nineteenth-century slavery controversy.

When the Congressional Committee took up slavery in 1787, only two issues concerned Southern delegates: (1) the status of blacks in the Southwest Territory, and (2) the authority of free jurisdictions over slaves. Adoption of a policy of gradual emancipation concerned Northern members on the committee. Thus, the sixth article of the Ordinance of 1787 pleased both groups. The first clause in the ordinance settled the gradual emancipation issue: "*There shall be neither slavery nor involuntary servitude in the [Northwest] Territory* [author's emphasis]."[11] In addition to gradual emancipation underway in the North, the United States had gone on record to favor emancipation in the general Union.

Southern delegates also obtained legal assurance on reclamation: "*Provided always, That any person escaping into the same, from whom labor or service is lawfully claimed in any one of the original States, such fugitive may be lawfully reclaimed, and conveyed to the person claiming his or her labor or service as aforesaid* [author's emphasis]."[12] Additionally, the prohibition against slavery applied to the Old Northwest only. With these compromises, the Ordinance of 1787 passed the Congressional Committee almost unanimously. Southern members voted solidly in favor of the clause. Only Abraham Yates, delegate from New York, voted against it. Daniel Webster, who became a nineteenth-century nationalist, aptly summed up the compromise: The sixth article of ordinance "applies equally to both [North and South] neither party has lost or gained."[13]

Scholars have been of two minds about the sixth article of ordinance. Neither school of thought is completely wrong. Some historians whom I call revisionists criticize Article 6 in the Ordinance of 1787. Paul Finkelman and Peter Onuf, leading revisionist scholars, argue that adoption of the article was coincidental, ambiguous, and did little to immediately affect slavery in the region. Other scholars disagree. Don E. Fehrenbacher and other traditionalists describe Article 6 as "plain language."[14] The themes precipitating this debate include the language of the clause, its operation in the territory, and the reality of bondage for most African Americans. This dispute notwithstanding, it is reasonable for historians to approach the Ordinance of 1787 as an antislavery document.

Contemporaries of the Ordinance acted to settle the slavery debate for various reasons. The ideals of the revolution stimulated some of them to oppose slavery and support at least a gradual emancipation policy. There can be little doubt that whites, including John Dickinson, John Jay, and Benjamin Franklin, actively opposed slavery. Dickinson prayed that Congress establish a government dedicated to freedom in the Old Northwest. He considered slavery costly, dangerous, and cruel.[15]

Article 6 intimidated some slave holders immediately. Some of them considered it an antislavery device, designed to liberate enslaved blacks. A farmer traveling through Illinois aptly summarized their sentiments: "Well, sir, your soil is fertile, but a man can't own niggers her, God-durn ye [*sic*]."[16] Slave holders had few illusions about Article 6. Soon after its adoption many fled into Spanish territories to preserve slavery. Some, like Edward Tiffin and Thomas Worthington, emancipated their slaves when they arrived in the Old Northwest, while others put up a fight to preserve their way of life by appealing to federal officers to modify the Article 6.

For example, slave holders sought assurance from government officers that the ordinance would not emancipate slaves already in the territory. Bartholomew Tardiveau carried their concerns to the President of the United States and to Congress where he applied a strict interpretation to the ordinance. He explained that Article 6 applied to slaves brought into the territory after 1787, an interpretation consistent with the gradual emancipation policy formulated by the Northern states. For in the North, the states did not do away with slavery immediately. They made plans for its ultimate demise. The federal government ignored Tardiveau, however. As historian Eugene H. Berwanger puts it, "No official statement was made."[17]

Tardiveau then turned to Governor St. Clair for help. In 1789, he asked St. Clair to endorse his interpretation of Article 6. In addition to Tardiveau's argument that Article 6 was prospective, he added that slavery was vital to economic development in the western territory. Enforcement of Article 6, Tardiveau argued, "would deprive a considerable number of citizens of their property acquired and enjoyed long before they were under the dominion of the United States."[18] He concluded that Article 6 could only be considered ex post facto law.

In fact, the threat to freedom in the Old Northwest did not originate with the ordinance itself; rather, political leaders in the territory emasculated America's first antislavery provision. An examination of the administration of territorial Governor Arthur St. Clair will illustrate the true source for the survival of slavery in the region.

Arthur St. Clair was an opportunist who had ambitions for high office in the new Republic. He had extensive political experience. He had been a magistrate in Pennsylvania before the revolution and had served as president of the congress. He accepted the appointment of territorial governor thinking it might lead to higher office. St. Clair was also a slave holder who continued to purchase slaves after 1787. In 1788, for example, he bought several Africans from Thomas Gailbreath, and held them in bondage in the Northwest Territory. It is not surprising that slave holders in the Old Northwest found him sympathetic to slavery.

St. Clair obtained little guidance on the status of Africans in the Northwest from President George Washington or Congress. Consequently, he developed his own interpretation of Article 6. St. Clair considered retrospective laws unjust; hence, he considered the slavery provision in the Ordinance of 1787 a prospective law. He doubted that Congress would have adopted a provision to deprive white Americans of their property without just compensation, so he upheld French and English statutes which had provided for slavery. It is imperative that scholars see his ruling as the opinion of Arthur St. Clair, territorial governor and slave holder.

Under St. Clair's construction of Article 6, Congress had adopted a gradual emancipation policy. Only slaves brought into the territory after 1787 were freed automatically. St. Clair supported this approach to emancipation. After all, Northern states had pursued gradual emancipation since 1783. His decree on the Article 6 was a concession that Congress could determine the future of slavery in the Old Northwest. This interpretation of American law proved devastating to African Americans. St. Clair's endorsement of slavery gave tacit approval to racial discrimination in future states organized in the

Old Northwest. As Fehrenbacher puts it, "The head start given to antislavery in the west was soon offset in several ways."[19] The reticence of the federal government and St. Clair's interpretation of the ordinance produced a political climate favorable for the black laws.

Although the majority of white Americans in the Northwest never owned slaves, the enslavement of Africans reinforced the color prejudice of whites. Slavery made racial discrimination inevitable. The American legal culture did not recognize Africans as Americans who had a natural right to life, liberty, and property. The Ordinance of 1787 made such an interpretation possible. Although a few black males enjoyed suffrage until the turn of the century, all prospects for liberty to African Americans disappeared as whites matured in a culture that recognized blacks as slaves.[20] It was only natural that in each state formed from the Old Northwest the political systems did not regard African peoples favorably.

The documents that follow illustrate the development of the black laws, thereby providing a documentary history of racial discrimination in the Old Northwest. They show that the states formed from the region denied African Americans suffrage, public education, benefits of welfare, testimony against a white, freedom to marry a white, and imposed restrictions on militia service, immigration, and employment. By enacting discriminatory statutes, white lawmakers intended to reserve their states for whites only. They went to great lengths to make blacks unwelcomed in their respective states. Yet the African-American population boomed throughout the region in spite of the laws. African Americans considered racial discrimination more tolerable than slavery.

In time, African Americans and their allies challenged the legal policy of states in the Northwest. Persons of mixed ancestry first won consideration for civil rights in the courts. Judges developed a visible admixture rule, declaring that persons who "looked white" should receive the privileges of white people. Next, African Americans tried to desegregate common schools, but legislatures rewarded them with a segregated school system. Once the states endorsed educational opportunities for blacks, a few integrated schools emerged in areas where too few blacks lived to form a separate school. By the end of the 1870s, each state adopted ineffective civil rights laws, which disappeared under the "separate but equal" ruling of the Supreme Court in *Plessy v. Ferguson* (1896).

NOTES

1. For a discussion of the western land problem see Merril Jensen, *The Articles of Confederation: An Interpretation of the Social-Constitutional History of the American Revolution 1774-1781* (Madison: University of Wisconsin Press, 1976).

2. Quoted in *A Documentary History of Slavery in North America*, edited by Willie Lee Rose (New York: Oxford University Press, 1976), pp. 15-16; for a discussion on the development of slavery during the Colonial Period see A. Leon Higginbotham, Jr., *In the Matter of Color; Race and the American Legal Process: The Colonial Period* (New York: Oxford University Press, 1978).

3. John C. Hurd, *The Law of Freedom and Bondage in the United States* (New York: Negro University's Press, 1968), p. 112; Carter G. Woodson, *A Century of Negro Migration* (New York: Russell and Russell, 1969), pp. 5-6; Fred Stephen Crum, "Edward Coles with Special Reference to His Influence Against Slavery in the Northwest," Master's thesis, Cornell University, 1893, p. 34.

4. Carl Degler, "Slavery and the Genesis of American Race Prejudice," *Comparative Studies in Society and History* 2 (October 1959); Oscar and Mary F. Handlin, "Origins of the Southern Labor System," *William and Mary Quarterly* 7 (January 1950); also of interest are Winthrop D. Jordan, *White Over Black: American Attitudes Toward the Negro 1550-1812*, (Chapel Hill: University of North Carolina Press, 1968); Edmund Morgan, *American Slavery-American Freedom: The Ordeal of Colonial Virginia* (New York: W.W. Norton, 1975); T.H. Breen, "Creative Adaptions: Peoples and Culture," in *Colonial British America: Essays in the New History of the Early Modern Era*, edited by Jack P. Greene and J. R. Pole (Baltimore: Johns Hopkins University Press, 1988), pp. 195-232; John B. Boles, *Black Southerners 1619-1869* (Lexington: University Press of Kentucky, 1984), pp. 3-16.

5. William M. Wiecek, "The Statutory Law of Slavery and Race in the Thirteen Mainland Colonies of British America," *William and Mary Quarterly* 34 (1977); Higginbotham, *In the Matter of Color*.

6. Higginbotham, *In the Matter of Color*, p. 310; Philip S. Foner, *History of African Americans from Africa to the Emergence of the Cotton Kingdom* (Westport, CT.: Greenwood Press, 1975), pp. 279-291; for a discussion of judicial emancipation in Massachusetts see Leonard W. Levy, *The Law of the Commonwealth and Chief Justice Shaw* (Cambridge: Harvard University Press, 1957); Paul Finkelman, *An Imperfect Union: Slavery, Federalism, and Comity* (Chapel Hill: University of North Carolina Press, 1981).

7. Quoted in "Slavery and the Founding Fathers," by Staughton Lynd in *Black History: A Reappraisal*, edited by Melvin Drimmer (New York: Anchor Books, 1969), pp. 119-121; also see John Fiske, *The Critical Period of American History 1783-1789* (New York: Houghton Mifflin, 1916), pp. 196-198; Peter S. Onuf, *Statehood and Union: A History of the Northwest Ordinance* (Bloomington: Indiana University Press, 1987), p. 110.

8. Rufus King, *Ohio: First Fruits of the Ordinance of 1787* (New York: Houghton Mifflin, 1903), p. 179; William H. Smith, (ed.), *The St. Clair Papers* (New York: Books for Libraries Press, 1970), 1:603-607; Julian Boyd, (ed.), *The Papers of Thomas Jefferson* (New Jersey: Princeton University

Press, 1950), 1:130, 604, 608; Jordan, *White Over Black*, pp. 321-322; Crum, "Edward Coles," pp. 39-40, 44.

9. King, *Ohio: First Fruits*, p. 179.

10. For a discussion of the *Somerset* case see Higginbotham, *In the Matter of Color*, pp. 313-352; William M. Wiecek, The Sources of Antislavery Constitutionalism in America, (1760-1848), pp. 20-61.

11. Northwest Ordinance, Article 6, 1787.

12. Ibid; Robert M. Taylor, (ed.), *The Northwest Ordinance 1787: A Bicentennial Handbook* (Indianapolis: Indiana Historical Society, 1987), pp. 72-74.

13. David G. Allen, (ed.), *The Papers of Daniel Webster* (Hanover, New Hampshire: University Press of New England), 7:28-29.

14. Paul Finkelman, "Slavery and the Northwest Ordinance: A Study in Ambiguity," *Journal of the Early Republic* (1986); Onuf, *Statehood and Union*; Peter Onuf, *The Origins of the Federal Republic: Jurisdictional Controversies in the United States 1775-1787*, (Philadelphia: University of Pennsylvania Press, 1983).

15. Lynd, "Slavery and the Founding Fathers."

16. Quoted in Walter Havighurst, *The Heartland: Ohio, Indiana, Illinois* (New York: Harper and Row, 1962), p. 155.

17. Smith, *The St. Clair Papers*, pp. 2:117-119; Eugene H. Berwanger, *The Frontier Against Slavery; Western Anti-Negro Prejudice and the Slavery Extension Controversy* (Urbana: University of Illinois Press, 1967), p. 7.

18. Smith, *The St. Clair Papers*, 2:118.

19. Don E. Fehrenbacher, *The Dred Scott Case: Its Significance in American Law and Politics* (New York: Oxford University Press, 1978), p. 84.

20. For a comment on black electors, see *Reports: The Black Laws*, in this volume, p. 58.

Part One

OHIO,
March 1, 1803

As the first state formed from the Old Northwest, Ohio was the paradigm for that territory's racial policy, especially on the question of slavery and civil rights. During Ohio's territorial phase, whites in the region had expressed strong reservations regarding slavery. Yet early on Ohio attracted a diverse mix of immigrants. Since the 1780s, Southern whites from the states of Virginia and North and South Carolina had trickled into the territory. These immigrants were divided in their sentiments regarding race and slavery. Some slave holders had immigrated to Ohio because of its agricultural potential, and they had hoped to retain their "peculiar institution" there. Others, who believed that slave laborers performed work which would normally go to whites, fled the South to avoid competition with enslaved blacks. Neither faction matured above the racial prejudice produced under slavery. And Ohioans with Southern antecedents were united in their determination to deny civil rights to blacks.

Whites with Northern antecedents, immigrating from the states of Pennsylvania and Massachusetts, also settled in Buckeye country. These immigrants had witnessed the development of a gradual emancipation policy in the North during the American Revolution. Although they were not all humanitarians, they were favorably disposed to the idea of freedom for enslaved blacks. A number of Ohio leaders, including Jacob Burnet, considered the slavery question in economic terms. As an investor in corporate enterprises in Ohio, Burnet wanted to populate the state quickly. He believed Ohio's primary advantage lay in the pecuniary opportunities it afforded white immigrants. Consequently, Burnet and other stockholders were willing to do away with slavery in order to further white immigration to Ohio.

Of all the immigrating groups to the Ohio country, African Americans were the only group to seek refuge there. Certainly they anticipated greater economic opportunities in a free zone than they had experienced under slavery.

But they were mainly interested in achieving personal liberty. Neither Ohio nor the other states in the Old Northwest welcomed black refugees. Nonetheless, they consistently crossed the borders of the free states located on the fringe of slavery. When the Constitutional Convention met in Ohio in 1802, therefore, it could not ignore the African-American presence in the state. Although no African American attended the convention, race and slavery proved to be contentious issues for the delegates.

Neither of the competing factions at the convention held a decisive majority on questions involving slavery and civil rights. Furthermore, delegates who favored slavery were disadvantaged by the sixth article in the Ordinance of 1787. *De jure* slavery was never a real possibility in Ohio. Antislavery leaders also held a slight majority on questions involving race and slavery. They anticipated that their civil rights agenda would succeed. However, to complicate matters, there was legal precedent for designing a government that was neutral on the issue of race. The territorial government under the ordinance had not abridged the rights of African Americans. Considering the prohibition of slavery in Article 6, it is reasonable to assume that the civil rights provisions in the ordinance applied to people of color. Ohio lawmakers later contended that enfranchised African Americans voted in the election for delegates to the 1802 Constitutional Convention. That notwithstanding, the matter of race and slavery was still an open question in Ohio.

The convention journal also makes it clear that some delegates were steadfast in their commitment to enfranchise African Americans. A resolution to grant suffrage to resident blacks actually passed. This was not an overwhelming endorsement of black suffrage, however, and the small African-American population would not have exerted much influence. Moreover, once enfranchised blacks died or left the state suffrage would have automatically become the instrument of white males. On the other hand, even a conservative endorsement of black suffrage might have ultimately advanced the cause for all African Americans in Ohio. But we will never know for sure. Imbued by their success, zealous delegates pushed to enfranchise the descendants of black voters. This initiative spelled the demise of the black suffrage movement at the Ohio Constitutional Convention because it brought on strong resistance from conservative whites. To avoid further delay in constitution-making and possibly fracture the Convention, the delegates agreed to table all discussions on civil rights, to enfranchise white males, and prohibit slavery. Presumably, the status of African Americans remained an open question after 1802.

Ohioans elected a conservative band of politicians to the State's General Assembly in 1803, and, beginning in 1804, the legislature produced the black laws. First, the legislature attempted to discourage blacks from migrating to Ohio. Statutes in 1804 and 1807 required newcomers to show proof of freedom as a condition for settlement and employment. Moreover, the law compelled legal immigrants to register their names with county officials. The 1807 statute mandated that immigrating blacks post a $500 bond for their welfare and security and obtain the signatures of persons responsible for their welfare should they become destitute. The immigration laws also compelled residents to comply fully with the federal Fugitive Slave Law of 1793 and the state's black employment policy. A list of black laws followed, denying African Americans access to public schools, welfare programs, suffrage, militia service, jury service, or testimony against a white. By adopting these policies, Ohio demonstrated to its neighbors across the Ohio River that it would not offer refuge to runaway slaves.

There were other considerations behind adoption of the black laws in the Buckeye State. Ohio, like other states in the Old Northwest, offered freedom to its residents. Enslaved African Americans interpreted this interdict against slavery as an opportunity to achieve liberty. Should Ohio have granted liberty to slaves unilaterally, slave holders would have considered Ohio a threat to their way of life. Slave holders from as far away as Louisiana had frequently visited Cincinnati, the pork capital in the Northwest, to buy meat and supplies. They no doubt wondered if Ohio would emancipate enslaved blacks who accompanied them? If so, slave holders would surely retaliate by suspending trade with Ohio. The prospect of losing this trade and impairing the state's commercial relations with Southern masters induced Ohio lawmakers to adopt the policy of appeasement.

Furthermore, Ohio whites believed that blacks who used their state as a highway to Native American communities in the West might precipitate balkanization in their region. The fear that Ohio might be thrust into armed struggles over runaway slaves also contributed to the adoption of black laws. So did the fact that slave holders sometimes brought destitute, aged, and ill slaves to the Old Northwest to emancipate them. Ohioans had strong feelings against African Americans. Whites did not want to offer them refugee status, because of their race. Other than the absence of *de jure* slavery, therefore, Ohio offered few amenities to African Americans.

Although the immigration and residency laws appeared the most menacing, they were not. Evidence indicates that the legislature did not intend to enforce them, because there was no administrative agency to implement them. This was prohibitive legislation, designed to discourage immigrating blacks. The black laws were not merely nuisance legislation, however. They provided whites the legal basis to assail African-American communities at will. After the Cincinnati riot of 1829, for example, whites compelled large numbers of its black residents to leave the state. And when conservatives wanted to teach abolitionists a lesson, they culled from the records laws most whites had forgotten. In 1837 James G. Birney was singled out for allegedly violating the state's employment law. Birney was indicted and convicted because of his politics. On appeal, the Ohio Supreme Court, sensing the ethical questions surrounding selective enforcement of the statute, found a technicality to dismiss the case.

With the adoption of the black laws, the legal system in Ohio furthered its policy of accommodation. Runaway slaves were returned after a summary process, and sometimes free blacks were illegally removed by professional slave catchers. In the name of comity, the state protected slave holders who brought black servants to Ohio temporarily. Visiting masters retained absolute control over enslaved blacks. Masters in transit with slaves also obtained passage through Ohio. And the state permitted masters in the South to hire-out slaves in the state. Obviously, these concessions violated Ohio law, which had prohibited slavery. Until the 1840s, public sentiment, the legislature, and the courts favored accommodation.

A movement to reform Ohio's conservative racial policy surfaced in public education during the 1830s. The black law that had denied African Americans access to common schools faced challenges. Human nature had a great deal to do with the problems facing the school system. Interracial marriages and assaults on black females had produced a noticeable mulatto population in Ohio. Mulattoes sued when schools denied their children education solely on account of race. The Ohio Supreme Court defended their cause, ruling that a person with a preponderance of white blood should not be subject to the disabilities of being black. Next, African-American children entered private schools along with whites. The courts defended them again, as long as they paid tuition to the proprietor. Similar civil rights questions surfaced, including suffrage, jury service, and testimony. As the documents will show, the legislature attempted to settle this controversy by adopting the Visible Admixture Law.

The fugitive slave debate was most controversial in Ohio. Before the 1840s, there were few whites who defended a black claimed by a slave holder. In 1835, the Common Pleas Court in Hamilton County approved the removal of Frank, an African American who had escaped to Ohio and had resided there for several years. There were many reasons to question his removal. He was born in Pennsylvania while his mother was in transit to a life of slavery in Kentucky. His owner, who had promised to free Frank, had died by 1835 when his heir mysteriously appeared to claim Frank. The court ignored these questions and approved the rendition. The black laws produced an environment in which whites were numb to the problems facing African Americans.

Nevertheless, Ohio was transformed, albeit grudgingly. The legislature created a segregated school system for blacks during the 1840s, a concession that the black laws did not deprive them of the right to education. The Supreme Court proclaimed freedom to slaves whose masters brought them, or allowed them, to enter Ohio. In 1849, the legislature repealed a portion of the black laws. And, after the Civil War, Ohio adopted civil rights laws. The following documents describe the pattern of discrimination in Ohio.

Obviously, the legislature made Ohio a province for whites soon after statehood. Black residents had few rights enforceable in court. And, because of incessant agitation after the Civil War, the state agreed to civil rights reform. Although integration did not come until the twentieth century, the reforms of the Reconstruction era did a great deal to transform Ohio.

I

Declaration of Rights

When white Ohioans examined their first constitution, they considered the state "a bastion of liberty." Salmon Portland Chase in A Preliminary History of Ohio extolled the virtues of the state. Ohio never required property for voting. It protected personal and property rights. It assured a trial by jury, peaceable assembly, an educational system, and it prohibited slavery. Ohio, however, was no bastion of liberty for African Americans. Along with its declaration of rights, the state constitution subtly decreed Ohio to be a white state. Its constitutional policy limited all rights and privileges to whites, particularly white males. The following documents show this dual policy.

NUMBER 1

Constitution of Ohio, Article 8, 1802.

That the general, great, and essential principles of liberty and free government may be recognized, and forever unalterably established, we declare:

Section 1. That all men are born equally free and independent, and have certain natural inherent and inalienable rights; amongst which are enjoying and defending life and liberty, acquiring, possessing and protecting property, and pursuing and obtaining happiness and safety; and every free republican government, being founded on their sole authority, and organized for the great purpose of protecting their rights and liberties, and securing their independence: to effect these ends, they have at all times a complete power to alter, reform or abolish their government, whenever they may deem it necessary.

Section 2. There shall be neither slavery nor involuntary servitude in this State, otherwise than for the punishment of crimes, whereof the party shall have been duly convicted; nor shall any male person, arrived at the age of twenty-one years, or female person arrived at the age of eighteen years, be held to serve any person as a servant, under the pretence of indenture, or otherwise, unless such person shall enter into such indenture, while in a state of perfect freedom, and on condition of a bona fide consideration received, or to be received for their service, except as before excepted. Nor shall any indenture of any negro or mulatto, hereafter be executed out of the State, or if made in the State, where the term of service exceeds one year, be of the least validity, except those given in the case of apprenticeships.

Section 7. That all courts shall be open, and every person, for an injury done him in his lands, goods, person or reputation, shall have remedy by due course of law, and right and justice administered without denial or delay.

Section 8. That the right of trial by jury shall be inviolate.

Section 19. That the people shall have a right to assemble together, in a peaceable manner, to consult for their common good, to instruct their representatives, and to apply to the legislature for a redress of grievances.

Section 25. That no law shall be passed to prevent the poor in the several counties and townships within this State from an equal participation in the schools, academies, and colleges, and universities within the State, which are endowed, in whole or in part, from the revenue arising from donations made by the United States, for the support of schools and colleges; and the doors of the said schools, academies and universities shall be open for the reception of schools, students, and teachers, of every grade, without any distinction or preference whatever, contrary to the intent for which said donations were made.

* * *

Constitution of Ohio, Article 1, 1851

Section 6. There shall be no slavery in this State nor involuntary servitude, unless for the punishment of crime.

II

Enumeration and Election

As an enclave for "whites only" Ohio denied blacks suffrage rights and ignored them when deciding taxation and representation issues. The adjudication of race proved disastrous for the state. The courts decided that there were persons with African ancestry who, by virtue of their complexion, might be entitled to "the privileges of white." This was called the Visible Admixture Law, enacted by the legislature in 1859, which caused more problems than it solved. The matter was the subject of litigation and incessant debate. Ohioans could find no common ground between the code of racism in the state and its law of freedom.

NUMBER 1

Constitution of Ohio, Article 1, 1802.

Section 2. Within one year after the first meeting of the General Assembly, and within every subsequent term of four years, an enumeration of all white male inhabitants, above twenty-one years of age, shall be made in manner as shall be directed by law. The number of representatives shall, at the several periods of making such enumeration, be fixed by the Legislature and apportioned among the several counties, according to the number of white male inhabitants above twenty-one years of age in each, and shall never be less than twenty-four, nor greater than thirty-six, until the number of white male inhabitants, above twenty-one years of age, shall be twenty-two thousand; and after that event, at such a ratio that the whole number of representatives shall never be less than thirty-six, nor exceed seventy-two.

* * *

Constitution of Ohio, Article 4, 1802.

Section 1. In all elections, all white male inhabitants above the age of twenty-one years, having resided in the State one year next preceding the election, and who have paid or are charged with a State or county tax shall enjoy the right of an elector; but no person shall be entitled to vote, except in the county or district in which he shall actually reside at the time of the election.

NUMBER 2

Constitution of Ohio, Article 5, 1851.

Section 1. Every white male citizen of the United States, of the age of twenty-one years, who shall have been a resident of the State one year next preceding the election, and of the country, township, or ward, in which he resides, such time as may be provided by law, shall have the qualifications of an elector, and be entitled to vote at all elections.

NUMBER 3

An act to prescribe the duties of judges of election's in certain cases, and preserve the purity of elections. Approved April 2, 1859, Laws of Ohio.

Section 1. Be it enacted by the General Assembly of the State of Ohio, That the judge or judges of any election held under the authority of any of the laws of this state, shall reject the vote of any person offering to vote at such election, and claiming to be a white male citizen of the United States, whenever it shall appear to such judge or judges that the person so offering to vote has a distinct and visible admixture of African blood.

Section 2. Any judge or judges of any such election, who shall receive the vote of any person when such person has a distinct and visible admixture of African blood, shall, on conviction thereof, be fined in any sum not exceeding five hundred dollars, nor less than one hundred dollars, and imprisoned in the county jail of the proper county not more than six months, nor less than one month.

Section 3. Any person who shall procure, aid, assist, counsel or advise another to give his vote at any such election when such person has a distinct and visible admixture of African blood, shall, on conviction thereof be fined in any sum not exceeding five hundred dollars, nor less than fifty dollars and be imprisoned in the county jail of the property county not more than six months, nor less than one month.

Section 4. All prosecutions under this act shall be by indictment in the court of common pleas of the court of grand jury at each term of the court.

Section 5. This act shall take effect from and after its passage.

III

Militia Policy

The constitution of Ohio (1802) ignored the racial makeup of the state's militia, and presumably an African American could enlist in the organization. African Americans had a history of military service since the colonial period. Without a statute banning their enlistment in Ohio militia service was conceivable. The constitution of 1851 supported this trend and restricted militia service to white males. Historically, white Americans had always taken a "needs analysis" before enlisting blacks for military service. Ohio entered the Union during peacetime and there was little motivation to enroll blacks in the militia. As the following documents show, the legislature revised this loophole and made it illegal to employ blacks in the state militia. Whether influenced by prejudice or fear, the state ultimately barred African Americans from militia service.

NUMBER 1

An act to organize and discipline the militia. Approved 1803, Laws of Ohio.

Section 1. Be it enacted by the General Assembly of the State of Ohio, That each and every free, able-bodied, white male citizen of the state, who is or shall be of the age of eighteen and under the age of forty-five years, except as hereinafter excepted, shall severally and respectively be enrolled in the militia; by the captain or commanding officer of the company within whose bounds such citizens shall reside, within twenty days next after such residence.

NUMBER 2

Constitution of Ohio, Article 9, 1851.

Section 1. All white male citizens, residents of this State, being eighteen years of age, and under the age of forty-five years, shall be enrolled in the militia, and perform military duty, in such manner, not incompatible with the Constitution and laws of the United States, as may be prescribed by law.

NUMBER 3

An act to organize and discipline the militia and volunteer militia. Approved March 28, 1857, Laws of Ohio.

Section 1. Be it enacted by the General Assembly of the State of Ohio, That all able bodied, white male citizens resident of this state, being eighteen years of age, and under the age of forty-five years, excepting persons exempt by law, shall be enrolled in the militia, and perform military duty in such manner, not incompatible with the Constitution and laws of the United States, as hereinafter prescribed.

IV

Immigration and Residency

The immigration and residency policy was designed to preserve Ohio as a white state. In addition to discouraging black immigration, the legislature made it a crime for whites to employ blacks who did not provide proof of freedom and demonstrate the ability to pay for their welfare should they become destitute. The state closed its public relief programs to blacks. There were many motivations for these laws. Some whites feared a loss of trade with Southern planters and merchants if they sympathized with blacks. Others envisioned a mass exodus of Southern blacks to Ohio. And still others feared that Native American communities just west of the Buckeye State might extend refuge to blacks. Such an event might have produced armed struggle with slave holders who lived in Virginia and Kentucky on the fringes of Ohio, a free state. Most whites excluded blacks from the state because of race prejudice.

NUMBER 1

An act to regulate black and mulatto persons. Approved January 5, 1804, Laws of Ohio.

Section 1. Be it enacted by the General Assembly of the State of Ohio, that from and after the first day of June next, no black or mulatto person, shall be permitted to settle or reside in this state, unless he or she shall first produce a fair certificate from some court with the United States, of his or her actual freedom, which certificate shall be attested by the clerk of said court, and the seal thereof annexed thereto, by the said clerk.

Section 2. That every black or mulatto person residing within this state, on or before the first day of June, one thousand eight hundred and four, shall enter his or her name together with the name or names of his or her children, in the clerk's office in the county in which he, she, or they reside, which shall be entered on record by said clerk, and thereafter the clerk's certificate of such record shall pay to the clerk twelve and an half cents: Provided nevertheless, That nothing in this act contained shall bar the lawful claim to any black or mulatto person.

Section 3. That no person or persons' residents of this state, shall be permitted to hire, or in any way employ any black or mulatto person, unless such black or mulatto person shall have one of the certificates as aforesaid, under pain of forfeiting and paying any sum not less than ten nor more than fifty dollars, at the discretion of the court, for every such offense, one half thereof for the use of the informer, and the other half for the use of the state; and shall moreover pay to the owner, if any there be, of such black or mulatto person, the sum of fifty cents for every day he, she or they shall in otherwise employ, harbor or be recoverable before any court having cognizance thereof.

Section 4. That if any person or persons shall harbor or secret any black or mulatto person, the property of any person whatever, or shall in anywise hinder or prevent the lawful owner or owners from retaking and possessing his or her black or mulatto servant or servants, shall, upon conviction thereof, by indictment or information, be fined in any sum not less than ten nor more than fifty dollars, at the discretion of the court, one-half thereof for the use of the informer and the other half for the use of the state.

Section 5. That every black or mulatto person who shall come to reside in this state with such certificates as is required in the first section of this act, shall, within two years, have the same recorded in the clerk's office, in the county in which he or she means to reside, for which he or she shall pay to the clerk twelve and an half cents, and the clerk shall give him or her a certificate of such record.

Section 6. That in case any person or persons, his or their agent or agents, claiming any black or mulatto person that now are, or hereafter may be in this state, may apply, upon making satisfactory proof that such black or mulatto person or persons is the property of him or her who applies to any associate judge or justice of the pace within this state, the associate judge or justice is thereby empowered and required, by his precept, to direct the sheriff or constable to arrest such black or mulatto person or persons, and deliver the same in the county or township where such officers shall reside, to the claimant or claimants or his or their agents, for which service the sheriff or constable shall receive such compensation as they are entitled to receive in other cases for similar services.

Section 7. That any person or persons who shall attempt to remove or shall remove from this state, or who shall aid and assist in removing, contrary to the provisions of this act, any black or mulatto person or persons, without first proving as herein before directed, that he, she or they, is or are legally entitled so to do, shall on conviction thereof, before any court having cognizance of the same, forfeit and pay the sum of one thousand dollars, one-half to the use of the informer and the other half to the use of the state to be recovered by action of debt, qui tam, or indictment, and moreover be liable to the action of the party injured.

NUMBER 2

An act to amend the last named act "An Act to Regulate Black and Mulatto Persons" Approved January 25, 1807, Laws of Ohio.

Section 1. Be it enacted by the General Assembly of the State of Ohio, that no negro or mulatto person shall be permitted to emigrate into, and settle within this state, unless such negro or mulatto person shall, within twenty days thereafter, enter into bond with two or more freehold sureties, in the penal sum of five hundred dollars, before the clerk of the court of common pleas of the county in which such negro or mulatto person may wish to reside, (to be approved of by the clerk), conditioned for the good behavior of such negro or mulatto, and moreover to pay for the support of such person, in case he, she or they should thereafter be found within any township in this state, unable to support themselves. And if any negro or mulatto person shall migrate in this state, and not comply with the provisions of this act, it shall be the duty of the overseer of the poor of the township where such negro or mulatto person may be found to remove immediately such black or mulatto person, in the same manner as is required in the case of paupers.

Section 2. That it shall be the duty of the clerk, before whom such bond may be given as given as aforesaid, to file the same in his office, and give a certificate thereof to such negro or mulatto person; and the said clerk shall be entitled to receive the sum of one dollar for the bond and certificate aforesaid, on the delivery of the certificate.

Section 3. That if any person, being a resident of this state, shall employ, harbor or conceal any such negro or mulatto person aforesaid, contrary to the provisions of the first section of this act, any person offending shall forfeit and pay, for every such offence, nay sum not exceeding one hundred dollars, the one half to the informer, and the other half for the use of the poor of the township in which such person may reside, to be recovered by action of debt, before any court having competent jurisdiction; and moreover be liable for the maintenance and support of such negro or mulatto, provided be, she or they shall become unable to support themselves.

Section 4. That no black or mulatto person or persons shall hereafter be permitted to be sworn or give evidence in any court of record, or elsewhere, in this state, in any cause depending, or matter of controversy, where either party to the same is a white person.

Section 5. That so much of the act, entitled "an act to regulate black and mulatto persons," as is contrary to this act, together with the sixth section thereof, be and the same is hereby repealed. This act shall take effect and be in force from and after the first day of April next.

NUMBER 3

An act to amend the act entitled "an act to regulate black and mulatto persons, passed January 5, 1804." Approved February 27, 1834, Laws of Ohio.

Section 1. Be it enacted by the General Assembly of the State of Ohio, That in all cases wherein a certificate is granted to any black or mulatto person, resident within this state, agreeably to the second section of the act to which this is an amendment, the clerk of the court issuing the same shall make or cause to be made, a record of the same, in a book provided for that purpose, and carefully preserved in said office, and on such record of the same being made, the said clerk shall endorse thereon the number of the same, the book in which, and the page or pages where such records is made, and shall forthwith, if required, deliver over the same to the individual for whose benefit it was intended, and it shall furthermore be the duty of the presiding judge of such circuit in which said certificate may be issued, on application being made to him by the holder of the same, to endorse thereon his certificate of the genuineness of the same; provided, that nothing in this act contained shall be so construed as to bar the lawful claim to any black or mulatto person thus obtaining a certificate with this state.

V

Colonization

The Northwest Ordinance of 1787 prohibited slavery, although some states in the territory found ingenious ways to circumvent the measure. Whites in Ohio recognized that they would be guided by the interdict in the Ordinance, and they ratified a clause prohibiting slavery at the Constitutional Convention of 1802. Most whites, especially migrants from New England, did not want to practice slavery. Some migrating Southerners shared this point of view. They left the South intending to live in a region that practiced free labor. Yet, whites in Ohio shared the prejudice of most southern and northern racists. They subjugated blacks in their laws and, as an alternative to slavery, proposed colonizating its African American and residents. Most whites--even liberal whites--doubted that blacks and whites could live peaceably in the same community. Consequently, most whites supported the colonization movement to expatriate African Americans. The following documents describe Ohio's commitment to colonization as a means to solve the slavery and race problem in the United States.

NUMBER 1

Resolution on colonization. Approved January 29, 1818, Laws of Ohio.

Whereas a number of the good people of this state, have by a memorial expressed their most ardent wishes for the emancipation and colonization of the people of color of the United States; Therefore,

Resolved by the general assembly of the State of Ohio, That our senators in Congress be instructed, and our representatives be requested, to use their best endeavors to procure the passage of a law which will effect the purposes aforesaid.

Resolved, That the governor be requested to transmit a copy of the foregoing preamble and resolution to each of our senators and representatives in Congress.

NUMBER 2

Resolution on colonization. Approved January 17, 1824, Laws of Ohio.

Resolved by the General Assembly of the State of Ohio, That the confederation of a system providing for the gradual emancipation of the people of color, held in servitude in the United States, be recommended to the legislatures of the several states of the American Union, and to the Congress of the United States.

Resolved, That in the opinion of this General Assembly a system of foreign colonization, with correspondent measures might be adapted that would in due time effect the entire emancipation of the slaves in our country without any violation of the national compact, or infringement of the rights of individuals; by the passage of a law by the general government (with the consent of the slave holding states) which should provide that all children of persons now held in slavery, born after the passage of such a law, should be free at the age of twenty-one years (being supported during their minority by the persons claiming the service of their parents) providing they then consent to be transported to the intended place of colonization.

Resolved, That it is expedient that such a system should be predicated upon the principle that the evil of slavery is a national one, and that the people and the states of this Union ought mutually to participate in the duties and burdens of removing it.

Resolved, That his Excellency the governor [*sic*] be requested to forward a copy of the foregoing Resolutions to his excellency the Governor of each of the United States, requesting him to lay the same before the legislature thereof; and that his Excellency will also forward a like copy to each of our senators and representatives in Congress, requesting their cooperation in all national measures having tendency to effect the grand object embraced therein.

NUMBER 3

Resolution on colonization. Approved January 24, 1828, Laws of Ohio.

Resolved by the General Assembly of the State of Ohio, That our senators in Congress be instructed, and our representatives be requested, to use their efforts to induce the government of the United States to aid the "American Colonization Society" in effecting the object of their institution which is so eminently calculated to advance the honor and interest of our common country.

Resolved, That the governor be, and he is hereby requested to forward to each of our senators and representatives in Congress, a copy of the foregoing resolution.

NUMBER 4

Joint resolution relative to excluding slavery from Oregon Territory, and any other territory which may hereafter be annexed to the United States. Approved February 8, 1847, Laws of Ohio.

Resolved, by the General Assembly of the State of Ohio, That the senators and representatives from this state, in the Congress of the United states, be and are hereby respectively requested to procure the passage of measures in that body providing for the exclusion of slavery from the territory of Oregon, and also from any other territory that is, or hereafter may be annexed to the United States.

Resolved, That the Governor be requested to transmit to each of the Senators and Representatives from this State, in the Congress of the United States, a copy of the above resolution, to be by them laid before their respective houses.

NUMBER 5

Resolution declaring that so much of the Ordinance of 1787 as relates to slavery, should be extended to the territory acquired from Mexico. Approved February 25, 1848, Laws of Ohio.

Resolved, by the General Assembly of the State of Ohio, That the provisions of the Ordinance of Congress, of one thousand seven hundred and eighty-seven, so far as the same relates to slavery should be extended to any territory that may be acquired from Mexico by treaty or otherwise.

NUMBER 6

House joint resolution relative to slavery and the trade in the District of Columbia. Approved March 24, 1849, Laws of Ohio.

Resolved, by the General Assembly of the State of Ohio, That our senators and representatives in Congress be instructed to use all constitutional means for the abolition of slavery in the District of Columbia.

Resolved, That the Governor be and he is hereby requested to communicate the foregoing resolutions to each of our Senators and Representatives.

NUMBER 7

House joint resolution relative to the oppressed people of color in the United States. Approved March 23, 1849, Laws of Ohio.

Whereas, the people of color of the United States have been oppressed and enslaved, by the several states, and thereby to do something for their elevation to that position nature's God designed for all men, therefore,

Be it resolved, by the General Assembly of the State of Ohio, That our Senators be instructed, and our Representatives in Congress be requested to inquire into the expediency of procuring the passage of a law, authorizing the survey and appropriation of a portion of the territory acquired from Mexico, for the benefit of all free persons of color who may become actual settlers of the same, and a title of eighty acres of land delivered to each of said persons, free of charge, and also to establish and provide for them a government of protection.

Resolved, That the Governor of this State be requested to forward a copy of the above preamble and resolutions to each of our senators and representatives in Congress.

NUMBER 8

Senate joint resolution relative to colonization. Approved March 23, 1850, Laws of Ohio.

Whereas, the settlement of the African coast with the colonies of civilized colored men, is the cheapest and best plan of suppressing the African slave trade, being likewise calculated to further the work of colonizing our people of color, as well as civilizing our people of color, as well as civilizing and christianizing the African race, which plan of suppressing the slave trade is true American policy: Therefore,

Be it resolved, by the General Assembly of the State of Ohio, to call for a change of National Policy on the subject of the "African Slave Trade," and that they require a settlement of the coast of Africa, with colored men from the United States, and procure such changes in our treaty relations with other nations, as will enable us to transport colored men from this country to Africa, with whom to effect settlement.

NUMBER 9

Preamble and joint resolution instructing our senators and representatives in Congress in relation to the independence of Liberia, and other purposes. Laws of Ohio, Approved February 5, 1850.

Whereas, the colored emigrants from the United States, who have settled on the coast of Africa by the agency of the American Colonization Society, are now organized into an independent Republic, and have been acknowledged as such by the governments of England and France; And whereas, the influence exerted by the colony in promoting civilization in Africa, has been very beneficial, and promises extensive usefulness; and whereas, intelligent colored men in the United States who might be eminently useful in Africa, are unwilling to emigrate to Liberia until its independence shall be acknowledged by the government of the United States; therefore,

Resolved by the General Assembly of the State of Ohio, That our senators in Congress are hereby instructed, and our Representatives in Congress requested to use their influence to induce the general government to acknowledge the independence of the Republic of Liberia; that they also be requested to use all honorable means to induce the free blacks of the United States to emigrate to that country.

NUMBER 10

Senate joint resolution relative to slavery and the extension thereof. Approved April 17, 1857, Laws of Ohio.

Resolved by the General Assembly of the State of Ohio, That the people of Ohio now, as they always have done, look upon the institution of slavery as an evil unfavorable to the full development of the spirit and practical benefits of free institutions; and that entertaining these sentiments they will feel it their duty to use all power consistent with the national compact, to prevent its increase, to mitigate, and finally to eradicate the evil.

2. Resolved, That the provisions of the ordinance of congress of 1787, so far as the same relates to slavery, should be extended to all territory of the United States not yet organized into states.

3. Resolved, That our senators and representatives in Congress are hereby requested to vote against the admission of any state in the union, unless slavery, or involuntary servitude, except for crime, be excluded in the constitution thereof.

NUMBER 11

Senate joint resolution relative to the decision of the Dred Scott Case. Approved April 17, 1857, Laws of Ohio.

Resolved by the General Assembly of the State of Ohio, 1st. That this general assembly has observed with regret that, in the opinion lately pronounced by Chief Justice Roger Taney in behalf of a majority of the Supreme Court of the United States in the case of Dred Scott against J.H. Sanford, occasion has been taken to promulgate extra judicially certain doctrines concerning slavery, not less contradictory to well-known facts of history, then repugnant to the plain provisions of the constitution, and subversive to the rights of freemen and free states.

2. That in the judgment of the general assembly, every free person born within the limits of an state of this union, is a citizen thereof, and to deny to any such person the right of suing in the courts of the United States, in those cases where that right is guaranteed by the constitution to all citizens of the United States, is a palpable and unwarrantable violation of that sacred instrument.

3. That the doctrine announced by the chief justice, in behalf of a majority of the court, the federal constitution regards slavery as mere property, and protects the claims of masters to slaves to the same extent, and in the same manner as the rights of owners in property, foreshadows, if it does not include the doctrine, that masters may hold slaves as property within the limits of free states, during temporary visits, or for purposes of transit, to the practical consequences of which doctrine no free state can submit with honor.

4. That the doctrine announced in behalf of a majority of the court that there exists no power in the general government to exclude slavery from the territories of the United States, subverts the spirit of the constitution, annuls the just authority of the people of the United States over their own territories, and contradicts the uniform practice of the government.

5. That the general assembly in behalf of the people of Ohio, hereby solemnly protest against these doctrines, as destructive of personal liberty, of states' rights, or constitutional obligations, and of the union; and so protesting, further declares its unalterable conviction that in the Declaration of Independence the fathers of the republic intended to assert the indestructible and equal rights of all men, without any exception or reservation whatever; to life, liberty, and the pursuit of happiness; and in the constitution, by the comprehensive guaranty that no person shall be deprived of life, liberty or property without due process of law, designed to secure these rights against all invasion by the federal government, and to make the establishment of slavery outside of slave states a constitutional impossibility.

Resolved, That the Governor be requested to transmit a copy of the foregoing resolutions to the President of the United States, to the governors of the several states respectively, and to each senator and representative of Ohio in Congress.

VI

Kidnapping Law

Gamaliel Bailey's description of abolitionists as a "steadfast minority" was an appropriate label for nineteenth-century antislavery reformers. Bailey, himself an abolitionist, joined his colleagues to condemn slavery. Although abolitionists were a minority, they were articulate speech-makers and editors who were determined to do away with slavery. They were a vociferous and talented group of reformers. Abolitionists created the doctrine of antislavery law, and called on lawyers sympathetic to their cause to argue their doctrine in court. They achieved the automatic emancipation of African Americans brought into Ohio by consenting slave holders. Ohio also faced the growing problem of kidnapping, and free African Americans were not safe. Federal fugitive slave legislation enabled professional slave catchers to chase runaway slaves to free states. Unscrupulous as they were, slave catchers sometimes apprehended and removed free blacks. Consequently, in order to protect free African-American residents, some states adopted personal liberty laws. Ohio did not adopt personal liberty laws per se. Nonetheless, the state legislature adopted laws against kidnapping. The following documents demonstrate how whites handled the problem of kidnapping in Ohio. These documents, along with other state statutes, suggests that whites were more concerned about violations of their free laws than they were about the legal rights of free blacks.

NUMBER 1

An act to punish kidnapping. Approved January 25, 1819, Laws of Ohio.

Whereas, it is provided by an Act of congress, passed the twelfth day of February one thousand seven hundred and ninety-three, that when a person held to labor in any of the United States, or in any of the territories north-west or south of the river Ohio under the laws thereof, shall escape into any other of the said states or territories the person to whom such labor or service may be due, his agent or attorney, is authorized and empowered to seize or arrest said fugitive from labor, and to take him or her before any judge of the circuit or district courts of the United States, residing or being within the state, or before any magistrate of a county, city or town corporate, wherein such seizure or arrest shall be made, and upon proof to the satisfaction of such judge or magistrate either by oral testimony, or by affidavit, taken before and certified by a magistrate of any such state or territory, that the person so seized or arrested, does under the laws of the state or territory from which he or she fled, owe service or labor to the person claiming him or her, it shall be the duty of such judge or magistrate, to give a certificate thereof, to such claimant, his agent or attorney, which shall be a sufficient warrant for removing the said fugitive from labor, to the state or territory from which he or she fled, and whereas it has been represented to this general assembly, that upon pretence of seizing fugitives from service, under the provisions of the before recited act, unprincipled persons have kidnapped free persons of color, within this state, and sell them into slavery; and whereas it is necessary and proper to put a stop to this nefarious and inhuman practice, therefore:

Section 1. Be it enacted by the general assembly of the state of Ohio, That if any person or persons, under any pretence whatsoever, shall by violence, fraud, or deception, seize upon any free black or mulatto person, within this state, and keep or detain such free black or mulatto person in any kind of restrain or confinement, with intent to transport such free black or mulatto person out of this state, contrary to law, or shall in any manner attempt to carry out of this state, any black or mulatto person before some judge of the circuit or district court, or justice of the peace, in the county wherein such black or mulatto person was taken, agreeably to the provisions of the above recited act of congress, and there prove his right to such black or mulatto person, every such person so offending, shall be deemed guilty of a high misdemeanor; and on conviction thereof before any court having competent authority to try the same, shall be confined in the penitentiary of this state at hard lobbyer, for any space of time not less than one nor more than ten years, at the discretion of the court.

This act to take effect from and after the first day of June next.

NUMBER 2

An act to prevent kidnapping. Approved February 15, 1831, Laws of Ohio.

Section 1. Be it enacted by the General Assembly of the State of Ohio, That no person or persons, under any pretence whatever, shall, by violence or fraud or deception seize upon any free black or mulatto person within this State, and keep such free black or mulatto person in any kind of restraint or confinement, with intent to transport such black or mulatto person out of the State.

Section 2. That no person or persons shall in any manner attempt to carry out of this State, or knowingly be aiding in carrying out of this State any black or mulatto person, without first taking such black or mulatto person before some judge or justice of the peace, in the county where such black or mulatto person was taken, and there agreeably to the laws of the United States, establish by proof, his or their property in such black or mulatto person.

Section 3. That any person or persons so offending against the provisions of this act shall, on conviction thereof, by indictment in the court of common pleas in any county in this State, be deemed guilty of a misdemeanor, and shall be confined in the penitentiary, at hard labor, for any space of time, not less than three, nor more than seven years, at the discretion of the court.

Section 4. That the act, entitled "An act to prevent kidnapping," passed January twenty-fifth, eighteen hundred and nineteen, be, and the same is hereby repealed.

NUMBER 3

Report of the committee on federal relations, respecting the kidnapping of certain citizens of this state. Approved February 16, 1846, House Journal. Mr. Phelps, from the committee on Federal Relations, made the following report:

The committee on Federal Relations, to whom was referred the correspondence between the Governor of the State of Ohio and the Governor of Virginia, in relations to the kidnapping of certain citizens of this State, have had the same under consideration, and now submit the following report:

The material facts in respect to the transaction, are briefly as follows: Certain citizens of this State, being upon the Ohio bank or shore of the Ohio river, where a canoe had landed with a number of negroes--the river then being several feet above low water, and the shore some distance from the margin of the channel at low water--five citizens of Virginia, who had previously placed themselves in concealment for that purpose, upon the Ohio side of the river, rushed forth, and, under the pretext of arresting them for an infraction of the criminal law of Virginia, then and there committee, forcibly seized, bound, and conveyed to the Virginia shore, and lodged in the jail of Parkersburg, three citizens of the State of Ohio. The five persons guilty of this act of kidnapping, were indicted therefor by the grand jury of Washington county, and a legal requisition made by the Governor of this State for the delivery over of said five persons to the authorities of this State, for trail on the above charge; which requisition was not complied with. Some two weeks afterwards, the Governor of this State addressed a letter to the Governor of Virginia, calling his attention to the subject, and requesting to be informed of his Executive action upon the requisition. This letter was replied to by the Governor of Virginia on the 21st of October last--more than a month after the requisition had been made--stating as a reason why it could not be complied with, that the said five persons were then under subpoena to testify against the very three citizens thus kidnapped. In the mean time, these three citizens of Ohio remained confined in the jail of Parkersburg, but were afterwards brought to rail before their county court, at Parkersburg, when the jury returned a special verdict; and, in December last, the case came up before the Virginia Court of Appeals, composed of fifteen Judges, on a question of jurisdiction, and, strange as it may seem, fourteen of these Judges were equally divided as to whether Virginia had jurisdiction at the place where the offence was alleged to have been committed, and where the said citizens were seized. The other Judge, by reasons of not having heard the whole case, gave no opinion; so that it resulted in continuing the imprisonment of these three citizens, to await another term of the court. The Court of Appeals, however, made a milder order than had been made by the county court, in respect to admitting them to bail; under which order in the month of January last, they were discharged, on bail of one hundred dollars each--a citizen of Ohio, of no responsibility, as your committee are informed, being received as the surety of all.

The only question for the determination of the Virginia Court of Appeals, was--Did the place, where the said supposed offence was alleged to have been committed by said citizens of Ohio, constitute a part of the territory, and was it within the jurisdiction of Virginia or not? It was upon the Ohio side of the river, and back from the margin at low water about sixty.

The deed of cession from Virginia to the United States, ceded to the latter all the territory northwest of the Ohio river. From this territory the States of Ohio and Indiana were subsequently erected, each being bounded upon the Ohio river. A deed of land to an individual, bounding him upon such a river, would vest in him the soil to low water mark. Without expressing an opinion whether the State of Ohio might or might not rightfully claim to the center of the river, it is sufficient, for the determination of this question, that she has, in the opinion of your committee, an undoubted right and title to the territory, and exclusive dominion over it, down to the margin of the river at this lowest stage of water; or, in other words, to what is always a river. This has been adjudicated and determined by the highest authority. In the case of Handley's Lessee v. Anthony (5th Wehat., 375) a claim was made, under a grant from Kentucky, to a peninsula on the Indiana side of the Ohio, connected with the main land by narrow neck, over which the Ohio flowed only when considerably above low water mark, so as then to convert the peninsula into an island. The court decided against the Kentucky claim, upon the ground that the margin of the river at low water mark was the boundary line of Indiana. Chief Justice Marshall, in pronouncing his decision, remarked, that, "when a great river is the boundary between two nations, if the original property is in neither, and no convention respecting it, each holds to the middle. But when, as in this case, one is the original proprietor, and against the territory, it retains the river in its own dominion, and the new State holds only to the river. It is, however, "the main permanent river which is the boundary." He further said: "If it be true that the river Ohio, not its ordinary bank, is the boundary of Indiana, the limits of that State can only be determined by the river itself. The same tract cannot be sometimes in Kentucky and sometimes in Indiana." Yet, with this case, so clear and strong, and no contradictory authority, the Virginia court were divided in opinion. In any view of the subject, your committee regard the place where these three citizens were seized as within the unquestionable territory and exclusive dominion of the State of Ohio; and they deem the transaction, irrespective of what may have been the character or conduct of the abducted citizens, a gross violation of the territory and sovereign authority of the State of Ohio.

The question then arises, what action, under all the circumstances, should this State adopt? And the question is not without its difficulties. Were the State of Ohio and Virginia perfectly independent of each other, and not standing, as they do, in the relation of sister States in the Federal Union, then, in conformity with international law, having demanded of Virginia the release of the citizens thus kidnapped, and the delivery over to justice of the persons guilty of kidnapping them, upon her refusal to comply with such demand, we should have just cause to make reprisals, or resort to war; but rashly to adopt such action, would be destructive of the harmony of our Union. The encroachments of the States upon each other, seem neither to have been expected, nor provided against by the framers of our national compact; but the several States, sovereign in all respects, except as to powers expressly surrendered, are left to settle all such controversies in the best manner they can. If, however, by reason of our union, we are to be restrained from seeking that redress for violations of our territorial rights, which of right appertains to all sovereign and independent States, it necessarily follows that the General Government should protect our rights in that respect, and redress all such injuries. Otherwise the Union, while it would confer upon us no protection, would only operate as a restraint upon our protecting ourselves.

Your committee, after much consideration, are of the opinion that when, as in this case, the territory of the State has been violated, and satisfaction refused by the violating State, it becomes the duty of the Executive authority to call upon the General Government for redress, and should the federal government neglect or refuse to interfere, whether such neglect or refusal arise either from want of will, or from a real or supposed defect of power, that then the injured State may justly redress her own injuries by her own power. There remains in fact no other remedy, and the necessity of the case imposes it upon her, if she would preserve her dominion over her own territory. Your committee, under all the present circumstances of this case, are not prepared to recommend any definite action in respect thereto, but would respectfully propose the adoption of the following resolutions:

Resolved by the General Assembly of the State of Ohio, That the forcible seizure of Peter Garner, Crighton J. Lorain, and Thomas, three citizens of Ohio, within the unquestionable territory of this State, their transportation and incarceration in the jail of Parkersburg, under the pretext of an infraction of the criminal law of Virginia, was an unwarrantable outrage upon the rights of this State.

Resolved, That when our territory is thus violated, the offending State refuses satisfaction, and, upon application to the federal government, interference and redress are neglected or refused, it then becomes our duty and just right, to take it into our own hands, and to redress the wrongs inflicted upon the sovereignty of the State by the power thereof, in conformity with international law.

NUMBER 4

An act to prevent slave holding and kidnapping in Ohio. Approved April 17, 1857, Laws of Ohio.

Section 1. Be it enacted by the General Assembly of the State of Ohio, That if any person shall bring into this state any other person, with intent to hold or control, or shall hold or control, or shall aid or assist in holding or controlling directly or indirectly, within this state, any other person as a slave; such person, so offending, shall be deemed guilty of false imprisonment in the county jail, not less than three, nor more than nine months, and by fine not less than two hundred, nor more than five hundred dollars; and every person coming within this state otherwise than as a person held to service in another state under the laws thereof, and escaping into this state, shall be deemed and held in all courts as absolutely free.

Section 2. If any person shall seize or arrest, or shall attempt to seize or arrest, or shall aid in seizing or arresting, or in attempting to seize or arrest, or shall use force or fraud for the purpose of holding, detaining or controlling any other person, upon any pretence or claim that such person is a fugitive from service, such person, so offending, shall be deemed guilty of false imprisonment, and shall be punished by imprisonment in the county jail, not less than three months, nor more than nine months, and by fine not less than three hundred, nor more than five hundred dollars.

Section 3. If any person shall seize or arrest, or shall attempt to seize or arrest, or shall aid in seizing or arresting, or in attempting to seize or arrest, or shall use any force or fraud for the purpose of holding, detaining, controlling, or influencing any other person with intent to carry or remove such person out of this state, or with intent to cause such person voluntarily to depart out of this state in order that such person may be taken, held, or controlled as a slave, in some other state, territory, or jurisdiction, such person so offending, shall be deemed guilty of kidnapping, and shall be punished by imprisonment in the penitentiary at hard labor, not less than three, nor more than seven years.

Section 4. Nothing in the preceding sections of this act shall apply to any act done by any person under the authority of the constitution of the United States, or of any law of the United States, made in pursuance thereof.

NUMBER 5

An act to prevent kidnapping. Approved April 17, 1857, Laws of Ohio.

Section 1. Be it enacted by the General Assembly of the State of Ohio, That no person or persons shall arrest and imprison, or kidnap, or forcibly or fraudulently carry off or decoy out of this state any free black or mulatto person or persons within this state, or attempt to kidnap or forcibly or fraudulently carry off or decoy out of this state any such free black or mulatto person, or shall arrest and imprison any such free black or mulatto person or persons with the intention of having such person or persons carried out of this state, unless it be in pursuance of the laws thereof.

Section 2. That no person or persons shall kidnap or forcibly or fraudulently carry off or decoy out of this state any black or mulatto person or persons within this state, claimed as a fugitive from service or labor, or shall attempt to kidnap, or forcibly or fraudulently carry off or decoy out of this state any such black or mulatto person or persons before the court, judge or commissioner of the proper circuit, district or county having jurisdiction, according to the laws of the United States, in cases of persons held to service or labor in any state escaping into this state, and there, according to the laws of the United States, establishing by proof his or their property in such person.

Section 3. That any person or persons offending against the provisions of this act shall be deemed guilty of a misdemeanor, and on conviction thereof by indictment in the court of common pleas of any county in this state, shall be confined in the penitentiary at hard labor for any space of time not less than three years nor more than eight years at the discretion of the court, and moreover be liable for all costs of prosecution.

Section 4. That the act entitled in act to prevent kidnapping, passed February 15th, 1831, be and the same is hereby repealed, but nothing in this act contained shall in any manner affect the prosecution or punishment for offenses committed before the taking effect of this act.

Section 5. This act takes effect on its passage.

NUMBER 6

An act to repeal an act therein named. Approved March 27, 1858, Laws of Ohio.

Section 1. Be it enacted by the General Assembly of the State of Ohio, That an act entitled An act to Prevent Slave holding and Kidnapping in Ohio, passed April 17, 1857, be and the same is hereby repealed.

Section 2. This act takes effect upon its passage.

NUMBER 7

Joint resolution relative to the kidnapping of the Polly family. March 10, 1860, Laws of Ohio.

Whereas, on the night of the 6th of June, 1850, seven of the children and one grand child of Peyton Polly, all free persons of color, residing in Lawrence county, were forcibly seized with the view of reducing them to slavery, that four of them were arrested in the State of Kentucky on their way to a southern slave market, and after protracted litigation were declared free persons by the courts of that State, and returned to their homes; and whereas, four of said persons of color were sold into slavery in the county of Wayne, in the State of Virginia, and are now held in bondage there; and whereas, suit was instituted in the county of Cabell, in the State of Virginia, for freedom of said last mentioned colored persons, and were declared free by the judgment of the circuit court of Cabell county, which judgment was afterwards reversed by the court of appeals, on the ground that the actual residence of the defendant was in Wayne county, and the Cabell county court had no jurisdiction of the cause; that said proceedings were removed to the county of Wayne, and are now pending: Therefore,

Be it resolved by the General Assembly of the State of Ohio, That the governor be and he is hereby authorized to expend any sum not exceeding one thousand dollars for the purpose of defraying expenses of said litigation; that the standing committee on finance be instructed to provide for the same in the general appropriation bill; and that the governor be requested to take such measures he, in his judgment, may deem necessary for the speedy and successful termination of said proceedings.

VII

Public Education

For African Americans, northern states offered their only prospect for freedom. Enslaved blacks escaped to the North by the thousands, hoping to find relief from slavery and discrimination. Many of them found freedom; but they hardly enjoyed a respite from racial prejudice. The North, for example, paved the way for legal segregation. Massachusetts led the way in 1849 in the case of Roberts v. the City of Boston. The law required Benjamin Roberts' six-year-old daughter Sarah to pass by at least two schools reserved for whites on her way to a school for African-American children. The State Supreme Court did not provide relief. It ruled that the existence of a school for black children satisfied the equal protection of the laws clause in the State Constitution. Such discrimination against African Americans was prevalent in Ohio. The state assembly initially closed all public schools to black youths. The Supreme Court revised this rule by admitting mulattoes to schools reserved for whites. The only condition was that those persons had to have a preponderance of white features. The state assembly approved this practice by enacting the Visible Admixture Law. Appearance, therefore, determined who could receive the privileges of being white. Antislavery lawyers prevailed on the Court to outlaw segregation. In Van Camp v. Logan (1859), the Court rejected their pleas. The following documents describe this problem of educating black children in the pubic schools of Ohio.

NUMBER 1

An act to provide for the support and better regulation of common schools. Approved February 10, 1829, Laws of Ohio.

Section 1. Be it enacted by the General Assembly of the State of Ohio, that a fund shall hereafter be raised in the several counties in this state, in the manner pointed out by this act for the use of common schools, for the instruction of youth of every class and grade without distinction, in reading, writing, arithmetic and other necessary branches of a common eduction: Provided, That nothing in this act contained shall be so construed as to permit black or mulatto persons to attend the schools hereby established, or compel them to pay any tax for the support of such schools; but all taxes assessed on their property, for school purposed, in the several counties in this state, shall be appropriated as the Trustees of the several townships may direct, for the education of said black and mulatto persons therein, and for no other purpose whatever.

NUMBER 2

An act in addition to the act entitled "an act to incorporate and establish the city of Cincinnati, and repealing all laws and parts of laws heretofore enacted on that subject," passed the twenty-sixth day of January in the year eighteen hundred and twenty-seven. Approved February 12, 1829, Laws of Ohio.

The significant portion of Section 5 says: That nothing in this act contained shall be so construed as to permit black or mulatto persons to attend said schools, or to receive instruction therein; but all taxes assessed on the property of black or mulatto persons in said city, or in the township of Cincinnati, for school purposes, shall be appropriated as the Trustees and Visitors, hereinafter mentioned, may direct, for the education of black or mulatto persons in said city, and for no other purpose whatever.

NUMBER 3

An act to provide for the support and better regulation of common schools. Approved March 10, 1831, Laws of Ohio.

Section 1. Be it enacted by the General Assembly of the State of Ohio, That a fund shall hereafter be raised in the several counties of this State, in the manner pointed out by this act, for the use of common schools, for the instruction of white youth of every class and grade, without distinction, in reading, writing and arithmetic, and other necessary branches of education.

Section 2. That, for the purpose and use aforesaid, there shall be annually levied and assessed, upon the ad valorem amount of the general list of taxable property, in each county of this State, the property of blacks and mulattoes excepted, three fourths of a mill on the dollar which assessment shall be made by the county auditor, and collected by the county treasurer, in the same manner as all other taxes for State and county purposes are directed by law to be levied and collected.

Section 28. That, the clerk of each school district shall, annually, in the month of November, take a list or enumeration in writing, of all white youth in the district, between the ages of four and twenty-one years, not including any who are married, and shall return the same to the auditor of his county with an oath or affirmation endorsed thereon, that the same is a true enumeration to the best of his knowledge.

Section 34. That when any appropriation shall be made by the director of any school district, from the treasury thereof, for the payment of a teacher, the school in such district shall be open to all white children residing therein for the space of three months, and as much longer as such appropriation will pay the teacher. . .

Section 38. That the act, entitled "an act to provide for the support and better regulation of common schools," passed February 10th, 1829 and the act entitled "an act to amend the act, entitled 'an act to provide for the support and better regulation of common schools', passed February 22nd, 1830," and all the acts contrary to the provisions of this act, be, and the same are hereby repealed.

NUMBER 4

An act for the support and better regulation of common schools and to create permanently the office of superintendent. Approved March 7, 1838, Laws of Ohio.

Section 1. Be it enacted by the General Assembly of the State of Ohio, That a fund shall hereafter be provided, in the manner hereinafter specified, for the education of all the white youth in this State, in such branches of learning as shall hereinafter be prescribed.

Section 2. That for the purpose aforesaid, there shall be annually levied and assessed upon the ad valorem amount of the general list of taxable property, in each county of this State, (the property of black and mulatto persons excepted), two mills on the dollar; which assessment shall be made by the county auditor, and collected by the county treasurer, in the same manner as other taxes are levied and collected: Provided, That if any tax for school purposes shall be levied on the property of any black or mulatto person, it shall be the duty of the county treasurer or other person charged with the collection of the same to abate said tax.

Section 3. That there shall be a State Common School Fund established, consisting of the interest on the Surplus Revenue, at five percent, the interest on the proceeds of Salt lands; the revenue from Banks, Insurance and Bridge Companies, and other funds to be annually provided by the State, to the amount of two hundred thousand dollars per annum; and that said sum of two hundred thousand dollars, shall be annually distributed among the several counties in this State, in the month of December, according to the number of white youth, (unmarried), between the ages of four and twenty years, resident in each county, under the restrictions and regulations herein after provided.

Section 9. Significant portion says: That in all cases during the periods when the public money is applied for the support of the schools, said schools shall be free for all the white children in the district, under such regulations as may be adopted to secure an equal participation therein.

NUMBER 5

An act to amend an act entitled "an act for the support and better regulation of common schools, and to create permanently the office of superintendent." Approved March 16, 1839, Laws of Ohio.

Section 8. That all white youth over four and under twenty-one years of age shall have equal privileges in all the common schools in this state, any other law or laws to the contrary not withstanding; and hereafter the enumeration shall be taken of all white youth between four and twenty-one years of age, not including such as are attending academies or colleges of the district in which is their home or permanent residence, and the directors of any such school district shall be authorized at their discretion to admit persons over twenty-one years of age as well as youths not residing in said district, on payment of such sum as said director may prescribe.

Section 20. That it shall be the duty of the county assessors, when taking a list of taxable property of the county, when he takes in the property of a black or mulatto person, to note the fact opposite to his or her name in the abstracts he makes out for the county auditor.

Section 22. This act to be in force from and after the first day of April next.

NUMBER 6

An act to provide for the establishment of Common Schools for the education of children of black and mulatto persons, and to amend the act entitled "an act for the support and better regulation of common schools, and to create permanently the office of superintendent," passed March 7, 1838 and the acts mandatory thereto. Approved February 24, 1848, Laws of Ohio.

Section 1. Be it enacted by the General Assembly of the State of Ohio, That all such property belonging to black or colored persons, as is liable to taxation when owned by white persons, be taxed for school purposes, and the taxes thereon assessed be collected in the same manner as similar taxes are by the acts to which this is an amendment, a separate account of which shall be kept by the several county auditors, and shall be paid out for the support of schools for black or colored persons in any district in which the children of black or colored persons are permitted to attend the common schools with the children of white persons, then such fund shall be added to the common school fund of the district from which it was collected, and paid over to the treasurer of said district on the order of the directors of said district.

Section 2. That every city, incorporated town or village, seat of justice, or organized township in the State, containing twenty or more black or colored children, of any age, and desirous of attending school, shall constitute a school district for such children; and it shall be lawful for colored persons residing in such school district as aforesaid, to assemble and organize said district, appoint school directors of their own number, to erect and repair a suitable school house of their own to procure suitable teachers, and in all respects, for such purposes only, to possess the same powers, and enjoy the same benefits that are possessed and enjoyed by white persons, by virtue of the acts to which this is an amendment.

Section 3. That if any of the said school districts, as herein provided, contain more than fifty black or colored scholars, the same may be divided by the school directors of said districts, into two or more districts, and each of such new districts shall have all the powers and privileges possessed by those from which said districts were taken: Provided, no school district shall contain a less number of black or colored scholars than twenty.

Section 4. That when any three or more of the black or colored taxpayers in a school district shall be desirous of dividing said district, as herein before provided, they shall first cause ten days' notice to be given, by posting up written or printed notices, in at least three public places within said district, of the time and place that the directors will meet for that purpose, which notice shall, also, contain a description of the boundaries of the proposed new division; and it shall be the duty of said directors to meet at the time and place named in said notice, and if a majority of black or colored taxpayers in said district are in favor of dividing said district, as described in said notice, it shall be the duty of said directors to make said division.

Section 5. That in every city, incorporated township or village, seat of justice, or organized township in this State, where there are less than twenty black or colored children desirous of attending the common schools, and the white inhabitants will not permit them to attend said schools, and in all other respects be entitled to the same privileges, and governed in the same manner as they would be if they were white, under the acts to which this is an amendment, in all such districts, no black or colored person's property shall be taxed for school purposes.

Section 6. That when any black or colored person or persons residing in any school district within this State, where there are less than twenty black or colored children of any age, desirous of attending the common schools in said district or districts, shall have paid a tax for school purposes, it shall be the duty of the county auditor in the county in which such district or districts are located, on application of such black or colored person or persons, and satisfactory proof thereof, to draw an order in favor of such black or colored person or persons, on the county treasurer, for the amount of said tax: Provided, in all cases, that the white inhabitants will not permit such black or colored children to have the benefit of the common schools in said districts, upon the same terms, and enjoy the same privileges, possess the same powers, in all respects, that they would if they were white, under the acts to which this is an amendment.

Section 7. That when the said schools are organized, as herein before provided, they shall, in all respects, be governed except as herein provided, and also, in their organization, according to the provisions of the act to which this is an amendment; the children of such schools shall be enumerated, and have the exclusive benefit of any donation or grant of land which shall be made by an person or persons, or by congress for the support of such schools, which shall be vested in the legislature of this State and appropriated to such schools only; and all the taxes levied and collected from the property of colored or black persons in the same manner that they would be entitled to were they white, and in all other respects have the same powers under the acts to which this is an amendment.

Section 8. That nothing in this act shall be so construed as to tax the property of white persons for the purpose of building school houses for black or colored children, or purchasing sites for such houses, or for tuition purposes, contrary to the wishes of such taxpayers.

Section 9. That all acts or parts thereof inconsistent with the provisions of this act are repealed; and, in no case, shall the property of black or colored persons be taxed for the support of schools organized to educate white youth except as herein provided.

NUMBER 7

An act to authorize the establishment of separate schools for the education of colored children, and for other purposes. Approved February 10, 1849, Laws of Ohio.

Section 1. Be it enacted by the General Assembly of the State of Ohio, That the trustees of each incorporated township in this State, and the trustees, visitors, and directors of schools, or other officers having authority in the premises, of each city and incorporated town or village, shall be and they are hereby authorized and required respectively, incase they shall not deem it expedient to admit the colored children resident in any such township, city, town, or village, into the regular common schools therein established, to create one or more school districts for colored persons, in every township, city, town, or village, which district or districts, shall include all the territories thereof; and in laying off said districts and in altering the same, they shall be governed in all aspects by the provisions of the act for the support and better regulation of common schools, etc. passed March 7, 1838.

Section 2. Whenever any district shall be established as aforesaid, the trustees or other authorities establishing the same, shall give notice, by public advertisement, to the adult male colored tax payers residing in such district, to meet at a time and place specified in the notice, and choose their school directors, and such meeting, and all subsequent meetings, for the election of directors, and for other purposes, shall be held and conducted as is directed in respect to meetings for like objects by the said act of March 7, 1838, and the acts amending the same: and the powers, rights, and duties of the directors so chosen, and of their successors, shall be the same respect to the school officers of their several districts, as are conferred upon, or required of school districts by said acts.

Section 3. The trustees or other authorities establishing separate districts, as aforesaid, shall cause an accurate list to be made as speedily as possible, of all colored taxpayers, and all of colored youth over four and under twenty-one years of age, resident therein, and shall certify it to the county auditor, who shall preserve the same in his office; and no property of any colored tax payer within said districts shall be charged with any special tax for district purposes, for the benefit of the schools in any regular district, composed wholly or in part of the same territory, and no property of any white person in any regular district shall be charged with any tax for the benefit of the schools in any separate district composed wholly, or in part, of the same territory.

Section 4. Every separate district, established as aforesaid, shall be held to include for school purposes, only the colored persons resident within its territorial limits, and from and after the establishment of the same, the colored youth resident therein, shall attend the schools organized under the directors of such district; and the powers and duties of county auditors, county treasurers, township trustees, officers in regard to such separate districts and the schools established therein, shall be the same as now are or may be exercised or performed by said officers respectively, in relation to the regular districts, and the schools established therein, and said districts and schools shall in all respects except so far as this act provides to the contrary, be governed by and have the benefits of all the provisions of said act of March 7, 1838, and the mandatory acts, and all acts relating to schools in cities, towns or villages modifying the same.

Section 5. The term colored as used in this act, shall be construed as being of the same signification as the term "black or mulatto" as used in former acts.

Section 6. The act entitled an act to provide for the establishment of common schools for the education of black and mulatto persons, etc. passed February 24th, 1848, and the act to regulate black and mulatto persons, passed January 5th, 1804, and the several acts to amend the same, passed January 5th, 1807, and February 27th, 1834, and all parts of other acts so far as they enforce any special disabilities or confer any special privileges on account of color, are hereby repealed, except the act of the 9th February, 1831, relating to juries and the act of the 14th March, 1831 for the relief of the poor; Provided, however, that if any person shall bring or cause to be brought, or shall aid in bringing or causing to be brought, or persuade or induce to come into this State, any person or persons, who is or are likely to become chargeable as paupers in any township of this state, or to become vagrants, every such person so offending shall forfeit and pay a fine not exceeding five hundred dollars, to be recovered, with costs of suit, in any court having jurisdiction by action of debt, in behalf of the State of Ohio, or by indictment, and shall also be imprisoned until such fine be paid, unless the court shall otherwise direct.

NUMBER 8

An act to provide for the maintenance and better regulation of the common schools in the city of Cincinnati. Approved January 27, 1853, Laws of Ohio.

Section 12. That the common schools in the several districts of the city, and all other grades of schools authorized or established and maintained in whole or in part from the school funds of said city, shall at all times be equally free and accessible to all white children not less than six years of age who may reside in said city, and subject only to such regulations for their admission, government and instruction, as the trustees and visitors may from time to time provide.

Section 17. The property of all colored persons in said city shall be listed and taxed for school purposes in the same manner as the property of other persons, and separate schools shall be established for the education of the colored children of said city, shall be appropriated as a fund, subject to the order of said board, for the support of schools for colored children.

Section 18. That the act entitled "an act supplementary to an act to increase the number of trustees and visitors of common schools in the city of Cincinnati, and for other purposes," passed March 7th, 1837, passed March 12, 1845, "the act entitled an act to authorize the appointment of a superintendent of common schools in Cincinnati, and for other purposes, passed March 13, 1850"; section one of the act entitled "an act for the better organization and classification of the common schools of Cincinnati and Dayton, and for other purposes," passed February 11, 1845, so far as the same relates to the common schools of the city of Cincinnati, and the act entitled "an act to authorize the establishment of separate schools for the education of colored children, and for other purposes," passed February 10, 1849, so far as the same relates to schools for colored children in the city of Cincinnati--be and they hereby are repealed.

Section 19. That this act shall take effect and be in force from and after the 15th day of March A.D., 1853.

NUMBER 9

An act to provide for the reorganization, supervision and maintenance of common schools. Approved March 14, 1853, Laws of Ohio.

Section 31. The township boards of education in this State, in their respective townships, and the several other boards of education, and the trustees, visitors, and directors of schools, or incorporated villages, shall be, and they are hereby authorized and required to establish within their respective jurisdictions, one or more separate schools for colored children, when the whole number by enumeration exceeds thirty, so as to afford them as far as practicable under all circumstances, the advantages and privileges of a common school education: and all such schools so established for colored children shall be under the control and management of the board of education, other school officers who have in charge the educational interests of the other schools; but in case the average number of colored children in attendance shall be less than fifteen for any one month, it shall be the duty of said board of education, or other school officer, to discontinue said school or schools for any period not exceeding six months at any one time; and if the number of colored children shall be less than fifteen, the director shall reserve the money raised on the number of said colored children and the money so reserved shall be appropriated for the education of such colored children under the direction of the township board.

NUMBER 10

An act to amend the "act to provide for the maintenance and better regulation of common schools, in the city of Cincinnati, passed January 27, 1853." Approved April 18, 1854, Laws of Ohio.

Section 1. Be it enacted by the General Assembly of the State of Ohio, That the seventeenth section of the act entitled "An act to provide for the maintenance and better regulation of common schools in the city of Cincinnati," passed January 27, 1853, be so amended as to read as follows: Section XVII. The property of all colored persons in said city shall be listed and taxed for school purposes in the same manner as the property of other persons and separate schools shall be established for the education of the colored children of said city, in such districts as the board of trustees and visitors of common schools shall, from time to time establish for that purpose; and the district schools so established, shall be conducted under the control and management of three directors in each of said districts, who shall be elected annually in the month of June, by the said board of trustees and visitors of common schools, at a regular meeting, from among the colored people resident in such districts respectively, and who shall take an oath of office. Said directors shall hold their office, or until their successors shall be elected and qualified, and vacancies in their number shall be filled by said trustees and visitors, and said directors shall have the care and management of the schools and school property of their respective districts, appoint teachers, and regulate their salaries, regulate the course of studies and textbooks, fix and determine the times and duration of such schools, and the vacations thereof, provide suitable accommodations, furniture and fuel, & c., for their due maintenance, and perform duties, necessary for keeping up such schools, and for the government and instruction of the colored children of their respective districts in such schools; said directors shall cause a record of their proceedings to be fairly kept in books, which they shall provide for that purpose, and transmit to their successors; and said directors shall render accounts monthly, in detail, of all their expenditures or liabilities, to said board of trustees and visitors of common schools, and if approved by said board, out of the fund for colored schools, provided by this; and so much of the school funds of said city, as upon an equal distribution of the same per capita under any such enumeration, shall be appropriated as a fund, subject to the order of said board of trustees and visitors, for the support of said schools for colored children; Provided, That no person shall be employed or paid, directly or indirectly, as a teacher or instructor, in any of said schools, until he or she shall first have obtained from the board of examiners created by this act, a certificate of qualification, as to his or her competency and moral character.

Section 2. That the original section seventeen of the act of which this act is mandatory, be and the same is hereby repealed.

NUMBER 11

An act to amend an act entitled "an act to amend the act to provide for the maintenance and better regulation of common schools in the city of Cincinnati, passed January 27, 1853, and April 18, 1854." Approved April 8, 1856, Laws of Ohio.

Section 1. Be it enacted by the General Assembly of the State of Ohio, That section seventeen of the act to which this is an amendment, be amended so as to read as follows: Section XVII. The property of all colored persons in said city shall be listed and taxed for school purposed in the same manner as the property of other persons, and the separate schools now established for the education of the colored children in said city, in such districts as the board of trustees and visitors shall have established, shall continue until changed as hereinafter provided, and the district schools so established shall be conducted under the control and management of three directors in each district, who shall be elected annually from among the residents in such districts respectively, by the adult colored males resident in each district, on the last Monday in June of each year, of which public notice of time and place of election shall be given by the clerk of the board for at least one week previous to each election, by publication in a newspaper published in said city; and hold their office one year, or until their successors shall be elected and qualified, and vacancies in their number shall be filled by said directors, and they shall have the care and management of the schools and school property of their respective districts, appoint teachers and regulate their salaries, regulate the course of studies and textbooks, fix and determine the times and duration of such schools, and the vacations thereof; provide suitable accommodations, furniture and fuel for their due maintenance, and perform all the duties necessary for keeping up such schools, and for the government and instruction of the colored children of their respective districts in said schools. Said directors shall cause a record of their proceedings to be fairly kept, in books which they shall provide for that purpose, and transmit to their successors; and all powers and duties, conferred or imposed upon the board of trustees and visitors, of common schools in said city by sections five, six, seven, eight, nine, ten, thirteen and fifteen, of the act entitled "an act to provide for the better regulation of the common schools in the city of Cincinnati"; passed January 14, 1853, be, and the same is hereby conferred and imposed upon said board of colored directors so far the same are applicable to colored schools, and so much of the school funds of said city, as upon an equal distribution of the same per capita, under any enumeration required by this act, as would fall to the share of the colored children; Provided, that no person shall be employed or paid, directly or indirectly, as teacher or instructor in any of said schools until he or she shall first have obtained form the board of examiners, created by this act, a certificate of qualification as to his or her competency and moral character. The said board of directors for colored schools; and said board of trustees and visitors shall include said estimate, or so much of it as they deem necessary in their annual certificate to the city council of the city of Cincinnati, of the amount necessary to be raised for school purpose in said city.

Section 2. The words "colored persons" and "colored children" as used in this act, and the act to which this an amendment, shall be deemed and held to mean those who are reputed to be in whole or in part of African descent.

Section 3. That the original section seventeen of the act of which this is mandatory, be, and the same is hereby repealed.

Section 4. This act shall take effect and be in force from and after the first day of June next.

NUMBER 12

An act to amend "an act for the reorganization and maintenance of common schools," passed May 1, 1873, and to repeal section thirty-one of "an act to amend and supplementary to an act entitled an act to provide for the organization, supervision, and maintenance of common schools," passed March 14, 1852, and acts mandatory thereto; also, supplementary to an act for the support and better regulation of common schools in the town of Akron, passed February 8, 1847, and the acts mandatory thereto; also, supplementary to an act for the better regulation of public schools in cities, towns, etc., passed February 21, 1849, and the acts mandatory thereto. Approved May 11, 1878, Laws of Ohio.

Section 1. Be it enacted by the General Assembly of the State of Ohio. That section fifty of the above recited act be amended to read as follows:

Section 50. Each board of education shall establish a sufficient number of schools to provide for the free education of the youth of school age within the district, at such places as will be most convenient for the attendance of the large number of such youth, and where in their judgment it may be for the advantage of the district to do so, they may organize separate schools for colored children; boards of education in two or more adjoining township districts may, in like manner, unite in a separate school for colored children, each board to bear its proportionate share of the expense of such school, according to the number of colored children from each district in said school, which shall be under the control of the board of education of the township in which the school house is situated; any board of education may establish one or more schools of higher grade than the primary schools whenever they deem the establishment of such school or schools proper or necessary for the convenience or progress in studies of the pupils attending the same, or for the conduct and welfare of the educational interests of such district; and the board shall continue each and every day school established by them for not less than twenty-four nor more than forty-four weeks in each school year: provided, that each township board of education shall establish at least one primary school in each sub-district of their township; and the boards of education of the districts in which a "children's home" is or may be established under an act entitled "an act for the establishment, support, and regulation of children's homes in the several counties of the state," etc, passed April 7, 1867, and in districts in which a county infirmary is or may be located, when requested by the board of trustees of such "children's home," or the directors of such county infirmary, are hereby authorized and required to establish in such home or infirmary a separate school so as to afford to the children therein, so far as practicable, the advantages and privileges of a common school education; and such school shall be continued in operation each year until the full share of all the school funds of the township or district belonging to said children, on the basis of the enumeration, shall have been expended; and all schools so established shall be under the control and management of the board of education or other school officers who have charge of the common schools of such district: provided, that in the establishment of said schools the county commissioners of the county in which such "children's home" or county infirmary may be established, shall provide the necessary school room or rooms, furniture, apparatus, and books, which they are hereby empowered to do; and provided, further, that such boards of education shall incur no expense in supporting said schools, except in the payment of the teachers.

Section 2. The said original section fifty, of the act of May 1, 1873, and section thirty-one of the above recited acts, are hereby repealed.

Section 3. This act shall take effect and be in force from and after its passage.

VIII

Jury Law

The Constitutional Convention of Ohio (1802) avoided a definitive statement on the status of African Americans. After debating the possibility of enfranchising black residents, the Convention tabled all matters referring to race. It did grantee suffrage to eligible white males. Aside from this, no one could have been absolutely certain about the future status of African Americans. The legislature, meeting in 1803, removed all doubts about its intentions for blacks. It adopted a series of measures called the black laws. In ensuing years, when the legislature refined these discriminatory measures, it adopted the jury law (1831). Unable to have a jury with at least one member of his race, African Americans were always at the mercy of whites. A white skin did not always mean that court decision would be rendered in favor of whites, however. The Supreme Court occasionally protected black residents. But there were limits to what the court could achieve. Consequently, the jury law made African Americans, in spite of their best efforts, an impotent under-class in Ohio.

NUMBER 1

An act relating to juries. Approved February 9, 1831, Laws of Ohio.

Section 1. Be it enacted by the General Assembly of the State of Ohio, That one hundred and eight judicious persons, having the qualifications of electors, shall be annually selected in each county, to serve as grand and petit jurors the ensuing year.

Section 2. That the clerks of the courts of common pleas, in their respective counties, shall, on the first Monday of September next, and on the first Monday of September, annually thereafter, cause the proportion of jurors to be ascertained from the number of white male inhabitants of the age of twenty-one years, in their respective townships and shall make, in writing, a statement of the number of jurors apportioned to each township, and shall deliver the same to the sheriff; and the sheriff, at the time he gives public notice of the general election to be held on the second Tuesday of October, shall insert a clause in his notification, to be set up at the place of holding the election in the several townships of his county, giving the trustees notice of the number of persons to be returned as jurors from such township.

IX

Reports: The Black Laws

Republican delegates to the Ohio Constitutional Convention of 1802 lost their campaign to enfranchise African-American residents. Their opponents not only succeeded in defeating their proposal, they also captured the legislature the following year. As lawmakers, they succeeded in drafting statutes to make blacks an under-class. Subsequently, social reformers in Ohio sent to the legislature a series of petitions demanding repeal of the black laws. Their supporters in the assembly kept this issue current before their colleagues. House and Senate journals of the legislature clearly show an uncompromising effort of a few lawmakers to persuade the assembly to nullify the black laws. The legislature studied this question carefully, and in 1837 produced its first report on the black laws. The legislature moved haltingly on the question. Finally, in a political compromise in 1849, it nullified the black laws. African Americans played a significant role in achieving the rescission of the black laws. They obtained few additional benefits, at least not immediately. The following documents, in addition to showing legislative review of the black laws, illustrates the role played by black and white petitioners for their repeal. Unfortunately for scholars, the whereabouts of these petitions is unknown.

NUMBER 1

Report on petitions to repeal the black laws. December 4, 1837, Senate Journal.

The select committee to which was referred the numerous petitions of the citizens of this State, asking the repeal of certain laws, imposing restrictions and disabilities, upon persons of color, not found in the constitution, and which the petitioners aver to be contrary to its principles; and also praying that the right of trial by jury, may be secured to all persons within its jurisdiction; respectfully present the following report:

That they are fully sensible of the difficulties and perplexities which have been thrown around this subject, from motives of State policy from popular prejudice, from self-interest, and from excited apprehension of impending danger; and also of the extreme sensitiveness of public feeling, upon the agitation and discussion of all questions, connected with it, and the suspicion and obloquy which attends this very effort, and attaches to every person, that contributes in the smallest degree, to present it to the consideration of the American people.

Notwithstanding this threatening array of vindictive feeling, and excited prejudice, your committee have proceeded calmly and dispassionately, but firmly and conscientiously, in discharging the duties assigned them, under a deep sense of all their responsibilities to their fellow beings, to their country and its constitutional authority, to the immutable principles of justice and equity, and to that Supreme Being, from whom all power is derived, and to whom all moral agents are amenable.

And while they are constrained to believe, that popular feeling has been perverted and led astray upon these important subjects, through mistaken views of public policy, and moral duty; they have no desire to animadvert upon the motives or causes which have induced it, and they would gladly avoid all those exciting questions, calculated to inflame the public mind. Their only wish has been, to present the several questions submitted to their consideration, fairly before the Legislature, for their deliberate examination, and if their judgment and reason do not urge them to act in the premises, the committee will seek no additional impulse from any appeal to their passions.

There was a time in the history of our county, when the privilege of "enjoying and defending life and liberty, of acquiring, possessing, and protecting property, of pursuing and obtaining happiness and safety, was declared to be the natural, inherent, and unalienable right of all men, and recognized as one of the great and essential principles of liberty and free government"; when the dissemination of these principles was every where acknowledged to be a public duty, and a moral virtue; when they met a cordial response from the breast of every American patriot; when their advocates were hailed as the "great apostles of civil liberty," when their total disregard was made the subject of repeated complaint and remonstrance against the parent government, from which we revolted; when they were relied upon, as a justification for abolishing a form of government in which they were not recognized; and when they were solemnly and officially promulgated to the world, as self-evident truths, on which all rightful governments should be based, and upon which our own was to be "forever unalterably established" and administered.

Nor were these sentiment, at that period, confined to any particular section of the country, or regarded as the mere abstract principles of a visionary theory, or speculative philosophy; but they were inculcated as practical maxims, applicable to the condition of man, suited to the state of human society, "essential to liberty and free government," and in numerous instances, incorporated into our political systems or forms of government. In accordance with these principles, the first act of Congress, on assuming jurisdiction over the North Western Territory, after its cession by the States of Virginia and Connecticut, by the Ordinance of 1787, declared, "There should be neither slavery or involuntary servitude, in said Territory, otherwise than in the punishment of crimes, whereof the party shall have been duly convicted," with a further provision, that whenever any portion of said Territory would be admitted as a State into the confederacy, "its constitution and government should be republican, and in conformity to the principles contained in said ordinance."

Actuated by the same spirit of liberty and equal justice, one State after another abolished the system which had been established while under a colonial government, of withholding from a portion of their fellow beings those natural and personal rights which, as a nation, we had declared to be inalienable, as emanating from Deity, and as the common inheritance of the whole human family.

So expanded was this feeling, so powerful was its impulse, and so practical its effects, that, within the short period of a few years, eight out of the thirteen States originally in the confederacy, and which subsequently united in forming the present federal constitution, had discarded this system from their constitutions and laws, and restored their fellow creatures to liberty and freedom. In these events we have a happy illustration of the facility with which public opinion and long established customs and modes of thought may be made to yield to the power of truth and moral obligation, when left to their free and unrestrained influence. It was owing to the spirit of the times, to the virtue of the people, to the freedom and firmness with which these principles were discussed and maintained, and to a readiness in the public mind to listen to the voice of reason, and yield to the conviction of duty, that such important results were effected. It was to the untiring energies and eloquent appeals of such men as Franklin and Jefferson, that America is indebted for the incorporation of these fundamental principles into our constitutional form of government, and for the emancipation of a portion of our territory from the evils of a system which had once pervaded the land. That fervency of zeal and philanthropy of feeling which appear to characterize all the writings of the latter, in the cause of civil liberty, seem to partake almost of the spirit of prophecy, when portraying the direful calamities and future consequences which would result from the continuance of this system. In reference to the evils of the system, he says: "The whole commerce between the master and slave is a perpetual exercise of the most boisterous passions, the most unremitting despotism on one part, and degrading submission on the other. Our children see this, and learn to imitate it; for man is an imitative animal. This quality is the germ of all education in him. From his cradle to his grave, he is learning to do what he sees others do. The man must be a prodigy, who can retain his manners and morals undepraved by such circumstances. With the morals of the people, their industry, also, is destroyed."

In relation to its injustice and impolicy, he observes: "That disposition to theft, with which they have been branded, must be ascribed to their situation, and not to any depravity of the moral sense. The man in whose favor no laws of property exist, probably feels himself less bound to respect those made in favor of others. When arguing for ourselves, we lay it down as a fundamental principle, that laws, to be just, must give a reciprocation of right; that without this, they are mere arbitrary rules of conduct, founded in force, and not in conscience; and it is a problem, which I give to the master to solve, whether the religious precepts against the violation of property were not framed for him as well as his slave; and whether the slave may not as justifiably take a little from one who has taken all from him, as he may slay one who would slay him. That a change in the relations in which a man is placed, should change his ideas of moral right and wrong, is neither new nor peculiar to the color of the blacks. "The opinion that they are inferior, in the faculty of reason and imagination, must be hazarded with great diffidence. And with what execration should the statesman be loaded who, permitting one half of citizens thus to trample on the rights of the other, transforms those into despots and these into enemies; destroys the morals of the one part, and the amor patriae of the other?"

In reference to the future consequences of a continuance of this system, the same writer remarks: "Deep-rooted prejudices, entertained by the whites; ten thousand recollections by the blacks, of the injuries they have sustained; new provocations; the real distinctions which nature has made, and many other circumstances, will divide us into parties, and provide convulsions which will probably never end but in the extermination of the one race or the other. And can the liberties of a nation be though secure when we have removed their only firm basis, a conviction in the minds of the people that these liberties are the gift of God? that they are not to be violated but with his wrath? Indeed, I tremble for my country when I reflect that God is just; that his justice cannot sleep forever; that, considering numbers, nature and natural means only, a revolution of the wheel of fortune, an exchange of situation, is among possible events; that it may become probable by supernatural interference. The Almighty has no attribute which can take side with us in such a contest."

On the subject of emancipation, and the natural tendency of governments to degenerate, he expresses the following sentiments:

"In the very first session held under the Republican Government, the Assembly passed a law for the perpetual prohibition of the importation of slaves. This will, in some measure, stop the increase of this great political and moral evil, while the minds of our citizens may be ripening for a complete emancipation of human nature.

"I think a change is already perceptible, since the origin of the present revolution. The spirit of the master is abating--that of the slave rising from the dust; his condition mollifying--the way, I hope, preparing, under the auspices of Heaven, for a total emancipation; and that this is disposed, in the order of events, to be with the consent of the masters, rather than by their extirpation.

"But the spirit of the times may alter, will alter. Our rulers will become corrupt, our people careless. A single zealot may commence persecution, and better men be his victims. It can never be too often repeated, that the time for fixing every essential right on a legal basis, is while our rulers are honest, and ourselves united. From the conclusion of this war, we shall be going down hill. It will not then be necessary to resort every moment to the people for support. They will forget themselves, but in the sole faculty of making money, and will never think of uniting, to effect a due respect for their rights. The shackles, therefore, which shall not be knocked off, at the conclusion of the war, will remain on us long, will be made heavier and heavier, till our rights shall revive or expire in a convulsion."

Such were the sentiments of Mr. Thomas Jefferson, on these questions, as openly avowed, and widely disseminated, during the struggle for independence.

At the commencement, and during the progress of the Revolution, and for many years subsequent, there was a general desire, expectation, and intention of abolishing this system. In the Articles of Confederation of 1777, formed for mutual union and defence, the right of citizenship and equal privileges was secured to all the free inhabitants, irrespective of color, in the several States; paupers, vagabonds, and fugitives from justice, only excepted. On the adoption of the present Constitution of the United States, the strongest objections arose in the several States upon this important subject. In Virginia, the following opinions were entertained and expressed, by her most eminent statesmen, in the convention held for the purpose of deliberating upon its provisions.

Upon the clause of the Constitution, restricting Congress from prohibiting the importation of slaves until 1808, Mr. George Mason remarked: "This is a fatal section, which has created more danger than any other. The first clause allows the importation of slaves for twenty years. Under the Royal Government this evil was looked upon as a great oppression, and many attempts were made to prevent it; but the interest of the African merchant prevented its prohibition. No sooner did the revolution take place than it was thought of. It was one of the greatest causes of our separation from Great Britain. Its exclusion has been a principal object of this State, and most of the States in this Union. The augmentation of slaves weakens the States, and such a trade is diabolical in itself, and disgraceful to mankind."

On the same subject, Mr. Tyler observed: "He thought the reasons urged by gentlemen, in defence of it, were inconclusive and ill-founded. It was one cause of the complaint against British tyranny that this trade was permitted. The revolution had put a period to it, but now it was to be revived. He thought nothing could justify it. His earnest desire was, that it should be handed down to posterity, that he had opposed this wicked clause."

Mr. Johnson, on the same occasion, remarked as follows: "Look at the 1st section of our bill of rights. It says that all men are, by nature, equally free and independent. Does the paper (the Constitution) acknowledge this? No, it denies it. They tell us that they see a progressive danger of bringing about emancipation. The principle has begun since the American Revolution. Let us do what we will, it will come round. Slavery has been the foundation of the impiety and dissipation which have been so much disseminated among our countrymen. If it were totally abolished it would do much good."

The opinions of George Washington, upon the question of emancipation, were equally explicit. In his correspondence with Marquis de Lafayette, and other eminent statesmen, after the close of the Revolutionary war, he says: "It is among my first wishes to see some plan adopted, by which slavery in this country, may be abolished by law. It certainly might, and assuredly ought to be effected, and that, too, by legislative authority. There are, in Pennsylvania, laws for the gradual abolition of slavery which neither Maryland nor Virginia have at present, but which nothing is more certain that they must have, and at a period not remote."

Mr. Iredell, afterwards a Judge of the Supreme Court of the United States, in the Convention of North Carolina, observed: "When the entire abolition of slavery takes place, it will be an event which must be pleasing to every generous mind and every friend of human nature."

William Pinckney, in the House of Delegates of Maryland, in 1789, in advocating the emancipation of slaves, declared that, "by the eternal principles of natural justice, no master in the State has a right to hold his slave in bondage for a single hour. I would as soon believe the incoherent tale of a school boy, who should tell me he had been frightened by a ghost, as the grant of this petition ought, in any degree, to alarm us. Are we apprehensive that these men will become more dangerous by becoming freemen? Are we alarmed, lest by being admitted into the enjoyment of civil rights, they will be inspired with a deadly enmity against the rights of others? How much more rational would it be to argue, that the natural enemy of the privileges of freemen is he who is robbed of them himself."

Such were the doctrine promulgated to the people and to the whole civilized world, on these ever interesting and exciting subjects, by those who were hailed, as the champions of liberty, and the rights of man, in the early history of our republic; and although their practical influence may have been lost upon their descendants, still their benign effects upon the destinies of this nation will endure and be felt to the latest posterity.

Had the same combined efforts been made to prevent the dissemination of these principles--to suppress all discussion of them--to proscribe their advocates--to stifle the press, and to excite public alarm and prejudice, as at the present day; instead of now seeing one half of our country freed from its demoralizing and withering influences, we might have beheld that system spread over the whole length and breadth of our land. Had the same spirit of intolerance, of self-interest, of sectional feeling, and of moral apathy and timidity, pervaded the breasts of the patriots of the revolution, and of those who swayed the councils of the nation, at that period when the memorable Ordinance of 1787, secured to our territory a population of freemen, instead of beholding, with emotions gratitude and patriotic pride, the rising eminence of our own State, its rapid progress in wealth, population, and enterprise; with its present moral, industrious, and intelligent yeomanry, we might have now witnessed it, intercepted in its lofty career, borne down with a servile population, shorn of its vigor and energy, and suffering under all the calamities and apprehensions, arising from a system which converts the productive, laboring class of the community, which should be its strength and defence, into the natural enemies of the State.

But it is said that Ohio, having never participated in this system, is exempted from its responsibilities, and absolved from all moral obligation, to extend shelter or protection to that portion of the human family, which has been made the peculiar victims of this policy; and that we may drive them from our borders by acts of outlawry, or subject them, in this land of their birth, to a state of perpetual degradation and suffering, by depriving them of the power of "acquiring, possessing, and protecting property," by arbitrary laws, notwithstanding the following declaration is found in the constitution of our State:

"That the general, great and essential principles of liberty and free government, may be recognized and forever unalterably established, we declare: That lo men are born equally free and independent, and have certain natural, inherent, and unalienable rights; amongst which are the enjoying and defending of life and liberty; acquiring, possessing, and protecting property, and obtaining happiness and safety."

Let us examine, for a moment, this claim of exemption from all participation in this system, and consequent discharge from all moral obligation, to this unfortunate and long abused race.

Their first introduction to this country was contrary to their wishes, and an act of force and oppression on the part of the government and people of these States. By our own people they were torn from their friends, their homes, and their country, transported to our shores, sold in our markets, and purchased by our ancestors; and notwithstanding this traffic was denounced by the philanthropists and statesmen of that day, in many of the colonies, and made the subject of complaint and remonstrance to the Royal Government; still, it was sustained by the people and their provincial Assemblies. For we are informed by Mr. Jefferson, that in Virginia, under the Royal Government, they had obtained a law, imposing such a duty upon their importation, as amounted nearly to a prohibition, when it was repealed by their Assembly.

In reviewing our history, down to the period of the revolution, we shall find but little cause to exonerate our ancestors from the responsibilities which are involved in the establishment and progress of this inhuman system. Although it was authorized and encouraged by the Crown of Great Britain, to which we were then subject, yet it could not have been sustained, unless sanctioned by the people.

During our own struggles for liberty and independence, the progress of this system was suspended. Its impolicy and injustice was every where admitted, and its origin and continuance was charged upon the British Government, as an act of tyranny and oppression. Personal liberty was proclaimed throughout the nation, as the birth-right of man, of which no human government could rightfully deprive him but for the punishment of crimes. In many of the States, including Virginia, laws were passed emancipating the slaves, on condition they would join the revolutionary army and fight for their own and their country's freedom.

By the moral force of these principles, the cause of liberty was sustained through the arduous conflict, and our independence established. By that event, we were freed from all foreign influence and control over our action upon this subject. On taking our rank among the nations of the earth, we assumed all the responsibilities of an independent sovereignty. It is true, that under the articles of union and confederacy, the powers of the national government were limited and defined. Yet it was during their existence, that the most effectual checks had been interposed, to the extension of this system, by the national authority. The rights of citizenship were secured to all men in the several States, except slaves, paupers, vagabonds and criminals.

The further extension of slavery was prohibited by an act of Congress, declaring it should forever be excluded from the Territory Northwest of the Ohio, which had been ceded to the United States, and out of which new States were to be formed and admitted into the Union. The justice and propriety of this prohibition was so universally admitted at that period, that it met with no opposition, and was carried into an ordinance, and declared unalterable, except by common consent, but with one dissenting vote. So far as the power had been conferred upon the National Government, it had been exercised, to interdict and restrain its further progress. In most of the State Governments, the same public feeling had been manifested. At the same period, the country was suffering under all the calamities growing out of protracted and desolating war, from financial embarrassment, from disaffection in a portion of the people, and from the want of an efficient power in the General Government to remedy and correct these disorders.

Under all these embarrassing circumstances, the people were invoked to appoint delegates to the National Convention, to revise the Articles of Confederation, and form a more efficient National Government.

Such a Convention was held, and the present Constitution of the United States was the production of their deliberations. By that instrument, the assent of the people, and the sanction of the National Government, were obtained, for the revival and continuance of this system for the period of twenty years.

The importation of slaves into the republic, was thus authorized by the people of the United States, in their national character, and made an item of general revenue, in which they were all to participate. By the same national authority, and with any constitutional obligation, but in direct contravention of its avowed policy, and determined purpose, solemnly, deliberately, and almost unanimously, expressed in the celebrated ordinance, this system has been extended over the Territories under its jurisdiction, from which new States have been formed and admitted into the Union, until it is claimed as a right, over which the General Government has no discretion or control. In this manner, seven new States, in which this system has been established, have been added to the union, since the Ordinance of 1787, and since the adoption of the Constitution; and the territory out of which most of them have been formed, has been acquired by purchase, since the half of the people of the State, we have also acknowledged our mutual obligations, in common with others, resulting from this system, by the passage of the following resolutions, which were transmitted to Congress, and to all the States in the Union:

"Resolved by the General Assembly of the State of Ohio, That the consideration of a system, providing for the gradual emancipation of the people of color held in servitude, in the United States, be recommended to the Legislatures of the several States of the American Union, and to the Congress of the Unites States."

"Resolved That it is expedient that such a system should be predicated upon the principle that the evil of slavery is a national one, and that the people, and the States of this Union, ought mutually to participate in the duties and burdens of removing it."

After having thus, in our national character, contributed to the extension of encouragement of this system; after having participated in the system of deriving a revenue from the importation of this class of our population; after seeing them emancipated by other States, and restored to their natural rights, for risking their lives in securing our liberties, and for subsequently defending them, and for other praiseworthy actions; we then seek to avoid the responsibilities and inconveniences arising from these measures, by assuming another character, and exercising the prerogatives of a separate sovereignty. With this view we have enacted, from time to time, the most odious and oppressive laws, to degrade and depress this portion of our population.

Regardless of the principles of justice, of natural rights, of moral duty, and of the provisions of the Federal and State Constitutions, the following provisions have been incorporated into our laws, and remain on our statute books at the present time: 1st. That no black or mulatto person shall be permitted to settle or reside in this State, unless he shall procure a certificate of his freedom, under the seal of a court of record. And no such person shall emigrate and settle within the State, until he shall enter into bonds, with two freehold securities, in the sum of five hundred dollars, conditioned for his good behavior, and the payment of all charges which may be incurred on his account; for which bond and certificate he is to pay one dollar; and it is made the duty of the officers of the township, to remove out of the State, any such emigrant, not complying with these laws; and no person, a resident of the State, is permitted to employ, in any manner, any black or mulatto, not having such certificate, under severe penalties.

2d. That no black or mulatto person shall be sworn, or give evidence, in any court, or elsewhere, in this State, in any cause where a white person is a party, or in any prosecution, on behalf of the State against a white person.

3d. They are deprived of all participation in the school fund, arising from donations made by Congress for the support of schools.

4th. The right of trial by jury is withheld from them, in cases involving their personal liberties.

Your committee propose to examine these several items in the order thus presented:

It has already been observed, that by the articles of confederation, the right of citizenship, of ingress and egress, to and from all the States, and the privileges of trade and commerce, were secured to all free persons within its jurisdiction, irrespective of color. From the formation of the Confederacy until the adoption of the present Constitution of the United States, there were no constitutional restrictions imposed upon this race, unless they were slaves. They were entitled to the rights and privileges of any other class, and recognized as citizens, in the several States of the Confederacy. Under the Territorial Government, they exercised the right of suffrage, in common with all other citizens, down to the time of the adoption of our Constitution, and formation of a State Government. They voted for delegates to attend the Convention, to form our present Constitution, in 1802.

And here the inquiry should be made, in what mode, by what instrument, and to what extent have these rights and privileges been restricted or taken away? Do we find any restrictions upon them in the Constitution of the United States? There are none to be found in that document. All free persons are numbered for representation, excluding Indians not taxed, to which were to be added three-fifths of the slaves. It is true, that the qualifications of citizens and electors are not defined, as in the Articles of Confederation, but the constitution does not preclude them from enjoying the same rights and privileges they held under the consideration; nor does it make any distinction on account of color. The qualifications of electors and citizenship, are left to the States. It declares, however, that "the citizens of each State shall be entitled to all privileges and immunities of citizens in the several States."

Under the State of things the convention assembled which formed the present constitution of this State. In the journal of their proceedings will be found the subjects which were brought into discussion, and the manner in which they were imposed of. The question of depriving the colored population of the right of suffrage, which they had hitherto enjoyed, was one on which the members were much divided. On a motion to insert a clause to continue this privilege to all males residing in the territory, it was carried in the affirmative, by a vote of nineteen to fifteen, every member being present. A motion to extend the same privilege to their descendants, was not by a vote of seventeen to sixteen, one member being absent. On the third reading of the article, a motion was made to strike out the clause which had been previously inserted, extending this privilege to persons of color as above stated, which was carried by the casting vote of the president, on a tie of all the members. On the question of striking out a clause which had been inserted, excluding them from giving testimony in courts of justice against white persons, it carried in the affirmative, by a vote of seventeen to sixteen, one member absent.

It will thus be seen how far their rights and privileges were intended to be restricted by the framers of the constitution, and the majorities by which the various propositions to circumscribe them were carried or rejected. The right of suffrage was taken from them by the casting vote of the presiding officer; but a majority of the convention decided that they would not exclude them from giving evidence in courts of justice. So far as their rights and privileges were restricted by the convention, and these restrictions incorporated, into the constitution which has been accepted by the people, and made the paramount law of the State, there have been no complaints made to the Legislature. It is for the repeal of those laws, which have been made in direct violation of the plainest provisions, the most essential principles and solemn declarations contained in that sacred instrument, which were to be "forever unalterably established," that these numerous petitions have been preferred. It is for the restoration of those natural and inalienable rights, which the constitution declares belong to "all men, of enjoying life and liberty, of acquiring, possessing, and protecting property, and obtaining happiness and safety," that appeals have been so constantly made to the Legislature by citizens from every section of the State. That requisition of the law compelling them to obtain certificates of freedom, under the seal of a court, as a condition of residence in the State, in numerous instances, could never be complied with by those on whom it was intended to operate. They have no power or authority by which they could procure such certificate. It is not made the duty which they have no power to perform. It reverses all the ordinary rules of justice and the maxims of law, by raising a presumption that every one is a slave until he shall prove himself to be free, in a State where slavery does not exist. It is derogative of the authority of our own constitution, which recognizes every person within its jurisdiction as freeman, and renders it subordinate to the laws of other States. It withholds the protection of our constitution and laws from freeman in our own State, and makes them subservient to the system of slavery.

It is a species of solemn mockery in legislation, unworthy the character and dignity of a free government, to impose upon any portion of the community such conditions of enjoying the rights and privileges secured by the letter and spirit of the constitution to all, as must necessarily exclude them from all participation in them.

That such was the design of these laws, and that such would be their practical effect, if carried into execution, few will deny.

It was never believed that the law, requiring bonds, with two freehold securities, in the penal sum of five hundred dollars, as a condition of residence, would ever be complied with, nor was it intended by the makers that it ever should be. Its evident design was to drive this portion of our population into other States. It was an unrighteous attempt to accomplish indirectly and covertly, what they would shrink from doing openly and frankly. Under the plausible pretext of disobedience to those requirements, they were to be cast out from amongst us, placed beyond the protection of law, and deprived of the means of procuring sustenance and support.

To effect this object, the citizens of the State were restricted in the exercise of privileges which are allowed to those out of the State.

All residents of the State were prohibited, by penal laws, from hiring or employing, in any manner whatever, any person subject to this law, who had failed to comply with its provisions, while the citizens of other States, who had not gained a residence, were exempted from such penalties.

Nor were the projectors of this measure satisfied with casting them out beyond the protection of law, and depriving them of the means of obtaining a lawful subsistence; but they made it the duty of the officers of townships to remove them by force out of the State, for disobedience to these laws. By the same process of legislation every right secured by the Constitution may be taken from the citizens of the State. The right of suffrage, the right to bear arms, the right of the people to assemble together and consult for the common good; the right to speak, write, and print, upon any subject, might be trammelled with such conditions, as to preclude their free exercise by a large portion of the citizens to whom they are secured. There is no greater security given for the right of suffrage, to those who now enjoy it, by the constitution, than is given to all men, of acquiring and protecting property, pursuing happiness and safety, and of enjoying personal liberty. The Constitution was formed with a full knowledge that our population was comprised of white and colored persons.

The rights and privileges of the one class were as clearly defined and settled, and as sacredly secured, as the other, by that instrument. That discrimination was distinctly made and expressed in unequivocal terms, whenever it was intended to confer any political privilege upon the one, from which the other was to be excluded.

That clause in the Constitution which declares, "in all elections, all white male inhabitants, above the age of twenty-one years, having resided in the State one year next preceding the election, and who have paid, or are charged with, a State or county tax, shall enjoy the right of an elector," has no greater force than those which secure to all others, not electors, the natural and unalienable rights which were extended to them, in terms equally clear and explicit. To restrain the exercise of either, by imposing conditions unjust and oppressive, would be equally repugnant to the Constitution. No person was to be transported out of the State for any offence committed within the State. Excessive fines were not to be imposed, nor cruel and unusual punishments inflicted. These rights and privileges, and these restraints upon the legislative power, were unalterably established by the Constitution, until our form of government should be changed. There were certain fundamental principles laid down, by which the various departments of the Government were to be guided, and which neither the Legislative, Judicial, or Executive powers, would transcend. No power was delegated to the Legislature to enact laws repugnant to those principles, or subversive of those rights, which had been defined and established by the Constitution. They were to be held inviolate under that instrument, as the paramount law of the State, to which all in authority should yield obedience.

But these laws are not only repugnant to the Constitution of this State, and to the principles of our free institutions; they are also in direct contravention of the Constitution of the United Sates. That document declares that "the citizens of each State shall be entitled to all the privileges and immunities of citizens in the several States." What is the plain and obvious import of this provision? What was the manifest design of its insertion? Can there be any doubt as to its construction or intention? Was it not intended to secure to all the citizens in each State the right of ingress and egress to and from them, and the privileges of trade, commerce, and employment in them, of acquiring and holding property, and sustaining and defending life and liberty, in any State in the Union? Does it not form one of the conditions of our national compact? It is true the phraseology is changed, from that found in the articles of confederation. The term citizens is substituted for "free inhabitants and people," but the right is as sacredly secured to all the citizens of each State, by that national charter of our liberties, as it was under the confederation. Under the confederacy, all the free inhabitants of each State were entitled to all the privileges of citizens, and the people of every State were allowed the privileges of ingress and egress, and of trade and commerce in the several States.

In many of the States those rights and privileges have been continued without change, and are still enjoyed by all persons, without distinction of color.

In other States, the colored population have been especially admitted to all the rights and privileges of citizens, by the constitutions which they have adopted.

In what manner have the claims to these privileges and immunities thus secured to the citizens of each State, been treated by the States, as separate sovereignties? In Ohio, where slavery was prohibited by the General Government--where political privileges and natural rights were well defined, and unalterably established by the Constitution--where exemption from all moral obligation to the colored race is claimed on account of having never participated in any system to oppress or enslave them, we have enacted arbitrary laws by which they are excluded from the rights and privileges, which are extended to the vilest criminal in the land. Our citizens are prohibited by penal laws, from giving them employment or sustenance, and are required to expel them by force from our State. It is believed that no free State in the Union, has adopted a system so oppressive and degrading to this unfortunate race--so repugnant to the spirit and genius of our government--so revolting to the feelings of humanity or so adverse to the know and settled principles of its constitution charter, as the Statute of Ohio. But to the honor and credit of the State, and the moral sensibilities of the people, some of these laws have been reprobated and denounced by the people.

The duties enjoined upon public officers have never been performed--the penalties imposed upon the citizens have been wholly disregarded--the essential requisitions of the laws have been disobeyed with impunity, until they have become a dead letter upon your statute books, to be regarded only as a record of the imbecility, timidity, and delinquency of legislators, and the moral virtue, intelligence and discernment of the people. As a measure of public policy, it has been wholly inoperative, because it was not sanctioned by the community. It has not driven them from the State, or placed any check upon their emigration. They have found their way into this State as readily, and numerously, as into others, where no such conditions have been imposed. It is contrary to sound policy, to enact laws so repugnant to the moral sense of the community, as to preclude their execution. It is degrading to the dignity of the State--it is trifling with the moral feelings of its citizens, to continue laws in existence, under which severe penalties are hourly incurred by the great mass of the community, under a belief and expectation that they will not be enforced.

In every light in which your committee have viewed this branch of the subject referred to them, they have been impelled to the belief that these provisions in our laws, should be repealed.

In relation to the law excluding persons of color from giving testimony in courts of justice, where a white person is a party, or in State prosecutions against a white person, your committee would observe, that the great end of all judicial tribunals should be to dispense justice to all, irrespective of rank or condition, and to arrive at the truth in all their investigations. That testimony is as necessary for defence, as for accusation; as essential to ascertain innocence, as to establish guilt. That every member of the community is equally interested in the due administration of justice--in the protection of innocence--in the punishment of crimes, and in securing all necessary and proper means of attaining these important objects. Any arbitrary laws which would take from the courts the power of hearing testimony, in their researches after truth, or which would deprive an individual of the means of obtaining a disclosure of facts and circumstances essential to his defence, when charged with a criminal offence, would be a denial of justice, fraught with more dangerous consequences to society, than if such facts were to be disclosed by witnesses who were not entitled to implicit confidence. Nor can any substantial reasons be discovered why such facts should be withheld on the trial of any cause, because they rested in the knowledge of colored persons alone. Is it because they are not entitled to credit, or for the want of capacity and intelligence; or because they are too deficient in moral sensibility, to understand and appreciate the obligations of an oath, that their testimony should be excluded? It will hardly be contended that many of these reasons will apply to the entire race; and if they would, then the law, to be consistent, should exclude their testimony in all cases. If their statements under oath will elicit facts, or elucidate the truth in one case, where equal and exact justice should be administered, by what equitable rule can they be excluded in others?

The Constitution secures to every person, the rights of an impartial trial, of compulsory process for obtaining witness in his favor, and of the due administration of justice, without denial or delay. By an act of legislation, we have impaired these constitutional rights, by depriving our citizens of the benefit of witness in their favor, in prosecutions for criminal trials, which, in many cases, might lead to a denial of justice.

In trials for capital offence, where the punishment is death, and in all others of minor importance, the same means of defence, and proof of innocence, are denied to the citizens, when they are extended to those who are disfranchised. A white citizen is prohibited from procuring a disclosure of facts within the knowledge of persons of color, which might be decisive of his fate, where life or death is suspended on the issue. And still the same facts might be disclosed, in the same court of justice, on the very next trial, provided the ministers of the law should, on personal inspection of the traverser at the bar, be satisfied that he had more of the African blood than of the European blood in his veins.

The same degrading duty is again imposed upon the ministers of justice, of making the discrimination from the tincture of the skin, in the reception of witness. How often do we witness in our halls of justice the humiliating spectacle of a score of witness, of various shades of color, before our judges, to ascertain whether they are white enough to testify, or whether their color is too dark to permit them to be sworn, in that particular cause. For it should ever be remembered that these questions are finally be decided by the court, not upon any proof of parentage, or admixture of the two races, but simply, upon proof being made of the person, they declare, whether his complexion approximates the nearest of the standard colors of white or black.

And upon these decisions, thus arbitrarily made, are suspended the rights of our citizens, to prove themselves guiltless of the most heinous offence, nd the power of the State to obtain evidence, necessary to procure the conviction of the most flagrant transgressors of the laws.

Instead of securing an impartial trial, and equal and exact justice to all, the most arbitrary and unjust distinctions are made in the fundamental rules by which the rights of property, of liberty, and of life, are determined.

And the application of these rules are not made to depend upon the important questions involved in the issue, but upon the character and color of the parties, a distinction which is utterly subversive of every well settled and established principle of justice and equity in civilized society.

The right of a party in court to the benefit of certain testimony, being dependent upon these nice distinctions, it becomes highly important that our judges should possess the requisite qualifications to analyze and determine the precise shade of color which is to form the dividing line between those who are to be denominated white, and those who shall be considered black.

The point upon which all these rights are to turn should be known and defined, and when the standard is fixed, it should be incorporated into the law, for the benefit of all suitors in court, that they might have an opportunity to bring themselves and their witness to the test, previous to the trial of their cause. And so long as those laws are in force, the propriety is suggested, of changing the ancient emblems of Justice, in conformity to these provisions, and instead of being represented as blind, it should assume the form of an argus, and in lieu of the suspended even balances, it should display a graduated scale of colors, by which its favors were to be dispensed, according to the condition and complexion of the humble supplicants in its temple.

Such are the absurdities into which we are led, whenever we undertake to change immutable principles, and make them bend to our prejudices, or conform to particular circumstances. The organization of our judicial tribunals, the manner in which our juries are constituted, the ordinary rules of evidence, and the power of our courts to scan the testimony of witness, and set aside a verdict, are sufficient safeguards of the due administration of justice, without the intervention of these arbitrary laws.

These tribunals are all necessarily composed of white citizens, and to their discriminating intelligence, we may safely confide the power of determining the credibility of witness, and the proper weight which should be given to the testimony, of either white or colored persons.

In many cases of frequent occurrence, the testimony of colored persons is required, to bring criminals to justice, and maintain the sovereignty of the laws, where they are neither parties to the suit, or in any manner connected with the transaction by which the laws have been violated. It is the only mode by which they can be protected in the enjoyment of life, liberty, or property. Their persons and property are constantly exposed to the lawless violence of the most profligate members of Society, without the hope of redress, unless the transactions have been witnessed by others, not of their color. They are deprived of the protection of law, and denied the means of obtaining justice in our courts, or a redress for "injuries done in their lands, goods, and persons," contrary to the provisions of the constitution, declaring they should be secured to "every person."

The question of excluding them from testifying in courts of justice against white persons, was also definitely settled, by a recorded vote, in the convention which formed the constitution of the State. It was there decided, on due deliberation by the members of the convention, that they should not be excluded from the exercises of this privilege; and they continued to enjoy it until the passage of the law in question. By what authority can the rights and privileges which were passed upon and settled by the constitution, be revoked by legislation?

That instrument, after defining and establishing the powers of the various departments of the Government; after fixing the qualifications of electors, and public officers; after enumerating that natural and political rights and privileges which should be extended to all persons; after declaring that certain great and essential principles recognizing these rights should be "forever unalterably established"--in the closing paragraph of the last article reads as follows: "To guard against the transgressions of the high powers which we have delegated, we declare that all powers not hereby delegated, remain with the people."

The right and privilege of testifying in courts of justice having been exercised by this class of our population previous to the adoption of the constitution of our State; the question having been raised in the convention which formed it, and after mature deliberation settled by a vote in a favor of the continuance of this right; and no power having been delegated by the constitution to the Legislature, to abridge in the rights of the people, as recognized and settled by that instrument, it would seem that a revocation of it would transcend the powers delegated to the Legislature.

The abrogation of this right does not affect the interests of the colored population alone. It involves the rights and privileges of every member of society. So far as the body politic is concerned in the protection of innocence and the punishment of guilt, its power is abridged by the suppression of testimony which might establish either the one or the other. The rights of every individual citizen are affected, because they are deprived of the constitutional privilege of obtaining the testimony of witness in their favor, where their property, reputation, and life are at stake.

The rights of the colored population are left wholly unprotected, and their property, persons, and lives, exposed to the lawless depredations of every abandoned member of the community, without the means of obtaining redress.

Believing such restrictions to be contrary to sound policy, injurious to public morals, an obstruction to the impartial administration of justice, an infringement of constitutional rights, and repugnant to the spirit and genius of our political institutions, your committee recommend a repeal of that section of the law excluding them from giving testimony.

On the subject of excluding the children of persons of color from participating in the benefits of the school funds, arising from donations made by the United States and from taxation, the following observations are submitted for the consideration of the Senate.

Before the organization of a State Government, the following proposition, with others, was incorporated into a law of Congress, for the acceptance or rejection of the then Territory (now State) of Ohio, on condition that the State would, by an irrevocable ordinance, exempt the lands of the United States from taxation for the term of five years from and after the day of sale: "That the section number sixteen in every township--and, where such section has been sold, granted, or disposed of, other lands equivalent thereto, and most contiguous to the same--shall be granted to the inhabitants of such township for the use of schools."

The State of Ohio, in convention assembled, accepted the above proposition, on condition "that all the lands before mentioned to be appropriated by the United States for the support of schools, shall be vested in the Legislature of this State in trust for said purpose."

This modification of the former proposition was agreed to by Congress, and the grants were made in accordance with it, and the title "vested in the Legislature of Ohio in trust for the use aforesaid, and for no other use, intent, or purpose whatever."

It should be noticed, that this grant of section sixteen in each town or its equivalent, was to be made to the inhabitants of such township, for the use of schools therein. That it was not to depend upon any section of the township, or upon the comparative number, character, or condition of the inhabitants; for at that period the country was a wilderness, and most of the townships were uninhabited. Still, that section or its equivalent was to be held in trust by the Legislature, for the inhabitants of the township, for the use of schools whenever it became inhabited. It was a donation secured to each township, for the benefit of its future inhabitants, without reservation or distinction, except it was to be applied to the use of schools.

The State had no control over the sale of the lands comprising the townships, nor could it make a selection of the purchasers, who were to constitute their future inhabitants. The lands might be taken up and settled by foreigners, or by persons not naturalized, who would nevertheless be entitled to the benefit of the donation, and could rightfully claim the execution of the trust. The beneficial interest arising from the grant enured to the inhabitants, whoever they might be.

The power of the Legislature was limited to the terms of the grant, and could only carry into execution its express stipulations.

If an entire township had been sold by the United States to persons of color alone, or to foreign immigrants not naturalized, and they should constitute its only inhabitants, would they not have been rightfully and legally entitled to all the benefits of the grant? If they would not, to whom would their interests have reverted? If, under such circumstances, it should have been withheld from the inhabitants, and declared forfeited to the State, or applied to other townships, would it revert back to the proper township, on the removal of some half dozen white citizens within its limits?

If the same grant had been made by an individual proprietor of a township of land, and he had subsequently sold every other section within it to colored persons, could they not have lawfully claimed the benefit of the trust estate? and would not their claims have been allowed and enforced by our courts, under the ordinary rules and principles of law?

These various questions must have forced themselves upon the consideration of the members of the convention which formed the constitution of the State. The terms and conditions of the proposed grant were before them, for their free acceptance or rejection. Before yielding their assent, they had the right of proposing any modification of its terms.

The only one upon which their acceptance was predicated, having any bearing upon the question now at issue, was, that the property conferred by the grant should be vested in the Legislature of the State, in trust for the purposes certified in the proposition.

With a perfect knowledge of all the conditions attached to the grant, and the duties involved in the trust, and of the mixed character of the rights and privileges of the people by a written constitution.

In discriminating between the political rights and privileges which were thereafter to be enjoyed by the various classes of a mixed population, the distinctions were made in the most appropriate language, and in explicit terms. In declaring these distinctions, the words "white inhabitants," or "white males," in contradistinction from those of color, are used six times, and the words "negro or mulatto" occur once in the constitution. After defining the qualifications of electors, citizens, and those eligible to office, the term "citizens," or "effectors," is frequently used, to mark the distinction between them and other persons or inhabitants; and these terms are constantly occurring throughout that instrument, in defining those distinct privileges which were intended to be conferred upon them, apart from those rights and privileges which were secured to all persons, without any discrimination.

But to show more clearly their views upon this subject, and as it would seem, to place it beyond the power of future legislation to disregard them, after having settled all the distinctions which should be made in the rights and privileges of white and colored persons, they incorporate the following section into the last article of constitution: "That no law shall be passed to prevent the poor in the several counties and townships within this State from an equal participation in the schools, academies, colleges and universities within this State, which are endowed, in whole or in part, from the revenue arising from donations made by the United States for the support of schools and colleges; and the doors of said schools, academies, and universities, shall be open for the reception of scholars, students, and teachers of every grade, without any distinction or preference whatever, contrary to the intent for which such donations were made."

From the first organization of our State Government down to 1829, there were no attempts made by the Legislature to change the application of these funds, or to make any distinction in the reception of scholars in the schools to which they were applied. The law of that year first excluded colored children from the property of color persons provided that all taxes assessed upon the property of colored persons should be appropriated, by the trustees of townships, for the education of such children. In 1831, the funds arising from these donations were appropriated "for the instruction of white youth of every class and grade, without distinction"; and the property of colored persons was exempted from taxation for school purposes. And upon these principles this fund has since been annually distributed, against the remonstrances and petitions of numerous citizens in various sections of the State.

Two questions will naturally present themselves to the consideration of every reflecting mind, in the investigation of this subject. First. Whether a portion of these funds does not rightfully belong to this class of our population, by the terms of the grant, the conditions of the trust, and the provisions of the constitution? Second. Whether public policy and moral duty do not require that legislative provision should be made for the education of this unfortunate portion of the human family?

Every casual observer must notice with surprise the clashing of the present law, as above quoted, with that clause in the constitution before referred to.

The constitution declares that these "schools shall be open for the reception of scholars, students, and teachers, of every grade, without any distinction or preference whatever." The law declares that they shall be "for the instruction of white youth of every class and grade, without distinction," thereby making a distinction which excludes a class of scholars who have enjoyed the right for more than a quarter of a century under the constitution. Strike out from our laws the interpolation which has thus been made in the constitutional provisions upon the subject, and the question is practically settled.

This class of our population are taxed, in common with all others, for the current expenditures of the government, and the support of common schools throughout the State. Although the law for raising a school tax exempts the property of blacks and mulattoes from taxation for that specific object, still it is not made the duty of any officer to ascertain the proper ownership of such property, and the tax is levied and collected, in most instances in the State, without any such discrimination.

These facts have been ascertained by communications from various county auditors, in different sections of the state, which have been laid before your committee. A proper investigation of this subject will show they have not only been excluded from all the benefits arising from the donations made by Congress to the inhabitants of each township in the State for the support of schools, and refused all opportunity of educating their own children, but that they have been compelled to contribute to the fund for the education of white children, and taxed for the support of schools from which they are excluded, and to sustain a government which refuses them the protection of its laws. Their manifest injustice and oppression have called forth the note of remonstrance, and the supplications of eight thousand petitioners, comprising some of the most respectable and conspicuous citizens of every profession in all parts of the State for their modification or repeal. Nor have we any reason to expect that they will cease from their exertions, or falter in their invocations to the Legislature, until the demands of justice shall be duly considered.

But, laying aside all legal and constitutional claims, what are the dictates of public policy and moral duty, in relation to this subject?

This unfortunate race constitutes a portion of our population, with every prospect of a proportionate increase. What shall be done with them? As a State, we have no more authority to restrict their residence than any other State in the Union. Their introduction to the country was a national act, the consequences of which must rest upon the nation collectively. We should consider this question, with reference not merely to local interests, sectional feelings, or present State policy, but to all its bearing upon the character, safety, and well-being of the people of the United States. We can now look back upon the course pursued by those who have gone before us, in directing public opinion, and settling the policy of the nation upon this subject, and discover the errors which they committed, and the threatening calamities they have entailed upon succeeding generations, for want of moral firmness in resisting, at the proper period, the establishment, continuance, and extension of the system from which all these evils have flowed. The same moral obligation rests upon the present generation, to adopt such measures as will most effectually secure the republic from the dangers which must inevitably result from a continuance of the present course of policy. We have this people amongst us, with every assurance that they will from a portion of our population for generations that will succeed us.

And shall we compel them to remain in their present degraded condition, without the hope or power of improvement?

Will the safety, well-being, and happiness of the people be promoted by withholding from them the means of education?

Will the power and strength of the State, or the stability and permanency of our free institutions be better secured by adopting a course of policy towards them which must force them to become the enemies of the government?

The suggestion that, as their privileges are enlarged, their rights protected, and their minds cultivated, they will become more dangerous to society, is unnatural, and contrary to all practical experience. Reason and observation teach us that the spirit of man becomes vindictive in proportion to the injuries he has received; and the truth of this observation is fully verified in the history of this race.

Wherever their rights have been respected, they have been peaceable and quiet.

As a measure of sound policy in reference to the present and future generations, as an act of public duty and moral obligation, as a matter of constitutional right and legal justice, your committee believe that the means of education should be extended to this degraded portion of our population.

In regard to the right of trial by jury, it may truly be said that it is one of inestimable value to freemen, "and unformidable to tyrants only." It constitutes the most effectual barrier against tyranny, injustice, and oppression, and the last hope of the innocent, the injured and the oppressed. It forms the best security against corruption, and the dangerous influence of power, and interposes no obstructions to the administration for justice. In any case whatever.

It had long been the boast of our ancestors, in the land of their fathers, and was transferred by them to this country to their adoption, as one of the vital elements of civil and religious freedom; affording the safest protection against the encroachments of power upon the rights and liberties of the people. It was the most invaluable concession ever wrested from despotic power, and should be the last to be relinquished by the people, under any pretence whatever. An attempt to restrict the exercise of this right in certain cases, was one of the prominent acts of usurpation and oppression on the part of the British crown, for which its sovereign was denounced as a tyrant by the unanimous voice of the representatives of the three millions of people, in 1776.

In subsequently framing our systems of government, it has never been lost sight of, but has been watched with jealous attention, and guarded with scrupulous care. By the Ordinance of 1787, certain fundamental principles were established, by which the people, and the States thereafter to be erected out of the territory, were to be governed, which were to "remain forever unalterable, unless by common consent."

Among which were the following: "There shall be neither slavery or involuntary servitude in said territory, otherwise than in punishment of crimes whereof the party shall have been duly convicted: Provided always, That any person escaping into the same, from whom labor or service is lawfully claimed in any one of the original States, such fugitive may be lawfully reclaimed, and conveyed to the person claiming his or her labor or service, as foresaid." "The inhabitants of said territory shall always be entitled to the writ of habeas corpus, and of trial by jury; no man shall be deprived of his liberty or property but by the judgment of his peers or the law of the land."

This was the first constitutional law which guaranteed these rights to the inhabitants of this State, and defined and settled their relative duties to the original States.

To whom were these benefits of trial by jury and the writ of habeas corpus secured? To all the future inhabitants of the territory, or States which should be formed out of it. No distinction was made; no preference was given, to any portion of the future population. It was extended to all persons, whether citizens or aliens, should thereafter reside within its limits, or be subject to its jurisdiction.

What was the tenure by which these rights were to be held? They were to remain forever unalterable, unless by common consent.

Did the free exercise and enjoyment of these rights conflict with the duties enjoined upon them in relation to fugitives from labor or service? Not in the least. They were bound to take cognizance of such claims, and make provision for their investigation and decision, as in all other cases. Whether they were fugitives from labor or service from another State, or whether such service as lawfully claimed, were preliminary questions for judicial decision. The law embraced all cases where service was claimed to be due from one person to another out of this State, whether by indenture, apprenticeship, or otherwise.

The claim could be set up against one person, as well as another, without distinction of color, rank or condition; and the mode of proceeding would be the same in all cases under the same law.

It would have been preposterous to suppose that the manner of determining these questions was to be dedicated by another by any other authority than the sovereign power of the State.

To have vested such power of dictation over their judicial proceedings in any other body, would have been irreconcilable with the privileges, and subversive of the rights guaranteed by that ordinance, to the people of the State.

The exercise of such authority, could limit, control, or suspend at pleasure, the right of trial by jury, and to the writ of habeas corpus, which had been secured to all the future inhabitants of the State or territory. So far from holding these rights subject to any foreign dictatorial power, they were placed not only beyond the control of our own legislation, but above the law-making power of any constituted authorities whatsoever. They existed by "compact between the original States and the people, and States in the territory, and were to remain forever unalterable, unless by common consent." The supposition that any person could be deprived of the benefit of a trial by jury, or of a writ of habeas corpus, on the allegation that he had fled from another State, where he owed service or labor, is adverse to every principle of law--to every dictate of reason. It would be determining his character by accusation, and establishing his delinquency, by averment. It would be deciding the question at issue, for the purpose of settling the mode by which it should be tried.

These guarantees were made for the benefit of the people, to protect them against any arbitrary exercise of power, on the part of the government, or those who should administer it. They were intended as limitations upon the law-making power, by whomsoever it should thereafter be exercised. They were as much restricted from abridging these rights, as they were precluded from passing any laws, discharging persons from service in any of the original States. The right of lawfully reclaiming persons from whom service was lawfully due, under the laws of other States, was never to be prohibited by the laws of this State. The existence of such lawful claim, however, could only be established by the judicial tribunals of the State, where the party was found, and in accordance with its own laws. There was no discretionary power vested in our own courts or legislature, to suspend the operation of one law, in carrying into execution the other, nor was there any necessity for so doing, to the full and perfect discharge of all our duties and obligations under both. Much less was there an investment of such extraordinary power over our own laws, in any superior tribunal, or independent government. Such authority was never claimed by the United States, under the confederation, when this compact was made between them and the people of the territory or States growing out of it.

No such power having been reserved, vested, or claimed by the General Government, under the ordinance or Articles of Confederation, let us examine how far our relative powers and duties have been changed, or our rights affected, by the formation of the present constitution of the United States, and the organization of our State Government.

The constitution of the United States was adopted soon after the passage of the ordinance to which we have referred. It did not supersede it, or absolve the parties from the obligations of the compact, or change the fundamental principles or abrogate the rights and privileges which had been established by it, for the guidance and government, and for the welfare and security, of the people of the Territory.

The controlling authority, and binding force of the ordinance, has been constantly recognized and admitted by the parties, in all their subsequent transactions. Every modification of its important provisions and stipulations, has been effected by negotiations and "common consent." Its force and validity was acknowledged by the first Congress under the constitution, in the act to provide for the government of the Territory. The preamble to this act reads as follows: "Whereas, in order that the ordinance of the United States, in Congress assembled, for the government of the Territory North west of the river Ohio, may continue to have full effect, it is requisite that certain provisions should be made, so as to adapt the same to the present constitution of the United States." The act then declares, that all information and communication from the officers of the Territory, required to be made to Congress by said ordinance, may thereafter be made to the President; and provides for other corresponding changes in the appointment and commission of officers, to adapt it to the system of the Government as re-organized. Under the Territorial Government, down to the time of the adoption of the State constitution, the ordinance was considered as the written constitution for the government of the Territory, by every federal and territorial officer. The powers of the Government, the constitutionality of its laws, were to be tested by their conformity or repugnance to the provisions of that instrument.

So clearly was this understood, that great embarrassments arose, in consequence of the want of power to repeal the laws once established by the Territorial Government; no provision having been made in the ordinance for such power, until the population became so numerous as to entitle them to organize a General Assembly.

In the act of Congress of 1802, authorizing the inhabitants of that portion of the territory constituting the present State of Ohio, to form a constitution and State government, for admission into the Union, the ordinance was referred to as containing the fundamental principles upon which the constitution should be established. It was required to be in conformity to its provisions, and not repugnant to its principles. Overtures were also made by the United States in said act, to the people of Ohio, for further mutual stipulations between the parties, on matters not embraced in the ordinance, which were offered for their free acceptance or rejection. If accepted by the State, they became obligatory upon the United States. If they were rejected, it was admitted Congress had no relative power to enforce them, because the relative powers and obligations of the parties had been established by the ordinance, and were forever to remain unalterable, unless by common consent. After various modifications, the propositions were accepted, and thereby became of equal validity with the ordinance, from which neither party had power to recede, unless by a violation of the solemn compact between them. With this written covenant in existence, acknowledged to be in full force by the parties, the constitution of this State was formed, with which it was admitted into the Union, which declares, "That all courts shall be open, and every person, for an injury done him in his lands, goods, person, or reputation, shall have remedy by due course of law, and right and justice be administered without denial or delay. The people shall be secure in their persons from unwarrantable seizures; that general warrants to seize any person or persons not named, whose offence are more particularly described, and without oath or affirmation, are dangerous to liberty, and shall not be granted. That the right of trial by jury shall be inviolate. That the privilege of the writ of habeas corpus shall not be suspended, unless when in case of rebellion or invasion, the public safety may require it. There shall be neither slavery nor involuntary servitude in this State, otherwise than for the punishment of crimes; nor shall any indenture of any negro or mulatto, hereafter made and executed out of the State, or if made in the State, where the term of service exceeds one year, be of the least validity, except those given in the case of apprenticeships."

We thus find incorporated into the constitution all the essential principles contained in the ordinance, to secure the rights and privileges, and protect the liberties of the people. No discrimination was made in the persons to whom these rights were extended, no distinction, or exception in, the cases to which they should be applied. Every person within its jurisdiction, was declared to be free, and slavery could have no existence within its borders. The right of trial by jury, was secured to all the inhabitants in the territory, by the ordinance; and it was declared to be inviolate by the constitution.

Down to this period, the ordinance had been the only constitutional authority, by which the relative powers and obligations of the contracting parties, could be ascertained. Both were equally bound by its stipulations and conditions, nor could either change the terms of the compact, or release themselves from its obligations, by an organization of its form of government. This could only be affected by mutual agreement, or concurrent action. It was irrevocable and coextensive with their corporate existence, unless altered by mutual consent.

But it is said, that an admittance into the Union, as one of the United States, nullified the ordinance, and substituted the constitution in its place. Such a conclusion is controverted by the whole tenor and import of the instrument itself. The declared object of the ordinance was, "to fix and establish the principles of civil and religious liberty, as the basis of all laws, constitutions, and governments, which forever hereafter shall be formed in the said territory; to provide also for the establishment of States, and permanent government therein, and for their admission to a share in the federal councils, on an equal footing with the original States." The preamble to the constitution of this State, also asserts the right of admission into the Union, on principles "consistent with the constitution of the United States, the Ordinance of 1787, and the law of Congress of 1802."

The law of Congress referred to, required that the constitution adopted by the State, should conform to the principles contained in said ordinance.

In all these solemn public acts, the controlling authority of the compact was duly recognized and admitted.

The State constitution was framed and submitted to public scrutiny, and by the subsequent admission of the State into the Union; it received the sanction of Congress, that its principles were not only in conformity to the ordinance, but that they were not inconsistent with the provisions of the constitution of the United States.

It is not the intention of the committee to controvert the position, that the State is bound to conform to the requisitions of the constitution of the United States, but to establish the fact, that the provisions of the ordinance and of those of the federal and State constitutions, harmonize and accord with each other, and that full force and effect can be given to each without infringing the authority of the other. They have each received the deliberate sanction of the same public authorities, and such construction should be given to them as would reconcile them with each other, if consistent with the fair import of their language, and the intentions of the respective bodies, from which they emanated.

Having examined the provisions of the ordinance and the constitution of the State, in relation to the right of trial by jury, and of personal security for unwarrantable seizures, let us refer to those of the constitution of the United States, to ascertain whether these personal rights have been annihilated, or whether any power has been vested in the general government, to suspend, limit, or abridge them in any case whatever.

One would naturally be led to conclude, if such extraordinary power was intended to be conferred upon Congress by the constitution, that it would have been given in express terms and in unequivocal language. A power which so directly infringes the sovereignty of the States, as to nullify the most essential provisions of their own constitutions, and deprive their people of those personal immunities, which had been thus secured to them, should not be permitted, silently, to be drawn to the federal government by inference, implication, or assumption, without due examination into the foundation of its claims.

In the constitution of the United States, the right of trial by jury is three times distinctly recognized and established, without making any personal discrimination.

It is twice extended to all criminal trials, except cases of impeachment; and in all civil suits, where the value in controversy shall exceed twenty dollars.

It also declares, that "the right of the people to be secure in their persons, houses, papers, and effects, against unreasonable searches and seizures, shall not be violated, and no warrants shall issue but upon probable cause, supported by oath or affirmation, and particularly describing the place to be searched, and the persons or things to be seized." It likewise provides, that "the powers not delegated to the United States by the constitution, nor prohibited by it to the States, are reserved to the States respectively, or to the people."

In all these provisions, we find nothing to limit or disparage this right, but a full confirmation of it to all persons, irrespective of rank or condition.

But the power to suspend, or restrict, the exercise of this right, and to set aside all those personal immunities, which had apparently been so well secured to all persons, both by the State and Federal constitutions, is claimed to be drawn from the two following clauses in the constitution of the United States.

"No person held to service or labor in one State, under the laws thereof, escaping into another, shall, in consequence of any law or regulation therein be discharged from such service or labor, but shall be delivered upon claim of the party to whom such service or labor may be due." "The Congress shall have power to make all laws which shall be necessary and proper, for carrying into execution all the powers vested by this constitution, in the government of the United States, or in any department, or office thereof."

And here the inquiry may well be made--What powers were vested in Congress, or any department of the General Government, by the foregoing clauses in the constitution? Was it the arbitrary power of annihilating, or abridging, the rights which had been secured to the people, in other sections of the same instrument? Was the dangerous power, of suspending the exercise and enjoyment, of the privileges and immunities which had been formally extended to them, conferred upon Congress, or any other department of the government, by these two paragraphs? Was the corrupting power, of subsequently making invidious discriminations, in the persons, or cases, to which these rights and privileges should be extended or withheld, cautiously concealed in these sections, to be called forth and exercised at pleasure?

Was the extraordinary power, of abrogating the most essential principles, and plainest provisions of the State constitutions, of dictating to the State sovereignties, the mode of their judicial proceedings, and of establishing rules by which their magistrates should be governed, in their official investigations and decisions, intended to be vested in General Government, by the clauses which have been recited? Did the framers of the constitution design to invest the Congress of the United States with the despotic power, of subjecting the people of the States, not chargeable with the commission of any crime, to lawless seizure and caption, without notice, without process of law, in a manner unknown in the history of even criminal jurisprudence, and expressly prohibited by the very instrument from which all their authority is derived, to be forced by the captors to a magistrate of their own selection, for the purpose of procuring a certificate, which might transfer them and their posterity, from a state of lawful freedom, to one of interminable and hopeless slavery?

Yet such are the powers assumed by Congress, in the passage of the law of 1793, which, it is claimed, they have the constitutional right of enforcing.

Nor can it, with truth, be asserted, that this law can only be applied to persons of the African race, and to those already in slavery. The law itself, when taken in connection with other acts of congress, precludes such a conclusion. The ordinance of Congress of prior date, prohibits slavery in the

Northwestern territories. There could have been no slaves to escape from those territories, on which the law could operate.

The law, however, declares, that any person held to labor in either of the northwestern or southern territories, who shall escape into any other State, may be seized without a warrant, by the person claiming such labor, his agent attorney, and taken before any magistrate, that such labor or service is due, and his official certificate shall be a sufficient warrant, to take the person from the remotest State in the Union.

To what persons escaping from a free State, was this law to apply? It could not be to slaves, as slavery did not exist, and was prohibited by an act of Congress in some of the Territories or States included in the law. It could be applied, however, and does embrace cases of indenture and apprenticeships, and reaches the acknowledged freeman, as well as the reputed slave; the white, as well as the colored population.

Indeed, in cases where they are claimed as slaves, the question at issue, would always be, whether they were freemen or slaves; whether they were freemen or slaves; whether they were fugitives or lawful residents. The rights and privileges of freemen, are necessarily involved in these extra-judicial proceedings by which they are deprived of all the constitutional securities and immunities, most sacredly guaranteed to them by the supreme law of the land.

The important principle involved in this law, is not, whether slaves should, or should not, be reclaimed; it is, whether freemen should be liable to be seized in this lawless manner, and consigned to perpetual bondage. The only condition required by the law, for such seizure is, that the person is held to service, or labor, in another State. By making such claim, without oath or affirmation, the claimant is authorized to seize any person in the community, and forthwith force him from his family and friends to a magistrate previously selected for the purpose, beyond the power of procuring any witness in his favor; and thus, without the benefit of witness, counsel or jury, his case may be decided, on the statement of witness already prepared by the person who has him in custody, and such decision is conclusive and final under the law, and the certificate of the magistrate a sufficient warrant for transporting such person to any other State, where the service is claimed to be due. To this extent, this law may be carried against any member of the community, without distinction of color or character, and without incurring any penalties under its provisions for preferring an illegal or improper claim. But as it regards persons of color, the consequences resulting from such a decision are still more inhuman, and revolting to every principle of justice. If taken by such certificate into a slave State, by the operation of their laws he is presumed to be a slave, and if the claimant cannot sustain the claim to his services, he may be cast into prison on the affirmation of any person, that he believes him to be a slave, and unless he can there in a strange land, separated from all his friends, prove his freedom, he is sold into slavery to discharge the costs arising from such illegal caption and imprisonment. Nor are the cases where freemen are claimed for slaves of uncommon occurrence. Several trials of this character have occurred in this State, where persons have been carried, under the sanctions of a certificate from our magistrates, into other States, where they have been declared to be free, and no redress for the wrongs and injuries they have sustained could be obtained under the law. An instance has been reported to the present General Assembly, by the Executive of the State, where a person was taken unto a neighboring State, under a claim that she was the slave of a person resident therein. On reaching the place, the pretended owner disclaimed all interest in the captive. She was then committed to prison, on the charge that she was the slave of another in the State of Louisiana, and unless claimed by that or some other person, she must under their laws, be sold, and become the slave of the purchaser. In this case, the Governor has been requested by the other branch of the legislature, to open a correspondence with the Executive of the sister State, to procure her restoration to freedom. Nor are instances wanting, where white persons have been claimed, and undergone the ordeal of a trial, under this sanguinary law. The dreadful consequences resulting from the exercise of such unusual powers, in a free government, should lead us to scan their constitutional authority.

The clause in the constitution of the United States in relation to fugitives from labor, vests no power in Congress to legislate on the subject. It is merely prohibitory of the exercise of certain powers by the State, and declaratory of certain reciprocal duties to each other. It restrains the State Governments from passing laws or making any regulations, by which fugitives from another State shall be discharged from their obligations to do service or labor under the laws of such State. It declares such legal claims for services shall be recognized in the different State, whenever persons owing such service shall escape into their jurisdiction. Its obvious design was to provide, that where claims for personal services were held valid under the laws of our State, they should not be invalidated by the laws of another.--That in their judicial investigations of such claims, their courts should have reference to the rights of the parties under the existing laws of such other State, and should render such judgment as would preserve and enforce such legal rights, by surrendering the person into the custody of the party who should prefer and substantiate such claim.

To sustain the correctness of this position, we have the highest authority. In the deliberations of the Virginia convention, on the adoption of the Constitution, every article and section was carefully scrutinized and canvassed by her most distinguished statesmen. The reputed father of the Constitution of Virginia, George Mason, declared that, "no real security could arise from the clause which provides that persons held to labor in one State, escaping into another, shall be delivered up. This only meant, that runaway slaves should not be protected in other States." The celebrated Patrick Henry also affirmed, in the Convention, that "he considered this clause as no security at all. It was not more than this: that a runaway negro could be taken up in Maryland and

New York." The construction thus given to this clause, was not controverted by the most ardent advocates of the adoption of the Constitution in that Convention, but was either tacitly or expressly admitted by all. Mr. James Madison stated that, "at present, if any slave elopes to any of those States where slaves are free, he now becomes emancipated by their laws." This clause was expressly inserted to enable owners of slaves to reclaim them. This is a better security than any that now exists.

It should be remembered that these men were all appointed members of the convention which formed the constitution of the United States; that they were among the most eminent statesmen in the union, and that two of them, Mason and Madison, took distinguished parts in the deliberations of that body, and that one was in favor of the adoption of the constitution and the other was opposed to it, in the Virginia Convention. And on that occasion, when every clause in the constitution underwent the scrutiny of these men, it was admitted, on full discussion, that its intended design and effect, would be to restrict the States from releasing persons from the obligations imposed upon them by the laws of another State, from which they had escaped. No one pretended that every power was vested in Congress to legislate on the subject.

In regard to the legislative powers of Congress, Mr. John Marshall, then a member of the convention, and afterwards chief justice of the United States, observed, that "Congress had not power to make laws on every subject. They could not go beyond the delegated powers. If they were to make a law, not warranted by any of the powers enumerated, it would be considered by the judges as an infringement of the constitution, which they are to guard. They would not consider such a law as coming under their jurisdiction. They would declare it void."

In what part of the constitution do we find the power delegated to Congress, of prescribing the manner by which the rights of persons to freedom shall be determined in the several States? Where is the power given them, of authorizing or requiring the judicial tribunals of a State to take jurisdiction under any law of Congress, or to establish any arbitrary rules, by which these judicial investigations shall be regulated? It is not to be found among any of the "enumerated powers vested in the government of the United States, or in any department or officer thereof." And yet, this constitutes their only warrant for making any laws upon the subject, according to the opinion expressed by Chief Marshall, in the Virginia Constitutional Convention. That the clause in relation, to fugitives from service was merely prohibitory on the States, that it meant nothing more than that runaway slaves should not be protected, or emancipated by the laws of other States--we have the express opinion of James Madison, George Mason, and Patrick Henry, and the tacit assent of the whole Virginia Convention. If it is not to be found among the enumerated powers, and is not vested in the general government, in some other part of the constitution, then it is not embraced in the sweeping clause, giving to Congress "power to make all laws necessary and proper, for carrying into execution all the powers vested in the government of the United States." The power of making laws was not extended by this clause to all the subjects embraced in the constitution, but to such subjects only, where the power had been vested in them. If no power had been vested in them over a particular subject, then they had no power to make laws upon that subject. There were powers delegated to Congress, over certain matters--there were others prohibited to the States, and others reserved to the States, and to the people. But it is claimed that the power is implied, in the clause we have recited, and that whenever the constitution declares an act shall be done, the power incidentally devolves upon Congress, to prescribe by law the mode by which it shall be accomplished.

Let us test the correctness of this position. In the same article, from which we have extracted the clause to which reference has been made the constitution declares that "the United States shall guaranty to every State in the Union a republican form of government." Does this vest Congress with the power to prescribe by law the details of the form, or to coerce the States to adopt any uniform system of government, or code of laws, which they may deem proper to dictate? Certainly not. The subject is left entirely to the power and discretion of the State, under the restrictions of the constitution; no law of Congress is necessary, nor would it be of any validity should one be passed, to compel them to observe uniformity, or adopt any particular model. The States are bound to conform to the constitution in this respect, but not to any law of Congress.

Again: the same article in the constitution declares, "the citizens of each State shall be entitled to all the privileges and immunities of citizens in the several States."

Has Congress passed any law, to enforce any observance of this mandatory clause? Could they add to its obligation upon State Legislatures, Judicial proceedings, by enacting it into a law? Being found in the Constitution, is it not the supreme law of the land, and could any action of Congress make it more sacred, or binding, however much it may have been disregarded by legislators or magistrates?

But the question recurs, has Congress any power to make laws to regulate the exercise of the privileges in the several States? By the constitutions of the States of New York, and Vermont, and perhaps of some others, colored persons are allowed the right of suffrage and the privilege of citizenship. They are recognized as citizens in those States. Let Congress pass laws to enforce the provisions of the constitution, declaring that they shall be entitled to all these privileges and immunities, in any other State, to which they shall remove, or even the privilege of removing, and we should soon have their constitutionality put to the test. And yet this clause is as imperative, and involves the same incidental power, of carrying it into execution as the other.

Both are equally mandatory upon the States; they vest no power in the General Government, and no legislative action of Congress could enhance or diminish their binding or legal obligations, upon the Legislatures, and Judicial tribunals of the several States.

But another clause in the same article of the Constitution, it would seem, should be decisive of the question at issue, and form a rule of construction for the whole.

The first section of the article reads as follows: "Full faith and credit shall be given in each State to the public acts, records and judicial proceedings of every other State. And the Congress may, by general laws, prescribe the manner in which such acts, records and proceedings, shall be provided, and the effect thereof."

By an examination of the journals of the proceedings of the convention, which formed the constitution, it will be found the original draft, as reported and considered in committee, contained the first clause of the above section only, and that it was re-committed to a committee of five, for the express purpose of vesting in Congress the power to regulate by law, the manner of authenticating such proceedings, and records, and declaring the effect of the same. As it stood in the first draft, it was considered merely a declaratory act, subject to such regulations as the States might adopt to carry it into effect. To produce uniformity, the power was subsequently vested in Congress, to legislate on the subject. Here then we have the strongest evidence, that the framers of the Constitution, did not consider the general grant of "power to make all laws necessary, and proper, for carrying into execution, all the powers vested by the constitution, in the Government of the United States, or in any department or officer thereof," as reaching the subject embraced in this clause, in its original form. --and [*sic*] for this reason, that section was recommitted, to attain that object by the additional clause. It would be difficult to express, in more explicit terms, the intention of limiting or extending, in the same degree, the power of Congress over different subjects, than was conveyed in the three sections we have recited, in their original form. The language is strikingly uniform. "Full faith and credit shall be given in each State, to the public acts, records and judicial proceedings of every other State."

"The citizens of each State shall be entitled to all privileges and immunities of citizens in the several States."

"No person held to service, or labor, in one State, under the laws thereof, escaping into another, shall, inconsequence of any law or regulation therein, be discharged from such service or labor, but shall be delivered up on claim of the party to whom such service or labor may be due."

In the first case, a special investment of power was considered necessary, to authorize Congress to make any laws upon the subject, and the additional clause was inserted. In the second case, they have never assumed any power to enforce its observance by law.

In the third case, they have claimed the power of making laws, to supersede the constitutional provisions and laws, of half the States in the Union.

But we have not only the opinions of the framers of the constitution of the United States, and the members of the Virginia Constitutional Convention, to sustain us in the position we have assumed, that there is no power vested in Congress to legislate on this subject; but we have the opinions of the Legislatures of several of the States, and of their highest judicial tribunals. The States of New York and Pennsylvania have prohibited their magistrates, under severe penalties, from taking jurisdiction under the law of Congress, or of carrying it into execution, according to its provisions.

In New York, Massachusetts, Vermont and New Jersey, they have made provisions by law, by which these questions, of personal liberty, may be determined by jury in accordance with the principles of their constitutions. In Ohio, the General Assembly have, on two different occasions, decided that the States had legislative jurisdiction over this subject. In 1804, a law was passed prescribing the mode of proceedings in the investigation of these claims, and requiring certain magistrates to take cognizance of them, and carry into effect the provisions of the law of the State.

In 1823, on application of the Governor of Kentucky, in pursuance of a resolution of the General Assembly of that State, that the States of Ohio, Indiana and Illinois, would appoint commissioners to take into consideration the subject of slaves that might escape, and also in relation to persons of color, and recommend to their several States the passage of such laws as would secure the rights of the people, and produce harmony in the States, the Legislature of Ohio, by adjoining resolution, approved of the plan, and requested the Executive to appoint such commissioners.

The following extracts are taken from the opinion delivered by Chancellor Walworth, (the successor of Chancellor Kent,) on the trial of a case, which had been taken from the Supreme Court to the Court of Errors, in the State of New York: "The decision of the Court below is put upon the ground that Congress not only has power to legislate upon this subject, but that their legislation must necessarily be exclusive in relation to this matter. If the decision of this cause turned upon these questions, I am not prepared to say that Congress has the power, under the Constitution, to make the certificate of a state magistrate conclusive evidence of the right of the claimant to remove a native born citizen of that State to a distant part of the Union, so as to deprive him of the benefit of a writ of habeas corpus, and the right of trial by jury in the State where he is found. I am one of those who have the habit of believing, that the State legislatures had the general powers to pass laws on all subjects, except those in which they were restricted by the Constitution of the United States, or their own local constitutions, and that Congress had no power to legislate on any subject, except so far as the power was delegated to it by the Constitution. I have looked in vain among the powers delegated to

Congress by the Constitution, for any general authority to that body to legislate on this subject. It certainly is not contained in any express grant of power, and it does not appear to be embraced in the general grant of incidental powers, contained in the last clause of the Constitution relative to the powers of Congress. The law of Congress respecting fugitives from justice and fugitive slaves, is not a law to carry into effect any of the powers vested by the Constitution in the Government of the United States, or any department or officer thereof."

Similar decisions have been made by the Chief Justice of the State of New Jersey, against the constitutionality of this law of Congress.

But setting aside this weight of concurring testimony, against the power of Congress to pass any laws upon this subject, there is another principle of still greater interest, and fraught with more danger to the people of the Union, involved in this law. If the power is vested in the General Government, to prescribe by law the manner in which these claims to personal liberty shall be investigated and decided, has it the power of annulling the most prominent provisions of the constitution, in carrying that power into execution? Has it the power of suspending the right of trial by jury, in cases involving liberty and slavery, when the Constitution declares, it shall be preserved in all criminal prosecutions, and in civil cases where the matter in controversy exceeds twenty dollars? Has it the power of authorizing the seizure and caption of persons, without warrant, oath or affirmation, and of causing them to be transported to a distant land, contrary to the express provisions to the Constitution? Has it the power of setting aside all the established forms of law, all the fundamental principles which have been settled for centuries, in the administration of justice? Is this power, thus acquired by implication, of such paramount authority as to transcend all the prohibitions, and annihilate all the securities contained in that sacred instrument? And to what purpose are all these alarming powers to be brought into requisition? Is it to provide for the common defence--to promote the public welfare--to enhance the national strength and prosperity, or to secure the safety and happiness of the people that these inestimable rights are to be invaded, and these constitutional privileges and immunities surrendered? Far from it. Its avowed purpose is to strengthen and sustain a system which is adverse to every principle upon which our Government was established, which is repugnant to the genius and spirit of all her free institutions, and which must demoralize and weaken the nation. It makes the defence and protection of this system the paramount duty of the Government, the chief end of our laws.

Wherever its interests are involved, the precepts of the Constitution, the rights of freemen, the privileges guaranteed to the whole American people must be held in abeyance, and become subordinate to its superior demands upon the Government for protection. The right of trial by jury, the writ of habeas corpus, of personal security from lawless arrest, without oath or affirmation, must all be suspended, during an investigation of these paramount claims for service and labor. The laws made for the protection of freemen, must be set aside by those made for the protection of slavery, in cases where the decision of the question at issue may consign the party, and his posterity after him, to perpetual servitude; when, under the general laws of the country, he might have substantiated his legal right to freedom,--and this in a State where slavery does not exist.

Your committee cannot believe that the framers of the Constitution intended to vest Congress with the legislative power of transcending any of its general restrictions--of disobeying any of its injunctions--of disregarding any of its prohibitions, or of violating or abridging any rights or privileges and immunities guaranteed to the people.

Believing that Congress is not vested with any legislative power upon this subject, that the Government of the United States has no other power in the matter than that of judicially enforcing an observance of these duties enjoined upon the States; that the Constitution secures to every citizen the right of trial by jury in cases involving personal liberty; that it prohibits the seizure and transportation out of a State of any person without a warrant supported by oath or affirmation, and that Congress has no power to require any State magistrate to take jurisdiction of these cases under its laws--your committee herewith report a bill prescribing the mode of proceedings, in all cases arising under that clause of the Constitution, respecting fugitives from service or labor. They also recommend the passage of the bill now pending in the Legislature, repealing the law excluding persons of color from testifying in courts of justice, and the adoption of the following resolutions:

Resolved, That the following declarations contained in the Constitution of the United States or of this State are applicable to all persons, and were intended by their respective framers to be practically extended to all free persons within their respective jurisdictions, and should be sustained and adhered to, by all persons exercising authority under them. To wit: "That all men are born equally free and independent, and have certain natural inherent and unalienable rights--that amongst these are the enjoying and defending life and liberty; acquiring, possessing and protecting property--that the right of the people to be secure in their persons against unwarrantable seizures, shall not be violated--that no warrants shall issue but upon probable cause supported by oath or affirmation--that the right of trial by jury shall be preserved."

Resolved, That in the administration of justice, and in the protection of these natural and constitutional rights, the same rules and principles of law should be extended to all persons, irrespective of color, rank or condition.

NUMBER 2

Report on the repeal of the black laws. February 7, 1838, House Journal.

The minority of the committee upon the Judiciary to which were referred the petitions of sundry citizens, praying a repeal of our laws against the colored population, having had the same under consideration, now report upon that branch of those laws which abridges the competency of black and mulatto persons to be sworn and give evidence in courts of justice or elsewhere.

The number and character of the petitioners, the theory and practice of our Government, and the questions involved, commend this subject to the calm and thorough examination of the Legislature. Three thousand eight hundred citizens of this State have asked us to repeal these laws. The constitution of the State declares that a frequent recurrence to the fundamental principles of civil government, is absolutely necessary to preserve the blessings of liberty, and the questions involved directly affect the rights and the obligations of our whole population. When men come together into communities, they yield up certain rights, in order more effectually to secure the remainder. They form governments to which they owe allegiance, because these governments extend to them protection; and that government is best which exacts a surrender of the fewest natural rights, and most effectually protects the reserved rights of the people. Civil and political rights are the creation of man; they are the incidents of human government, and the power which forms this government can extend these privileges to others, or they can confine them to their own number. Natural rights spring from a higher source; they are the creation of God; and though they may, perhaps, in many instances, be yielded up by their possessor, they can only be taken away by that Power which confers them. Hence, our constitution justly proclaims that all men are born equally free and independent, and have certain natural and inalienable rights, among which are the enjoying and defending life and liberty, acquiring, possessing, and protecting property, and pursuing and obtaining happiness and safety. If these views are correct it follows that we, as a people, can extend to others or confine to ourselves the mere civil and political rights which we enjoy. We may spread our arms and invite to the privilege of citizenship the whole family of man; we may extend or abridge the right of suffrage; and we may qualify or disqualify for official station. But when we attempt to go further, and to abridge, by legislation, the natural rights of man, both the fundamental laws of our State and of our nature say to us, hitherto shalt thou come, and no further.

The first and most important question, then, in our present inquiry, is, does the law under consideration infringe either natural or constitutional rights! It is the opinion of that branch of your committee now reporting, that it does infringe both these rights. At the time the Constitution was adopted, and for more than four years afterwards, no such law existed. Colored persons were then competent witness; and by that clause in the Constitution, giving to the accused in criminal prosecutions, compulsory process to obtain witness in his favor; and, by the process of our courts, the white man, as well as the colored, could call before the court and substantiate his innocence by the testimony of the black or mulatto person. But, under this law, the white man can, in no possible case, have the benefit of their testimony; every avenue to fact from these sources is shut; the mouths of these persons are as effectually sealed, when they could disclose facts which would acquit, as when they would condemn. The law is equally effectual to cover guilt and to conceal innocence. In the one case, it would send the murderer out of court acquit; in the other, it would send innocence to the gallows. In this aspect of the law, in its effect to deprive the white man of the power to prove his innocence of crime by the testimony of colored persons, it seems there cannot be a doubt but what it deprives him both of his natural and his constitutional rights. Life and liberty are unquestionably natural as well as constitutional rights, (of the white men at least;) and they are as effectually violated when he is stripped of them by not being permitted to show his innocence by testimony, as if the law directly took them away. In our view, these considerations fully establish the position that so much of the law in question as provides that no black or mulatto person shall be permitted to be sworn or give evidence in any prosecution which shall be instituted in behalf of this State against a white person, is unconstitutional and void, and should be repealed. The unconstitutionality of the remaining branch of this provision of the law, which enacts that no black or mulatto person shall be permitted to be sworn or give evidence in any court of record or elsewhere in this State, in any cause depending or matter of controversy where either party to the same is a white person, is also apparent. First, (and this applies to the first, as well as to the last proposition,) as before intimated, the law in question did not exist at the time the constitution was formed, nor until several years afterwards. The clause in the constitution which provides that the accused shall have compulsory process to obtain witness in his favor in all criminal prosecutions, guaranteed his right to this species of evidence. This law then, curtails the right which the white man had guaranteed to him by that instrument--a right which all enjoyed under that instrument, up to the time of the enactment of this law.

Further: The constitution plainly recognizes the natural rights of colored persons; and its enumerates amongst these rights, not only the enjoying and defending life and liberty, but the acquiring, possessing, and protecting property, and pursuing and obtaining happiness and safety. How can these rights be protected and enjoyed? We answer, they can be only in the same way that all our other rights are protected, or the violation of them redressed--by the laws, through the medium of the Courts of Justice. We but mock the people, then, with these provisions of our constitution, if our laws will permit lawless white men to enter a community of colored persons, commit crimes too horrible to mention, or despoil them of their goods, and when the matter is submitted to a legal investigation, we seal their mouths; we make it unlawful, for a black or mulatto person to be sworn, or to testify. We profess to guarantee these rights by our constitution; we license their violation by our laws, as effectually, though not as directly, as if these people were outlawed, and given up to plunder and to violence. Destroy evidence, and you can neither substantiate guilt, innocence, nor rights. It may be here urged, that these results are only imaginary. This is not so. There is credible evidence that crimes of almost every grade have been committed; that clause in our constitution which provides that the people shall be secure in their persons, houses, papers and possessions, from unwarrantable searches and seizures, has been infringed; that property has been plundered; and that, too, with impunity, under the practical operation of this law. We, therefore, pronounce it to be in derogation of the natural rights of our whole population--rights sacredly guaranteed and recognized by our Creator and our constitution--and for these, if for no other reasons, the entire enactment should be repealed.

There are, also, further, and other reasons for its appeal. The enactment is against sound policy. This requires that the truth should be brought to light, that the guilty should be punished, and that the innocent should be shielded. These desirable objects are defeated by the enactment which curtails the competency of witness, except for good cause. The laws of evidence proceed upon this principle. They exclude those convicted to infamous crimes, and those interested in the event of suits. The law under consideration violates every principle of the common law of evidence, by making a mere physical quality a ground of exclusion. But, further, the common law rule shows its extreme solicitude to elicit all the facts which may throw light upon the question under investigation, by authorizing persons proved to be not equal in point of veracity to their fellow men, to testify, while the fact of impeachment goes only to their credibility, not to their exclusion. Our law, then, which carries the rule further and makes color a ground of incompetency, without respect to moral character, is an anomaly which should be removed from our statute book.

Does the objector meet us at this point with the allegation, that the rule is a valuable one, because these people are not equally credible with the rest of mankind? In the first place, we say, that the testimony which has been spread upon our tables, composed of certificates from respectable men, seems to fail to sustain such a position; and we pronounce, without fear of contradiction, that there are some of their number in whom the community have implicit confidence in their characters for truth. But if, for the sake of the argument, we admit the position that they are not equally credible as a class, how can we exclude them entirely from the privilege, whilst we admit the white man, after his neighbors have sworn that they would not believe him under oath? And the fact that he is impeached, goes only to his credibility, not to his exclusion. The rules of law, of reason, and of sound policy, all cry out against such an invidious distinction.

It is also a dictate of sound policy to do equal and exact justice, and to spread the shield of protection alike over all, the lowest as well as the highest: this is the only security for anyone. Once we break down the barriers which protect the poor, the weak, and the despised, and a landmark is removed from the boundaries of right; and pride, cupidity, and wrong will riot almost unrestrained over the whole field. Make such distinctions as are made, not only by the enactment here referred to, but by all our laws against colored persons, and you do what you can to detach them from the Government--to alienate their affections from it--and to break down that protection which equal laws always find implanted deep in the heart, the affections, and the judgment of the whole human family. The minority of your committee would be glad to see this boundary fixed by Ohio, upon this subject, upon what they think the exact line of right. They would rejoice to see her laws, as well as her constitution, protecting all the rights of all mankind. They are, however, of opinion that the branch of the law upon which they have reported is so manifestly unjust, inexpedient, and unconstitutional, that the plea for its repeal would be weakened by a union with any other branch of the subject; and for the present they will content themselves with the recommendation of the accompanying bill for its repeal.

NUMBER 3

Report of the select committee, to which was referred petitions and memorials relating to the disabilities of persons of color. March 3, 1842, House Journal.

The select committee to which numerous petitions and memorials, relating to the disabilities of persons of color, have been referred, report:

That, believing fully in the right of the people, or of any portion of them, to petition the General Assembly in relation to any matter upon which that body has the constitutional power to legislate, and that all petitions, respectfully addressed, should be respectfully received and considered, we have endeavored to give the various petitions and memorials referred to us, all the consideration that petitions upon any other subject, of equal importance, should receive.

We had intended to present to the House the result of our deliberations at an earlier day; but, after delaying action upon the subject for a while, in order that all the petitions designed to be presented during the present session, which, under the resolution of the House, would be referred to the same committee, might be before us at the same time, we were still further delayed by the protracted illness of one member of the committee, whose counsel and co-operation the others desired to obtain.

To ascertain the appropriate duties of the committee, we have referred to the resolution under which it was appointed, which was adopted on the 30th day of December last, and reads as follows:

"Resolved, That all petitions or memorials relating to slavery, or disability of persons of color, presented to the House, shall be referred, without debate or reading, to a select committee of five members, to be appointed by a vote of the House."

Finding in the petition to incorporate the Red Oak Seminary, nothing relating to slavery, or the disability of persons of color, we conclude that the petition did not receive an appropriate reference; therefore, without further action upon it, we return it to the House, and recommend its reference to the committee on corporations.

The other petitions and memorials, referred to us, belong to two classes: First--such as pray that the disabilities now imposed on persons of color, may be lessened; and, second--such as pray that they may be increased to such an extent as will effectually prevent the further immigration and settlement, amongst us, of the race of people. The first class may be further divided as follows: First--such as ask a repeal of the "act relating to fugitives from labor or service, from other States," passed February 26, 1839. Second--such as ask that the right of trial by jury may be extended to every human being. Third--such as ask a repeal of that provision of the law which prohibits blacks and mulattoes from giving testimony in any case in which a white person is a party to the controversy. Fourth--such as ask that towns and cities may be made liable for all damages done by mobs. Fifth--such as ask that blacks and mulattoes may be permitted to participate in the benefits of our school funds; and last--such as cover the whole ground, and pray a repeal of all laws which make distinction on account of color.

Taking up these petitions in the order of the foregoing division and subdivision, we are called upon, first, to determine whether the fugitive law, as it is commonly called, ought to be repealed. Upon this branch of the subject, the committee unanimously adopt the argument contained in the report made upon the same subject, in the House of Representatives, on the 18th day of January, 1841, by Mr. Bliss, from the Judiciary committee, to be found in the House Journal of 1840-41, page 213, and which, being already in possession of the people of the State, may as well be referred to, as to be here repeated. We have, also, come to the same conclusions to which that argument brought him, that as the constitution of the United States directs that "persons held to service or labor in one State, under the laws thereof, escaping into another, shall be delivered up, on claim of the party to whom such service or labor may be due"; it is the duty of the States to deliver up such fugitives, and, to that end, it is their duty to provide, by law, a mode of ascertaining the facts necessary to show who are such fugitives, and whether the claim to their services, upon which the delivering up is asked, be well founded. That the law in question, designed for this purpose, and containing many necessary and wise provisions ought not to be repealed, but may be amended and improved.

We are next, and in connection with the amendment above suggested, led to consider whether the right of trial by jury ought to be extended as prayed for in these petitions. Here, again, your committee adopt the argument in the same report, and arrive at the same conclusions, that, as the fact, whether the person who is alleged to be a fugitive from labor or service, who is claimed to be delivered up, be in truth held to such labor or service--be a slave or a freeman, should be fully ascertained before such delivery; that it should be ascertained in a court of justice--and should be ascertained in the same manner that facts of the same importance are usually ascertained in courts of justice. We, therefore, cannot offer any good reason why an inquiry, involving such important consequences as the personal liberty of a human being for life, next in value to life itself, should not, if desired by the party interested, be determined by a jury; that mode of trial, which we, as well as our English ancestors, boast of as one of the principal bulwarks of liberty. We, therefore, conclude that the law of 1839, above mentioned, would be improved by so amending it as to provide for the trial of facts, under it, by a jury, if desired by either party. We do not report a bill making such an amendment, for the reasons which will be given in the sequel.

The next branch of the subject is, ought blacks and mulattoes to be permitted to give testimony in case wherein a white person is a party to the controversy? In this matter, the committee not unanimous. On the one hand, it is urged that by reason of this prohibition, crimes committed by white persons, often go unpunished--frauds are successfully committed in matters of contract between persons of different colors; and that, in many instances, the testimony of a colored person, is essential for the purposes of justice in controversies, where both parties are white; and that the degree of credibility to which any person is entitled, is so easily estimated, that no greater fears may be entertained from perjury being committed by blacks than by whites. On the other hand, it is said, that crime is vastly more common among blacks, than among the white population, their numbers being compared; that the low state of both their moral and intellectual culture, render them unsafe witness; and especially their envy of what they are led to consider the superior condition of the whites, from whose society they are, in a manner, excluded, leading them to harbor feelings of hostility towards the whites, and a clannish attachment to those of their own color and condition, would be very likely to lead them aside from the truth, in cases where the controversy is between whites and blacks. These arguments, both pro and con, have some truth for their support. In some parts of the state, where the blacks are few, and where their moral and intellectual culture has been attended to, no great evil would be likely to result from their being permitted to give testimony in all cases; and, indeed, the cause of justice might be advanced by admitting their testimony. But in other places, where they are more numerous, and less cultivated--where they have been treated with less kindness, and are more clannish in their disposition and habits, the white population would consider the security in their rights of person and property, greatly weakened, by placing the blacks on an equal footing with them, in regard to giving testimony. In addition to this, if this disability tends in any degree, to prevent the increase among us of this class of our population, by immigration into this, from other states, so far, it is beneficial. They, who, knowing the existence of this disability, come voluntarily and settle down under it, have no right to complain of it. Upon the whole, a majority of the committee entertain the opinion that, taking the state at large, and the sentiments of all our people, into consideration, and considering the great length of time, during which this disability has existed with the approbation of a majority of the people, it is inexpedient now to remove it. And were we satisfied that it ought to be removed, still we should deem it inexpedient to attempt it at the present session.

Upon the fourth branch of the subject embraced in the petitions, to wit: the making of towns and cities liable for damages done by mobs, we shall say but little; indeed we might, with propriety, pass it over without a single remark, for there is, in truth, nothing in that branch of the subject relating exclusively to slavery, or the disabilities of persons of color. This matter is foreign to the purposes for which the committee was raised, and the reference of such petitions was inappropriate. Mobs are not frequently raised by the blacks, nor is mob violence always directed against the persons or property of the blacks. Another class of our people, and who are now being put under many disabilities too, seem to be in greater danger from mob violence, at present, than the colored race, or their particular friends.

Whether a town or city should be made liable for the damages resulting from mob violence committed in it, should, in our judgment, be made to depend on the fact, whether such violence could have been prevented by proper vigilance on the part of the police officers, or proper authorities of such town or city. But as the matter does not properly belong to us, and involves some nice questions of constitutional and legal rights, and as some members of the committee on the Judiciary have already given the subject of mobs some attention, we recommend that committee as a more appropriate one for such further consideration of this branch of the subject, as the House may think proper to direct.

In regard to the proposition of allowing the colored population to participate in the benefits of our school fund, we hold, that inasmuch as God and Nature have marked that people with such distinctive characteristics, they should be forever considered a distinct race, and those distinctive characteristics perpetuated, by keeping the race as distinct and exclusive in their associations as circumstances and the laws of humanity will permit. We cannot, therefore, believe that our colleges, academies and schools, in which white youths are educated and taught, should be thrown open to the colored population. Public sentiment, or public prejudice, if you choose so to call it, forbids it. Consequently, the admission of the blacks would operate as an exclusion of the whites, and the cause of education would be obstructed and hindered, instead of being promoted and advanced. But if the moral and intellectual culture of the blacks, who are settled among us, is to be desired, and we believe that it is; if such culture would, in its results, prove beneficial to the whites around them, as well as to the blacks themselves, and we believe it would, then we can offer no good reason or argument why blacks and mulattoes, where they are numerous enough to have schools exclusively of their own color, to be supported by their own means, should not have the aid of laws for that purpose, and we should be exempted from contributing to theirs, and they should not be required to contribute to ours. This is the case now, to a certain extent, but not so fully as might be provided.

Those petitioners who ask for a repeal of all laws creating any distinction on account of color, will find a sufficient answer in the remarks already made. Doubtless, those petitioners are aware that most of the disabilities imposed upon the colored people of our state, and not alluded to in the foregoing remarks, are such disabilities as are imposed by our state constitution, and we do not understand the petitioners as asking any thing in violation of that instrument.

We now proceed to consider, briefly, that class of petitions which pray the enactment of laws creating additional disabilities, such as will effectually prevent the further immigration, into this state, of persons of color. Some of those petitions suggest the passage of laws to prohibit blacks and mulattoes from purchasing and holding real estate within our state, and to declare all contracts made by, or with them, after a given time, entirely null and void.

We agree with the petitioners, in relation to the natural distinctive characteristic of the two races--"that to each was assigned a different sphere in the great plan of creation." We regret the necessity of their mingling, in any degree, or occupying the same territory. We believe that the comfort and happiness of both races would be promoted by their entire separation, were such separation practicable. But these people are among us--no adequate provision has been made for their separate colonization, and none is likely soon to be made; and until such shall be made, the principles of humanity forbid that we should deny them the right of existence, or the means of sustaining that existence. Whatever restraining laws it might be proper for us to enact, might, with equal propriety, be enacted by other states. And should all the states deprive the free blacks of the power of contracting, and being contracted with, they would effectually deprive them of all the means of subsistence, excepting such as might be bestowed by the hand of charity. This, we believe, would be carrying the matter too far. We are not, however, prepared to say but that some amendment of those laws, designed to discourage and prevent the increase amongst us, of this class of people by immigration, would be salutary; but we forbear going more fully into the consideration of the matter, because we believe this is not a proper time for any legislative action upon any branch of the subject referred to us.

It is not the proper time, because the House is not, and has not, during this session, been in the proper temper to legislate upon this subject, with that coolness of deliberation which a subject of so much perplexity demands. This was evidenced, by the feeling manifested upon the presentation of some of the petitions, at an early day in the session. It was also further evidenced upon the election of this committee. Apparently, an extraordinary liberality was manifested by the majority, towards the minority, in this House, and the committee was elected, entirely, from the minority. It was, in effect, saying to the petitioners, we, the majority, cannot deign to consider your petitions; we will turn them over to the minority, the only matter that we are willing to entrust them with the exclusive consideration of. "Let them go; blacks, mulattoes, abolitionists, and Whigs, all together, and manage their affairs in their own way."

Who could doubt, after the selection of this committee, that the House was not in the proper temper for calmly legislating upon this subject?

Further, it is not the proper time for legislation on this subject, because the people of the State are not in the proper temper for it. This subject seems to be a sort of tinder box--whenever touched, it produces a flame. On the one hand, the friends of liberty, as they style themselves, press their doctrines and views with a zeal and energy, in many instances, as we conceive, ill-timed and misdirected. They petition the Legislature, and ask too much. On the other hand, those who oppose them, carry their opposition, in many instances, to quite as great an extreme--manifest the same impatience and intemperate zeal; and they, also, ask too much. To yield to the demands of the first, would excite a flame among the last; and to yield to the demands of the last, would add fuel to the fire of the first. In either case, evils greater than those now complained of, would be produced. An excitement, which has already, in many instances, destroyed the harmony of neighborhoods, and disturbed the public peace, would be greatly increased. Upon this, as well as most other subjects, extremes should be avoided as dangerous, and the middle course should be pursued as the safest. This middle course is, in our opinion, to leave things as they are for the present. When the public mind becomes tranquil--when men in the Legislature, as well as out of it, can approach this subject dispassionately, and deliberate upon it, freed from enthusiasm on the one hand, and deep rooted prejudice on the other, then, and not till then, can any good results be expected from legislating upon it. To produce this desirable tranquility, it seems to us to be necessary that ultraists, upon both sides, should be discountenanced, and the counsel of cool and discreet heads--lovers of our country--lovers of our cherished institutions--lovers of peace, and yet friends of humanity, should be sought and pursued.

Entertaining these views, the committee ask to be discharged from the further consideration of the subject, and the petitioners have leave to withdraw their petitions.

NUMBER 4

Report of the minority of the select committee upon the subject of the laws relative to people of color. January 18, 1845, House Journal.

Mr. Archbold, from the minority of the select committee, to which the subject had been referred, made the following Report:

The select committee to whom were referred divers petitions and memorials, asking for a radical change in the longstanding policy of this State with regard to its colored population, having had the same under consideration, and, after an interchange and comparison of sentiments, finding it impossible to harmonize their opinions, the minority think it due to the occasion, and to themselves, to render their reasons for opposing a change of that policy, which commenced with the early infancy of our State, and has continued to this day.

The committee will indulge in but one preliminary observation, and that is, that, as a great majority of the petitioners appear to be animated by feelings of benevolence, a quality always respectable to generous opponents, we intend to treat them and their arguments with all possible respect; but, as to the fierce bigots who have endeavored to kindle the flames of civil war, by employing the arm of this government to punish men for obeying the national government, not feeling any sentiments of respect. It is not likely that we shall express any.

The majority of the committee have laid down some abstract principles, to which, as mere abstractions, we can have no possible objection. But they considerably underrate the sagacity of the minority, if they suppose that we are going to advance into the arena to do battle with them concerning these propositions. On the contrary, did stern realities permit, we should be delighted to accompany the majority in their reveries--we are perfectly capable of tasting the deliciousness of a day dream. And not infrequently, when scorched by the heat, annoyed by the dust, and fatigued by the toils of life's long work-day, we cast a wistful glance towards the shades of philosophy, and the groves of the academy; and we freely admit that, if we could meet the majority there, we should anticipate nothing but unmixed pleasure from their social qualities. But such is not our destiny--labor, labor is our lot; and we are not called to indulge in the pleasing speculations of philosophers, but to perform the active duties of statesmen. We must, therefore, turn our reluctant gaze from the beautiful, green fields of imagination, to the diversified landscape of real life. It is worthy of remark, that human polity and institutions may be contemplated with reference to two very different standards. The one we shall call the standard of absolute theoretical perfection, the chief good, the "beau ideal" in human conduct; the other, the standard of that which is practicable and attainable. The difference is in degree, not in kind. But it behooves us to use circumspection as to which standard we aim to direct the energies of society; for, it is unfortunately true that, by indiscreetly aiming at the former, both communities and individuals have often miserably failed, and fallen far below the latter. An intelligent consideration and appreciation of the circumstances by which we are surrounded, are almost indispensable to the right discharge of our duties as legislators. We may be said, almost, without a trope, to be yet engaged in laying, broad and deep, the foundations of empire. We live in the midst of new institutions, and witness new forms of society--in one word, our State is in its youth, but it is the youth of a Colossus. It contains, at present, scarcely less than two millions of people. If populated as densely as Britain or Holland, it would contain eight or ten millions; but, a more genial climate, and a more fertile soil, give assurance that its population will not stop short of the ratio of those countries. Suppose it propounded to an intelligent and benevolent legislator that it lies in his breast to choose of what materials this mighty mass of population shall be composed--that it lies with him to determine whether it shall consist of one mighty, homogeneous mass, or of two or three diverse and repugnant castes, of unequal rank and civil condition, and as incapable of combination as oil and water. Could materials for a commonwealth be thought of more discordant than the Saxon and the son of Ham?--the one restless, turbulent, ambitious, aspiring; meditating, even in his amusements, some high enterprise, and making his amusements subservient to the advancement of his designs; the other gay, thoughtless, improvident, and reckless of the future. Let none say that this picture is too highly colored. Is it not drawn from fact? Do not other European races coalesce with the negro on much easier terms than the Saxon? Witness Mexico and South America. And does not every man know that the intercourse between the two races is, to the last degree, unpleasant--poisoned by incurable suspicions of haughtiness, overbearing, and injustice on the one side, and of insolence, meanness, and petty vices on the other. This unhappy feeling ordinarily spends itself in petty annoyances, poisoning the happiness of life. It sometimes terminates in tragic occurrences. It is not about two years since the wagon of a black drive was overturned by that of a white, in the streets of one of our principal cities. The white man got down to help him to right it again. The negro, fired with jealousy that a deliberate prank had been played upon him, seized an iron bar, and laid the unfortunate man dead at his feet. A rencontre took place in our own country of Belmont last summer, between a white mower and a black one, which terminated in the loss of an ear to the former, and which originated in a trifling jest about going to supper. In these instances, and in hundreds of similar ones, no anger or jealousy would have been kindled had the parties both been of the same race.

If illustrations on a larger scale be necessary to a right understanding of the principle, the last few years of the history of Philadelphia and Cincinnati, will furnish those illustrations.

These facts are not alluded to for the purpose of showing that the black race is naturally baser, or more depraved in moral faculties, than the white. The committee has never so believed, nor ever seen any good reason so to believe. To place the argument on a wrong basis, would materially injure its force. The evil arises from the incompatibility of the two races; and, surely, the petitioners, themselves, will admit, that this incompatibility can not be removed by amalgamation, except to the shame and perdition of the superior race. Guided by these, and similar considerations, perhaps, of more cogency, can we doubt what the determination of such a legislator, place of that legislator, and it is our highest duty to bring to the determination of this question whatever of benevolence and whatever of wisdom nature or providence may have awarded to us, unbiased by prejudice of preconceived opinions. Our black population fortunately consists of less than twenty thousand, and the real question at issue is, whether we shall invite all the straggles of that unhappy race, from Cape Florida to our own southern border, here to congregate.

Although, as before observed, our State and our institutions are new, we are surrounded by an older world, and other institutions; and, unfortunately, some of those institutions are as old as sin. The untamed barbarity of our British ancestors has left for the solution of their posterity the most knotty questions--has left us nothing but a choice of difficulties; and evils of greater or less magnitude, will press upon us, be our determination what it may. But, when we consider what a vast mass of these unfortunate people exists immediately on our southern border, in the States of Virginia, North Carolina, Kentucky, and Tennessee, the lights which ought to guide our steps, would not seem to be difficult of attainment. In the year of our Lord, 1830, one of those states, Virginia, alone, contained largely more than forty thousand free blacks. If, therefore, in the language of the petitioners, "we abolish all distinctions on account of color," and raise that race to a perfect equality with the white, we may expect a deluge of that "undesirable species of population" to set in upon us. Not only the free born blacks, but old worn out emancipated negroes and fugitive slaves, will crowd to our shores, and we shall pay the penalty of ill-advised and undiscerning benevolence. Is it possible that the General Assembly can seriously intend to entertain such a proposition as this? To call such an uncouth, untutored, undisciplined mass to a full participation in all the privileges, and duties for which ages of self direction and self-control have scarcely sufficed to prepare our own people! Let not our opponents object that we recommend a policy to the House not in accordance with the standard of abstract, absolute, moral perfection, but with that of mere expediency.

The petitioners, themselves, do not propose to go all lengths against slavery. They do not propose, themselves, nor do they ask this government to do all that might be done to subvert that institution. Why do they not? It is an institution which, as they contend, and we admit, is utterly inconsistent with the abstract principles of natural justice. But one answer can be given to this question. They are overcome by the force of circumstances with which they are surrounded. In other words, they yield to overbearing considerations of expediency. It is manifest that we are recommending to the House principles of action, the cogency of which is tacitly perceived and acknowledged by the petitioners, themselves. Another circumstances will tend to show that the petitioners can comprehend this train of reasoning. They complain, in some of their petitions, of the ready reception which European paupers, vagrants, and refugees experience when they land on our shores; and they term these unfortunates an "undesirable species of population." This may be, in some measure, true, but the inconvenience, in the nature of things, can be but temporary. A few generations will obliterate all distinctions, and it will never be known whose ancestors first, or whose last, trod the soil of the land of liberty. Very different is the case of the negro population, or the minority of the committee would instantly unite with the majority to recommend a bill in accordance with the prayer of the petitioners.

The foregoing considerations relate, in a great measure, to the present situation and future prospects of our own beloved State; other considerations of equal cogency, in the opinion of the committee, relate more immediately to the destinies of the African race. We feel convinced that the voice which calls the merry, humble, menial negro to remain here in a state of semi-servitude, in a state of unequal competition with a superior race, in a situation which cultivates his vices and defects, and represses his virtues and his energies, is a serene voice, which calls him not to his highest or happiest destiny. Africa should be looked to as the ultimate home of the black man. In the language of the great orator of the West, "we should regard him as the stray child of another's family, to be treated with kindness and compassion while he remains, but to be returned as soon as possible to his original home." There his long dormant energies might be awakened, there his habits of self management and control might be strengthened and confirmed and there he would be placed in circumstances much more, nearly resembling our own that he can be in our midst. To return to Africa our whole black population, free and enslaved, is regarded by many as a hopeless task, on account of its magnitude. But this consideration loses its force, when the enterprise of benevolence and philanthropy is confined to the free black population. When we consider the immense and continued increase of the European race upon this continent, that the next census will show twenty millions of that race within the present boundaries of the United States, we must pronounce such an enterprise as speedily falling within the capacity of our benevolence and philanthropy, or the conclusion will be inevitable, that our benevolence and philanthropy are neither very ardent nor persevering.

It is consoling to the committee to reflect that, in shaping our policy with a view of the ultimate return of the black man to the home of his ancestors, as the missionary of a pure faith, and a beneficent civilization, we will in our humble sphere, and at an almost infinite distance, be imitating that Great Being, whose government of the world appears to be a system of benevolence and amelioration but not of optimism. Had it suited the purposes of his inscrutable will, when that "felon of the human race," the miscreant manstealer, first guided his bark to the shores of unhappy Africa, his red right hand might have grasped its thunderbolts and sunk him in the deep. It is the divine prerogative to bring good out of evil; and now that the gracious plans of His providence begin to unfold themselves, we perceive that, however atrocious may have been the character of the first intercourse, between the races of Europe and Africa, that intercourse, by a gradual process of amelioration, is to end in bestowing the blessings of civilization and religion on that benighted continent. It is for the people of the Union, and of this State in particular, to determine whether, listening to the suggestions of a short sighted and undiscerning philanthropy, they will vainly oppose. Is not this an enterprise of benevolence sufficiently sublime to dilate the hearts and stimulate the energies of a great and Christian people? Let none object, that these views are merely visionary and chimerical, and the object attainable. History does not warrant such an objection; on the contrary, the man who is most conversant with her pages, will be the first to pronounce such an objection untenable.

Had some old philosopher in the Augustan age, pointed out to a polished Greek or haughty Roman, some fair haired Goth or sinewy Saxon, and ventured the prediction that his race would subdue the proud mistress of the world; would seize upon the victor's garland the civic wreath, and would carry the arts of peace and war to a degree of perfection which the day dreams of Greece and Rome had not then conceived possible, he would have incurred the penalty of laughter and ridicule, and would have been suspected of hallucination. Yet all this, and more, have been accomplished; for, as ages rolled on, that restless race awaked from the sleep of centuries, and, in due time, a Milton, a Newton, and a Washington appeared.

The majority of the committee has submitted an elaborate argument on the supposed hardship of excluding the children of the colored population from our district schools, and has appealed to a certain clause of our State Constitution, which secures to the poor a proper participation in the benefits of those literary institutions which are supported in whole, or in part, by the bounty of the United States.

The minority has weighed this argument, but without feeling its cogency, and, of course, without conviction. When we reflect that the convention declared that they adopted the Constitution "to secure the blessings of liberty to themselves and their posterity," and, in the same instrument, disqualified the blacks and mulattoes from all participation in the government, by confining the right of suffrage to white persons, it is difficult to conceive that, under this covert phrase, "the poor," they intended to throw open the doors of our colleges and universities to a class of persons who were never to perform the duties of electors, or elected. If, by the term "poor," they really meant negroes and mulattoes, how easily might they have employed such phraseology as would have placed their meaning beyond all doubt. This view of the case is strengthened by the well known fact, that a number of the members of the convention sat in the General Assembly which passed the very first of that series of statutes, now by the petitioners sought to be repealed.

The minority is at a loss to conceive the object of the majority in pressing this matter upon the attention of the House. Do they, or does any man, seriously suppose that the children of the two races could be educated together? That they could stand in the same classes, sit on the same forms, or associate in the study of the same lessons? We hazard nothing in affirming that the presence of a single negro, unless under very peculiar circumstances, would turn our schoolrooms into deserts. A different state of feeling may prevail at the north, but, certainly, in the southern, eastern and western parts of our State, it would require the terrors of the bayonet to people the schoolroom with a mixed assemblage of whites and blacks. We cannot permit ourselves to doubt, that gentlemen would shrink back with horror from the idea of sending, their own children to associate with negroes and mulattoes. Do they conceive their constituents to be less fastidious, or less delicate than themselves?

The minority might feel more sympathy with the blacks, in their exclusion from our common schools, but for the well known fact, that myriads of our white fellow citizens would regard the same exclusion as a precious boon, if they could enjoy it on the same terms, i.e., exemption of their property from taxation for school purposes. It is well known that, in all our populous neighborhoods and considerable villages, two systems of education are constantly going forward--the public and the private schools; or, perhaps we should say, the district and the subscription schools. The district schools are crowded to excess; the energies of the teacher are wasted amongst such a multitude as to be rendered altogether inefficient. Parental affection, ever wakeful, ever enduring, soon discovers that adequate mental training and discipline can not be had in those institutions, and, as an expedient to secure the blessings of thorough and sound eduction to its beloved objects, subscriptions are made, and competent teachers employed, on a scale of liberality somewhat commensurate with the end in view. It should be remembered, that both these systems of schools are mainly supported by the toils and the frugality of the same class of men, that is, the tax payers and small proprietors. It is true, our citizens do not greatly complain of this state of things. They pay their school taxes with comparative cheerfulness, from a conviction that those taxes constitute a necessary fund, to be employed in affording the lights of eduction, imperfect and unfinished, perhaps, yet better than none to the children of their fellow citizens, who are to compose a large portion of the future electors and sovereigns of the land, and whose opportunities are greatly increased by the withdrawal of the large numbers who attend the subscription schools. But they pay those taxes, as taxes, that is for the sake of an indirect and future benefit; they are not sufficiently stupid to suppose that they have any direct or immediate interest in the matter. But are the already overtaxed and overburdened energies of our industrious people, to be charged with the education of all the black population, who will crowd here from the east and from the west, and from the north and from the SOUTH, [*sic*] if invited here by an abolition of all laws making a distinction on account of color, and enticed by the premium of that education, bestowed without money and without price? The committee can not but regard with astonishment, the coolness and composure with which gentlemen sometimes bring forward propositions for direct, and indirect additions to the pecuniary burthens of our people, already intolerable. The calmness of their countenances, and the rectilinear arrangement of the muscles of their faces, discover them to be in earnest, but this circumstance only demands additional earnestness and energy of resistance. Those gentlemen, perhaps, represent very opulent constituencies. It is said that extremes are prone to meet; certain it is, that none are so ready to vote pecuniary burthens upon society, as the extremely indigent; and for an obvious reason, neither of them are in a situation, adequately, to appreciate the pressure of those burthens. Need we add, that the House should yield a willing and favorable attention to the remonstrances of the representatives of the small property holders, who feel those burthens in their full weight.

The minority think it right to make themselves understood on one point, lest their reasoning should labor under a prejudice, from which its earnestness, sincerity and directness, should rescue it. They are not conscious of recommending to the House any policy which would have even a remote tendency to promote, or perpetuate slavery. They do not wish to unchristianize their southern fellow citizens, not doubting that while chivalry, generosity, and manly spirit are abundant at the north, so the mild virtues of benevolence, compassion, and human kindness, are frequently found to flourish at the south. But it is believed that no good man, out of the circle of its immediate influence, can look upon the image of slavery with complacency. It has features essentially forbidding and deformed, and in spite of all attempts at smoothing and painting, the sight of those features is calculated to repel, and not to attract. Cherishing and expressing these sentiments, the committee will not be suspected of having any sympathy with that atrocious and brigand spirit which ruthlessly dedicates three millions of men, and their posterity, to the demon-god of everlasting slavery. It is an institution to be tolerated and excused from the invincible necessity of the case, not to be recommended, or approved. And those documents, whether originating in high places, or in low places, which boldly defend the institution as righteous, patriarchal, and agreeable to the will of heaven, are offensive to the enlightened moral feelings of the nineteenth century. Some of those literary efforts, from the high source in which they originated, were, no doubt, expected to produce a great effect upon the public mind, and verily, their authors have not been mistaken; they have filed the highest order of minds, and the most generous spirits, with unutterable horror and disgust.

But while we acknowledge ourselves hostile to the permanency of this institution, and would gladly give a direction to the policy of this great State, consistent with its federal and fraternal relations, yet tending to its final extinction, we feel that the duty of circumspection, in tracing the adaptation of means to ends, is imposed upon us by weight considerations. We are not at liberty to surrender ourselves to the blind impulses, even of benevolence, without carefully weighing the consequences. We cannot, therefore, join with the petitions in recommending the abolition of all distinctions here, on account of color. We think that such an ill-advised procedure would make this State the general rendezvous of the African race in the United States. The free blacks, and old worn out slaves from the southern States, would be poured in upon us in such numbers, as to weigh down and exhaust the charities of our people, and materially to relieve slavery from a burthen which it ought to bear. In the language of an estimable gentleman now in our city, "such a course of policy would effectually prune the tree of slavery, and keep it green and flourishing, but would lay no axe to its root." A great many of the petitioners appear to belong to the Society of Friends; a society of persons very amiable and estimable, no doubt, in the walks of private life, but whose mental discipline has not been such as to render them very accurate, or profound, in training the consequences of human actions. A friend of southern slavery, would join them in their petitions.

The report of the majority indulges in some acrimony of phraseology in regard to the supposed tendency of the policy of the southern States, to keep the indigent classes of white people in ignorance, in order that they may labor contentedly by the side of the slave. It is believed that great delicacy is demanded in speaking of the institutions of our sister States, lest that kindly and fraternal spirit should receive a wound, which now contributes so essentially, to strengthen and support our glorious Union. It must be expected that censures contained in solemn documents emanating from committees of our General Assembly, and other responsible sources, will have far more power of irritation, than the writings of anonymous and obscure individuals. The minority can speak from personal knowledge of the institutions of the first, and most considerable of those States. That great and magnanimous commonwealth, has an immense school fund dedicated to the express purpose of the education of the children of indigence, and it is efficiently and economically managed. Would to Heaven as much could be truly said of our own.

We find it impossible to follow the majority in detail through all their reasoning, without extending this report to an inconvenient length. They misquote the second section of the fourth article of the Federal Constitution; that article reads thus: "The citizens of each State shall be entitled to all the privileges and immunities of citizens in the several States." We apprehend that the present order of things, in the British West India Colonies, is too new to afford any safe lights of history for the guidance of the conduct of statesmen in other countries. There, as well as in Canada, a strong government, aided by glittering bayonets, may preserve a degree of apparent order and quiet; and a happy destitution of minute and local knowledge, in the House and in the committee, leaves open a wide field for conjecture.

It must be obvious to the House, that if we regard the interests of our own home-bred black population, who would seem to have the fairest claims upon us, we shall pause before we invite, by the premium of free schools and munificent poor laws, and absolute legal equality, that countless host of rude and uncultivated foreign negroes, who will pour in upon us and compete with our present black population in all their employments and pursuits. That they will rue the change, we have no doubt. In deprecating--in most earnestly remonstrating against a measure so ultra, so visionary, so hostile to all the sober deductions of reason, as the attempt, by legal enactment, to equalize two races--whom God and nature, and habits, and previous institutions, and history, and ten thousand recollections have rendered so utterly unequal and incompatible--it affords real pleasure to the committee to be able to say, that there is nothing shocking to humanity or torturing to the feelings of compassion in the condition of our black population. Their own moderate exertions, aided by the generosity of their white neighbors, in a land of abundance, obtain a plentiful supply for all their corporeal wants, and they appear to pass gaily down in the stream of time, enjoying the sunshine of an almost perpetual infancy. Their rotundity of outline and evident good keeping contrast advantageously with the meager visages and careworn countenances of some of their white neighbors.

Were it possible to inspire the negro with the hopes and the fears, the turbulent ambition and the restless enterprise, and to load him with the responsibilities of the white man, it might well be doubted whether he would not be a great loser in striking the balance sheet of happiness. It is true that the all-powerful force of habit has reconciled the latter to his situation; in the pursuit of some object, in his estimation great and engrossing, he resigns a thousand minor gratifications otherwise within his reach. But while he bows a willing devotee at the shrine of ambition, he is perfectly conscious of the value of the sacrificed which he brings to the altar. It is no less true that the same kindly power has reconciled the former to his humble lot, and bestowed upon him a degree of mental vivacity and cheerfulness to which many of his sympathizers are utter strangers; and if unassisted by the benevolent but misjudging clamor of the petitioners, he would regard that lot without envy and without repining.

But if it determined to elevate the black man to a new theater, and to make him a participant in the hopes, the fears, the cares and the aspirations of the white man, why should not this House give a direction to its policy, which will return him to that stage where alone he can attempt to act a similar part, and to hasten on to a similar destiny, with the slightest hopes of success. We have no ambition to level all inequalities in society, whether created by nature or by those long enduring habits as powerful as nature. The practiced eye of one of her votaries delights to dwell upon the silver rivulet and the green round knoll, as well as upon the towering mountain and the majestic river. Delighted with the perpetual succession and every varying prospect of hill and dale, and winding stream, and brake, and copsewood, and green meadows and brown fallow field, and sunshine and shade; such a one would regard as the artificer of unmixed mischief, the rude projector who would propose to smooth the face of nature into one unvarying outline of endless and cheerless uniformity; to dig down the mountains and to fill up the valleys. So we feel perfectly willing to leave the superior race to their exciting pursuits and their self-directed labors, and the inferior race to their humble enjoyments without indulging in that pragmatical spirit which vainly attempts to produce uniformity and equality where uniformity and equality are absolutely unattainable.

Impressed with a belief that a majority of the petitioners are influenced by kindly and amiable moral motives, we have endeavored to combat their arguments with calmness and serenity, and to treat them with all possible respect. But we almost despair of producing conviction in their minds. We well know that monomania, whether of a benevolent or malevolent character, rushes blindly to its object, regardless of consequences. We do not doubt that, if the black race be specially invited to assume new responsibilities, and perform new duties, they will accept the invitation. That the points of collision between the two races will be indefinitely multiplied, we have little doubt. That tragedies will be re-enacted, such as we have recently witnessed in the two cities before named, we have the utmost reason to fear. That the annoyances of life will be indefinitely increased, in every neighborhood in the State, we consider certain as the laws of nature herself. And, we must warn the House that it greatly deceives itself if it supposes that the community at large, or the committee itself, will be able to restrain those ebullitions of feeling which the innumerable collisions consequent upon the new order of things will be so well calculated to produce; and that, if it supposes that it cost the committee no sacrifice of feeling, no exercise of mental discipline and self restraint to repress that natural indignation which the proposition of the petitioners is so well calculated to inspire, it will do the committee injustice. It is a proposition which must appear, and does appear, and monstrous and outrageous to those who do not assent to the reasoning of the petitioners, nor drink into their spirit, and to whom the proposition must necessarily wear a different aspect.

We say, most emphatically, in the language of our ancestors across the deep, that we are "unwilling to change the laws of this great commonwealth"; and if the House should resolve to govern itself by other counsels, our supineness will not be to blame. We shall content ourselves with replacing our protest on the journals, and will abide the judgment of our contemporaries and our posterity with that composure which arises from a clear conscience and an honest discharge of duty.

NUMBER 5

Report of the select committee, on the subject of repealing the laws which make distinctions on account of color. January 9, 1846, House Journal.

Mr. Harvey, from the select committee to whom was referred sundry petitions for the repeal of the black laws, made the following report:

The select committee, to whom were referred the petitions of numerous, citizens of Ohio, praying for the repeal of all laws which impose restrictions and disabilities on the colored inhabitants of the State, and also that part of the Governor's message which has relation to the same subject, have had the matter under consideration, and now report:

That they have endeavored to bestow upon the subject that amount of reflection and investigation which its importance demands, and a majority of the committee have come to the conclusion that the request of the petitioners should be granted, and the recommendation of the Governor carried out, in the repeal of the laws in question.

We deem it unnecessary to consume any time in preliminary remarks, the committee will therefore proceed directly to call the attention of the House to those parts of the Statutes sought to be repealed by your petitioners, which operate with the greatest severity on the colored inhabitants of the State.

By the act of January 5, 1804, it is provided, "that no black or mulatto person shall be permitted to settle or reside in this State, unless he or she shall first produce a fair certificate from some court within the United States, of his or her actual freedom; which certificate shall be attested by the clerk of said court, and the seal thereof annexed thereto by said clerk."

The act of January 25, 1807, provides, "that no negro or mulatto person shall be permitted to emigrate into, or settle within this State, unless such negro or mulatto person shall, within twenty days thereafter, enter into bonds, with two or more freehold sureties, in the penal sum of five hundred dollars, before the clerk of the Court of Common Pleas of the county in which such negro or mulatto may wish to reside, conditioned for the good behavior of such person or persons, and to pay for their support in case they should come to want. And in case any negro or mulatto shall migrate into this State, and not comply with the conditions of this act, it shall be the duty of the overseers of the poor of the township to remove, immediately, such person, in the same manner as is required in the case of paupers."

Section 4, of the same act, provides, that no black or mulatto person shall hereafter be permitted to be sworn, or give evidence, in any court of record, or elsewhere, in this State, in any cause depending, or matter of controversy, where either party to the same is a white person; or in any prosecution, which shall be instituted in behalf of the State, against any white person.

Again: By the act for the support and regulation of common schools, blacks and mulattoes are excluded from the privileges of the system, the door of the district school house is closed against their scholars, and the privilege is denied to them of educating their children out of the public fund.

The sections of the statutes above quoted, contain, it is believed, the principal parts of the laws which bear oppressively on the colored population of our State.

The majority of the committee have come to the conclusion that the laws in question should be repealed. The reason and arguments in support of this opinion, they will bring to the attention of the House under the following divisions:

1st. These laws are inconsistent with the provisions and spirit of the constitution, as well as unjust in principle.

2d. They are opposed to the dictates of a sound and enlightened public policy.

In order to a right apprehension of the spirit and provisions of the constitution of our State, we must go back to those organic laws and ordinances of the general government of our country, on which this constitution is founded.

By the Articles of Confederation of the United States, adopted July 9, 1778, [*sic*] it is declared, "that the free inhabitants of each of these States shall be entitled to all privileges and immunities of free citizens in the several States."

By the ordinance for the government of the territory northwest of the river Ohio, passed in Congress, July 13, 1787, it is provided that for every five hundred free male inhabitants there shall be one representative in the General Assembly.

The territorial government passed an act, December 6, 1799, entitled, "an act to ascertain the number of free male inhabitants of the age of twenty-one years, and regulate the election of representatives for the same." This act provides for taking the number of free male inhabitants; and the 12th section, defining the qualifications of electors, speaks of every free male inhabitant. In the several organic laws and legislative enactments, no allusion whatever is made to color; every free inhabitant is designated, without any distinction at all of that kind. Now, under these laws, what were the rights of the blacks? Most clearly they were precisely the same with those of the whites. The terms free inhabitants-free male inhabitants, certainly include all within the bounds of the territory; these are words of most general signification, and the rule of construction is, that the words are to be taken in their most general and common acceptation.

From this examination it appears, that previous to the adoption of the constitution of the State blacks and mulattoes within the territory enjoyed all civil privileges and immunities in common with the whites. They were sworn and gave evidence in courts of justice, they were enumerated with the other citizens, for representation, they even had the right of suffrage.

We will now proceed to show the manner in which the rights of the colored people were treated, in the convention which formed the constitution of the State of Ohio, and the civil franchises, of which they were deprived, under that constitution. This is the more necessary, because it is sometimes said that those who framed the constitution did not contemplate the blacks, or take them into account as a part of the people, and that there is no direct allusion to them in that instrument.

The convention assembled at the town of Chillicothe, in the county of Ross, on the first Monday of November, 1842, to form a constitution for the State of Ohio. On the 27th page of their journal it is recorded, (the 4th article of the constitution, designating the qualifications of electors being under consideration,) "that a motion was then made further to amend the said article, by striking out, after the word all, in the first line of the first section, the word, white," which would extend the right of suffrage to all the male inhabitants of the State. This amendment was rejected by a vote of 19 to 14. On the 28th page we find," another motion was then made further to amend said section, by adding to the end of the section, a proviso, in the words following--Provided, that all male negroes and mulattoes, now residing in this territory, shall be entitled to the right of suffrage, if they shall, within months, make a record of their citizenship." This was carried in the affirmative, by a vote of 19 to 15.

After this, a motion was made to secure the same right to their male descendants, and lost, by a vote of 17 to 16.

Page 29. The seventh article being under consideration, "a motion was made further to amend said article, by adding a new section as the seventh section, in the words following--"No negro or mulatto shall ever be eligible to any office, civil or military, or give his oath in any court of justice against a white person, be subject to do military duty, or pay a poll tax in this State." This amendment was at first adopted, by a vote of 19 to 16. But four days after it was stricken out, by a vote of 17 to 16.

Page 34. A motion was made to strike out the proviso added to the first section of the fourth article, extending the right of suffrage to all male negroes and mulattoes now residing in the territory. On this question the convention was equally divided, and it prevailed only by the casting vote of the President. These quotations from the journal of the convention, provide that the members of that body were not unmindful of the colored inhabitants of the territory, that they were fully aware of the existence of that class of the population, and that the consideration of the rights of the blacks held a prominent place in their deliberations. And as the results of their deliberations, it appears they saw fit, under the constitution, to deprive the blacks of the right to vote at elections, and to exclude them from the enumeration in making out the representative population. In all other respects it evidently was the intention of the framers of the constitution to leave the colored inhabitants of the State in the full possession and enjoyment of the same rights with the whites. But how do our laws accord with the provisions of the Constitution?

The voice of the constitution proclaims, "all men are born equally free and independent, and have certain natural, inherent, and inalienable rights; amongst which are the enjoying and defending life and liberty, acquiring, possessing, and protecting property, and pursuing and obtaining happiness and safety." But your law meets the colored man at the threshold of our State and says to him, you cannot come in here without "first producing a fair certificate, from some court of record, of your actual freedom." Can there be a more odious inconsistency than this? Certainly this is one bow to the demon of slavery which is entirely superfluous, which we are under no obligation to make, by any existing compact or compromise. Most surely, a free State, promulgating such liberal and glorious principles, is bound to consider every man, whose foot touches her soil, as free, until proof is made to the contrary.

Again: The constitution declares, "That all courts shall be open, and every person, for any injury done him in his lands, goods, person, or reputation, shall have remedy by due course of law, and right and justice administered without denial or delay." Is it possible for language to be broader and more unrestricted than this? Every person, not the white man or the black man alone, but every person may redress his injuries by due course of law. How is it possible to reconcile this with the law which forbids any colored person to give evidence in any case in which a white person is concerned? How can the colored man have remedy by the due course of law, and right and justice administered without denial, when his witness, although of good character, are excluded? When his opponent, because he is white, is allowed to testify to his book account, while he is not permitted to swear to his own. How can he protect his property, when the white man may rob him in open day, in the presence of his family and friends, and yet he be unable to prove the outrage, because his witness are of another color.

Again: The constitution provides, "that all schools, which are supported, in whole or in part, by revenues arising from donations made by the United States, shall be open to scholars and teachers of every grade, without any distinction or preference whatever, contrary to the intent for which such donations were made." Now, what was the intent for which these donations were made? Let the law of Congress determine. Land Laws of the United States, page, 201, section 7, provides, "That the section, No. 16, in every township, and when such section has been sold, granted or disposed of, other lands equivalent thereto, shall be granted to the inhabitants of such township, for the use of schools." Here is no distinction of white or black, one class has just the same right as the other. Under these provisions of the law of the United States, and of our own constitution, what right or what authority had the Legislature to go on and enact laws establishing schools for white children and youth, while those of a darker hue were excluded? If we, should propose to make the law the other way, that no white children should be educated out of the public fund, that the doors of the district school should be open only to children of color, the numerous expounders of the constitution, in this House, would all start up in alarm, they would all open their mouths at once to pronounce such a law unconstitutional and void. And yet, would not the Legislature have the same right to enact such a law in the one case as in the other?

In view of the utter inconsistency of the laws in question, with the provisions and spirit of the constitution, it is to us a matter of wonder and astonishment, that any law-makers, professing to be governed by the principles of that instrument, could ever give their sanction to the enactment of such laws. But there is another thing equally wonderful and amazing, and that is, that men should now be found in our legislative body, obstinately bent in persevering in the support of such laws, and refusing to lend their aid in their repeal.

The committee are irresistibly brought to the conclusion, that the laws under discussion are contrary to the letter and spirit of the constitution, and should therefore be repealed without delay.

We shall now consider the subject under our second proposition, that the laws in question are opposed to a sound and enlightened public policy.

It is always bad policy in any government to enact, and continue in force, an unjust law, and peculiarly so in a government like our own, where, to insure regard and efficiency to our laws, we are wholly dependent on the moral sense and power of the people. Whatever support men may give to such laws, for the time being, from interested or mercenary motives, the government which enacts them is sure to fall into contempt with the people at large, and in the eyes of the world. And there is no disguising the fact, that the existence of the black laws on the statute book of our State, is disgracing the government in the eyes of our citizens, and weakening the authority of all our legislation. And who is benefitted by such measures? Does the white portion of our community derive any advantage from denying to the blacks a participation in those privileges secured by our organic laws, to every inhabitant of the State? We trow not. The evil effects of these laws must fall on all classes of our people. Cases are of frequent occurrence in which we need the aid of colored persons as witness, in deciding controversies between one white man and another, and in bringing white offenders against the State to justice.

The least degree of reflection must convince every one that the ends of justice must often fail of being accomplished, unless every person is allowed to give evidence, in any court, who is capable of understanding the nature and obligation of an oath, and who has honesty enough to tell the truth, let the tincture of his skin be what it will.

Do we find recorded in history a single instance where evils have resulted to any community, by reason of extending to all its people equality of political privilege? It requires no labored argument to show that the education, and the consequent elevation of the colored people of our State, will increase the whole amount of intelligence, and extend more widely the moral influence of the people.

But it is objected, "that the children of the two races cannot be educated together in the same school, that they will not stand in the same classes, nor associate in the study of the same lessons." We reply, that all this has been done in other States, and amongst people quite as refined and intelligent as our own, and we hear of no evils arising therefrom. We deem all such prejudices unreasonable, and therefore trust they would not be of long continuance; but while they exist, they can be no excuse for injustice.

Admitting that this kind of prejudice is now so inveterate in some parts of our State, that white and colored children could not be associated in the same school, still this is no good reason why we should deprive the latter of their just right in the public fund. Some other arrangement might be made, by which injustice might be avoided. And it is believed the provisions of our school law, as it now stands, would afford an adequate remedy for this difficulty. The directors of each school district are authorized to establish such number of schools, and employ such teachers, and to divide off the scholars, assigning such number and grade to each teacher as they may think proper.

But we are met with another object--"It is said to be in vain to attempt to elevate the moral and intellectual condition of the colored race"--"that the blacks have a greater share of depravity"--"that they are more addicted to vice"--"that the records of crime show a frightful disproportion in the number of black and white offenders." Admit this last assertion to be true, and does it not afford the strongest evidence that our whole system of treatment towards that race is wrong, and attended with the worst effects, and that it is high time to change the whole course of our policy in relation to them?

What evidence have we that the negro race are worse by nature than any other portion of the human family? On the contrary, we have the testimony of every intelligent traveler who has visited them in their native wilds of Africa, that this race is the most mild and inoffensive of all the uncivilized tribes on the face of the earth. What other portion of the human family, with the same kind of treatment, oppressed and down trodden, denied the rights and privileges of men, as the negroes have been in this country, would have made improvements in knowledge or virtue more than they? Like the tyrant of Egypt, we have been requiring bricks without straw. No man has any right to say it is in vain to attempt to elevate the condition of the blacks, so long as we refuse them a participation in those facilities and means of moral and intellectual improvement, which are so much the pride and boast of our State. Let us give the experiment a fair trial, and if it fails, then, and not till then, will we admit that the negro is incapable of improvement.

Against: It is objected, "that the repeal of the laws in question would make this State the general rendezvous of the African race in the United States. That the free blacks and worn out slaves would be poured in upon us in such numbers as to exhaust the charities of our people."

To this we reply, that there is no evidence at all that our black laws have ever kept one negro out of the State. Notwithstanding these barriers, our black population is steadily on the increase.

Pennsylvania, with no such laws, and with a location equally favorable for the influx of refugees from the slave holding States, does not increase her black population so fast as Ohio.

We have now laws to protect ourselves from the influx of foreign paupers, and, if it is necessary to strengthen that protection, the same law which keeps the white pauper out of the State will serve to keep the black pauper out too; and it is not needful, on that account, to make any invidious distinction of color.

In conclusion, the majority of the committee would express a decided opinion that there is no cause, founded in reason or justice, for the continuance of the black laws on our statute book, and believe them to be unconstitutional and contrary to sound public policy; we therefore report a bill for their repeal.

X

Runaway Slaves

For decades, Ohio accommodated its policy of freedom with slave holders who used fugitive slave legislation to apprehend runaway slaves. The federal Fugitive Slave Act of 1793 and Ohio fugitive slave laws enabled slave holders to control alleged runaways in Ohio. Abolitionists in Ohio challenged state policy beginning in during the 1830s. Abolitionist editor and antislavery lawyer James G. Birney played a decisive role in converting skillful attorneys to antislavery reform. Salmon P. Chase was Birney's most eminent convert to reform in Ohio. Attorneys such as Chase produced the legal field of antislavery law. Ultimately, they weakened the ability of slave holders to control enslaved blacks in Ohio. According to their doctrine, any slave who entered Ohio with the knowledge and consent of a master became automatically freed. Moreover, they declared the federal Fugitive Slave Act unconstitutional. This was a futile effort, however. State and federal courts consistently upheld the validity of the Act of 1793. The following documents describe the process whereby the law authorized slave holders to capture and remove runaway slaves.

NUMBER 1

An act relating to fugitives from labor or service from other states. Approved February 26, 1839, Laws of Ohio.

Whereas, the second section of the fourth article of the constitution of the United States declares, that "no person held to service or labor in another state, under the laws thereof, escaping into another, shall, in consequence of any law or regulation therein, be discharged from such service or labor, but shall be delivered up on claim of the party to whom such service or labor may be due": And, since, the laws now in force within the State of Ohio are wholly inadequate to the protection pledged by this provision of the constitution to the southern states of the Union: and, whereas, it is the duty of those who reap the largest measure of benefits conferred by the constitution, to recognize, to their full extent, the obligation which that instrument imposes: And, whereas, it is the deliberate conviction of this general assembly, that the constitution can only be sustained as it was framed, by spirit of just compromise: Therefore,

Section 1. Be it enacted by the General Assembly of the State of Ohio, That when any person held to labor or service in any of the United States under the laws, thereof, shall escape into this state, the person to whom such labor or service is due, his or her agent or attorney, is hereby authorized to apply to any judge of any court of record in this state, to any justice of the peace, or to the mayor of any city or town corporation, who on such application, (supported by the oath or affirmation of such claimant, his or her agent or attorney, that said fugitive has escaped from his or her service, or from the service of the person for whom he is agent or attorney, and which oath or affirmation shall be reduced to writing, and shall specify the name and place of residence of the person to whom such labor or service is due, and also the name and supposed age of such fugitive, with a pertinent description of his or her person) shall issue his warrant, under his hand and seal, and directed to the sheriff or constable of any county in this state, authorizing and directing said sheriff or constable to seize and arrest the said fugitive, who shall be named in the said warrant; and in case the said fugitive, who shall be named in the said warrant; and in case the said fugitive shall be arrested in the county in which said warrant may be issued, to bring him or her before some judge of a court of record of this state residing within such county, or in case not in the county in which the warrant may be issued, then to take him or her before some judge of a court of record in this state, residing in the county in which such arrest is made; provided, however, that no such warrant shall be returned before any officer residing out of the county in which the same may have been issued, unless the official character of the judge or justice, issuing the same, shall be duly authenticated by the seal and certificate of the clerk of the supreme court or court of common pleas; and if issued by a mayor of any city or town corporate, the official character of said warrant shall be duly authenticated under the seal of said city or town corporate; which said warrant shall be in the form and to the following, that is to say:

The State of Ohio, ________________ County:

To any sheriff or constable of the State of Ohio, greetings: This is to authorize and require you to seize and arrest the body of ___________ sworn [or affirmed] to be a slave [or servant, as the case may be] of ___________ of the state __________; and in case such arrest be made in this county, to bring such person so arrested forthwith before some judge of a court of record of this state residing within this county, or in case such arrest be made in any other county in this state, then to take said person so arrested before some judge of a court of record of this state, residing within the county in which such arrest may be made, to be dealt with as the law directs.

To which warrant shall be annexed a copy of the oath or affirmation hereinbefore specified; by virtue of which warrant the said fugitive named therein shall be arrested by the officer to whom it is directed, in any county of this state; provided, that no such arrest shall be made by any sheriff or constable of this state without the limits of his own proper county.

Section 2. The said person so claimed as a fugitive, when so arrested, shall be brought before the officer as directed in the first section of this act; and the said claimant; his or her agent or attorney, having first given security for the costs; and having proved to the satisfaction of such officer, that the person so seized and arrested does, under the laws of the state from which he or she fled, owe service or labor to the person claiming him or her, it shall be the duty of such judge to give a certificate thereof to such claimant, his or her agent or attorney, which shall be sufficient authority for removing the said fugitive to the state from which he or she fled; but no such certificate shall be deemed a sufficient authority for the removal of such fugitive under the provisions of this act, in relation to the issuing of warrants.

Section 3. If any person shall knowingly and willfully prevent such sheriff or constable from arresting such fugitive from labor or service as aforesaid, or shall knowingly and willfully obstruct or hinder such sheriff or constable in making such arrest; or shall knowingly and willfully hinder or obstruct any claimant his or her agent or attorney, having the certificate provided for in the second section of the act, in the removal of such fugitive to the state from which he or she fled; or shall rescue or aid and abet in the rescue of such fugitive from sheriff, constable, claimant, agent or attorney; or if two or more persons shall assemble together with intent to obstruct, hinder or interrupt such sheriff or constable in arresting such fugitive, or with intent to obstruct, hinder or interrupt such claimant, agent or attorney, having the certificate aforesaid, in the removal of such fugitive to the state from which he or she fled, and shall make any movement or preparation therefor, every person so offending shall upon conviction thereof, by indictment, be fined in any sum not exceeding five hundred dollars, or be imprisoned in the jail of the county not exceeding sixty days, at the discretion of the court, and shall moreover be liable in an action at the suit of the person claiming such labor or service.

Section 4. That when said fugitive shall be brought before the judge, agreeably to the provisions of this act, on the return warrant, if the claimant, his or her agent or attorney, shall not be prepared for trial, and shall make oath or affirmation that he or she does verily believe that the person so arrested is a fugitive from labor or service in another state, and that if allowed time, he or she will be able to produce satisfactory evidence that the person so arrested does owe such labor or service, it shall be the duty of such judge to postpone the trial to such time as he may deem reasonable, not exceeding sixty days; and in case of such postponement, it shall and may be lawful for said judge (unless the person so arrested shall enter into bond, with one or more sufficient securities, to be approved of by such judge, in the penal sum of one thousand dollars to the person claiming the person so arrested as aforesaid, conditioned for his or her appearance on the day to which the trial shall be postponed, and that he or she will then and there abide the decision of the judge who shall try the case,) to commit the party arrested to the jail of the county where the trial is pending, there to be detained until the day set for trial by said judge. And in case the party arrested shall be committed to the jail of the county, the claimant, his or her agent or attorney shall pay down to said judge for the use of the person entitled thereto, the amount of the jail fees and the sheriff's fees for keeping and providing for such person during the period that he or she shall be imprisoned as aforesaid. And the said judge shall, in like manner, give time, not exceeding sixty days for the production of evidence on the behalf of the arrested party, if he or she shall file affidavit that he or she does not owe labor or service to the claimant, and that affiant verily believes that he or she will be able to produce evidence to that effect: provided, that the person so arrested shall give bond and security as, aforesaid, in the penalty of one thousand dollars, and conditioned for his or her personal appearance at the time and place of trial, and that he or she will abide the decision of the judge who shall try the case; and on failure to give such bond and security, the party arrested shall be committed to the jail of the county, there to be detained until the time fixed for trial as aforesaid. And on the day appointed for the trial, if such fugitive, if committed to jail shall be brought before said judge, or in case of his absence, sickness or inability to attend, before some other judge of a court of record of this state residing within such county, by written order of such judge, directed to the sheriff or jailor of the proper county, for final hearing and adjudication; and in case there shall be a breach of the condition of either of said bonds, the claimant shall have a right of action thereon, and recover as in other cases; and on said trial, either party shall be entitled to be heard by counsel, and shall have compulsory process to compel the attendance of witness.

Section 5. It shall be the duty of the said judge at the time to which the case is postponed as aforesaid, to proceed to hear the parties, and if it shall be proven to his satisfaction that the party arrested does owe labor or service to the claimant, he shall give such claimant, his or her agent or attorney, a certificate of that fact, which shall be a sufficient authority for such claimant, his or her agent or attorney to remove such fugitive from the state; but no certificate shall be deemed a sufficient authority for the removal of such fugitive, unless the official character of the officer giving the same be duly authenticated, according to the provisions of this act in relation to the issuing of warrants. And if the party thus arrested shall not appear, according to the conditions of his or her bond, it shall be the duty of said judge to deliver the same to the claimant, his or her agent or attorney, to enable him or her to bring suit thereon.

Section 6. If any person or persons in this state shall counsel, advise, or entice any other person, who, by the laws of any other state, shall owe labor or service to any other person or persons, to leave, abandon, abscond or escape from the person or persons to whom such labor or service, according to the laws of such other state, is or be due, or shall furnish money or conveyance of any kind, or any other facility, with intent and for the purpose of enabling such person, owing labor or service as aforesaid, to escape from or elude the claimant of such person, owing labor or service as aforesaid, every person so offending shall, upon conviction thereof by indictment, be fined in any sum not exceeding five hundred dollars, or be imprisoned in the jail of the county not exceeding sixty days, at the discretion of the court; and shall moreover be liable in an action at the suit of the party injured.

Section 7. If any person or persons shall falsely, fraudulently and without proper authority, give to any other person, who by the laws of any other state, shall owe labor or service to any person or persons, any certificate or testimonial of emancipation, with the intent to defraud the person or persons to whom such labor or service may be due, knowing such person to owe labor or service as aforesaid; or shall harbor or conceal any such person owing labor or service as aforesaid, who may come into this state without the consent of the person or persons to owe labor or service as aforesaid, every person so offending shall upon conviction thereof by indictment, be fined in any sum not exceeding five hundred dollars, or be imprisoned in the jail of the county not exceeding sixty days, at the discretion of the court; and shall moreover be liable in any action at the suit of the party injured.

Section 8. Any sheriff, or constable, who shall execute any process directed and delivered to him and under the provisions of this act, or any clerk of a court, or mayor, who shall authenticate any certificate or warrant under the provisions of this act, shall receive the same fees as are now allowed by law for similar services in other cases.

Section 9. It shall be the duty of all officers proceeding under this act, to recognize, without proof, the existence of slavery or involuntary servitude, in the several states of this union, in which the same may exist or be recognized by law.

Section 10. If any person, in any deposition or affidavit, or other oath or affirmation, taken pursuant to the provisions of this act, shall willfully and corruptly depose, affirm, or declare any matter to be fact, knowing the same to be false; or shall in like manner, deny any matter to be fact, knowing the same to be true, every person so offending shall be deemed guilty of perjury, and upon conviction thereof, shall be imprisoned in the penitentiary, and kept at hard labor not more than seven, nor less than three years.

Section 11. If any person or persons shall in any manner attempt to carry out of this state or knowingly be aiding in carrying out of this state, any person, without first obtaining sufficient legal authority for so doing, according to the laws of this state or of the United States, every person so offending shall be deemed guilty of a misdemeanor, and upon conviction thereof, shall be imprisoned in the penitentiary, and kept at hard labor, not less than three, nor more than seven years.

Section 12. That the fourth section of an act to regulate black and mulatto persons, passed January 5, 1804, and so much of the second section of the act to prevent kidnapping, passed February 15, 1831, as is inconsistent with the provisions of this act, be and the same is hereby repealed.

Section 13. That a trial and judgment under the act of congress, entitled "an act respecting fugitives from justice, and persons escaping from the service of their masters" approved February 12, 1793, or a trial and judgment under the provisions of this act, shall be adjudged a final bar to any subsequent proceeding against the fugitive under the provisions of this act.

Section 14. This act to take effect from and after the first day of May next.

NUMBER 2

Report on fugitive slaves. January 18, 1841, House Journal.

The standing committee on the Judiciary, to whom was referred a large number of petitions, praying the repeal of the act entitled "an act relating to fugitives from labor or service from other states," and, also, sundry petitions that the right of trial by jury may be extended to every human being, have had the same under consideration, and now report:

That the questions necessarily involved in the consideration of the subject, if thoroughly examined, would lead into an extensive field of inquiry. That the committee have not, perhaps, given it that full, and perfect investigation that the subject demands, is owing more to a want of time, and opportunity to investigate, than from any lack of an earnest desire, on the part of the committee, to arrive at a just conclusion. It not only involves the great question of person rights, but the equally important consideration, of the relations that exist between the different states of the confederacy, and the obligations each state is under to preserve, inviolate, the letter and spirit of the provisions of our constitution, in reference to those relations. The constitution recognizes the existence of slavery in the Union, and, as a protection to those states in which it exists, it provides, in article 4th section 2d, that "No person held to labor or service in one state under the laws thereof, escaping to another, shall in consequence of any law, or regulation therein, be discharged from such service or labor, but shall be delivered up on claim of the party to whom such service or labor may be due." No one will be found to contend that this provision of the constitution is not binding on the states. However strongly the sympathy of individuals may incline them to regret, and their moral feelings to condemn, yet the fact, based upon a rock, still exists, that a state cannot, by law, constitute a person, escaping from service or labor from another state, a FREE MAN, while, by laws of the state from which he escapes, he is a SLAVE.

In considering the propriety of repealing the law, the repeal of which the petitioners ask, we should take into consideration the object of the law as it exists, and the effect of a repeal of its provisions. The object of the law was undoubtedly to fulfill the obligation the law makers supposed the state to be under, to assist, on her part, to carry out the provision of the constitution given above. The obligation to deliver up fugitives from service or labor, being conceded, this law was intended to prescribe the manner in which the claimant should substantiate his claim, by proving himself entitled to the services of the individual claimed to point out the forms of legal proceeding necessary to be gone through for the protection of the rights and interests of the claimant, and the person claimed. Whether this law does this in the best manner, will be considered hereafter.

If this is the object of the law, where should we find ourselves, were the law repealed? Would the situation of any of the parties interested, be bettered? Could the same object be accomplished in a better way? Would the rights of the parties be more fully protected? If so, the question should most certainly be considered; and if not, its consideration is not less important.

Those who ask for the repeal of this law, will not contend that this would release us from the obligation imposed by the constitution, to deliver up fugitives from service or labor, when the fact of being fugitives, is properly ascertained. The repeal of this law cannot release us from the obligations imposed by the constitution. It would not only not release us from our obligations to do a particular thing, but it would not even prevent the thing being done. It only releases us from doing it in a particular manner, and operates to substitute a different mode to do the same thing.

Is the mode substituted, better than the one provided by the present law?

The only law in existence, which can, in any possible contingency, bind the people of this state on this subject, other than the one now sought to be repealed, is the law of Congress, passed February 12, 1793, relating to fugitives from labor. The section of that law which points out the manner in which fugitives shall be arrested and delivered up, to which we wish particularly to advert, is the 3d section, as follows: That "when a person held to labor in any of the United States, or in either of the territories northwest or south of the river Ohio, under the laws thereof, shall escape into any other of the said states or territories, the person to whom such labor or service may be due, his agent or attorney is hereby empowered to seize or arrest such fugitive from labor, and to take him or her before any judge of the circuit or district courts of the United States, residing or being within the state, or before any magistrate of a county, city or town corporate, wherein such seizure or arrest shall be made, and upon proof, to the satisfaction of such judge, or magistrate, either by oral testimony or affidavit, taken before, and certified by, a magistrate of any such state or territory, that the person so seized or arrested, does, under the laws of the state or territory from which he or she has fled, owe service or labor to the person claiming him or her, it shall be the duty of such judge or magistrate to give a certificate thereof to such claimant, his agent or attorney, which shall be sufficient warrant for removing such fugitive from labor, to the state and territory from which he or she fled." The next section imposes a penalty of $500 upon any person who shall hinder such arrest, or rescue the fugitive.

By the provisions of the above law, an arrest and seizure of an alleged fugitive, may be made without oath or affidavit, without the description of the person, and without any warrant, or other process of court, by the claimant himself, or by his agent or attorney, and without the intervention of any office of the law whatsoever. While under the law now sought to be repealed, the claimant, his agent or attorney, must make oath that said fugitive has escaped from his service or labor, or from the service or labor of the person for whom he is agent or attorney, which oath shall be reduced to writing, and shall specify the name, and place of residence, of the person to whom such service is due, with the name and supposed age of the fugitive, with a pertinent description of his person, when, and not before, the magistrate shall issue his warrant for the arrest of the fugitive, which is to be served by a sheriff or constable. These, in the opinion of your committee, are all salutary checks, that do not exist under the operation of the law of the United States, and so far render the law of our own state decidedly preferable to the United States' law. While these checks are incorporated in the law, as a protection to the rights of the alleged fugitive, they do not, in the least degree, prejudice the rights of the claimant. He is only entitled to the individual who has, in fact, escaped from service or labor, and he cannot complain that he is required to establish this fact, in the way the law points out.

But there is another view of the law of '93, that may be taken, of paramount importance in the examination of this question--a view that has been taken by the ablest jurist of the country, and in accordance with which, many of the judicial tribunals of the land have uniformly adjudicated. The view now taken by the committee, is this:

That so far as that law purports to confer power upon state Magistrates, it is unconstitutional.

It seems to be a well settled principle, that Congress cannot, by law, confer any portion of the judicial power of the United States, on State Magistrates, or other State officers. This is entirely beyond the power of Congress. It has no power except that granted by the constitution, and unless the constitution provides that Congress can confer judicial power upon State Magistrates, the power does not exist. The states are sovereign and independent. Each state is as wholly foreign and alien to every other state, as is the government of the Union, to the Empire of China except so far as the states are confederated together by the bonds of the constitution. It is this constitution, adopted in a spirit of mutual compromise, that gives to the General Government all the power it possesses. Can there then be any power conferred by it, upon the judicial, or other officers of separate and independent states?

In what is the judicial power of the United States vested? Is there any doubt on this point? Article III, Sec. 1, of the constitution provides, that "the judicial power of the United States shall be vested in one Supreme Court, and in such inferior courts as the Congress may from time to time ordain and establish." Here the constitution provides that the judicial power of the Union shall be vested in one Supreme Court. Section 2 of the same article, says: "The judicial power shall extend to all cases, in law and equity, arising under this constitution; the laws of the United States, and treaties made, or which shall be made under their authority; to all cases affecting ambassadors, other public ministers and consuls; to all cases of admiralty and maritime jurisdiction," &c., &c.,&c. It is in reference to this provision of the constitution, that the learned Mr. Justice Story, in the case Martin v. Hunter's Lessees, (1 Wheaton, 304,) in his opinion, says: "Congress cannot vest any portion of the judicial power of the United States, except in courts ordained and established by itself." And if this power cannot be vested in any other than a court ordained by itself, it follows that no judicial or other officer of a state, can act as such under the laws of the United States. The object of the constitution was to establish three great distinctive departments of the government. The Legislative, the Executive, and the Judicial. The line of distinction between these three departments, is marked and clear. It was meant to confer all the legislative power upon Congress, all the executive power upon the President, and all the judicial power upon the Supreme and other Courts. The three departments must not interfere with each other. One cannot perform the duties of the other. And when the constitution says, that "the judicial power shall be vested," &c., it means that the whole judicial power shall be so vested. In the language of Mr. Justice Story, in the celebrated case above alluded to: "If, then, it is a duty of Congress to vest the judicial power of the United States, it is duty to vest the whole judicial power. The language, if imperative as to one part, is imperative as to all. If it were otherwise, this anomaly would exist, that Congress might successively refuse to vest the jurisdiction in any one class of cases enumerated in the constitution, and thereby defeat the jurisdiction as to all; for the constitution has not singled out any class on which Congress are bound to act in preference to others."

This question has not only been solemnly decided in the Supreme Court of the United States, but there are a multitude of decisions in the courts of the several states, that go to establish the same general proposition.

But, there is not only an abundance of Judicial Authority on this subject, but in addition to all this, we have the legislative action of many of the independent States on this very point. Wherever we find a state law directly contravening this law of the United States, we must come to the conclusion, that in the opinion of the Legislature enacting the law, the law of Congress was of no force. For it is an absurdity to suppose that a state legislature would enact a law in direct violation of a law of Congress, at the same time knowing that the law of the United States created a paramount obligation. We may, then, take it for granted, that whenever we find a state law contravening a law of the Union, it was the opinion of the state legislature enacting it, that the United States law was of no validity.

On the 21st of January, 1801, the Legislature of Virginia enacted a Law forbidding any of her Magistrates from acting under any Law, except the Law of the Commonwealth. The Law provided that no person, "either by his own authority, or under color of any office whatever, held or claimed to be held under the authority of this Commonwealth, should surrender or deliver up any citizen of the Commonwealth, entitled to the protection of its Laws, to be sent beyond the sea or elsewhere within the United States, under a penalty, upon conviction, of imprisonment in the Penitentiary, of not less than one, nor more than ten years. This Law undoubtedly expressed the opinion of the Legislature of Virginia on the point, whether any other authority except the authority of the Commonwealth itself, could confer any power upon its own Judicial Officers.

But let us look, for a moment, at our own Legislation. Your committee are of the opinion, that the Law now asked to be repealed, is at least in its spirit in direct contravention of the Law of Congress on the same subject. The one provides that a fugitive may be arrested without any of the forms of law, and brought before any Justice of the Peace; that such Justice shall adjudicate upon the fact of his being fugitive and his certificate, that he is so, is sufficient authority for the claimant to take the fugitive beyond the State. While the Law of our State provides that the claimant shall first make affidavit and procure a warrant from a Magistrate, and that warrant must be served either by a Sheriff or Constable, both the ministerial officers of our courts, and the warrant commands that the person executing it take the alleged fugitive before a Judge of a Court of Record of this State, who is authorized to adjudicate upon the matter. It is so far salutary and just. It gives the fugitive this protection, that it requires the affidavit of the claimant, as the prerequisite of a warrant, while it fulfills the constitutional obligation of the State in giving the claimant the advantage of a process, and the services of a public officer to execute it.

In view of all these authorities, ought we not, to say the least give the question a careful consideration. Here, by the solemn adjudication in the Supreme Court of the United States, and the courts of several of the States, and by the independent Legislative action of many of the States, we have the principle decided, that the Congress has not the power to confer any authority, nor to impose any obligation, upon any State officers; and that the law of

1793, so far as it purports to confer authority, and to impose obligations, upon officers of a State, is unconstitutional.

It is true, there are many cases where the officers of the several States and of the United States may act concurrently; and the State Courts and the Courts of the United States may exercise concurrent jurisdiction. But in no such case do the State Courts derive their authority from Congress; and in no such case can the power be conferred by Congress.

But, in addition to the authorities here given, there are other reasons, that will naturally suggest themselves to every reflecting mind, why Congress should not exercise this authority. The Constitution gives Congress no power to confer any such authority.

The tenth amendment to the Constitution says: "The powers not delegated to the United States by the Constitution, nor prohibited by it to the States, are reserved to the States, respectively, or to the people."

All will admit that Congress has no power to legislate, except such as is delegated by the Constitution; and if that instrument does not delegate to Congress any such power, nor prohibit it to the States, it is reserved to the States, and Congress can, of course exercise no such authority. All that the Constitution says on the subject is in article four, section two, which provides, that if a slave escapes from one State into another, that he shall not be released from such service by any law of the State into which he escapes, but shall be delivered up. Does this provision delegate any authority to Congress to legislate upon the subject? It imposes an obligation upon the States not to pass any law releasing slaves from service. But it cannot be tortured into the semblance of an authority for Congress to legislate, so as to confer power, or impose obligation, upon State authorities.

But further: Among the various principles, arising out of our peculiar form of Government, there is no one more obvious and important than the principle of responsibility. This is a principle that ought to be guarded in every department of the Government. Whatever will tend to enfeeble it, should be looked upon with watchful jealousy; and any thing that is calculated wholly to destroy it, should be utterly condemned, as tending to subvert our cherished institutions. All the officers of the United States, whether their duty is to defend the country, to adjudicate upon, or carry into execution, the laws of the land, are appointed by the authority of the United States; they are paid by the appointing power; and are, in all cases, responsible, directly or indirectly, to it, and are punishable by it for official misconduct. Here the doctrine of responsibility is fully carried out. But, if the United States can make use of an officer of an independent State to adjudicate upon, or to execute, their laws, then this principle is wholly destroyed. Can a State Judge be impeached for official misconduct, while acting under a law, and in behalf of the United States? Can any State officer be removed from office by any authority of the United States? If not, then, in these cases, the officer is wholly irresponsible to the power under whose authority he acts.

It is also equally clear, that, while acting under the law of the United States, he cannot be made responsible to the superior Power of the State, by which he is appointed and commissioned; for, he can only be made to answer to the authorities of the State for the faithful discharge of the trust they have committed to him; and he is not answerable to them for the faithful discharge of a trust committed to him by the United States. And the admission, on our part, that Congress has the right to confer authority or impose obligation upon State officers, is destructive to this great principle of responsibility.

But further: If the United States can impose any obligation upon a Judicial officer of a State, to act in his official capacity, under a law of Congress, they can, with equal authority, make use of the Legislative and Executive officers of a State to accomplish their purposes. They have the same power in the three cases. If they can require a Justice of the Peace of the State to adjudicate upon a law of the General government, they can require the Executive of a State to see the laws of Congress are faithfully executed; and also require the Legislatures of the several States to make laws for the United States. All the power of the General Government is made up of power conceded by the States; it has no original power; its powers were all granted by the States; and what powers the States did not grant, they reserved to themselves. And it cannot be presumed, that they intended to grant, powers to the General Government, by the Constitution, which must necessarily interfere with the full and perfect authority requisite to the due administration of their own affairs. It would, then, seem, from all that we can gather of the intention of the framers of our Constitution--from the Judicial decisions and Legislative action since that period--from the Judicial decisions and Legislative action since that period--from a consultation of the true spirit and meaning of the constitution itself, that Congress does not possess the power to confer authority upon any State officer. Any other doctrine would be dangerous in the extreme; it would tend most directly to convert our Confederated Republic into a Consolidated Government. A wicked and ambitious Executive could desire the prevalence of no better doctrine than this to aid him in his unholy aspirations.

If the General Government can swallow up the powers of the States--can contract or dilate them at pleasure, what more will they soon be than mere subordinate appendages to the Great Central Power; all humbly subservient to these mandates that emanate from the consolidated head. This should never be. A free people should ever repudiate doctrines that can tend to such a result. They should be jealous of their liberties; watch every avenue by which encroachment can enter; and, possessing the same spirit that actuated the heroes who bled, and the immortal sages who, by a Constitution, labored to perpetuate that for which those heroes bled, their sons can gloriously consummate the perpetuation of that liberty for which those heroes and sages battled and died.

But, whatever conclusion may be arrived at with regard to the constitutionality of the law of Congress, so far as it purports to give authority to State Magistrates to act judicially under its provisions, still, the obligation we are under to the slaveholding States--an obligation imposed by the Constitution--exists, and will continue to rest upon us, as long as the Constitution binds the States together. The Constitution expressly enjoins:

That no person, held to labor or service in one State, under the laws thereof, escaping into another, shall, in consequence of any law or regulation therein, be discharged from such service or labor, but shall be delivered up on claim of the party to whom such service or labor is due.

Here the question very naturally arises, upon whom does this clause of the constitution impose an obligation--upon Congress or upon the states? Does it enjoin upon Congress to act in any manner? It expressly says that the states shall not pass any law by which a person held to service or labor in another state, shall be released from that service or labor. So far this is an obligation upon the states, not to enact certain laws. Does it authorize Congress to enact any law on the subject? But this clause not only prohibits the states from passing any law by which the slave can be released, but it says, the fugitive shall be delivered up. This is an express provision. Who is to do it? Is he to be delivered up by authority of Congress, or are the state authorities bound to provide for the delivery. The states are bound not to pass a law to prevent his being delivered up; but he "shall be delivered up," and of course by the authorities of the state into whose bounds he has escaped.

But who is to be delivered up? Most manifestly every person, who, by the laws of a state, is held as a slave, and who escapes from such service into another state. Not every person who is alleged to be a fugitive, but who in fact is a fugitive from service or labor. If, then, a mere allegation that an individual is a slave, is not sufficient to justify his being delivered up, of course the fact should be ascertained, whether or not he is a fugitive from service. And how is that fact to be ascertained? Most certainly by a tribunal competent to adjudicate upon that fact. And how and where shall that tribunal be created? Without question, by the authorities in the state where the fact is to be determined. It is absolutely necessary, that there be legislation on the subject, not only to protect the rights of the person alleged to be a slave, but to secure to the master the perfect enjoyment of the rights guaranteed him by the constitution. The State Legislatures are fully competent to legislate on the subject, and it is their duty so to do. The members thereof, and all other state officers, both executive and judicial, take an oath to support the constitution of the United States. The provisions of that constitution, in reference to the rights of the parties, stand out clear and prominent, and it is not to be presumed the Legislature will violate their duty.

We now come to ask the question, ought the present law to be repealed? Your committee think they have shown, that a law enacted by the law making power of the State, on the subject, ought to exist. If so, shall this law be repealed? Or if the present law does not meet the exigencies of the case, in the best manner, shall we strike it from our statute book, or by modifying, and amending it, make it what it ought to be?

They are of the opinion, FIRST, that there should be a law on the subject; and, SECOND, that the present law is not what it should be, but that it is much better to amend than to repeal it.

In what particular is the present law defective? The object of the law should be to fulfill, to the fullest extent, our obligations to the slaveholding states, imposed by the constitution, while we protect the personal rights of those who, under a pretence of requiring a fulfillment of those obligations, may have their liberty endangered. But what is this obligation that we are so scrupulously to fulfill? It is that we deliver up those who have escaped from service or labor. Who are we to deliver up? Those who are in fact, what they may be alleged to be, slaves, who have escaped. This is the extent of our obligation. We are to deliver up fugitives from service or labor, not those who are merely claimed as such. All then that can be asked, is, that when the fact is ascertained, that the person claimed is a slave, that then he shall be delivered to the claimant. Where shall that fact be ascertained? In a court of justice. How shall it be ascertained? It would seem that that fact ought to be found in the same manner that facts of the same importance are usually found in courts of justice. The laws that should govern the practice of our courts in this case, should be the same that governs them in adjudicating upon facts in all other cases. Why not? Is not the fact in this case to be determined, of sufficient importance? All that the claimant can ask is, that the person claimed be delivered up when the fact is determined that he is entitled to him. Is it of no importance to the person claimed? What, the question that involves his personal liberty, and the liberty of his posterity, forever, of no consequence! His all depends upon it. That which may be dearer to him than life, hangs upon the issue! If the decision be erroneous, how terrible may be the consequences. It may be to consign a free man, one, who, from his cradled infancy has breathed the free air of Heaven, to hopeless bondage; while on the other hand, it can be no more than to deprive the owner of his value in money. Ought not then every guard be thrown around the forms of justice, that both parties may have a full guarantee that the adjudication shall be fairly made.

In what manner then ought this question of fact to be ascertained? A majority of your committee are of the opinion, that when either party desire it, they ought to have the right to demand, that it be tried by a jury.

Your committee would here remark, that in all cases the presumption of the law is in favor of freedom. The law presumes every man while in this State, a free man. Slavery can never exist except by positive institution. Its foundation is not in natural rights. Slavery is not instituted in this State, and therefore its laws always presume every man free. And the only reason why every man in the State is not in all cases in fact free, is the provision of the

Constitution heretofore alluded to. Were it not for this provision, every man, by setting his foot upon the soil of Ohio would become free. In the language of Judge Story, in his work on the conflict of Laws, page 92, "Independent of the provisions of the Constitution of the United States for the protection of the rights of masters in regard to domestic fugitive slaves, there is no doubt that the English principle pervades the common law of the non-slaveholding States in America; that is, foreign slaves would be no longer deemed such after removal thither."

The legal presumption being always in favor of freedom, in this respect, the black and the white man are on the same level. The law presumes the colored man free, it can presume no more of the white. The affidavit of the claimant, and the arrest in pursuance of it does not destroy that presumption. He is entitled to the full benefit of it, until the fact of his being a slave is determined by a competent tribunal. If in this respect the law places the black and the white side by side, why not give one the same remedy that the other possesses, in every case where the liberty of either is endangered.

Our Constitution says, "that there shall be neither slavery nor involuntary servitude in this State, otherwise than for the commission of crimes," and further, that no alteration of the Constitution shall ever take place so as to introduce slavery or involuntary servitude into this State. By these provisions, slavery, in this State, can never exist.

The case of Birney v. the State, 8 Ohio 230, was a writ of error from Hamilton county. The plaintiff in error was indicted for harboring a fugitive slave. The indictment did not aver that he knew her to be a slave. In deciding this point, the court say, "such is not the legal inference in a State whose Constitution declares that all are born free and equal, and that there shall be neither slavery nor involuntary servitude within its limits, except as a punishment for the commission of crime. On the contrary, the presumption is in favor of freedom."

The legal presumption, then, is always in favor of liberty. If so, as far as the Judiciary throws its protection over the rights of the people, why should one color be the recipient of that protection and the other be cast beyond its pale. Here, an individual is charged with not being entitled to his liberty. In fulfillment of the obligations imposed upon us by the Constitution, that charge must be judicially investigated. Is he guilty or not guilty. The fact is to be tried. How shall it be investigated? The charge is a heinous one, and the truth must be arrived at your committee believe that it ought to be judicially investigated, and a verdict of an impartial jury rendered upon it, as would be the case on any other charge of the most petty insignificance. Let the fact be found by a jury. As they regard their oaths they will do justice between the parties. We are too prone to lose sight of the important principles involved in the right of trial by jury. It is a sacred right, and one that can never be yielded. When gone, freedom is buried with it. It is in fact, itself the fire brightly burning upon the altar of liberty. It is an ancient right.

This is all in reference to this right under the common law. But let it be remembered, that with us the common law is in full force, except where it is restrained by positive enactment. We are in the enjoyment of the rich blessings of the right of trial by jury--by our fathers held so sacred, by the common law. But the people of this country, from its first settlement, seemingly fearful that this common law right, might be stripped from them, have continued to provide that the right should remain inviolate. The very first law of the Colony of New Plymouth, in 1623, was "that all criminal acts and also all matters of trespasses and debts between man and man, should be tried by the verdict of twelve honest men, to be impaneled by authority, in form of a jury upon their oath."

From the time the crew of the Mayflower first planted their feet upon Plymouth Rock, to the present moment, the people have guarded, as with a wall of fire, this inestimable right. Even while colonial dependents upon the British Crown, that privilege was guaranteed to us. And when the mighty spirits of our Revolution plucked from that Crown its brightest jewel, they did not forget that unless this right could be perpetuated, the blood they had shed for freedom would have been in vain. In the declaration of national rights in 1774, the people claimed the trial by jury as their birthright and inheritance; and when the Colonies had become independent, the right was constitutionally guarded in every State in the Union. The Constitution of the United States having been adopted, it was found that by it, this right was only established in the trial of crimes. The people were dissatisfied, and the very first Congress proposed amendments, which were ratified by the States, that "in suits at common law, where the value in controversy should exceed twenty dollars, the right of trial by jury shall be preserved.

No one, then, will be found to question the importance of the preservation of the right of jury trial. The great principle is one in which all will acquiesce. The only question that can arise in the consideration of the subject is, the application of the principle.

The question then again occurs, ought an alleged fugitive to have the privilege of having the fact determined by a jury? As has been before remarked, the law presumes every man free, until the contrary is proven. The law presuming him to be a freeman, shall this freedom be taken from him, without a jury trial? But he may be what the law presumes him to be in fact--a freeman. Shall a judicial investigation be permitted, in which the fact of his freedom is jeopardized, and he not have the right of a jury trial? No colored man, however infamous may be his character, can be convicted of the commission of a petty theft, except by the verdict of a jury. He is charged with the crime of larceny; he is presumed innocent, until he is proved guilty. Here the law throws its shield around him, and declares that he shall never be convicted of even such a charge as this, without being entitled to all the benefits of a jury trial.

The alleged fugitive is charged with being a slave; the law presumes him to be free. The charge, if true, will not merely subject him to the infliction of a petty fine, and perhaps to a few days' imprisonment, but it strips him of his freedom forever. Which of the two cases involves the greatest consequences? Which of the greatest importance? In the one case, we allow the negro, on a charge of theft, all the solemnities of a jury trial to vindicate himself; while, in the other case, when charged with that which, if true, will take from him, perhaps a wife and family, and certainly his freedom, as dear to him as to us, we deny him the safeguard of a jury trial. And, besides, he is allowed this right on the trial of a charge, which, if true, involves him not only in the punishment but the guilt of a crime. While, in the case of the fugitive, the consequences of the charge, if true, are infinitely worse than the punishment in the other case; yet, at the same time, the truth of the charge does not fix any guilt upon his skirt--it does not involve any moral wrong. In the one case, if the charge is true, the individual deserves the punishment inflicted; while, in the other case, the punishment is infinitely worse, with this aggravating circumstance, that, morally, he deserves no punishment at all. Ought we to allow a jury in the case comparatively trifling, and deny it in the other?

In every case of litigation, where the matter in controversy is but the amount of a single dollar, the parties, whether black or white, have the right of a trial by jury: and shall it be denied to the same individual, when the amount in controversy is the value of the labors of a whole life? Suppose the proposition should be brought forward, to deprive the colored man of the right of trial by jury in all cases of a civil or criminal nature: would it be entertained for a moment? Yet, how trifling would be the right of which we should deprive him, compared with the one which is now forbidden him--the right of having the question of his personal liberty determined by a jury.

It may be said, that they are of an inferior race, and not entitled to the privileges we enjoy. Admitting their inferiority, is this a reason why they should be deprived of the right now proposed to be granted them? If so, why allow them a jury trial in any case? Let us not make a mockery of justice, by permitting them to enjoy it in cases where it is now permitted them, while we refuse it to them in cases where, to them it is infinitely more important that they should have it. And, besides, it is noble, is it manly, is it generous, is it magnanimous, for superiors, whether in station, in intellect, or in whatever the superiority may consist, to monopolize the rights of the human race--to trample upon the defenseless, and grasp, with rigorous exaction, privileges that should be common to all? But, further, does not the spirit of our constitution require, that, even in this case, the right of trial by jury shall be inviolate?

The 8th article, section 1, of our constitution, declares, "That all men are born equally free and independent, and have certain natural, inherent and unalienable rights; amongst which are the enjoying and defending life and liberty." It declares that all men are born equally free, &c., and as there can neither be slavery, nor involuntary servitude, in this state, all men are, by the constitution, in fact, equally free, till the contrary is clearly proven. It also declares that it is a natural, inherent and unalienable right, that all men possess, to defend life and liberty. Does not then the spirit of the constitution require that the greatest possible facilities be given to "all men," by law, to defend their liberty? The constitution also, in the same article, declares, "that the right of trial by jury shall be inviolate." As the trial by jury is always one of the most powerful weapons in the defence of liberty, does not the constitution guarantee to all men the right to use it to defend their liberty? The constitution, in this article, it provides that electors shall be "white male" inhabitants, but in the 8th article, in speaking of unalienable rights, it declares that all men possess them, and the same article provides that the right of trial by jury shall be inviolate. What is the meaning of the constitution? Your committee believe, that although to refuse an alleged fugitive the right of a jury trial, might perhaps not violate the letter of the constitution, yet its spirit requires that the right be guaranteed them.

The question should be stripped of every thing of an extraneous character. It is intimately connected with a subject upon which the people are extremely excitable. Yet it is believed they are not only able, but willing, to discriminate between prejudice and reason. The views and feelings naturally engendered by the one, should always yield to the sound deductions of the other. The misguided efforts of many of those who are laboring for that which we all, in the abstract, desire, have undoubtedly induced many to doubt the policy of the course the committee recommend. The evils resulting from those misguided efforts, we are not able to palliate. But however great they may be, they should not swerve us from the course of right. The proposition is before us. The simple provision to allow the question of personal liberty to be tried by a jury. Shall that provision be placed upon our statute book? The parties interested can neither of them reasonably object to it. The effect can only be, that the case shall be fairly adjudged, in accordance with the spirit of our constitution and laws. Shall this be refused? Shall a magnanimous people--a people whose own freedom was bought with blood, refuse these facilities for the preservation for liberty? Tell it not! We appeal not to the sympathies, nor do we ask the aid of feeling, but with the demands of stern justice we would comply. There she stands, in her robes, and with her scales. Her mandates strike upon our ears. It is enough!

In accordance with the views here expressed, a majority of the committee report a bill to amend the act relating to fugitives from service and labor from other states, so as to allow the question of their liberty to be tried by a jury.

NUMBER 3

An act to repeal the act entitled "an act relating to fugitives from labor and service from other states passed February 26, 1839." Approved January 19, 1843, Laws of Ohio.

Section 1. Be it enacted by the General Assembly of the State of Ohio, That the act entitled "an act relating to fugitives from labor or service from other states," passed February twenty-six, one thousand eight hundred and thirty-nine, be and the same is hereby repealed, provided that nothing herein contained shall in any manner affect any prosecution, or proceeding in court, instituted and now pending under the provisions of said act, for which purposes the same shall continue and remain in force.

Section 2. That the second section of the act entitled "an act to prevent kidnapping" passed February fifteen, one thousand eight hundred and thirty-one, be and the same is hereby revived.

NUMBER 4

Resolution relative to slavery and the fugitive slave law. March 24, 1851, Laws of Ohio.

Resolved by the General Assembly of the State of Ohio, That while this General Assembly would urge the faithful observance of law upon all the people of this State, and of her sister States of the Union, as the most effectual mode of promoting their best interest, as well as a duty they owe alike to themselves and their common country, would most earnestly recommend to Congress, the necessity of so amending and modifying the provisions of the "Fugitive Slave Law," that while it secures a faithful compliance with all the obligations imposed by the constitution of the United States, it will, as becomes a free government, guard with zealous care the rights of the freeman. And if said law, in the opinion of Congress, cannot be so amended as to give to persons claimed as fugitives from labor, the benefit of every legal defense of their liberty, we then recommend the repeal of said law.

Resolved, That the law commonly called the "Fugitive Law," being a law that makes ex parte evidence conclusive of the master's right to recapture and return his slave; that denies a jury trial here or elsewhere; that provides for the appointment of swarms of petty officers to execute it; that gives double compensation to find every claim set up in favor of the master; and pays the expenses in any case from the public treasury; ought never receive the voluntary cooperation of our people, and ought therefore to be immediately repealed.

NUMBER 5

Joint resolution relative to the fugitive slave law. April 11, 1856, Laws of Ohio.

Whereas, in the judgment of this General Assembly the act of Congress usually called the Fugitive Slave Act, approved September 18, 1850, is inconsistent with and unwarranted by the constitution of the United States, and is repugnant to the plainest principles of justice and humanity; therefore

Resolved by the General Assembly of the State of Ohio, That our representatives in Congress be requested, and our Senators be instructed, to use their best exertions to procure the repeal of said act at the earliest practicable time.

NUMBER 6

An act to prohibit the confinement of fugitives from slavery in the jails of Ohio. Approved April 16, 1857, Laws of Ohio.

Section 1. Be it enacted by the General Assembly of the State of Ohio, That it shall be unlawful to confine in prison, or to detain in the penitentiary of this state, or in the jails of any county in this State, or in a calaboose, lock-up, guard house, or station, in this State, any person or persons charged with simply being a fugitive from slavery.

Section 2. Any officer or person who shall violate the provisions of the preceding section shall be deemed guilty of a misdemeanor, and upon conviction thereof, by indictment by the grand jury of the proper county, shall be imprisoned in the jail of the county not less than thirty nor more than ninety days, and be fined in any sum not exceeding five hundred dollars.

NUMBER 7

An act to repeal an act entitled "an act to prohibit the confinement of fugitives from slavery in the jails of Ohio, passed April 16, 1857." Approved February 23, 1858, Laws of Ohio.

Section 1. Be it enacted by the General Assembly of the State of Ohio, That the act entitled "an act to prohibit the confinement of fugitives from slavery in the jails of Ohio," passed April 16, 1857, be and the same is hereby repealed.

Section 2. This act shall take effect and be in force from and after its passage.

XI

Relief for the Poor

Ohio denied African Americans the benefit of its welfare programs. State officials responsible for the poor could order indigent blacks to leave. Those so warned could not obtain public assistance, and, if they did not leave the state voluntarily, could be escorted out by local authorities. The state policy on welfare also made it easier for whites to resort to extralegal means to drive out African Americans. Race riots broke out sporadically. The welfare policy of Ohio also had a salutary effect on blacks, who formed self-help organizations. Lydia P. Mott, a Quaker-abolitionist from Pennsylvania, encouraged local leaders to provide special programs for African Americans, particularly black youths. In Cincinnati, prominent, black and white citizens such as Salmon P. Chase and Peter Clark, organized the Cincinnati Colored Orphan Asylum in 1847. This association provided relief for indigent black Americans into the 1980s. Currently, it offers scholarships for needy students seeking a college eduction.

NUMBER 1

An act to amend the act entitled "an act for the relief of the poor." Approved February 12, 1829, Laws of Ohio.

Section 1. Be it enacted by the General Assembly of the State of Ohio, That any person or persons, other than those hereinafter provided for, residing three years in any township in the State without being warned by the Overseer of the Poor for said township, to depart the same, shall be considered as having gained a legal settlement in such township: every indented servant or apprentice, legally brought into this State, shall obtain a legal settlement in the township where such servant or apprentice first served his master or mistress three years; and every married woman, during coverture and after her husband's death, shall be considered legally settled in the place where he was last legally settled; but if he shall have, or shall have had no known legal settlement, then she shall be considered as settled in the place where she was last legally settled before marriage: but nothing in this act shall be so constructed as to enable any black or mulatto person to gain a legal settlement in this State: Provided, That the provisions of this section shall not be construed to exclude any person from voting at elections who would otherwise, by the constitution and laws of this State, be entitled to vote.

NUMBER 2

An act for the relief of the poor. Approved March 14, 1831, Laws of Ohio.

Section 1. Be it enacted by the General Assembly of the State of Ohio, That any person or persons, other than those hereinafter provided for, residing one year in any township in this state, without being warned by the overseer of the poor, for said township, to depart the same, or three years after being once so warned, without being again warned as aforesaid, shall be considered, as having gained a legal settlement in such township. Every indented servant or apprentice, legally brought into this state, shall obtain a legal settlement in the township where such servant or apprentice first served his master or mistress three years; and every married women, during coverture, and after her husband's death, shall be considered legally settled in the place where he was last legally settled; but if he shall have, or shall have had, no known legal settlement, then she shall be considered as settled in the place where she was last legally settled before marriage.

Section 2. That nothing in this act shall be so construed as to enable any black or mulatto person to gain a legal settlement in this state.

NUMBER 3

An act to amend the act entitled "an act to incorporate the trustees and subscribers of the new orphans' asylum of colored children in the city of Cincinnati." Approved February 3, 1847, Laws of Ohio.

Section 1. Be it enacted by the General Assembly of the State of Ohio, That all persons who shall subscribe and pay, each the sum of ten dollars at one time, or in such installments as the board of trustees may determine, shall be life members of the corporation created by the act hereby amended; and all persons who may subscribe and pay, annually, if males, the sum of one dollar each, and if female, the sum of fifty cents each, shall be members so long as they regularly pay such subscription; but no person not a life member shall be entitled to vote at any annual election, unless he or she shall have paid the amount of his or her subscription for the year next ensuing, on or before the fifth day of April next preceding such election.

Section 2. The board of trustees shall have custody and control of all children admitted into said asylum, until they shall attain, if females, the age of sixteen years, and if males, the age of eighteen years; and if any child, admitted into said asylum, shall signify to said board of trustees a desire to continue therein after attaining said age, the said board of trustees may consent thereto: and in such case, the child electing to remain shall continue under the control of said board of trustees, until the age of majority as established by law; but nothing herein contained shall prevent said board of trustees from discharging any beneficiary of said asylum for mal-conduct or immoral character, or shall prevent the discharge of any person from said asylum, upon complaint made as in the case of the apprentices.

Section 3. So much of the act hereby amended as is inconsistent with the provisions of this act is repealed.

NUMBER 4

An act for the relief of the poor. Approved March 14, 1853, Laws of Ohio.

Section 1. Be it enacted by the General Assembly of the State of Ohio, That any person or persons, other than those hereinafter, provided for, residing one year in any township in this State, without being warned by the trustees of said township to depart the same, or three years without being again warned as aforesaid, shall be considered as having gained a legal settlement in such township. Every indented servant, or apprentice, legally brought into this State, shall obtain a legal settlement in the township where such servant or apprentice, first served his or her master or mistress three years, and every married woman, during coverture and after her husband's death, shall be considered legally settled in the place where he was legally settled; but if he shall have had, no legal settlement, then she shall be considered as settled in the place where she was last legally settled before marriage.

Section 2. That nothing in this act shall be so construed as to enable any black or mulatto person to gain a settlement in this state: Provided that nothing in this section shall be so construed as to prevent the directors of any county or city infirmary, in their discretion, from admitting any black or mulatto person into said infirmary.

Section 12. That the act entitled "an act for the relief of the poor," passed March fourteenth, one thousand eight hundred and thirty-one, and the amendatory act thereto, passed March eight, one thousand eight hundred and fifty, be and they are hereby repealed; provided that all rights which have occurred, and all suits and proceedings now pending under the provisions of said acts repealed, shall be prosecuted and determined agreeably to and under the provisions of said acts, and all judgments which have been recovered, or which hereafter may be recovered, under the provisions of said acts, shall be carried into execution under the provisions of the acts hereby repealed.

XII

Miscegenation of the Races

For Americans, legal and social proscriptions against interracial sex is as old as America itself. Beginning in the colonial period, local laws forbade cohabitation between the races. Violators incurred punishments ranging from public beatings, penance, to banishment. Ohio also adopted this social value, although the legislature did not ratify a law against interracial sex until 1861. It also prohibited interracial marriages. There is no evidence that Ohio miscegenation law predated the 1861 statute. This was probably not an over sight. The black laws, like slavery, were so overwhelmingly oppressive that state lawmakers doubted that further legislation was necessary. When the racial code of Ohio relaxed in 1849, some whites feared the prospect of racial mixing. Consequently, the Ohio assembly adopted a law. However, state and federal law did not stop interracial mixing. Laws against miscegenation appeared frequently in the Old Northwest, suggesting that they did little to stop interracial sex. Ohio officials continued to frown on social relations between the races during the Reconstruction period, when federal and state governments adopted civil rights statutes.

NUMBER 1

An act to prevent the amalgamation of the white and colored races. Approved January 31, 1861, Laws of Ohio.

Section 1. Be it enacted by the General Assembly of the State of Ohio, That hereafter it shall be unlawful for any person of pure white blood to intermarry with or have illicit carnal intercourse with any negro, or person having a distinct and visible admixture of African blood; or for any negro or person having a distinct and visible admixture of African blood to intermarry with or have illicit carnal intercourse with any person of pure white blood; and any person offending against either of the provisions of this section shall be deemed guilty of misdemeanor, and on conviction thereof, shall be fined in any sum not exceeding one hundred dollars, or be imprisoned in the jail of the county for any period not exceeding three months, or both, at the discretion of the court.

Section 2. That any person who shall, knowingly, solemnize a marriage forbidden by this act, or any probate judge who shall, knowingly, issue a license for the solemnization of any marriage forbidden by this act, shall be deemed guilty of a misdemeanor, and on conviction thereof, shall be fined in any sum not exceeding one hundred dollars, or imprisoned in the county jail for a period not exceeding three months, or both, at the discretion of the court.

Section 3. This act shall take effect and be in force from and after its passage.

NUMBER 2

Marriages. Laws of Ohio, (1877).

Section 50. A person of pure white blood, who intermarries, or has illicit carnal intercourse, with any negro or person having a distinct and visible admixture of African blood, and any negro, or person having a distinct and visible admixture of African blood, who intermarries, or has illicit carnal intercourse, with any person of pure white blood, shall be fined not more than one hundred dollars, or imprisoned not more than three months, or both.

Section 51. A probate judge who knowingly issues a license for the solemnization of any marriage made penal by the last section, and every person who knowingly solemnizes any such marriage, shall be fined not more than one hundred dollars, or imprisoned not more than three months, or both.

XIII
Civil Rights

Congress took the leadership in adopting civil rights laws after the Civil War. The Ohio legislature followed along haltingly. It did not produce its first civil rights statute until 1884. Although more than two decades behind the federal government, the assembly adopted a series of laws prohibiting racial discrimination in jury selection, admission to public places, and it prescribed penalties for violators. The will of Congress to protect civil rights did not go beyond the 1880s. In a series of decisions, the Supreme Court struck down federal protection for civil rights. Ohio then slowed its reform movement. It had never actually decriminalized intimate contact between the races. Consequently, Ohio entered the twentieth century following a conservative racial policy.

NUMBER 1

An act to protect all citizens in their civil and legal rights. Approved February 7, 1884, Laws of Ohio.

Whereas, it is essential to just government that we recognize and protect all men as equal before the law, and that a democratic form of government should mete out equal and exact justice to all, of whatever nativity, race, color, persuasion, religious or political; and it being the appropriate object of legislation to enact great fundamental principles into law, therefore,

Section 1. Be it enacted by the General Assembly of the State of Ohio, That all persons within the jurisdiction of said state shall be entitled to the full and equal enjoyment of the accommodations, advantages, facilities and privilege of inns, public conveyances on land or water, theaters and other places of public amusement, subject only to the conditions and limitations established by law, and applicable alike to citizens of every race and color.

Section 2. That any person who shall violate any of the provisions of the foregoing section by denying to any citizen, except for reasons applicable alike to all citizens of every race and color, and regardless of color or race, the full enjoyment of any of the accommodations, advantages, facilities, or privileges in said section enumerated, or by aiding or inciting such denial, shall, for every such offense, forfeit and pay a sum not to exceed one hundred dollars to the person aggrieved thereby, to be recovered in any court of competent jurisdiction, in the county where said offense was committed; and shall also, for every such offense, be deemed guilty of a misdemeanor, and upon conviction thereof, shall be fined not to exceed one hundred dollars ($100), or shall be imprisoned not more than thirty days, or both; and provided, further, that a judgement in favor of the party aggrieved, or punishment upon an indictment, shall be a bar to either prosecution respectively.

Section 3. That no citizen of the state of Ohio, possessing all other qualifications which are or may be prescribed by law, shall be disqualified to serve as grand or petit juror in any court of said state, on account of race or color, and any officer or other person charged with any duty in the selection or summoning of jurors, who shall exclude or fail to summon any citizen for the cause aforesaid, shall on conviction thereof be deemed guilty of a misdemeanor, and be fined not more than one hundred dollars, or imprisoned not more than thirty days, or both.

Section 4. This act shall take effect and be in force from and after its passage.

NUMBER 2

An act to amend section 1 of an act entitled an "act to protect all citizens in their civil and legal rights, passed February 7, 1884." Approved March 27, 1884, Laws of Ohio.

Section 1. Be it enacted by the General Assembly of the State of Ohio, That section one of said act to protect all citizens in their civil and legal rights, be amended as follows:

Section 1. That all persons within the jurisdiction of said state shall be entitled to the full and equal enjoyment of accommodations, advantages, facilities and privileges of inns, restaurants, eating-houses, barber-shops, public conveyances on land or water, theaters and all other places of public accommodation and amusement, subject only to the conditions and limitations established by law, and applicable alike to all citizens.

Section 2. That section 1 of the above entitled act be and the same is hereby repealed.

Section 3. That this act shall take effect and be in force from and after its passage..

NUMBER 3

An act to prevent discrimination by life insurance companies against persons of color. Approved March 28, 1889, Laws of Ohio.

Section 1. Be it enacted by the General Assembly of the State of Ohio, That no life insurance company now organized or doing business, or that may hereafter be organized and do business within this state, shall make any distinction or discrimination between white persons and colored, wholly or partially of African descent, as to the premiums or rates charged for policies upon the lives of such persons; nor shall any such company demand or require greater premiums from such colored persons than are at that time required by such company from white persons of the same age, sex, general condition of health and hope of longevity; nor shall any such company make or require any rebate, diminution or discount upon the sum to be paid on such policy in case of the death of such colored person insured, nor insert in the policy any condition, nor make any stipulation whereby such person insured shall bind himself or his heirs, executors, administrators and assigns to accept any sum less than the full value or amount of such policy in case of a claim accruing thereon by reason of the death of such person insured, other than such as are imposed upon white persons in similar cases; and any such stipulation or condition so made or inserted shall be void.

Section 2. Any such company which shall refuse the application of any such colored person for insurance upon such person's life, shall furnish such person with the certificate of some regular examining physician of such company who has made examination of such person, stating that such person's application has been refused, not because such person is a person of color, but solely upon such grounds of the general health and hope of longevity of such person as would be applicable to white persons of the same age and sex.

Section 3. Any corporation, or the officer or agent of any corporation, violating any of the provisions of this act, either by demanding or receiving from such colored person such different or greater premium, or by allowing any discount or rebate upon the premium, or by allowing any discount or rebate upon the premiums paid or to be paid by white persons of the same age, sex, general condition of health and hope of longevity, or by making or requiring any rebate, diminution or discount upon the sum to be paid upon a policy in case of the death of such colored person insured, or by failing to furnish the certificate required by section second, shall for each offense be fined not less than one hundred nor more than two hundred dollars. But nothing in this act shall be so construed as to require any agent or company to take or receive the application for insurance of any person.

Section 4. This act shall take effect upon its passage.

NUMBER 4

An act to amend an act entitled "An act relating to life insurance companies doing business in the state of Ohio, passed April 10, 1889." Approved April 27, 1893, Laws of Ohio.

Section 1. Be it enacted by the General Assembly of the State of Ohio that an act entitled "An act relating to life insurance companies doing business in Ohio," be so amended as to read as follows:

Section 1. That no life insurance company doing business in Ohio, shall make or permit any distinction or discrimination in favor of individuals between insurants of the same class and equal expectation of life in the amount or payment of premiums, or rates charged for policies of life or endowment insurance, or in the dividends or other benefits payable thereon, or in any other of the terms and conditions of the contract it makes; nor shall any such company, or any agent thereof, make any contract of insurance, or agreement as to such contract, other than is plainly expressed in the policy issued thereon; nor shall any such company or agent pay or allow, or offer to pay or allow, as inducement to insurance, any rebate of premium payable on the policy, or any special favor or advantage in the dividends or other benefits to accrue thereon, or any valuable consideration or inducement whatever not specified in the policy contract of insurance.

Section 2. Every corporation which shall violate any of the provisions of this act shall be fined in any sum not less than one hundred dollars nor exceeding five hundred dollars, to be recovered by action in the name of the state, and the amount so recovered shall be paid into the county treasury for the benefit of the common school fund.

Section 3. Every officer or agent of any such corporation who shall violate any of the provisions of this act, shall be deemed guilty of a misdemeanor, and, upon conviction thereof, shall be fined in any sum not less than one hundred dollars nor exceeding five hundred dollars, or imprisoned in the jail of the county not exceeding thirty days, or both, at the discretion of the court, and shall pay the costs of prosecution.

Section 4. It shall be the duty of the superintendent of insurance, upon being satisfied that any such corporation, or any agent thereof, has violated any of the provisions of this act, to revoke the license of the company, or agent, so offending, and no license shall be granted to such company, or agent, for one year after such revocation.

Section 5. That said original act is hereby repealed; and this act shall take effect on its passage.

NUMBER 5

An act to amend sections 2 and 3 of an act entitled "An act to protect all citizens in their civil and legal rights, passed February 7, 1884 and amended March 27, 1884." Approved February 7, 1894, Laws of Ohio.

Section 1. Be it enacted by the General Assembly of the State of Ohio that sections 2 and 3 of an act entitled "An act to protect all citizens in their civil and legal rights," passed February 7, 1884, and amended March 27, 1884, be amended so as to read as follows:

Section 2. That any person who shall violate any of the provisions of the foregoing section by denying to any citizen, except for reasons applicable alike to all citizens of every race and color, and regardless of color or race, the full enjoyment of any of the accommodations, advantages, facilities or privileges in said section enumerated, or by aiding or inciting such denial shall, for every such offense, forfeit and pay a sum not less than fifty ($50) dollars nor more that five hundred ($500) dollars to the person aggrieved thereby, to be recovered in any court of competent jurisdiction in the county where said offense was committed; and shall also, for every such offense, be deemed guilty of a misdemeanor, and upon conviction thereof shall be fined not less than fifty ($50) dollars nor more than five hundred ($500) dollars, or shall be imprisoned not less than thirty (30) days nor more than ninety (90) days, or both; and provided further, that a judgment in favor of the party aggrieved, or punishment upon an indictment, shall be a bar to either prosecution respectively.

Section 3. That no citizen of the state of Ohio, possessing all other qualifications which are or may be prescribed by law, shall be disqualified to serve as grand or petit juror in any court of said state on account of race or color, and any officer or other person charged with any duty in the selection or summoning of jurors, who shall exclude or fail to summon any citizen for the cause aforesaid, shall on conviction thereof be deemed guilty of a misdemeanor and be fined not less than fifty ($50) dollars nor more than five hundred ($500) dollars, or imprisoned not less than thirty (30) days nor more than [ninety] (90) days, or both.

Section 4. That sections 2 and 3 of an act entitled "an act to protect all citizens in their civil and legal rights," passed February 7, 1884, and amended March 27, 1884, be and the same are hereby repealed.

Section 5. That this act shall take effect and be in force from and after its passage.

Summary of Cases

Ohio, the first state formed from the Old Northwest, also became the first state in the Territory to test the slavery prohibition in the Ordinance. Other territories had petitioned Congress to rescind or modify Article 6 during the 1790s, but none had yet voted on the status of African-American residents at the dawn of statehood. A resolution to enslave African-Americans came up at the Ohio Constitutional Convention (1802), but the proposal never stood a chance. Opponents of slavery had a majority. The Constitutional Convention of Ohio endorsed the slavery prohibition in the Ordinance. Yet, their decision did not immediately eliminate slavery from Ohio soil.

For the first four decades as a State, Ohio allowed slave holders to control enslaved blacks in Ohio. Moreover, slave holders sent enslaved blacks into the state as hired-out workers. Nothing in the federal or state constitutions warranted these courtesies. Rather, state leaders depended on southern trade, and they believed that any threat to slavery might jeopardize their revenue. Every year when slave holders came, they brought along their "chattels." From time to time, therefore, enslaved blacks stayed on Ohio soil. Whether their presence violated the Ordinance or the state constitution would be decided by the courts.

Initially, whites paid little attention to the presence of slaves in their state. African-Americans certainly did, but they were powerless to change state policy. Whenever possible, they lured away enslaved blacks, provided them food, clothing, and shelter before sending them along on the Underground Railroad. White abolitionists were capable of changing state policy. For most of the 1830s, abolitionist James G. Birney argued that certain conditions automatically freed slaves brought into Ohio. Birney had gotten this idea from England, where a court had freed a man because he had been brought onto the free soil of the nation. Birney had witnessed the successful use of this doctrine in Massachusetts. And he preached the doctrine of automatic emancipation in Ohio.

As the following annotated cases will show, Birney did not personally argue the doctrines he taught in antislavery law. He believed that his political activities would further prejudice any case wherein he might serve. He introduced Salmon P. Chase to this branch of constitutional law, and Chase argued his first case in 1837 in Matilda v. Lawrence. Matilda had entered Ohio in 1836. She found temporary refuge among black residents, who advised her to seek advice from Birney. When she discovered Mrs. Birney needed a maid and nurse, Matilda concealed her identity as a runaway slave until she won the Birney's trust. When she disclosed her status, they advised her to stay close to their home.

After one year of freedom, a slave catcher apprehended Matilda as a runaway slave. This episode thrust southwest Ohio into its first major case involving runaway slaves. Salmon Chase argued the case, but, in addition to Chase's inexperience in antislavery law, the Common Pleas Court and the County Justice of the Peace were not ready to endorse the doctrine of automatic emancipation. The Supreme Court on circuit did so in 1841 in the case of State v. Farr. The justices agreed that any person who entered Ohio with the consent of a slave holder, he or she was automatically free. The policy of accommodation collapsed in Ohio. As the following documents will show, the fugitive slave issue was the most controversial dispute litigated in Ohio. Once the Supreme Court approved automatic emancipation by the 1850's, it declared that Ohio law liberated every slave who entered Ohio. Only slave holders who showed indisputable proof that his bondsman or bondwoman was covered by federal law were returnable.

Antislavery lawyers also challenged federal fugitive slave legislation. In Birney v. Ohio (1837), In re Mary Townes (1841), and Jones v. Van Zandt (1843), they launched an attack on the validity of the Federal Fugitive Slave Act. They declared that only states had authority to legislate the return of runaway slaves. The Constitution, they advised, made Congress impotent over slavery. It could not create or destroy the "peculiar institution." Antislavery lawyers believed that a federal law which provided for the survival of slavery was the same as creating slavery. Such a law, they concluded, was unconstitutional. Ohio courts, and the courts in other northern states, disagreed. Consequently, runaway slaves coming from a slave jurisdiction were always returnable by the courts.

Ohio judges, more often than not, reviewed the black laws favorably. For example, the courts approved the testimony law (contemporaries called it the Negro Evidence Law). In a series of cases such as Gray v. Ohio (1831) and Jordan v. Smith (1846), the Supreme court ruled that a black could not testify against a white. The court did recognize exceptions to this rule of evidence. In the case of mulattoes, the court believed that a person who looked white should receive all the privileges of being white. But the Court denied visibly black residents this consideration.

The Supreme Court maintained this same point of view in elections and public education. The Court supported visibly white electors and visibly white children who were turned away by school masters. When a registrar turned away an elector because the registrar considered the man an Indian, the elector sued. In Jeffries v. Ankeny (1842), the Supreme Court ruled in the plaintiff's favor, holding that it considered a "near white" person white. The Court reached a similar opinion in Williams v. School District of Green County (1836). Williams, a mulatto, married a white woman. Their children were visibly white to all except to those who knew of Williams' part-African ancestry. A school master who knew Williams, denied admission to his children. The court did not approve, and ordered their admission. "Near white" children, the Court concluded, should not be subject to the disability of being black.

Although the court might have appeared liberal on some issues, it did not favor desegregation. In Van Camp v. Logan (1859) and Garnes v. MaCann (1871), the Court rejected the idea of integrated schools. The justices explained that the history of Ohio favored separation of the races.

The cases which follow describe the litigation of race and slavery in Ohio. They show that fugitive slave disputes were debated more extensively than any other issue. Although confronted by a conservative court, Ohio became a liberated zone. Only enslaved blacks who escaped from a slave state were returnable under federal law. This doctrine was a victory for the antislavery movement.

Select Annotated Cases

<u>Ohio v. Carneal</u> (1817) in Ervin H. Pollack, ed., <u>Ohio Unreported Judicial Decisions Prior to 1823</u> (n. d.).
Thomas Carneal held a black in bondage in Ohio in violation of state law. Although the court did not approve of slavery, it initially believed that comity protected a master's claim. The court, however, freed the slave on a technicality found in Carneal's title.

<u>In re Jacob Kounts</u> (1817) in Pollack, <u>Ohio Unreported Decisions</u>
A Virginia master held blacks in bondage in violation of Ohio law. An Ohio court rejected his claim that they were merely in transit to a slave jurisdiction. Although freed by Ohio law, the slave owner managed to return the slaves to Virginia where a court confirmed their status as slaves.

<u>Gray v. Ohio</u>, 4 Ohio 353 (1831)
A jury convicted Polly Gray of murder on the testimony of a mulatto witness. Attorneys for Gray complained that Ohio law barred the testimony of a black against a white. On appeal, the state supreme court reversed the conviction, concluding that "the witness was improperly admitted. The statute compels courts of justice to reject black and mulatto witnesses, where a white person is a party."

<u>Tom v. Daily</u>, 4 Ohio 368 (1831)
Thomas Daily purchased his sister Kate from a Kentucky slave holder, claiming that he made the purchase only to free her from slavery. Later, when Kate gave birth to a son, her brother Thomas betrayed her, and sold his nephew to Joseph Desha. Kate shielded the boy by sending him to Ohio for

safety. Daily pursued him there, and the dispute went before the state supreme court, the court declared the boy free because of his mother's status.

Lawson v. Perry, 1 Wright 242 (1833)
Lawson's employer defrauded him of wages earned as a steward on a steamboat that operated on the Ohio River. Lawson sued, and the matter went before the state supreme court. The court ruled that Lawson was entitled to "common wages," his color notwithstanding. Justice Wright advised the jury: "You have nothing to do with the color of the plaintiff." The jury awarded Lawson full pay.

Woods v. Green, 1 Wright 503 (1834)
This case involved a dispute between a black person and a white person, both of them claiming ownership of the horse. The black woman identified the animal before witnesses who testified that the animal seemed to recognize her. The supreme court accepted this testimony and advised the jury to overlook color in its deliberations. The jury ruled in favor of the black woman.

Williams v. School District, 1 Wright 578 (1836)
A school district in Greene County, Ohio, denied admission to school to the mulatto children of a Mr. Williams. Williams was "one-quarter negro, and his wife [was] a white woman." A lower court rejected his plea on the grounds that Ohio law prohibited admission of blacks to the public schools. On appeal, the supreme court ruled that the children were "white" within the meaning of the law.

Matilda Lawrence v. Larkin Lawrence, reported in Daily Cincinnati Republican, March 16, 1837
A Hamilton County court remanded Matilda, a slave who had escaped from her master while in transit through Ohio. The Common Pleas Court in Hamilton County and a justice of the peace both refused the argument that Ohio law freed slaves by virtue of their entering the state with the permission of a slave owner.

State of Ohio v. James Birney, reported in Cincinnati Daily Gazette, April 5, 1837
Opponents of abolition brought charges against James G. Birney in Hamilton County for allegedly harboring and concealing a runaway slave. The Common Pleas Court convicted him, mainly because of his antislavery politics. Subsequently, the state supreme court overturned the conviction.

Birney v. Ohio, 8 Ohio (1837)
The Hamilton County Common Pleas Court convicted James Birney for harboring a runaway slave. The law had been a dead letter and most

contemporaries believed Birney's politics influenced the court's judgment. On appeal the supreme court overturned his conviction, holding that there was no proof that Birney knew that the woman he aided was a runaway slave.

In re Mary Towns, reported in Cincinnati Gazette, May 12, 1841
Towns allegedly escaped from a Kentucky plantation in 1831 and was captured in Ohio in 1841. Abolitionists contested her removal from Ohio. The court released Towns on a technicality--an affidavit did not state that she had escaped from a slave jurisdiction.

State v. Farr, reported in Cincinnati Gazette, May 21 and June 1, 1841
Reversed the convictions of abolitionists who had rescued blacks belonging to slave holders in transit through Ohio. The supreme court declared slaves to be automatically free the moment they entered Ohio with the knowledge and consent of a slave owner.

Jeffries v. Ankeny, 11 Ohio 372 (1842)
Ohio law denied suffrage to people of color, and a registrar in Xenia refused to allow the plaintiff to vote because of his part-Indian ancestry. The court rejected this policy, holding that proper construction of Ohio law recognized that persons who were near white were eligible to the benefits of a white person.

Thacker v. Hawk, 11 Ohio 376 (1842)
This case involved the question of whether a person of mixed ancestry could vote in Ohio. Election officers refused to let the plaintiff vote, just as they had done in the Jeffries case. The judge in a lower court supported their action, instructing the jury that if the plaintiff had "any negro blood" he was ineligible to vote. The state supreme court rejected this construction of Ohio law, "explaining that it was wrong, and the judgement must be reversed."

Chalmers v. Stewart, 11 Ohio 386 (1842)
A public school teacher admitted black children to a common school where white children attended. The parents of one of the children complained, and removed their children from the school. Following the opinion in the Williams case, a lower court ruled in favor of the school district. On appeal, the supreme court reversed the judgment, explaining that Ohio law barred blacks from attending schools with whites. Consequently, teachers who admitted a black child violated their contract.

Jones v. Van Zandt, 13 Federal Cases (1843); Jones v. Van Zandt, 5 Howard 215 (1847)
A Kentucky slave holder sued John Van Zandt, a resident of Ohio, who had allegedly harbored and concealed runaway slaves. The court upheld the

fugitive slave law and a jury awarded the plaintiff damages. Van Zandt appealed the case to the U.S. Supreme Court, but the Court affirmed the validity of the statute and upheld Van Zandt's conviction.

Lane v. Baker, 12 Ohio 237 (1843)
Thomas Lane sued when a school district refused to admit his children on account of their mixed ancestry. The court found that the children had "more than one half white blood," which qualified them as white under the law. The court ordered their admission under the visible admixture rule.

Greathouse v. Dunlap, 10 Federal Cases 1062 (3 McLean 303) (1843)
Slaves belonging to Greathouse, a Kentucky slave owner, escaped to Ohio, where Mahan Dunlap allegedly harbored and concealed them. On a requisition from Kentucky officials, Ohio officials surrendered Mahan to be tried in Kentucky as a fugitive from justice. A Kentucky court convicted him. After a few months in jail, Mahan arranged to pay a cash settlement. When he reneged on the agreement, an Ohio court found the contract valid and ordered him to pay.

State v. Hoppes, 2 Western Law Journal 279 and 333 (1845)
This case involved the slave-transit question. The justice in the case agreed that Ohio law automatically emancipated a slave when he entered Ohio with the knowledge and consent of a master. Nonetheless, the court remanded the litigant in this case because he escaped from a boat on the Ohio River, a neutral jurisdiction.

Driskell v. Parish, 7 Federal Cases 1100 (3 McLean 631) (1845); 1093 (10 Law Reporter 395) (1847); 1095 (5 McLean 64) (1849)
Peter Driskell, a Kentucky slave holder, brought action against the defendant for allegedly harboring runaway slaves. Jane Harrison and her children had escaped from Kentucky and found employment with Parish in Ohio. The court ruled that Parish, after learning that the persons he employed were runaway slaves, did not surrender them to the claimant. Such an action constituted a violation of the fugitive slave law.

Jordan v. Smith, 14 Ohio 199 (1846)
This case involved the Negro Testimony Law, which forbade a black from testifying against a white. The court refused the testimony of a black against a white. It admitted that under Ohio law "the white man may now plunder the negro . . . [H]e may abuse his person; he may take his life . . . and he must go acquitted, unless . . . there . . . be some white man present."

Woodson v. State, 17 Ohio 161 (1848)
This case involved the estate of a mulatto named John Woodward. State officers charged that the administrator of the estate had not properly executed the will or discharged debts. A lower court made several errors in trying the case, including admitting blacks as witnesses, to reach a decision for the state. The state supreme court reversed the decision.

Stuart v. Southard, 17 Ohio 402 (1848)
Southard complained that a school district deprived him of educating his children when it "wrongfully" admitted black children to the school. A lower court ruled in his favor and awarded him damages. The supreme court reversed the opinion, holding that compensation for the error went beyond the scope of the law.

Campbell v. Kirkpatrick, 4 Federal Cases 1174 (5 McLean 175) (1850)
This case involved the federal Fugitive Slave Act of 1850, which provided for the capture and return of runaway slaves. A resident of Ohio had allegedly aided runaway slaves, and the plaintiff sued "to recover a penalty." The court discovered a conflict in jurisdiction, however, holding that the dispute rightfully belonged in a district court, and could not be turned over to a circuit court for trial.

State v. Cincinnati, 19 Ohio 178 (1850)
The city of Cincinnati collected taxes from black property holders to finance a common school created to educate their children. Once the city collected the money, however, it refused to turn it over to the school board. The directors of the school sued. The court ruled in their favor and issued a writ of mandamus against the city.

Smith v. Swornmstedt, 22 Federal Cases 663 (5 McLean) (1852)
The slavery controversy permeated religious organizations. The debate split the Methodist Episcopal Church into liberal and conservative factions. The liberal faction considered slavery a moral evil and prohibited church members from holding people as slaves. In this case a minister inherited slaves through marriage, and the church suspended him. The matter ended up in court, and the court upheld the action of the church.

Miller v. McQuerry, 17 Federal Cases 335 (5 McLean 469) (1853)
George Washington McQuerry, an enslaved African American, escaped from a Kentucky farm in 1849, and took up refuge in Ohio. His owner hunted him, and finally captured him in 1853. Abolitionist efforts to abort his removal failed, and the court ordered McQuerry's return to slavery under the federal fugitive slave law.

Weimer v. Sloane, 29 Federal Cases 599 (6 McLean 259) (1854); Gibbons v. Sloane, 10 Federal Cases 294 (6 McLean 273) (1854)
The plaintiff charged that Sloane harbored and concealed runaway slaves, in violation of federal law. Upon evidence that the persons had escaped from Kentucky, the court ordered their return. Had the enslaved blacks entered Ohio with the consent of their owner, the court would have released them from bondage.

Ex parte Robinson [The Rosetta Case], 20 Federal Cases 969 (6 McLean 355) (1855); 965 (1 Bond 39) (1856)
On a writ of habeas corpus, abolitionists brought action against a slave holder traveling through Ohio with Rosetta Armstead. A judge emancipated Rosetta, a minor, and assigned her a guardian. A U.S. commissioner intervened and ordered a federal marshal to recapture Rosetta under the federal fugitive slave law. Although ultimately federal courts successfully asserted their supremacy, Rosetta gained her freedom.

Anderson v. Poindexter, 6 Ohio 622 (1856)
Anderson, a slave holder who had promised to free Poindexter, accepted a promissory note from Poindexter for $400 for his freedom. Plaintiff then allowed Poindexter to enter Ohio so that he could earn money. When the note was due, Poindexter refused to pay, and the dispute ended up in court. The defense argued that by allowing Poindexter to enter Ohio he became a free man under state law. The court concurred.

Ex parte Sifford, 22 Federal Cases 105 (5 American Law Register 659) (1857)
The federal fugitive slave law authorized federal marshals to hunt down runaway slaves. Local residents considered their authority an infringement of state law. Clark County abolitionists attempted to punish federal marshals who had arrested Hiram Gutridge for allegedly harboring runaway slaves. Federal and state courts, however, upheld the fugitive slave law. Hence, the court discharged the federal officers.

Ex parte Early, 3 Weekly Law Gazette 234 (1858)
Ohio courts underwent a transformation during the 1840s and no longer supported reclamation, although judges there still recognized the validity of the federal fugitive slave law. In the Early case, the Common Pleas Court in Hamilton County refused to interfere with a federal officer remanding a black to slavery.

Ex parte Bushnell, Ex parte Langston, 9 Ohio 77 (1859)
Federal officers arrested Simeon Bushnell and Charles Langston for allegedly violating the fugitive slave law. Defense argued that the law itself was unconstitutional. The court held that "the power of Congress to legislate on

this subject is . . . fully settled by the . . . Supreme Court of the United States."

Van Camp v. Logan, 9 Ohio 406 (1859)
This case was an effort to win admission of mulatto children to an Ohio public school. In previous cases, the court had ordered the admission of children whose complexion was near white. A mulatto named Van Camp sued a school district for denying admission to his "two white children." They were all nearly "one-half African blood." The court revised its early doctrine of visible admixture to affirm segregation. The court concluded that since the Williams case the legislature had provided for the education of black and mulatto children in separate schools.

Anderson v. Milliken, 9 Ohio 568 (1859)
The plaintiff, whose father was white, sued when an election official denied him suffrage. The plaintiff was visibly white. A lower court, however, considered him black under Ohio law and affirmed the action of the registrar. On appeal, the state supreme court reversed this opinion, holding that "a person having less than half black blood shall have the rights of a white man."

Monroe v. Collins, 17 Ohio 665 (1867)
Collins, a person of mixed ancestry, attempted to vote under the visible admixture law. Election officers agreed that he had white features, but they considered his African color dominant. By this time the court had become weary with the question of the amount of color a person needed in order to deprive him of the privileges of a white person. Hence, it nullified the visible admixture law.

Coolidge v. Guthrie, 6 Federal Case 461 (8 American Law Register, N.S. 22) (1868)
The army did not ignore enslaved African Americans during the Civil War. General Curtis sympathized with them and sold contraband merchandise acquired from the Confederacy to feed hungry blacks. As he put it, his object was to raise funds to "support the starving negro population in the neighborhood of his camp" at Helena, Arkansas.

Garnes v. McCann, 21 Ohio 198 (1871)
Civil rights litigation commenced soon after the Civil War. The Garnes case was an effort to test segregation in light of the Civil War amendments. The plaintiff asked the court for mandamus against a school district that denied admission to his children. He alleged that there were no nearby "colored schools." The court upheld segregation, concluding that the practice "is too firmly established to be now judicially disturbed."

Suggested Readings

Blue, Frederick. Salmon Portland Chase: A Life in Politics, 1987.

Cayton, Andrew R. L. The Frontier Republics: Ideology and Politics in the Ohio Country, 1780 - 1825, 1986.

Chaddock, Robert. Ohio Before 1850, 1908.

Cheek, William and Amiee L. John Mercer Langston and the Fight for Black Freedom, 1989.

Erickson, Leonard. "Politics and Repeal of Ohio's Black Laws," 92 Ohio History (1972).

Gerber, David A. Black Ohio and the Color Line, 1860-1925, 1976.

Granger, Moses M. The Judiciary of Ohio, 1803-1903, 1903.

Hickok, Charles T. The Negro in Ohio, 1802-1870. Ph.D. diss., Western Reserve University, 1986.

Malvin, John. North into Freedom: The Autobiography of John Malvin, 1795-1880, 1966.

Marshall, Carrington T. A History of the Courts and Lawyers of Ohio, 1934.

Middleton, Stephen. Ohio and the Antislavery Activities of Attorney Salmon Portland Chase, 1990.

Quillin, Frank U. The Color Line in Ohio: A History of Race and Prejudice in a Typical Northern State, 1913.

Thurstun, Helen M. "The 1802 Constitutional Convention and the Status of the Negro," 81 Ohio History (1972).

Part Two

INDIANA,
December 11, 1816

The celebrated Article 6 in the Ordinance of 1787 did not dampen the enthusiasm of whites in Indiana for slavery. They pursued slavery vigorously, thinking that slave labor was vital to the economic development of their state. The rationale of proslavery leaders in Indiana was the antithesis of antislavery leaders in Ohio. Leaders in both states were motivated by race prejudice, and the consideration of what was best for whites. Ohio whites considered slave labor an institution which would absorb jobs that would normally go to white males. Indiana whites considered the agricultural potential of their region and the enormous labor required to exploit the land. Racism was prevalent in the minds of whites in both communities. Yet there was a significant distinction between Ohio and Indiana. Whites in Ohio were willing to recognize African Americans as freemen; whites in Indiana wanted to make them slaves.

As the petitions and statutes in Part Two will show, Indiana whites pressured Congress for decades to either rescind or modify Article 6. Their arguments were not persuasive, and some were quite ludicrous. For example, proslavery whites pretended that any work performed by slaves in Indiana would be much easier on blacks than the burdens enslaved blacks shouldered in Southern states. White petitioners also complained that Indiana residents had been treated unfairly because the Ordinance of 1787 denied them the opportunity to practice slavery while the "peculiar institution" was legal elsewhere. White Hoosiers also insisted that they were benevolent masters who were willing to place restrictions on slavery, including age limits and specified terms of service. Indiana, therefore, provided a major test on the effectiveness of America's first antislavery document.

Article 6 in the Ordinance was not a perfect clause. It had at least one significant weakness: It lacked coercive powers. The framers did not empower the territorial legislature as to enforce the antislavery provision with appropriate legislation. Because Congress rejected the pleas of proslavery leaders in Indiana to modify Article 6, Hoosiers designed an elaborate scheme to obviate it. There can be no question that the indentured servitude system in Indiana amounted to *de facto* slavery.

Initially, the indentured servitude law authorized masters to hold a person in a state of bondage for life. Later modifications required masters to free servants at age twenty-eight if female and thirty-five if male. There were a few other restrictions. For example, territorial and state law required that a bond servant be at least fifteen years old when brought into Indiana. These policies enabled masters to reduce African-American servants to a state of slavery. Nonetheless, Article 6 was a powerful barrier to *de jure* slavery in Indiana.

Indiana law discouraged the immigration of free African Americans, primarily by requiring a black immigrant to produce a certificate of freedom in order to obtain legal residence or employment. Such policies were designed to keep blacks out of Indiana. The black laws of Indiana also oppressed free African Americans already in the state. The law denied blacks citizenship rights and made them vulnerable politically and socially. Blacks could not testify against whites in a court of law, nor serve as jurors, militiamen, voters, officers of the state, or marry outside their race. Indiana also closed its schools and welfare programs to blacks.

Indiana was unusually hostile to people of color, and Negrophobia pervaded every quarter of the state. Although the black laws had effectively subjugated blacks in Indiana, whites there held irrational fears regarding social relations between the races. They assumed that if they permitted African Americans to enter the state freely, miscegenation would automatically occur. This was not an unusual fear for white males in the Old Northwest. Most were haunted by the notion that their women might be drawn away by vigorous black males. A second assumption of whites was that crime and other social ills would increase if Indiana allowed blacks to freely settle there. For example, slave holders sometimes brought aged and destitute slaves to the Old Northwest and then emancipated them. Indiana did not want to assume responsibility for this population. Whites mainly wanted to preserve the State as a province for whites.

The antislavery movement eventually reached Indiana, but it evolved slowly. At first, only a few whites who opposed slavery and the black laws supported the colonization movement--the removal of blacks to Africa. From this perspective, the colonization movement in the Hoosier State was similar to the state's black immigration policy. Sincere proponents of colonization, for example, antislavery Christians supported the movement, thinking that blacks might prefer a life in Africa, to racial discrimination in America. But most colonizationists were racists who considered people of color inferior to whites. They wanted to avoid social contact with blacks. The colonization movement in Indiana, like elsewhere, never became a powerful force.

The Indiana black laws were not successful. Some runaway slaves followed the Underground Railroad through Indiana to other destinations, while others stayed and joined African-American communities. By the 1820s, a few whites had begun to speak out against slavery; some even condemned the black laws. At first, Quakers led the abolition and civil rights movement in Indiana. They participated in the Underground Railroad, directing runaway slaves to freedom. Some participated in rescues and tore enslaved blacks away from slave holders. Others formed committees to provide employment opportunities for blacks. Still others joined political abolitionists to publish antislavery newspapers and form the Indiana Antislavery Society in 1838. They were a dedicated and vociferous minority.

The Civil War accelerated the civil rights reform movement in Indiana, but it remained a racially conservative state. The state legislature struck down the black laws, although the term "white" remained in the constitution until 1926. The general assembly provided for a segregated educational system. Nonetheless, in communities where too few blacks lived to create a segregated school, black children attended schools for whites. But the courts endorsed segregation and considered federal laws, including the Fourteenth Amendment of the U.S. Constitution, of no force in Indiana. The courts also considered interracial mixing, especially intermarriage, contrary to the laws of nature.

I

Declaration of Rights

The Indiana Constitution of 1816 contained a bill of rights, which provided civil rights protection for its citizens. The Constitution guaranteed rights including trial by jury, protection from illegal search and seizure, freedom of speech, and free elections. Indiana also prohibited slavery, albeit reluctantly. Yet the state constitution made African Americans exceptions. The bill of rights protected only white Americans. Like Ohio, and the rest of the states in the Old Northwest, Indiana began as a white state. Constitutional and statutory law subjugated African Americans.

NUMBER 1

Constitution of Indiana, Articles 1, 1816.

Section 1. That the general, great, and essential principles of liberty and free government may be recognized, and unalterably established: We declare, That all men are born equally free and independent, and have certain natural, inherent, and unalienable rights; among which are, the enjoying and defending life and liberty, and of acquiring, possessing, and protecting property, and pursuing and obtaining happiness and safety.

Section 2. That all power is inherent in the people; and all free governments are founded on their authority, and instituted for their peace, safety and happiness. For the advancement of these ends, they have, at all times, an unalienable and indefeasible right to alter or reform their government in such manner as they may think proper.

Section 3. That all men have a natural and indefeasible right to worship Almighty God according to the dictates of their own consciences: That no man shall be compelled to attend, erect, or support any place of worship, or to maintain any ministry against his consent: That no human authority can, in any case whatever, control or interfere with the rights of conscience: And that no preference shall ever be given by law to any religious societies, or order of worship; and no religious test shall be required as a qualification to any office of trust or profit.

Section 4. That elections shall be free and equal.

Section 5. That in all civil cases, where the value in controversy shall exceed the sum of twenty dollars, and in all criminal cases, except in petit misdemeanors, which shall be punished by fine only, not exceeding three dollars, in such manner as the legislature may prescribe by law, the right of trial by jury shall remain inviolate.

Section 6. That no power of suspending the operation of the laws shall be exercised, except by the legislature, or its authority.

Section 7. That no man's particular services shall be demanded, or property taken or applied to public use, without the consent of his representatives, or without a just compensation being made therefor.

Section 8. The rights of the people to be secure in their persons, houses, papers, and effects, against unreasonable searches and seizures, shall not be violated; and no warrant shall issue but upon probable cause, supported by oath or affirmation, and particularly describing the place to be searched, and the persons or things to be seized.

Section 9. That the printing presses shall be free to every person who undertakes to examine the proceedings of the legislature, or any branch of government; and no law shall ever be made to restrain the right thereof. The free communication of thoughts and opinions is one of the invaluable rights of man; and every citizen may freely speak, write, and print, on any subject, being responsible for the abuse of that liberty.

Section 10. In prosecutions for the publication of papers investigating the official conduct of officers or men in a public capacity, or where the matter published is proper for the public information, the truth thereof may be given in evidence; and in all indictments for libels, the jury shall have a right to determine the law and the facts, under the direction of the court, as in other cases.

Section 11. That all courts shall be open, and every person, for an injury done him, in his lands, goods, person, or reputation, shall have remedy by the due course of law; and right and justice administered without denial or delay.

Section 12. That no person arrested, or confined in jail, shall be treated with unnecessary rigor, or be put to answer any criminal charge but by presentment, indictment, or impeachment.

Section 13. That in all criminal prosecutions, the accused hath a right to be heard by himself and counsel, to demand the nature and cause of the accusation against him, and to have a copy thereof; to meet the witnesses face to face, to have compulsory process for obtaining witnesses in his favor; and in prosecutions by indictment or presentment, a speedy public trial by an impartial jury of the county or district in which the offence shall have been committed; and shall not be compelled to give evidence against himself, nor shall be twice put in jeopardy for the same offence.

Section 14. That all persons shall be bailable by sufficient sureties, unless for capital offenses when the proof is evident, or the presumption great; and the privilege of the writ of habeas corpus shall not be suspended, unless in case of rebellion or invasion, the public safety may require it.

Section 15. Excessive bail shall not be required, excessive fines shall not be imposed, nor cruel and unusual punishments inflicted.

Section 16. All penalties shall be proportioned to the nature of the offence.

Section 17. The person of a debtor, where there is not strong presumption of fraud, shall not be continued in prison after delivering up his estate, for the benefit of his creditor or creditors, in such manner as shall be prescribed by law.

Section 18. No ex post facto law, nor any law impairing the validity of contracts, shall ever be made, and no conviction shall work corruption of blood [*sic*], nor forfeiture of estate.

Section 19. That the people have a right to assemble together, in a peaceable manner, to consult for their common good, to instruct their representatives, and to apply to the legislature for redress of grievances.

Section 20. That the people have a right to bear arms for the defence of themselves, and the state; and that the military shall be kept in strict subordination to the civil power.

Section 21. That no soldier shall, in time of peace, be quartered in any house without the consent of the owner, nor in time of war, but in a manner to be prescribed by law.

Section 22. That the legislature shall not grant any title of nobility, or hereditary distinctions, nor create any office, the appointment to which shall be a longer term than good behavior.

Section 23. That emigration from the state shall not be prohibited.

Section 24. To guard against any encroachments on the rights herein retained, we declare, that everything in this article, is exempted out of the general powers of government, and shall forever remain inviolable.

NUMBER 2

Constitution of Indiana, Article 8, 1816.

Every twelfth year after this constitution shall have taken effect, at the general election held for governor, there shall be a poll opened, in which the qualified electors of the state, shall express, by vote, whether they are in favor of calling a convention or not; and if there should be a majority of all the votes given at such election, in favor of a convention, the governor shall inform the next general assembly thereof, whose duty it shall be, to provide by law for the election of the members to the convention, the number thereof, and the time and place of their meeting; which law shall not be passed, unless agreed to by a majority of all the members elected to both branches of the general assembly; and which convention, when met, shall have it in their power to revise, amend, or change the constitution. But as the holding any part of the human creation in slavery, or involuntary servitude, can only originate in usurpation and tyranny, no alteration of this constitution shall ever take place so as to introduce slavery or involuntary servitude in this state, otherwise than for the punishment of crimes whereof the party shall have been duly convicted.

***

Article 11.

Section 7. There shall neither be slavery, nor involuntary servitude in this state, otherwise than for the punishment of crimes whereof the party shall have been duly convicted. Nor shall any indenture of any negro or mulatto, hereafter made and executed out of the bonds of this state, be of any validity within the state.

II

Slavery

Indiana whites showed considerable interest in slavery, especially during its territorial phase. Proslavery leaders assembled at a convention in the town of Vincennes, to pursue suspension of Article 6, which banned slavery in the Northwest Territory. The petitioners asked Congress to either rescind or modify the article. They also made ridiculous assertions about their benevolence and concern for the welfare of blacks. They argued that the prohibition in the ordinance discouraged immigration to Indiana and they urged Congress to allow slave holders who came there to maintain control over enslaved persons. Congress did not approve of their petitions. Consequently, Indiana lawmakers devised a complex indentured servitude system that produced quasi-slavery for African Americans. The following documents include their petitions, reports, and memorials.

NUMBER 1

Proclamation calling for a convention to petition Congress to allow slavery in the Indiana Territory. Governor's messages, Executive Journal, November 22, 1802. Indiana Historical Collections, (1922).

Petitions having been presented to the Governor by a Considerable number of the Citizens of the Territory praying that a proclamation should Issue from the Executive authority for Calling A General Convention for the purpose of taking into consideration the propriety of repealing the sixth article of Compact between the United States and the people of the Territory, and for other purposes, and proof having been adduced to the governor that a very large majority of the Citizens are in favor of the measures: the Governor in

Compliance with their wishes Issued his proclamation notifying all whom it may concern that an Election will be held at the Respective Court Houses in Each county of the Territory on Tuesday the 11 day of December for choosing Representatives from the several Counties to be as follows: from the county of Knox, four; from the county of Randolph, three; from the county of St. Clair, three; and from the county of Clark, two; and the Sheriffs of the several counties are authorized and required to hold the elections in their respective counties, and in case of any of the sheriffs are candidates, then the election to be held by the coroners.

NUMBER 2

Resolution of Vincennes Convention, December 25, 1802. Indiana Historical Collections, (1922).

We the People of Indiana Territory inhabiting the middle and western Divisions of the Country Northwest of the Ohio, do by our Representatives in general Convention assembled, hereby agree that the operation of the Sixth Article of Compact between the United States and the people of the Territory [Ordinance of 1787] should be suspended for the space of ten years from the Day that a law may be passed by Congress giving their Consent to the Suspension of the said Article.

By a subsequent proclamation, dated November 24, the time for opening this convention was changed to Monday, December 20. On December 25, the convention adopted a resolution in favor of a ten year suspension of the article of the Ordinance of 1787 which prohibited slavery; and on the 28th the substance of this resolution, together with some additional requests concerning the grant of lands, provisions for education, roads, salt springs, the franchise, etc., was embodied in a petition to Congress, which was transmitted to that body by the Governor with an accompanying letter on the same day. An adverse report to the request concerning slavery (and most of the other matters) was returned in the House of Representatives by a committee presided over by John Randolph, on March 2, 1803; but a year later (February 17, 1804), second committee reported in favor of it. The desired authorization for the introduction of slavery, however, was not obtained, either at this time or later, when the petition was several times renewed. The documents cited above are here printed as necessary to an understanding of this proclamation.

Provided, however, that should no law be passed by Congress for suspending the said article before the 4th day of March 1805, then the consent of the people of this Territory hereby given shall be void and of no effect.

Done at Vincennes in the Indiana Territory the twenty-fifth day of December, one thousand Eight hundred and two, and in the twenty-seventh year of the Independence of the United States.

NUMBER 3

Petition of the Vincennes Convention, December 28, 1802. Indiana Historical Collections, (1922).

That nine-tenths of your memorialists being of opinion, that the sixth article of Compact contained in the ordinance for the Government of the Territory has been extremely prejudicial to their Interest and welfare, requested the Governor by petitions from each of the several counties to call a general convention of the Territory for the purpose of taking the sense of the whole People by their Representatives on a subject to them so interesting and of afterwards taking such measures as to them might seem meet by petition to your honorable Bodies not only for obtaining the repeal or suspension of the said article of Compact but also for that of representing and Petitioning for the passage of such other Laws as would in the opinion of the Convention be conducive to the general welfare, population and happiness of this distant and unrepresented portion of the United States.

This convention is now sitting at Vincennes and have agreed to make the following representations to the Congress of the United States, not in the least doubting but that everything they can desire (not prejudicial to the Constitution or to the Interest of the General Government) will readily be granted them.

The Sixth Article of Compact between the United States and the people of the Territory which declares that there shall be neither slavery nor involuntary servitude in it has prevented the Country from populating and been the reason of driving many valuable Citizens possessing Slaves to the Spanish side of the Mississippi, most of whom but for the prohibition contained in the ordinance would have settled in this Territory, and the consequences of keeping that prohibition in force will be that obliging the numerous Class of Citizens disposed to emigrate, to seek an Asylum in that country where they can be permitted to enjoy their property.

Your memorialist however and the people they represent do not wish for a repeal of the article entirely, but that it may be suspended for the Term of the Ten Years and then to be again in force, but that the slaves brought into the Territory during the Continuance of this Suspension and their progeny, may be considered and continued in the same state of Servitude, as if they had remained in those parts of the United States where Slavery is permitted and from whence they may have been removed.

Your memoralists beg leave further to represent, That the quantity of lands in the Territory open for Settlement is for the purpose of Civil Government. They therefore pray that the Indian titles to the land lying between the general Indian boundary line running from the mouth of the river Kentucky [Greenville Treaty Line] and the tract commonly called Clark's Grant [Clark county, Indiana] and between and below the said Clark's Grant and the Ohio and Wabash Rivers, may be extinguished; and as an encouragement for a speedy population of the Country; that those lands and all other public lands in the Territory may be sold in Smaller Tracts and at lower price than is now allowed by the existing Laws. A purchase of most of the Country above mentioned but more especially of that part lying between the Illinois and the Ohio it is conceived may be easily obtained from the Indians and on very moderate and advantageous Terms.

Several persons (as your memoralists are informed) having settled on the public lands in this Territory with the intention of purchasing the same when offered for sale by the United States are fearful that advantages may be taken of their Improvements to enhance the Price. Your Petitioners therefore pray, That a law may be passed for their relief, giving the right of Pre-emption to all those who may have so settled on the public lands, and also as one of the more sure means of populating the Country as of enhancing the value of the United States lands remaining undisposed of in the Territory. They further pray, that provision may be made in the said Law for securing a certain part of every Section of Such public land to those who will actually settle and cultivate the same.

The United States having pledged themselves in the Ordinance that schools and the means of Education should be forever encouraged, and having in all the Sales of land heretofore made, reserved considerable portions thereof for that purpose.

Your memorialist, therefore, humbly pray that a law may be passed making a grant of lands for the support of the Schools and Seminaries of learning to the several Settlements in the Illinois, the Settlement of Vincennes, and that of Clark's Grant, near the Rapids of the Ohio.

The means of communication as well between the several Settled parts of the Territory as between the territory and the State of Kentucky, being extremely difficult and inconvenient, as well for want of good Roads as for want of houses of Entertainment, and neither of those objects can be obtained otherwise than by application of the United States who own or may own the lands through which the said Roads must pass.

Your memorialist, therefore, further pray that a law may be enacted granting to such persons as the Governor of the Territory may recommend, Four Hundred acres of land to each in such places as the said Governor may designate, not exceeding the distance of Twenty miles from each other, on the road leading from Clark county to Knox county, and from Vincennes in the said County to the Bank of the Ohio opposite to the town of Henderson, in Kentucky; also from Vincennes to Kaskaskia, in Randolph county, and from thence to Lusk's Ferry on the Ohio [15 miles above the mouth of Cumberland river], who will open good wagon roads and Establish houses of Entertainment thereon for Five Years, under such restrictions as to your Wisdom may Seem Necessary.

And your Memorialist further beg leave to represent that one of the most indispensable articles of life (Salt) is very Scarce and difficult to be obtained,

That for the want of a sufficient number of Salt Springs in their country, that difficulty must increase with the population, and if effectual methods are not taken to secure the Timber in the neighborhood of the Salt Springs [near Shawneetown] from being willfully or carelessly wasted and destroyed, they will in a very few years indeed be utterly destitute of that very valuable article; that there is but one Salt Spring known in the Country of any value, and that is situated below the mouth of the Wabash River, Commonly called the Saline, and is very advantageously placed for the accommodation of most of the Inhabitants of the Territory, and has, moreover, been lately ceded by the Indians to the general Government.

Your memoralists, therefore, humbly pray the Congress of the United States to extend their Bounty to this Territory as they have lately done to that Northwest of the Ohio, and vest the said Salt Spring in the Legislature of the Territory, as soon as it is formed in trust, for the use of the Territory, and until the Legislature be formed, that the management of said spring be committed to the Governor of the Territory, or to such other person as the President of the United States may think proper to appoint.

By a Resolve of Congress of the 29th August, 1788, confirmed by an Act of the United States of the 3d March, 1791, a donation of Four hundred acres of land is given to each of those persons who were heads of Families in the Illinois Country on or before the year 1783, which the Governor of the Territory was directed to cause to be laid off to the several claimants in a form of a Parallelogram adjoining the several Villages therein mentioned.

The whole of the lands adjoining those Villages were before the passage of the above Resolve the private property of Individuals who claimed the same by virtue of old grants made to them and their ancestors during the time of the French government so that the Governor could not cause the said donation to be laid off in the form and manner designated by the said Resolve.

This has been very detrimental to the several Grantees, and in a great measure prevented the further population of the Country, your memorialist however beg leave to observe, that if the said donation lands are directed to be laid off in distinct Bodies for each Village, by far the greatest part of them must from the very large and extensive Prairies with which the whole of that country abounds be wholly and absolutely useless through the entire want of Timber.

Your memorialist therefore pray you to take the situation of the ancient Inhabitants of the Illinois Country into Consideration and as the humane Intention of Congress was to give such lands as would be useful, that you will permit the said Grantees, their Heirs and assigns especially after a period of Fourteen years, to locate their said donation of Four hundred acres of land in separate Tracts, in such parts of the Illinois Country to which the Indian titles may have been extinguished, and that the Governor of the Territory may be authorized to issue Patents therefor. This permission to locate the lands in separate tracts, will not it is conceived be prejudicial to the United States, as the value of lands in the neighborhood of each settled tract will thereby be considerably augmented.

Your memorialist further show that they view that part of the ordinance for the Government of the Territory which requires a freehold qualification in fifty acres of land as Electors for members to the general assembly as subversive of the liberties of the Citizens and tending to throw too great a weight in the Scale of wealth. They therefore pray that the right of Suffrage (in voting for representatives to the general assembly) may be extended to the free male Inhabitants of the Territory of the age of Twenty one years and upwards, but under such Regulations and Restrictions as to you in your Wisdom may seem proper.

Since the Erection of the Territory into a separate Government, the Attorney General [John Rice Jones] thereof has prosecuted not only for offenses committed against the Municipal Laws of the Territory but also against the Laws of the United States, and has been obliged at three different Times to travel one hundred and sixty miles, from his home to the seat of the Territorial Government to prosecute offenders against those Laws, and yet he has received no Compensation for his Services either from the United States or the Territory, nor is it probable that the Territory can afford to allow him any Salary for his future services.

Your memorialist, therefore, pray that a Law may be passed allowing a Salary to the Attorney-General of the Territory adequate to the important services which are rendered by that officer to the United States as well as to the Territory.

Your memorialist are well aware that the consideration of the numerous objects contemplated by this memorial will require more time than can well be spared from the important and general concerns of the Union, but when they reflect upon their neglected and orphan-like situation they are emboldened to hope that their wants and wishes will meet with all the indulgence and attention necessary to secure to them the relief which is so essential to their welfare and happiness.

Done at Vincennes in the Indiana Territory the twenty-eighth day of December in the Year of our Lord One Thousand Eight Hundred and Two, and of the Independence of the United States the Twenty-Seventh.

NUMBER 4

Vincennes Convention of the Indiana Territory. William Henry Harrison to The Honorable Speaker of the House of Representatives of the United States, December 28, 1802. Indiana Historical Collections, (1922).

The people of the Indiana Territory, having by their representatives in general convention assembled, determined to suspend, for a term of years, the operation of the sixth article of Compact between the United States and the people of the Territory, I have the honor herewith to inclose for you the information of the House of Representatives, the instrument declaratory of their consent.

***

Randolph's report on slavery in Indiana, March 2, 1803.

Mr. John Randolph, from the committee to whom were referred a letter from William Henry Harrison, President of the Convention, held at Vincennes, declaring the consent of the people of Indiana to the suspension of the sixth article of compact between the United States and the people of that territory: also, a memorial and petition of the inhabitants of the said territory; made the following report:

"That the rapid population of the State of Ohio sufficiently evinces in the opinion of your committee, that the labor of slaves is not necessary to promote the growth and settlement of colonies in that region. That this labor, demonstrable the dearest of any, can only be employed to advantage in the cultivation of products more valuable than any known to that quarter of the United States: that the committee deem it highly dangerous and inexpedient to impair a provision wisely calculated to promote the happiness and prosperity of the Northwestern country, and to give strength and security to that extensive frontier. In the salutary operation of this sagacious and benevolent restraint, it is believed that the inhabitants of Indiana will, at no very distant day, find ample remuneration for a temporary privation of labor and of emigration.

NUMBER 5

Slavery in Indiana. William Henry Harrison to Thomas Jefferson, November 26, 1803. Indiana Historical Collections, (1922).

The Governor of the Indiana Territory presents his respectful compliments to the President of the United States and requests his acceptance of the enclosed map which is a copy of the manuscript map of Mr. Evans' who ascended the Missouri River by order of the Spanish Government much farther than any other person.

***

James Madison to Congress, December 1, 1803.

The Secretary of State to whom by a resolution of the House of Representatives of the 2d March last was referred a Petition of sundry inhabitants of Post St. Vincennes in the Indiana Territory; has examined the same, and thereupon makes the following reports, viz. The petitioners assert a right to a tract of land which they describe as extending along the Wabash River from Point Coupee to the Mouth of the White River comprising about seventy-two miles above and below Post St. Vincennes, and on both banks of the said River from the little Wabash to the Protoeas River, forming according to their computation an extent in this direction of two hundred and twenty-six miles. This right they pretend to derive from an Indian grant to their predecessors as the first settlers of that District, as well as from a subsequent confirmation of it by the Indians. It is on the basis of these pretensions that they express their hopes that congress will "allow them at least a part in the grants which have lately been made by the Indians to the United States" and they add the request that a small tract of Woodland on the banks of the Wabash may be annexed to the villages Commons, which is now become destitute of Wood."

It would be unnecessary to contest the validity of this Indian grant and confirmation, since the inhabitants have repeatedly and formally renounced all the right they possessed to the tract in question, particularly in their address to Congress of the 26 July 1987 in which they use the following words: "Reposing the most unbounded confidence in the justice, humanity and benevolence of the honorable Congress we solemnly surrender our charter whatever it is, and throw ourselves upon your mercy." An extract from this source documents and others from Mr. Tardiveau's address to Congress in their behalf dated 7th August 1787, and 28th Feb. 1788, and also the powers given to him by the inhabitants of St. Vincennes as their agent are annexed. This renunciation as far as it might be supposed by the inhabitants to relate to a valid title in themselves was doubtless one of the motives to the grant and confirmations made to them by Congress in their acts of 20th June and 29th August 1788, and 3d March 1791, the latter of which ought to be considered as closing the claims of the settlers of St. Vincennes.

For these reasons the Secretary of State is of opinion that the petition ought not to be granted, which is respectfully submitted.

NUMBER 6

Second report on petition of the Vincennes Convention, February 17, 1804. Indiana Historical Collections, (1922).

Sr. Caesar Rodney, from the committee to whom were referred a letter From William Henry Harrison, President of the general convention of the representatives of the people of the Indiana Territory, also a memorial and petition from the said convention, together with the report of a former committee on the same subject at the last session of congress made the following report:

That taking into their consideration the facts stated in the said memorial and petition, they are induced to believe that a qualified suspension, for a limited time, of the sixth article of compact between the original States and the people and States west of the river Ohio, might be productive of benefit and advantage to the said Territory.

They do not conceive it would be proper to break in upon the system adopted for surveying and locating public lands, which experience has proved so well calculated to promote the general interest. If a preference be given to particular individuals in the present instance, an example will be set, by which future claimants will obtain the same privilege. The committee are, nevertheless, of opinion that after those lands shall have been surveyed a certain number of township should be designated, out of which the claims stated in the memorial ought to be satisfied, and that, for the encouragement of actual settlers, and right of pre-emption should be secured to them.

They consider the existing regulations contained in the ordinance for the government of the Territory of the United States, which requires a freehold of fifty acres as a qualification for an elector of the General Assembly, as limiting too much the elective franchise. They conceive the vital principle of a free Government is, that taxation and representation should go together after a residence of sufficient length to manifest the intention of becoming a permanent inhabitant, and to evince, by conduct orderly and upright, that a person is entitled to the rights of an elector. This probationary period should not extend beyond two years.

It must be the true policy of the United States, with the millions of acres of habitable country which she possesses, to cherish those principles which gave birth to her independence, and created her a nation, by affording an asylum to the oppressed of all countries.

One important object desired in the memorial, the extinguishment of the Indian title to certain lands, has been happily accomplished; whilst the salt spring below the mouth of the Wabash river has also been placed in a situation to be productive of every reasonable advantage.

After a careful review and an attentive consideration of the various subjects contemplated in the memorial and petition, the committee respectfully submit to the House the following resolutions, as embracing all the objects which require the attention of Congress at this period:

Resolved, That the sixth article of the Ordinance of 1787, which prohibited slavery within the said Territory, be suspended, in a qualified manner, for ten years, so as to permit the introduction of slaves, born within the United States, from any of the individual States: Provided, That such individual State does not permit the importation of slaves from foreign countries: And provided further, That the descendants of all such slaves shall, if males, be free at the age of twenty-five years, and, if females, at the age of twenty-one years.

Resolved, That every white free man, of the age of twenty-one years, who has resided within the Territory, two years, and within that time paid a territorial tax which shall have been assessed six months before the election, shall enjoy the right of an elector and vote for members of the General Assembly.

Resolved, That in all cases of sales of land within the Indiana Territory, the right of pre-emption be given to actual settlers on time.

Resolved, That the Secretary of the Treasury be, and he is hereby, required to cause an estimate to be made of the number and extent of the claims to be lands under the resolution of Congress of 1796, and to lay the same before this House.

Resolved, That provision, not exceeding one thirty-six part of the public lands within the Indiana Territory, ought to be made for the support of the school.

Resolved, That it is expedient to grant lands to individuals for the purpose of establishing houses of entertainment, and opening certain roads.

Resolved, That it is inexpedient, at this time, to vest in the Legislature of Louisiana [misprint for Indiana] Territory the salt spring below the mouth of the Wabash river.

Resolved, That compensation ought to be made to the attorney general of the said Territory for services performed by him on behalf of the United States.

NUMBER 7

House report on slavery in Indiana, February 14, 1806. Indiana Historical Collections, (1922).

Mr. Garnett, from the committee appointed Dec. 18, 1805, to whom was referred the report of a select committee, made on the 17th of February, 1804, at a convention held at Vincennes, in the Indiana Territory, declaring the consent of the people of the said territory to a suspension of the sixth article of compact between the United States and the said people; above also on a memorial and petition of the inhabitants of the said Territory; also on the petition of the Legislative Council and House of Representatives of the said territory; [see Feb. 12, 1807, and Sept. 19, 1807, above] together with the petition of certain purchasers of land, settled and intending to settle on that part of the Indiana Territory; west of Ohio, and east of the boundary line running from the mouth of the Kentucky river; and on two memorials from the inhabitants of Randolph and St. Clair--made the following report:

That having attentively considered the facts stated in the said petitions and memorials, they are of opinion that a qualified suspension, for a limited time, of the sixth article of compact between the original States and the people and States west of the river Ohio, would be beneficial to the people of the Indiana

Territory. The suspension of this article is different from the one between slavery and freedom, inasmuch as it would merely occasion the removal of persons, already slaves, from one part of the country to another. The good effects of this suspension, in the present instance, would be to accelerate the population of that Territory, instead of seeking as they are now compelled to do, settlements in other States or countries permitting the introduction of slaves. The condition of the slaves themselves would be much ameliorated by it, as it is evident, from experience that the more they are separated and diffused, the more care and attention are bestowed on them by their masters, each proprietor having it in his power to increase their comforts and conveniences in proportion to the smallness of their numbers. The dangers, too, (if any are to be apprehended,) from too large a black population existing in any one section of country, would certainly be very much diminished, if not entirely removed. But whether dangers are to be feared from this source or not, it is certainly an obvious dictate of sound policy to guard against them as far as possible. If this danger does exist, or there is any cause to apprehend it, and our Western brethren are not only willing but desirous to aid us in taking precautions against it, would it not be wise to accept their assistance? We should benefit ourselves, without injuring them, as their population must always so far exceed any black population which can ever exist in that country, as to render the idea of danger from the source chimerical.

Your committee consider the regulation, contained in the ordinance for the government of the territory of the United States, which requires a freehold of fifty acres of land as a qualification for an elector of the General Assembly, as limiting too much the elective franchise. Some restriction, however, being necessary, your committee conceive that a residence continued long enough to evince a determination to become a permanent inhabitant, should entitle a person to rights of suffrage. This probationary period need not extend beyond twelve months.

The petition of certain settlers in the Indiana Territory, [Dearborn County] praying to be annexed to the State of Ohio, ought not, in the opinion of your committee be granted.

It appears to your committee that the division of the Indiana Territory, in the manner directed by the Ordinance of 1787, and for which the people of Randolph and St. Clair have petitioned your honorable body, would be inexpedient at this time.

It appears to your committee that the division of the Indiana Territory, in the manner directed by the Ordinance of 1787, and for which the people of Randolph and St. Clair have petitioned your honorable body, would be inexpedient at this time. The people of the two sections have lately entered into the second grade of government, the whole expense of which would fall on the pole of one section, if a division were now to be made. This, in the opinion of your committee, would be neither politic nor just. But, although a division of the Territory appears improper at this time, we think it should be made as soon as the population of either section has increased so far as to entitle them to form a State Government. The petition which prays that such a Government may be formed, by uniting the two sections as soon as their inhabitants shall have authorized it. A territory, when once erected into a state, cannot be divided or dismembered without its own consent; the formation therefore, of two States out of this Territory, originally intended by the Ordinance of 1787, could not constitutionally be effected, if the two sections were once permitted to form one State, without the consent of that State, however necessary the extent and population of that Territory might render such division.

After attentively considering the various objects desired in the memorials and petitions, the committee respectfully submit to the House the following resolutions:

Resolved, That the sixth article of the Ordinance of 1787, which prohibits slavery within the Indiana Territory, be suspended for ten years, so as to permit the introduction of slaves, born within the United States, from any of the individual States.

Resolved, That every white freeman of the age of twenty-one years, who has resided within the Territory twelve months, and within the county in which he claims a vote, six months, immediately preceding the election, shall enjoy the rights of an elector of the General Assembly.

Resolved, That the petition of certain settlers in the Indiana Territory, praying to be annexed to the State of Ohio, ought not to be granted.

Resolved, That it is inexpedient, at this time, to grant that part of the petition of the people of Randolph and St. Clair [counties in Ill.] which prays for a division of the Indiana Territory.

Resolved, That so much of the petition of the Legislative council and House of Representatives of the Indiana Territory as prays that the two sections may be united into one State Government, ought not to be granted.

NUMBER 8

Slavery petition. Annals of Congress, February 12, 1807.

That the resolutions of the Legislative Council and House of Representatives of the Indiana Territory relate to a suspension of the term of ten years, of the sixth article of compact between the United States and the Territories and States northwest of the river Ohio, passed the 13th July, 1787. That article declares "there shall be neither slavery nor involuntary servitude in the said Territory."

The suspension of the said article would operate an immediate and essential benefit to the Territory, as emigration to it will be inconsiderable for many years except from those States where slavery is tolerated; and although it is not considered expedient to force the population of the Territory, yet it is desirable to connect its scattered settlements, and, in regard to political rights, to place it on an equal footing with the different states. From the interior situation of the Territory, it is not believed that slaves would ever become so numerous as to endanger the internal peace or future prosperity of the country. The current emigration flowing to the western country, the Territories ought all to be opened to their introduction. The abstract question of liberty and slavery is not involved in the proposed measure, as slavery now exists to a considerable extent in different parts of the Union; it would not augment the number of slaves, but merely authorize the removal to Indiana of such as are held in bondage in the United States. If slavery is an evil, means ought to be devised to render it least dangerous to the community, and by which the hapless situation of the slaves would be most ameliorated; and to accomplish these objects, no measure would be so effectual as the one proposed. The committee, therefore, respectfully submit to the House the following resolution:

Resolved, That it is expedient to suspend, from and after the 1st day of January 1808 the sixth article of compact between the United States and the Territories and States northwest of the river Ohio, passed the 13th day of July, 1787, for the term of ten years.

NUMBER 9

In the Legislative Council and House of Representatives of the Indiana Territory. Petition on slavery from Indiana, Sept. 19, 1807. Indiana Historical Collections, (1922).

Great solicitude has been evidenced by the Citizens of this Territory on the subject of the introduction of Slaves. In the year 1802 a special convention (December 25, 1802) of Delegates from the respective Counties petitioned Congress for a suspension of the sixth article of Compact, contained in the Ordinance of 1787: in 1805 a majority of the members of the Legislative Council and House of Representatives remonstrated with Congress on the subject (February 7, 1805). In 1806 the Legislative Council and House of Representatives passed sundry resolutions (February 14, 1806) which were laid before Congress, declaratory of their sense of the propriety of admitting slaves: and as the Citizens of the Territory decidedly approve of the toleration of Slavery the Legislative Council and House of Representatives consider it incumbent on them, briefly to state, on behalf of themselves and their constituents, the reasons which have influenced them in favor of the measures.

In the first place candor induces us to premise that in regard to the right of holding slaves a variety in opinion exists; whilst some consider it decent and Just to acquire them either by purchase or conquest, others consider their possession by either tenure as a crime of the deepest stain; that it is repugnant to every principle of nature. Justice of political rights and to every sentiment of humanity. Without entering into the merits of this controversy it need only be remarked that the proposition to introduce Slavery into the Territory is not embraced by them. It is not a question of liberty or Slavery. Slavery now exists in the United States and in this Territory. It was the crime of England, their misfortune. And it now becomes a question merely of policy in what way the slaves are to be disposed of, that they may be least dangerous to the community, most useful to their proprietors, and by which their situation may be most ameliorated.

As the law of Congress prohibiting the further importation of slaves into the United States takes effect the first of January next [1808], it is evident that the proposed toleration will not increase the number in the United States.

It is believed, and has not experience verified the fact, that such is the number of slaves in the Southern States that the safety of individuals as well as the political institutions of those States are exposed to no small hazard. However desirable it may be to emancipate them, it can never be done until they are dispersed; it would be equally impolitic for the whites as for the slaves;--The great current of emigration is constantly flowing from the Eastern & Southern States to the Western States and Territories. The increase of population in the Western Country for the last twenty years may afford some idea of its probable amount in the course of the present century;--It must be immense; and were all the Territories opened to the introduction of slaves, a large proportion of them would naturally be drawn from the southern States.

From a reference to the States of Kentucky and Tennessee and at the time of the last United States Census, it is not believed that the number of Slaves would ever become so great as to endanger either the internal peace or future prosperity of the Territory. It is also rendered improbable from the interior situation of the Territory its climate and productions.

Slavery is tolerated in the Territories of New Orleans, Mississippi, and Louisiana;--Why should this Territory be excepted?

It is believed that Slaves possessed in small numbers by farmers are better fed and better Clothed than when they are crowded together in quarters by hundreds;--their situation in Kentucky, Tennessee, and the back parts of Maryland and Virginia verify this belief.

Resolved by the Legislative Council and House of Representatives of the Indiana Territory That it is expedient to suspend for a given number of years the sixth article of compact contained in the Ordinance for the Government of the North-Western Territory passed the 13th day of July in the year 1787.

Resolved that a Copy of the foregoing be forwarded to the Vice President of the United States with a request that he will lay the same before the Senate and that Copy be forwarded to the Speaker of the House of Representatives with a request that he will lay the same before the said House of Representatives; and that the Governor of this Territory be requested to forward the same as aforesaid. Passed the Legislative council September 19, 1807.

NUMBER 10

Senate report on slavery in Indiana, November 13, 1807. American State Papers, I.

Mr. Franklin, from the committee to whom was referred the representation and resolution of the Legislative Council and House of Representatives of the Indiana Territory, bearing the date of 13th of July, 1807; and, also, the remonstrance of the citizens of Clark county, of the Territory aforesaid, reported:

The Legislative Council and House of Representatives, in their resolutions, express their sense of the propriety of introducing slavery into their Territory, and solicit the Congress of the United States to suspend, for a given number of years, the sixth article of compact, in the ordinance for the government of the Territory northwest of the river Ohio, passed the 13th day of July, 1787. That article declares: "there shall be neither slavery nor involuntary servitude in the said Territory."

The citizens of Clark county, in their remonstrance, express their sense of the impropriety of the measure, and solicit the Congress of the United States not to act on the subject, so as to permit the introduction of slaves into the Territory; at least until their population shall entitle them to form a constitution and State Government.

Your committee, after duly considering the matter, respectfully submit the following resolution:

Resolved, That it is not expedient at this time to suspend the sixth article of compact for the government of the territory of the United States northwest of the river Ohio.

NUMBER 11

House of Representatives report on slavery in Indiana, November 17, 1807. Indiana Historical Collections, (1922).

The Committee, to whom were referred the letter from William Henry Harrison governor of the Indiana Territory, inclosing certain resolutions passed by the Legislative Council and House of Representatives of said territory, relative to the suspension for a certain period, of the sixth article of compact [Ordinance of 1787] between the United States and the territories and states north-west of the river Ohio, made the 13th of July 1787. And the Memorial of the inhabitants of Clark county in the Indiana territory report:

They have attentively considered the Resolution of the Legislative council and House of Representatives of the Indiana territory--stating the expediency of suspending for a given number of years--the sixth article of Compact--contained in the ordinance for the government of the North Western territory--passed the 13th of July in the year 1787--together with the reasoning in favor of said resolution--And also--a counter memorial of a number of Citizens of Clark county in the said Territory of Indiana (October 10).

It appears to the committee as well from the statement of the Legislative council & House of Representatives of said territory--as from the Memorial of the Citizens of Clark county,--that a difference of opinion exists in the territory, as to the right of holding slaves--and as to the propriety of introducing them within the said territory.

On a subject of such magnitude, as the introduction of slavery (which by numbers is considered as a serious evil, and to be cautiously avoided) the voice of the citizens should be clearly ascertained. How far the introduction of slavery in said territory would operate to the prejudice, & injury of one part of the Citizens; and to the advancement & prosperity of the other, your committee cannot undertake to say--but the policy of a measure, that probably would have that tendency, without promoting the public-good, is at least questionable.

In a few years, from the rapid growth of population in the territory, its numbers, will entitle it to be admitted into the Union, as an Independent State, when the Citizens will have a right to adopt such measures, as may comport with their wishes on the subject.

Your Committee is of the opinion--that it would be improper at this time for Congress to legislate on the subject--And submit the following:

Resolved, That it is inexpedient to suspend for a given number of years, the sixth article of Compact, contained in the ordinance for the government of the North-Western territory, passed the 13th day of July in the year 1787.

NUMBER 12

A joint resolution in relation to the slave trade. Approved January 16, 1850, Indiana Acts.

Whereas, The policy of suppressing the African Slave Trade by an armed blockade, has upon the whole proved an entire failure, said trade being as vigorous now as it was before the blockade was attempted: And whereas, It is likely that England will soon make overtures to our General Government, demanding a release from all treaty stipulations whereby she is obliged to keep her expensive fleet on the African coast, for the suppression of the slave trade: And whereas, Both the governments of the United States and England are convinced that some other plan must be adopted to check that traffic: And whereas, The settlement of the African coast with colonies of civilized colored men is the cheapest and best plan of suppressing said traffic, being likewise calculated to further the work of colonizing our people of color, which plan of suppressing the trade is true American policy; Therefore,

Section 1. Be it resolved by the General Assembly of the State of Indiana, That our Senators and Representatives in Congress be, and they are hereby requested, in the name of the State of Indiana, to call for a change of national policy on the subject of the African Slave Trade, and that they require a settlement of the coast of Africa with colored men from the United States, and procure such changes in our relations with England as will permit us to transport colored men from this country to Africa, with whom to effect said settlement.

III

Indentured Servants and Laborers

Lawmakers in the Indiana Territory adopted the province's first black law in 1803. They drafted the statute to assure slave holders that they would not loose their slaves when they entered Indiana. The slavery prohibition in the Northwest Ordinance had intimidated slave holders, who feared that Article 6 in the Ordinance would automatically free their "chattels" the moment they entered Indiana. Legislators in the Territory recognized the validity of Article 6, although they did not consider it good law. To circumvent the clause, they introduced the practice of indentured servitude. Indiana law compelled in-coming slaves to complete labor contracts, which required them to work for their masters. The law also granted slave holders coercive powers over blacks, giving them license to use the lash when exacting labor or administering punishment. Lawmakers in the territory made only token gestures of civility to African Americans brought into the province. For example, the law required the whites to provide the blacks with adequate food, shelter, and clothing. These necessities were hardly any better than what blacks had received before, while living in a state of de jure slavery. Indiana, therefore, came as close to recognizing slavery as possible under the laws of the Northwest Ordinance which prohibited slavery.

NUMBER 1

Indiana Territory. A Law concerning Servants. [This law also applied to Illinois, a part of the Indiana Territory.] Approved September 22, 1803, Laws of the Indiana Territory.

Section 1. All negroes and mulattoes (and other persons not being citizens of the United States of America,) who shall come into this territory under contract to serve another in any trade or occupation, shall be compelled to perform such contract specifically during the term thereof.

Section 2. The said servants shall be provided by the master with wholesome and sufficient food, clothing and lodging, and at the end of their service if they shall not have contracted for any reward, food, clothing and lodging, suited to the season of the year, to wit: a coat, waistcoat, pair of breeches and shoes, two pair of stockings, two shirts, a hat and blanket.

Section 3. The benefit of the said contract of service, shall be assignable by the master to any person being a citizen of this territory, to whom the servant shall in the presence of a justice of the peace freely consent that it shall be assigned, the said justice attesting such free consent in writing, and shall also pass to the executors, administrators and legatees of the master.

Section 4. Any servant being lazy, disorderly, guilty of misbehavior to his master or his masters family shall be corrected by stripes on order from a justice of the county wherein he resides; or refusing to work, shall be compelled thereto in like manner, and moreover shall serve two days for every one he shall have so refused to serve, or shall otherwise have lost without sufficient justification. All necessary expenses incurred by a master for apprehending and bringing home any absconding servant, shall be repaid by further service after such rates as the court of the county shall direct; unless such servant shall give security to be approved of by the court for repayment in money, within six months after he shall be free from service, and shall accordingly pay the same.

Section 5. If any master shall fail in the duties described by this act, or shall be guilty of injurious demeanor towards his servant, it shall be redressed on motion, by the court of the county wherein the servant resides, who may hear and determine such cases in a summary way, making such orders thereupon as in their judgment will relieve the party injured in future.

Section 6. All contracts between master and servant during the time of service, shall be void.

Section 7. The court of every county shall at all times receive the complaints of servants, being citizens of any one of the United States of America, who reside within the jurisdiction of such court, against their masters or mistresses, alleging undeserved or immoderate correction, insufficient allowance of food, raiment or lodging, and may hear and determine such cases in a summary way, making such orders thereupon, as in their judgment will relieve the party injured in future; and may also in the same manner hear and determine complaints of masters or mistresses against their servants for desertion without good cause, and may oblige the latter for loss thereby occasioned, to make retribution, by further services, after the expiration of the times for which they had been bound.

Section 8. If any servant, shall at any time, bring in goods or money, or during the time of their service, shall, by gift or other lawful means acquire goods or money, they shall have the property and benefit thereof, to their own use. And if any servant shall be sick or lame, and so become useless or chargeable, his or her master or owner, shall maintain such servant until his or her whole time of service shall be expired. And if any master or owner shall put away a lame or sick servant under pretence of freedom, and such servant becomes chargeable to the county, such master or owner shall forfeit and pay thirty dollars to the overseers of the poor of the county when such offence shall be committed to the use of the poor of the county, recoverable with costs, by action of debt in any court of common pleas of this territory; and moreover shall be liable to the action of the said overseers of the poor, at the common law for damages.

Section 9. No negro, mulatto or Indian shall at any time purchase any servant, other than of their own complexion; and if any of the aforesaid, shall nevertheless presume to purchase a white servant, such servant shall immediately become free, and shall be so held deemed and taken.

Section 10. No person whatsoever shall buy, sell, or receive of, to, or from any servant, any coin commodity whatsoever, without the leave or consent of the master or owner of such servant; and if any person shall presume to deal with any servant without such leave or consent, he or she so offending, shall forfeit and pay to the master or owner of such servant four times the value of the thing so bought, sold or received; to be recovered with costs by an action upon the case in any court of common pleas of this territory; and shall also forfeit and pay the further sum of twenty dollars to any person who will sue for the same; or receive on his or her bare back, thirty nine lashes, well laid on, at the public whipping post, but shall nevertheless be liable to pay the costs of such.

Section 11. In all cases of penal laws, where free persons are punishable by fine, servants shall be punished by whipping, and receive no more than forty lashes at any one time, unless such offender can procure some person to pay the fine.

Section 12. Every servant upon the expiration of his or her time, and proof thereof made before the court of the county where he or she last served, shall have his or her freedom recorded, and a certificate thereof under the hand of the prothonotary, which shall be sufficient to indemnify any person for entertaining or hiring such servant; and if such certificate shall happen to be torn or lost, the prothonotary, upon request shall issue another, reciting therein the loss of the former. And if any person shall harbor or entertain a servant, not having and producing such certificate, he or she, shall pay to the master or owner of such servant, one dollar for every natural day he or she shall so harbor or entertain such runaway; recoverable with costs, by action of debt, in any court of common pleas of this territory. And if any runaway shall make use of a forged certificate, or after delivery of a true certificate to the person hiring him or her, shall steal the same, and thereby procure other entertainment, the person entertaining or hiring shall not be liable to the said penalty, but such runaway besides making reparation for loss of time, and charges of recovery, shall stand two hours in the pillory, on a court day, for making use of such forged or stolen certificate, and the person forging the same shall forfeit and pay thirty dollars; one moiety to the territory, and the other moiety to the owner of such runaway, or the informer, recoverable with costs, in any court of common pleas of this territory; and on failure of present payment, or security for the same within six months such offender shall receive thirty-nine lashes on his or her bare back, well laid on, at the common whipping post. And where a runaway shall happen to be hired upon a forged certificate, and afterwards denies the delivery thereof the agnus probandi shall lie upon the party hiring such runaway.

Section 13. This law shall commence and be in force from and after the first day of November next.

NUMBER 2

An act concerning servants. [This law also applied to Illinois, a part of the Indiana Territory.] Approved September 17, 1807, Laws of the Indiana Territory.

Section 1. All negroes and mulattoes, (and other persons not being citizens of the United States of America) who shall come into this Territory, under contract to serve another, in any trade or occupation, shall be compelled to perform such contract specifically during the time thereof.

Section 2. The said servants shall be provided by the master with wholesome and sufficient food, clothing and lodging, and at the end of their service, if they shall not have contracted for any reward, food, clothing and lodging, shall receive from him, one new and complete set of clothing, suiting to the season of the year, to wit: a coat, waistcoat, pair of breeches, and shoes, two pair of stockings, two shirts, a hat and blanket.

Section 3. The benefit of the said contract of service, shall be assignable by the master to any person being a citizen of this Territory to whom the servant shall in the presence of a Justice of the Peace freely consent, that it shall be assigned; the said Justice attesting such free consent in writing, and shall also pass to the executors, administrators, and legatees of the master.

Section 4. Any servant being lazy, disorderly, guilty of misbehavior to his master, or master's family, shall be corrected by stripes, on order from a Justice of the county wherein he resides; or refusing to work, shall be compelled thereto in like manner, and moreover shall serve two days for everyone he shall have so refused to serve, or shall otherwise have lost, without sufficient justification, all necessary expenses incurred by any master for apprehending and bringing home any absconding servant, shall be repaid by further service, after such rates as the court of Common Pleas, of the county shall direct, unless such servant shall give security, to be approved of by the court for the payment in money within six months, after he shall be free from service, and shall accordingly pay the same.

Section 5. If any master shall fail in the duties prescribed by this act, or shall be guilty of injurious demeanor towards his servant it shall be redressed on motion, by the court of Common Pleas, of the county wherein the servant resides who may hear and determine such cases in a summary way, making such orders thereupon as in their judgment will relieve the party injured in future.

Section 6. All contracts between masters and servants, during the time of service shall be void.

Section 7. The court of Common Pleas of every county shall at all times receive the complaints of servants, being citizens of any of the United States of America, who reside within the jurisdiction of such court, against their masters or mistresses, alleging undeserved or immoderate correction, insufficient allowances of food, raiment, or lodging, and may hear and determine such case in a summary way, making such orders thereupon as in their judgment will relieve the party injured in future, and may also in the same manner hear and determine complaints of masters and mistresses against their servants, for desertion without good cause, and may oblige the latter for loss thereby occasioned, to make restitution for further services, after the expiration of the time, for which they had been bound.

Section 8. If any servant shall at any time bring in goods or money, during the time of their service, shall by gift, or other lawful means, acquire goods or money, they shall have the property, and benefit thereof, to their own use; and if any servant shall be sick or lame and so become useless or chargeable, his or her master or owner shall maintain such servant, until his or her whole time of service shall be expired; and if any master or owner shall forfeit and pay thirty dollars, to the overseers of the poor of the county wherein such offence shall be committed, to the use of the poor of the county, recoverable with costs, by action of debt in any court of Common Pleas of this Territory, and moreover shall be liable to the action of the said overseers of the poor at the common law for damages.

Section 9. No negro, Mulatto or Indian shall at any time purchase any servant, other than of their own complexion, and if any of the persons aforesaid shall nevertheless presume to purchase a white servant, such servant shall immediately become free, and shall be so held deemed and taken.

Section 10. No person whatsoever shall buy, sell or receive of, to or from any servant any coin or commodity whatsoever, without the leave or consent of the master or owner of such servant; and if any person shall presume to deal with any servant without such leave or consent, he or she so offending, shall forfeit and pay to the master or owner of such servant, four times the value of the thing so bought, sold and received, to be recovered with costs by an action upon the case, in any court of Common pleas of this territory; & shall also forfeit & pay the further sum of twenty dollars to any person who will sue for the same, or receive on his or her bare back, thirty-nine lashes well laid on, at the public whipping post, but shall nevertheless be liable to pay the costs of such suit.

Section 11. In all cases of penal laws where free persons are punishable by fine, servants shall be punished by whipping, after the rate of twenty lashes for every eight dollars, so that no servant shall receive more than forty lashes at any one time, unless such offender can procure some person to pay the fine.

Section 12. Every servant upon the expiration of his or her time, and proof thereof made before the court of Common Pleas of the county, where he or she last served, shall have his or her freedom recorded and a certificate thereof, under the hand of the Clerk, which shall be sufficient to indemnify any person for entertaining or hiring such servant; and if such certificate should happen to be torn or lost, the Clerk upon request, shall issue another, reciting therein the loss of the former; and if any person shall harbor or entertain a servant not having and producing such certificate, he or she shall pay to the master or owner of such servant one dollar for every natural day he or she shall so harbor or entertain such runaway, recoverable with costs, by action of debt, in any court of Common Pleas of this Territory; and if any runaway shall make use of a forged certificate, or after delivery of a true certificate to the person hiring him or her, shall steal the same and thereby procure other entertainment, the person entertaining or hiring shall not be liable to the said penalty, but such runaway, besides making reparation for loss of time and charges of recovery, shall stand two hours in the pillory on a court day for making use of such forged or stolen certificate, and the person forging the same shall forfeit and pay thirty dollars, one moiety to the Territory and the other moiety to the owner of such runaway, or the informer, recoverable with costs, in any court of Common Pleas of this Territory; and on failure of present payment, or security for the same within six months, such offender shall receive thirty-nine lashes on his or her bare back well laid on, at the common whipping post; and where a runaway shall happen to be hired upon a forged certificate and afterwards denies the delivery thereof, the onus probandi shall lie upon the party hiring such runaway.

Section 13. If any slave or servant shall be found at the distance of ten miles from the tenement of his or her master, or the person with whom he or she lives, without a pass or some letter or token, whereby it may appear that he or she is proceeding by authority from his or her master, employer or overseer, it shall and may be lawful for any person to apprehend and carry him or her before a Justice of the Peace, to be by his order punished with stripes, not exceeding thirty five, at his discretion.

Section 14. If any slave or servant shall presume to come and be upon the plantation or at the dwelling house of any person whatsoever, without leave from his or her owner, not being sent upon lawful business it shall be lawful for the owner of such plantation, or dwelling house to give, or order such slave or servant ten lashes on his or her bare back.

Section 15. Riots, routs, unlawful assemblies, trespass and seditious speeches, by any slave or slaves, servant or servants, shall be punished with stripes, at the discretion of a Justice of the Peace, not exceeding thirty-nine, and he who will may apprehend and carry him, her or them before such Justice.

Section 16. If any person shall harbor any servant or slave of color, who is bound to service, without the consent of his or her master first obtained, he or she so offending, shall be fined in any sum not exceeding one hundred dollars, at the discretion of the court, to be recovered by indictment or information; and if any person shall aid and assist any servant, or slave to abscond from his or her master, upon conviction thereof, he or she so offending, shall be fined in any sum not exceeding five hundred dollars, at the discretion of the court, for the use of the party aggrieved, to be recovered as aforesaid.

NUMBER 3

An act concerning the introduction of Negroes and mulattoes into this Territory. [This law also applied to Illinois, a member of the Indiana Territory.] Approved September 17, 1807, Laws of the Indiana Territory.

Section 1. It shall and may be lawful for any person being the owner or possessor of any negroes or mulattoes of and above the age of fifteen years, and owing service and labor as slaves in any of the states or territories of the United States, or for any citizen of the said states or territories purchasing the same, to bring the said negroes or mulattoes into this territory.

Section 2. The owner or possessor of any negroes or mulattoes, as aforesaid, and bringing the same into this Territory, shall within thirty days after such removal, go with the same before the clerk of the court of Common Pleas of the proper county, and in the presence of the said clerk, the said owner or possessor shall determine and agree to and with his or her negro or mulatto, upon the term of years, which the said negro or mulatto will and shall serve his or her said owner or possessor, and the said clerk is hereby authorized and required to make a record thereof in a book which he shall keep for that purpose.

Section 3. If any negro or mulatto removed into this Territory as aforesaid, shall refuse to serve his or her owner as aforesaid, it shall and may be lawful for such person, within sixty days thereafter to remove the said negro or mulatto to any place, which by the laws of the United States, or territory, from whence such owner or possessor may or shall be authorized to remove the same.

Section 4. If any persons shall neglect or refuse to perform the duty required in the second, or to take advantage of the benefit of the preceding section hereof within the time therein respectively prescribed such person or persons shall forfeit all claim and right whatever, to the service and labor of such negroes or mulattoes.

Section 5. Any person removing into this territory, and being the owner or possessor of any negro or mulatto, as aforesaid under the age of fifteen years, or if any person shall hereafter acquire a property in any negro or mulatto under the age aforesaid, and who shall bring them into this territory; it shall and may be lawful for such person, owner or possessor to hold the said negro or mulatto to service or labor, the male until they arrive at the age of thirty-five, and the females until they arrive at the age of thirty two years.

Section 6. Any person removing any negro or mulatto into this territory, under the authority of the preceding sections, it shall be incumbent on such person within thirty days thereafter, to register the name and age of such negro or mulatto, with the clerk of the court of Common pleas, for the proper county.

Section 7. If any person shall remove any negro or mulatto from any one county to another county within this Territory, who may or shall be brought into the same under the authority of either the first or fifth sections hereof it shall be incumbent on such person to register the same, and also the name and age of the said negro or mulatto, with the said Clerk of the county, from whence, and to which such negro or mulatto may be removed, within thirty days after such removal.

Section 8. If any person shall neglect, or refuse to perform the duty required by the two preceding sections hereof, such person for such offence, shall be fined in the sum of fifty dollars, to be removed by indictment or information, and for the use of the property county.

Section 9. If any person shall neglect or refuse to perform the duty and service herein required, he shall for every such neglect or refusal, be fined in the sum of fifty dollars, to be recovered by information or indictment, and for the use of the county.

Section 10. It shall be the duty of the clerk of the court of Common Pleas aforesaid, when any person shall apply to him to register any negro or mulatto, agreeably to the preceding section, to demand and receive the said applicants bond, with sufficient security in the penalty of five hundred dollars, payable to the governor or his successor in office, conditioned that the negro or mulatto, negroes or mulattoes, as the case may be, shall not after the expiration of his or her time of service, become a county charge, which bond be lodged with the county treasurers respectively, for the use of the said counties: Provided always, That no such bond shall be required or requirable, in case the time of service of such negro or mulatto, shall expire before he or she arrives at the age of forty years; if such negro or mulatto, be at that time capable to support him or herself, by his or her own labor.

Section 11. Any person who shall forcibly take or carry out of this territory, or who shall be aiding or assisting therein any person or persons owing or having owed service or labor, without the consent of such person or persons, previously obtained, before any Judge of the court of Common Pleas of the county, where such person owing, or having owed such service or labor resides, which consent shall be certified by said Judge of the Common Pleas, to the Clerk of the court of Common Pleas, where he resides, at or before the next court, any person so offending, upon conviction thereof, shall forfeit and pay one thousand dollars; one third to the use of the county, and two thirds to the use of the person so taken or carried away, to be recovered by action of debt, or on the case: Provided, That there shall be nothing in this section so construed as to prevent any master or mistress from removing any person owing service or labor, from this territory, as described in the third section of this act.

Section 12. The said Clerk for every register made in manner aforesaid, shall receive seventy-five cents from the applicant therefor.

Section 13. The children born in this territory of a parent of color, owing service or labor by indenture, according to law, shall serve the master or mistress of such parent, the male until the age of thirty, and the female until the age of twenty-eight years.

Section 14. The provisions contained in a law of the territory, respecting apprentices, entitled "An act respecting apprentices," shall be in force, as to such children, in case of this misbehavior of the master or mistress, or for cruelty or ill usage.

IV

Suffrage and Election

The election policy of Indiana is one example of the state's pattern of racial discrimination. The state declared all elections to be free and equal, yet it enfranchised white males only. Along with blacks, the state disfranchised persons considered to have no stake in the community, including soldiers, women, and transients. Excerpts from the state constitutions of 1816 and 1851 describe Indiana's suffrage policy. From this perspective, Indiana was typical in its election laws. Most states, especially those organized before 1800, were cautious when assigning suffrage rights. This does not excuse Indiana, however; rather, it shows that discrimination was widespread in the United States.

NUMBER 1

Constitution of Indiana, Article 6, 1816.

Section 1. In all elections, not otherwise provided for by this constitution, every white male citizen of the United States, of the age of twenty-one years and upwards, who has resided in the state one year immediately preceding such election, shall be entitled to vote, in the county where he resides; except such as shall be enlisted in the army of the United States, or their allies.

NUMBER 2

Constitution of Indiana, Article 2, 1851.

Section 1. All elections shall be free and equal.

Section 2. In all elections, not otherwise provided for by this Constitution, every white male citizen of the United States, of the age of twenty-one years and upwards, who shall have resided in the State during the six months immediately preceding such election; and every white male, of foreign birth, of the age of twenty-one years and upwards, who shall have resided in the United States one year, and shall have resided in this State during the six months immediately preceding such election, and shall have declared his intention to become a citizen of the United States, conformably to the laws of the United States on the subject of naturalization, shall be entitled to vote in the township or precinct where he may reside.

Section 3. No soldier, seaman, or marine, in the army or navy of the United States, or of their allies, shall be deemed to have acquired a residence in the State, in consequence of having been stationed within the same; nor shall any such soldier, seaman, or marine have the right to vote.

Section 4. No person shall be deemed to have lost his residence in the State by reason of his absence, either on business of this State or of the United States.

Section 5. No Negro or Mulatto shall have the right to suffrage.

V

Militia Policy

The state of Indiana closed its militia organization to African Americans. The constitutions of 1816 and 1851 authorized only "able-bodied" white males to enlist in the militia. Remarkably, the state legislature did not enact this policy. There was no doubt, however, that the state constitution carried the force of law, and African Americans in Indiana would not carry weapons as soldiers until the Civil War. Why would the state bar blacks from the militia when African Americans had fought in colonial wars and the American Revolutionary War? It is likely because state militia organizations were reserved as clubs for white men. Its members received privileges and immunities denied to other whites. Consequently, it is not surprising that Indiana denied African Americans access to the "high calling" of the militia, a para-military organization.

NUMBER 1

Constitution of Indiana, Article 7, 1816.

Section 1. The militia of the state of Indiana shall consist of all free, able-bodied male persons, negroes, mulattoes, and Indians excepted, resident in the said state, between the ages of eighteen and forty-five years; except such persons as now are, or hereafter may be, exempted by the laws of the United States, or of this state; and shall be armed, equipped, and trained, as the general assembly may provide by law.

NUMBER 2

Constitution of Indiana, Article 12, 1851.

Section 1. The militia shall consist of all able-bodied white male persons, between the ages of eighteen and forty-five years, except such as may be exempted by the laws of the United States, or of this state; and shall be organized, officered, armed, equipped, and trained in such a manner as may be provided by law.

VI

Immigration and Residency

For enslaved African Americans in Southern states, Indiana must have been seen as a haven. After all, territorial and state law prohibited slavery. Indiana lawmakers, however, did not consider slaves who crossed into its borders refugees. They were fugitives; or worse, they were considered slaves. The immigration and residency laws of the state reinforced this policy. Consequently, Indiana voided any contract made by an immigrating black, unless the person satisfied the state's rigid immigration and residency policy. A slave holder could legally bring enslaved blacks into the state, but state law compelled free blacks to prove their freedom. Consequently, it was easier for a slave to become a resident of Indiana than a free black. As the following documents, will show, neither free nor enslaved blacks benefitted from the state's civil rights laws.

NUMBER 1

An act concerning the introduction of Negroes and mulattoes into this Territory. (This law also applied to Illinois, a part of the Indiana territory.) Approved August 26, 1805, Laws of the Indiana Territory.

Section 1. Be it enacted by the Legislative Council and House of Representatives, and it is hereby enacted by the authority of the same, That it shall and may be lawful for any person being the owner or possessor of any negroes or mulattoes of and above the age of fifteen years, and owing service and labor as slaves in either of the states or territories of the United States, or for any citizen of the said states or territories purchasing the same, to bring the said negroes or mulattoes into this territory.

Section 2. That the owner or possessor of any negroes or mulattoes, as aforesaid, and bringing the same into this territory, shall within thirty days after such removal, go with the same before the clerk of the court of common pleas of the proper county, and in the presence of the said clerk the said owner or possessor shall determine and agree to and with his or her negro or mulatto upon the term of years which the said negro or mulatto will and shall serve his or her said owner or possessor, and the said clerk is hereby authorized and required to make a record thereof, in a book which he shall keep for the purpose.

Section 3. That if any negro or mulatto removed into this territory as aforesaid, shall refuse to serve his or her owner as aforesaid, it shall and may be lawful for such person within sixty days thereafter, to remove the said negro or mulatto to any place, which by the laws of the United States, or territory from whence such owner or possessor may or shall be authorized to remove the same.

Section 4. That if any person or persons shall neglect or refuse to perform the duty required in the second, or to take advantage of the benefit of the preceding section hereof, within the time therein respectively prescribed, such person or persons, shall forfeit all claim and right whatever, to the service and labor, of such negroes or mulattoes.

Section 5. That any person removing into this territory, and being the owner or possessor of any negro or mulatto as aforesaid, under the age of fifteen years, or if any person shall hereafter acquire a property in any negro or mulatto under the age aforesaid, and who shall bring them into this territory, it shall and may be lawful for such person, owner or possessor, to hold the said negro or mulatto to service and labor, the males, until they arrive at the age of thirty five, and the females, until they arrive at the age of thirty two years.

Section 6. Any person removing any negro or mulatto into this territory under the authority of the preceding sections, it shall be incumbent on such person within thirty days thereafter, to register the name and age of such negro or mulatto, with the clerk of the court of common pleas of the proper county.

Section 7. That if any person shall remove any negro or mulatto from one county to another county within this territory, who may or shall be brought into the same under the authority of either the first or fifth sections hereof, it shall be incumbent on such person to register the same, and also the name and age of the said negro or mulatto with the said clerk of the county from whence, and to which such negro or mulatto may be removed within thirty days after such removal.

Section 8. That if any person shall neglect or refuse to perform the duty required by the two preceding sections hereof, such person for such offence, shall be fined in the sum of fifty dollars, to be recovered by indictment or information, and for the use of the proper county.

Section 9. That if any clerk shall neglect or refuse to perform the duty and service herein required, he shall for every such neglect or refusal be fined in the sum of 50 dollars to be recovered by information or indictment & for the use of the county.

Section 10. And be it further enacted, That it shall be the duty of the clerk of the court of common pleas aforesaid, when any person shall apply to him to register any mulatto or negro agreeably to the preceding section to demand and receive the said applicant's bond with sufficient security in the penalty of five hundred dollars, payable to the governor or his successor in office, conditioned that the said mulatto or negro, or mulattoes or negroes as the case may be, shall not after the expiration of his or her time of service become a county charge, which bond shall be lodged with the county treasurers respectively, for the use of the said counties; provided always, that no such bond shall be lodged with the county treasurers respectively, for the use of the said counties; provided always, that no such negro or mulatto shall expire before he or she arrives at the age of forty years, if such negro or mulatto, be at that time capable, him or herself, by his or her own labor.

Section 11. Any person who shall forcibly take or carry out of this territory, or who shall be aiding or assisting therein, any person or persons, owing, or having owed service or labor, without the consent of such person or persons, previously obtained before any judge of the court of common pleas, of the county where such person owing, or having owed such service or labor resides which consent shall be certified by said judge of the common pleas, to the clerk of the court of common pleas where he resides, at, or before the next court, any person so offending, upon conviction thereof, shall forfeit and pay one thousand dollars, one third to the use of the county, and two thirds to the use of the person so taken or carried away, to be recovered by action of debt, or on the case; Provided, That there shall be nothing in this section so construed, as to prevent any master or mistress from removing any person owing service or labor from this territory, as described in the third section of this action.

Section 12. That the said clerk, for registry made in manner aforesaid, shall receive seventy five cents from the applicant therefor.

Section 13. And be it further enacted, That the children born in this territory of a parent of color, owing service or labor by indenture according to law, shall serve the master or mistress of such parent, the males, until the age of thirty, and the females, until the age of twenty eight years.

Section 14. And be it further enacted, That the provisions contained in a law of this territory respecting apprentices, and passed at this session of the legislature, shall be in force as to such children in case of the misbehavior of the master or mistress, or for cruelty or ill usage. This act shall be in force from the passage thereof.

NUMBER 2

An Act concerning Free Negroes and Mulattoes, Servants and Slaves. Approved February 10, 1810, Laws of Indiana.

Section 1. Be it enacted by the General Assembly of the state of Indiana that from and after the first day of September next, no black or mulatto person coming or brought into this state, shall be permitted to reside therein, unless bond with good and sufficient security be given on behalf of such person of color, to approved of by the overseers of the poor of some township in this state, payable to the state of Indiana, in the penal sum of five hundred dollars, conditioned that such person shall not at any time become a charge to the said county in which said bond shall be given, nor to any other county in this state, as also for such person's good behavior; which bond shall be filed in the clerk's office of the county where the same may be taken. And a conviction of such negro or mulatto, of any crime or misdemeanor against the penal laws of this state, shall amount to a forfeiture of the condition of such bond: Provided, That on any suit brought upon such bond for the penalty thereof, a less sum than the penalty, may, in the discretion of the jury trying such action, be assessed against any defendant or defendants, by way of damages.

Section 2. If any negro or mulatto coming into this state as aforesaid, shall fail to comply with the provisions of the first section of this act, it shall be and is hereby made the duty of the overseers of the poor, in any township where such negro or mulatto may be found, to summon him, her or them, to appear before some justice of the peace, to show cause why he, she or they shall not comply with the provisions of this act; which summons shall be issued by a justice of the peace, on the application of any overseer of the poor in this state, and shall be executed by the proper constable. And if such negro or mulatto shall still fail to give the bond security required by the first section of this act, after being brought before such justice as aforesaid; it shall be the duty of the overseers of the poor of such township, to hire out such negro or mulatto for six months, for the best price in cash that can be had. The proceeds arising from such hiring shall be paid into the county treasury of the proper county, for the use of such negro or mulatto, in such manner as shall be directed by the overseers of the poor aforesaid: Provided however, That it shall be lawful for the overseers of the poor, to remove such negro or mulatto, out of the jurisdiction of this state, in the same manner and under the same rules and the regulations as are pointed out in the act for the relief of the poor, instead of hiring such negro or mulatto out, at the discretion of said overseers.

Section 3. Any sheriff or jailer, who shall hereafter commit or suffer to be committed to prison, any negro or mulatto, without a lawful warrant, or being otherwise authorized by law for that purpose, or under the provisions of this act, shall be fined, upon presentment or indictment, in any sum not less than one hundred, nor more than five hundred dollars.

Section 4. Should any person or persons knowingly engage or hire, or harbor such negro or mulatto hereafter coming or being brought into this state, without such colored person first complying with the provisions of this act, such person or persons so offending, shall pay a fine of not less than five, nor more than one hundred dollars, to be recovered by presentment or indictment.

Section 5. That the right of any person or persons to pass through this state, with his, her or their negroes or mulattoes, servant or servants, when emigrating or travelling to any other state or territory, or country, making no unnecessary delay, is hereby declared and secured.

NUMBER 3

An act to repeal the act entitled "An act for the introduction of Negroes and mulattoes into this territory, and for other purposes." Approved December 14, 1810, Laws of Indiana.

Section 1. Be it enacted by the Legislative Council and House of Representatives of Indiana Territory, and it is hereby enacted by the authority of the same, That the act of this territory entitled "An act for the introduction of negroes and mulattoes into this territory," approved on the seventeenth day of September, eighteen hundred and seven, be, and the same is hereby repealed.

Section 2. And be it further enacted, That if any person or persons shall attempt to remove from this territory, or shall aid or assist in removing any negro or mulatto person or persons, without first proving before one of the Judges of the court of Common Pleas, or Justice of the Peace, who shall give a certificate thereof, to be filed in the Clerk's office in the county wherein such proof shall be made, that he, she or they are legally entitled so to do according to the laws of the United States and of this territory, shall, on conviction thereof before any court having cognizance thereof, forfeit and pay the sum of one thousand dollars, one half to the use of the informer, and the other half to the use of the territory, to be recovered by action of debt or indictment, and shall be moreover liable to the action of the party grieved, and shall be forever disqualified from holding any office of honor, profit, or trust under this territory.

Section 3. And be it further enacted, That the first section of the law of this territory, entitled "An act concerning servants of color," be, and the same is hereby repealed, saving however to such persons as may heretofore have executed indentures of servitude, their right under the same, and the master his remedy thereon.

NUMBER 4

Constitution of Indiana, Article 13, 1851.

Section 1. No Negro or Mulatto shall come into, or settle in, the State, after the adoption of this Constitution.

Section 2. All contracts made with any Negro or Mulatto coming into the State, contrary to the provisions of the foregoing section, shall be void; and any person, who shall employ such Negro or Mulatto, or otherwise encourage him to remain in the State, shall be fined in any sum not less than ten dollars, nor more than five hundred dollars.

Section 3. All fines which may be collected for a violation of the provisions of this article, or of any law which may hereafter be passed for the purpose of carrying the same into the execution, shall be set apart and appropriated for the colonization of such Negroes and Mulattoes, and their descendants, as may be in the State at the adoption of this Constitution, and may be willing to emigrate.

Section 4. The General Assembly shall pass laws to carry out the provisions of this article.

NUMBER 5

An act to enforce the 13th Article of the Constitution. Approved June 18, 1852, Revised Statutes.

Section 1. Be it enacted by the General Assembly of the State of Indiana, That it shall not be lawful for any negro or mulatto to come into, settle in, or become an inhabitant of the state.

Section 2. The clerks of the several circuit courts in this state shall give notice, by publication in the newspaper published in their respective counties having the greater circulation, and if no newspaper be published therein, then by printed hand-bills posted up in three of the most public places in each township of such county, requiring all negroes and mulattoes who were inhabitants of the state prior to the first day of November, A.D. 1851, and entitled to reside therein, to appear before him for registry.

Section 3. It shall be the duty of each clerk of the said circuit courts to provide a suitable book, to be called the register of negroes and mulattoes, in which he shall record the name, age description, place of birth and residence of each and every mulatto who may present himself or herself before him for the purpose of being registered, and, also, the names of the witnesses by whom the right of such negro or mulatto to reside in the State of Indiana shall have been proven.

Section 4. The clerk of the said circuit court, when any negro or mulatto shall come before him for the purpose of being registered, shall have power to cause to come before him such witnesses as may be necessary to prove the right of inhabitation of such negro or mulatto, by process of subpoena, and shall proceed to hear and determine the right of such negro or mulatto.

Section 5. When the right of any such negro or mulatto shall have been proven to the satisfaction of such clerk he shall register the said negro or mulatto in his register of negroes and mulattoes, and shall also issue to such negro or mulatto a certificate, under the seal of the said court and attested by such clerk, setting forth the facts contained in such register; which certificate shall be conclusive evidence of the facts therein stated in all prosecutions against the employers of negroes or mulattoes, unless it is shown that said employer had notice that the same was obtained by fraud or other undue means, or was not genuine, and the same shall be prima facie evidence only in all other cases, and shall be issued to such negro or mulatto without charge.

Section 6. All contracts made with negroes or mulattoes who shall have come into the State of Indiana subsequent to the first day of November A.D. 1851, are hereby declared null and void.

Section 7. Any person who shall employ a negro or mulatto who shall have come into the State of Indiana subsequent to the thirty-first day of October in the year one thousand eight hundred and fifty-one, or shall hereafter come into said state, or who shall encourage such negro or mulatto to remain in the state, shall be fined in any sum not less than ten dollars nor [more] than five hundred dollars.

Section 8. This act shall apply only to contracts made with negroes and mulattoes subsequent to the passage of this act.

Section 9. Any negro or mulatto who shall come into or settle in this state contrary to, and in violation of the provisions of the constitution, and of the first section of this act, shall be fined in any sum less than ten, nor more than five hundred dollars.

VII

Miscegenation Laws

Although interracial marriage violated all social conventions developed by whites, blacks and whites sometimes overstepped these customs. The exact number of interracial marriages in pre-Civil War Indiana is unknown. The state assembly considered such marriages a significant problem. The Amalgamation Act proscribed intercourse and any sort of cohabitation between blacks and whites. It also provided penalties for violators, including the persons who might perform such marriages. The statute required that newspapers print the state's declaration against interracial marriages. The problem was not easily solved, however. The following documents will show repeated efforts to stamp out interracial sex in Indiana.

NUMBER 1

An act to prohibit the amalgamation of whites and blacks.
Approved February 24, 1840, General Laws of Indiana.

Section 1. Be it enacted by the General Assembly of the State of Indiana, That hereafter no negro man, mulatto, or any man having one-eighth part of negro blood, shall be permitted to marry any white woman of this State; nor shall any white man be permitted to marry any black woman, mulatto, or any woman having one-eighth part of negro blood.

Section 2. No clerk of this State shall issue any marriage license to any such persons named in the first section of this act, under pain of a fine of not less than five hundred, nor more than five thousand dollars for each offence, to be recovered by presentment or indictment in the proper circuit court. And said shall work a forfeiture of his office.

Section 3. All such marriages, as are prohibited by this act, shall be null and void.

Section 4. Each and every person who shall aid, counsel, abet, or in any manner be known to assist in any such marriage as is by this act prohibited, shall be subject to a fine of not less than one hundred nor more than one thousand dollars, to be recovered as aforesaid.

Section 5. Each and every person who shall marry in contravention to the provisions of this act, shall be subject to a fine of not less than one thousand, nor more than five thousand dollars, and be confined in the State's prison for not less than ten nor more than twenty years.

Section 6. Any officer of this State, or minister of the gospel, who shall celebrate the bands of matrimony in cases prohibited by this act, shall be subject to a fine, if a minister, of not less than one thousand nor more than ten thousand dollars, to be recovered as aforesaid; and an officer, he shall be subject to a fine of not less than five hundred nor more than five thousand dollars, to be recovered as aforesaid, and such offence shall work a forfeiture of his office.

Section 7. This act shall be in force from and after its publication in the Indiana Journal and Democrat, and it is hereby respectfully requested that each and every newspaper in this State publish this act free of charge, that the world may know our laws upon this subject.

NUMBER 2

An act defining felonies and prescribing punishment thereof. Approved June 10, 1852, Revised Statutes.

Section 47. No person having one eighth part or more of negro blood shall be permitted to marry any white woman of this state, nor shall any white man be permitted to marry any negro woman, or any woman having one eighth part or more of negro blood, and every person who shall knowingly marry in violation of the provisions of this section, shall upon conviction thereof, be imprisoned in the state's prison not less than one, nor more than ten years, and be fined not less than one thousand nor more than five thousand dollars.

NUMBER 3

An act defining misdemeanors and prescribing punishment thereof. Approved June 14, 1852, Revised Statutes.

Section 39. Every person who shall knowingly counsel, or assist in any manner, in any marriage between any person having one eighth part or more of negro blood, and any white person, shall be fined not less than one hundred, nor more than one thousand dollars.

NUMBER 4

An act declaratory of the law regulating marriages, and enforcing the provisions thereof by proper penalties. Approved March 5, 1852. Revised Statutes.

Section 1. Be it enacted by the General Assembly of the State of Indiana, That marriage is declared to be a civil contract into which males of the age of seventeen and females of the age of fourteen, not within the prohibited degrees of consanguinity, are capable of entering.

Section 2. The following marriages are declared void:

First. When either party had a wife or husband living at the time of such marriage.

Second. When one of the parties is a white person, and the other possessed of one-eighth or more of negro blood.

Third. When either party is insane or idiotic, at the time of such marriage.

Section 3. Marriages may be solemnized by ministers of the gospel and priests of every church throughout the state, judges of courts of record, and justices of the peace, within their respective counties, by the Society of Friends, and German Baptists, according to the rules of their societies; Provided, That no marriage, legal in other respects, shall be void on account of the incapacity of the person solemnizing the same.

Section 4. Before any persons, except member of the Society of Friends, shall be joined in marriage, they shall produce a license from the clerk of the circuit court of the county in which the female resides, directed to any person empowered by law to solemnize marriages, and authorizing him to join together the persons therein named, as husband and wife.

NUMBER 5

Domestic relations: marriages. Revised statutes, 1843.

Section 4. No white person shall intermarry with a negro or mulatto, and no insane person or idiot shall be capable of contracting marriage.

Section 19. If any person empowered to solemnize marriage shall join any persons in marriage contrary to the provisions of this article, knowing that the marriage is not duly authorized, he shall, upon conviction thereof upon indictment in any court having jurisdiction, be fined in any sum not exceeding five hundred dollars, and costs of suit; and shall moreover be declared forever after incapable of solemnizing marriages.

Section 22. All marriages which are prohibited by law, on account of consanguinity or affinity between the parties, or on account of either having a former wife or husband then living; all marriages between a white person and a negro or mulatto, if solemnized within this state, shall be absolutely void without any decree of divorce or other legal proceeding.

Section 44. No negro man, or person having one eighth part or more of negro blood, shall be permitted to marry any white women of this state; nor shall any white man be permitted to marry any negro woman, or any woman having one eighth part or more negro blood; and each and every person who shall knowingly marry in violation of the provisions of this section, shall, upon conviction thereof, be imprisoned at hard labor in the state prison for not less than one year nor more than ten years, and be fined in any sum not less than one thousand dollars nor more than five thousand dollars.

Section 112. Every person who shall knowingly aid, counsel, abet, or assist in any way or manner whatever in any marriage between any negro and white person, or between any person having one eighth part or more of negro blood and any white person, shall, upon conviction thereof, be fined in any sum not less than one hundred dollars nor more than one thousand dollars.

NUMBER 6

An act to amend an act entitled, "An act to amend the first section of an act concerning real property, and the alienation thereof, Approved May 6, 1852," and to legalize conveyances made by Indians, Negroes and mulattoes, and other persons of mixed blood, Approved May 2, 1859. Laws of Indiana.

Section 1. Be it enacted by the General Assembly of the State of Indiana, That said act, which reads as follows, to-wit: "That section first of an act entitled, 'an act concerning real property and the alienation thereof,' approved May 6, 1852, which reads as follows, to-wit: "That no person except a citizen of the United States, or an alien who shall be at the time a bona fide resident of the United States, shall take, hold, convey, devise or pass by descent lands, except in such cases of descent or devise as are provided for by law: And provided, further, That the marriage of a woman with an alien, and her residence with her husband in a foreign State or country, shall not bar her right to hold, convey, devise and pass by descent lands which may come to her by descent or purchase," be amended as to read as follows:

That no person except a citizen of the United States, or an alien who shall be at the time a bona fide resident of the United States, or an Indian, or a negro or mulatto, or other person of mixed blood, shall take, hold, convey, devise or pass by descent lands, except in such cases of descent or devise as are provided for by law: And provided further, That the marriage of a woman with an alien, and her residence with her husband in a foreign State or country, shall not bar her right to hold, convey, devise and pass by descent lands which may have come to her by descent or purchase.

Section 2. That all bona fide sales, conveyances, purchases and devises heretofore made by any Indian, negro or mulatto or other person of mixed blood, and all estates heretofore acquired by any Indian, negro, mulatto or other person of mixed blood, by conveyance, devise or descent, be and the same are hereby legalized, and such tenants are hereby declared to hold the same as fully and to the same extent as though there was no disability to the contrary: Provided, That nothing herein contained shall affect any suit or proceeding now pending in any of the courts of this State.

Section 3. Whereas, an emergency for the immediate taking effect of this act exists, the same is hereby declared to be in force from and after its passage.

VIII

Taxation and Enumeration

Blacks did not benefit from welfare programs administered by Indiana. The state counted only poor whites when determining appropriations for charity or apportioning representatives to the assembly. Unlike the federal Constitution which considered African Americans in terms of a ratio, three-fifths of free persons, Indiana law exempted blacks from such enumeration. The state also exempted blacks from paying taxes to fund social programs. Consequently, the state conducted its policy of social engineering as if black people did not reside in Indiana. As these documents suggest, philanthropic organizations provided welfare to aid the black poor. Later, the legislature provided state funds to assist those associations. In spite of these initiatives, African Americans remained outside of the mainstream in Indiana society well into the twentieth century.

NUMBER 1

An act to provide for taking the enumeration of the white male inhabitants, above the age of twenty-one years, in this state. Approved February 7, 1840, General laws of Indiana, (1839).

Section 1. Be it enacted by the General Assembly of the State of Indiana, That on or before the twenty-fifth day of November next, it shall be the duty of each and every clerk of the circuit court, within and for their respective counties, under the seal of their said courts, to certify to the Secretary of State, the whole number of white male paupers, and insane persons, and persons exempt from a poll tax, who are not certified to the Auditor of Public Accounts, that belong to, or are inhabitants of their several counties, together with the number furnished by the list of the collector, in pursuance of the provisions of the fifth section of this act.

Section 2. It shall be the duty of the Auditor of Public Accounts, on or before the first Monday in December next, to certify to the Secretary of State, the whole number of polls returned from each county for the present year.

Section 3. That it shall be the duty of the Secretary of State, on the second Monday of the next session of the General Assembly to furnish the Speaker of the House of Representatives, and the President of the Senate each, for the inspection of their respective Houses, with a certified statement, exhibiting the whole number returned from each county, agreeably to the provisions of this act.

Section 4. That if the clerk of any circuit court, the Auditor of Public Accounts, Secretary of State, or collector of any county, shall refuse to discharge the duties enjoined upon them in this act, he or they so offending, shall forfeit and pay, for the use of the proper county seminary, the sum of fifty dollars, to be recovered by presentment or indictment in any court having jurisdiction thereof.

Section 5. It shall be the duty of the several collectors of the State and county tax, up to the twenty-fifth day of November next, to take a list of all the white male inhabitants above the age of twenty-one years, that may not have been entered on the list of taxables, whether the same be subject to the payment of tax or not, and to enter their names alphabetically, in a book to be kept for that purpose, which book shall be returned by the collector, to the clerk of the circuit court of the proper county, on or before the twentieth day of November, 1840, whose duty it shall be forthwith to certify the whole number so returned, including those enumerated in the first section of this act, to the Secretary of State. And the board doing county business shall allow to such collectors a reasonable compensation for such services, to be paid out of the county treasury of their respective counties.

Section 6. In addition to the duties herein before required, it shall be the duty of the clerks aforesaid, forthwith after the said twentieth day of November next, to make and furnish the senator, or some one of the representatives of the proper county, with a certificate, certifying under his hand and seal of the circuit court, the whole number of polls, paupers, insane persons, persons exempt from poll tax, and persons returned by the collector as aforesaid, which certificate shall be handed over by said senator or representative, to the Secretary of State, within the first week of the next General Assembly.

Section 7. In all cases where counties have territories attached thereto, or have jurisdiction over any new county, which is unorganized, it shall be the duty of the several officers whose services are required in the aforementioned returns, severally to keep, make out, or transmit, as the case may be, separately, the numbers in said attached territory, or new county, and be governed in all other respects by the provisions of this act.

Section 8. This act to take effect and be in force from and after the first day of May next.

NUMBER 2

An act to amend section three of "An act supplemental to an act concerning the organization and perpetuity of voluntary associations," and repealing an act entitled "An act concerning the organization of voluntary associations," and repealing former laws in reference thereto, Approved February 12, 1855. Approved March 21, 1879, Laws of Indiana.

Section 1. Be it enacted by the General Assembly of the State of Indiana, That section three of said act be amended so as to read as follows: Section 2. In administering the charity of any association, organized as herein contemplated, no distinction shall be made in selecting the objects of its care on account of the nativity of such orphan, and no orphan shall be excluded from the benefits of such association on account of its religious or political associations or connections. And associations formed for the purpose of maintaining an asylum for colored orphan children, exclusively, shall be entitled to the allowance provided for in this act, and under its provisions for each colored orphan child cared for and maintained by such association.

Section 3. Inasmuch as an emergency exists, requiring the immediate taking effect of this act, it shall therefore take effect and be in force from and after its passage.

IX

Colonization

Whites in the Old Northwest considered persons of African descent inferior and incapable of living peaceably among them. In lieu of slavery, which to many Northern whites was morally wrong, they proposed resettlement of the black population. Even in Indiana, where many whites had a strong interest in slavery, a large number of them favored colonization. Whites were less concerned with the destination of resettled blacks than they were with their removal, which they hoped would diminish the immigration of black refugees from the South. Colonization societies sprang up in the state, and the legislature appropriated funds to implement the scheme. By 1865, however, the whites recognized that colonization was impractical. Unscrupulous agents obtained salaries from the state but provided little service. It is not surprising that state supported policies to expatriate blacks virtually disappeared after the Civil War.

NUMBER 1

Colonization. Senate Journal, (1829-1830).

The colonization of free blacks, dispersed through our country in the native land of their fathers, is passing the ordeal of philanthropic reflection, and gradually rising to public view, under the patronage of the American Colonization Society. No period in the annals of our history, would be hailed with more universal acclamation, than that one, which shall accomplish the return of these long degraded and unhappy members of the human family, to the country in which their God has placed them; from which they have been oppressively torn by the hand of tyranny, to gratify the most sacrilegious cupidity. We long to celebrate the jubilee of freedom--of general and unconditional emancipation, of every soul held in bondage, because his skin is dark. We look forward, with fervent hope, to the important era, when we shall see them wending their way across the atlantic, bearing with them the religion of the cross, and the eternal principles of liberty and equality, to a country where they may organize a government of their choice, and take their stable stand among the nations of the earth. But this is not the work of a day. And if in attempting to identify the colonization and emancipation of our colored population with the politics of the country, as a popular hobby, before the public mind and resources are prepared to yield to the good work, their effectual sanction, we shall touch the sensitive chord with too bold a hand, so as to endanger our magna charta, the great cause in hand, and the union, and thus effect the overthrow of our own liberties, the premature zeal affected on the subject must be long a fruitful source of perpetual lamentation. If there were no latent intention in the end, of levying a tax upon the free States, for the purchase of slaves, or in some other way, forcing a manumission--thereby strengthening the inducement and obstinacy of their holders to continue their bondage, until remuneration or compunction of conscience might reach them, they would have excited less jealousy. If, instead of this, the talent of the country were fairly enlisted to convince the people of the slave states, of what their own experience will ultimately show, that free labor is more profitable than slave labor, so as to produce a voluntary abandonment of the unnatural and unchris[tian] practice, without looking to the treasury of the nation, and the consequent introduction before Congress, of a question more dangerous to the constitution than enemy we have ever yet encountered, ten[d]ing to incite the blacks to the perpetration of the most horrid insurrections and murders, means would have, ere this, flowed into the coffers of the society in greater profusion. With such modifications, distrust would give place to general support; and the next generation might be saved the mortifying spectacle, of beholding the manacled African writhing in his fetters, in the temple of human freedom. I lay before you, at the request of the Governors of Missouri, Georgia, and South Carolina, resolutions of those states, denying the right of the general government, by the constitution, to appropriate money for the use of the society.

Colored People in Indiana

Duty of the State of Indiana, requires me to remark, that the scourge of the oppressed is not confined, as it should be, exclusively to the land of the oppressor. But, that this State, in common with her other free sisters, is not exempt from the lash of our crying national sin. A non-productive and in many instances, a super-annuated population, is pouring in upon us possessing all the affirmative bad qualities of the uneducated immoralised bondsman, without affording any of his advantages, living without visible means, or labor--most of whom are paupers on society. This, being the consequence of expulsion of laws of other States, less humane than ours, renders corresponding measures on our part necessary and inevitable. Whilst our laws and institutions proclaim the State an asylum for the good, virtuous, and useful of all nations and colors, it is due to ourselves and the rights of posterity, that we should not tamely submit to any imposition, which is the direct effect of foreign legislation. Though it might savor somewhat of injustice to interfere with any that are already here, it will still become your province as it is your right to regulate for the future, by prompt correctives, the emigration into the State, and the continuance of known paupers, thrown upon us from any quarter. Such, if they cannot afford, by sureties, indemnity to our citizens in a reasonable time, should be thrown back into the State or country from whence they came. To effect this, it may be proper to require them, on entering the State, to file a proclamation of particulars with evidence. No terms, however, should be demanded which could not, in the nature of things be complied with. For to those of them who will fill up the measure of duties of good citizens, the land of fellowship should be offered; and to such a proper and necessary portion of the citizens' privileges should be extended, that they may have some inducements to the performance of virtuous deeds. But shorn as they now are, of every incentive of the kind, they can do but little more than agonize in silent despair.

NUMBER 2

An act authorizing the state librarian to send surplus copies of public documents to Liberia. Approved January 21, 1850, Indiana Acts (1850).

Section 1. Be it enacted by the General Assembly of the State of Indiana, That the State Librarian be and he is hereby authorized to hand over to the agent of the American Colonization Society, a single copy of any surplus public documents now in the library, not required by the present and future wants of the State, for the purpose of being sent to Liberia.

Section 2. This act to be in force from and after its passage.

NUMBER 3

An act providing for the colonization of Negroes and mulattoes and their descendants, and appropriating 5,000 dollars thereof, constituting a State Board of Colonization, declaring the duties of said board, and of state treasurer and county treasurer in relation thereof. Approved April 28, 1852, Revised Statutes.

Section 1. Be it enacted by the General Assembly of the State of Indiana, That for the purpose of colonizing negro and mulattoes and their descendants that were residents of this state on the first day of November, one thousand eight hundred and fifty-one, and shall continue to reside in this state, that the sum of five thousand dollars is appropriated out of the state treasury for the year one thousand eight hundred and fifty-two, [which] together with all fines collected for the violation of laws passed to carry out the provisions of article thirteen of the constitution of this state, and the voluntary contributions received for said purposes, shall constitute a state colonization fund, and be applied to the colonization in Africa of said negroes, mulattoes, and their descendants.

Section 2. Three thousand dollars of the money appropriated out of the state treasury shall be used for the purchase of land in Africa, to be styled the Indiana colony, which shall be appropriated in one hundred acre lots, to such negroes, mulattoes, and their descendants, as designated in the first section of this act, as shall emigrate from this state to Africa, and occupy such land or control the same by resident acts of ownership, and the first emigrants shall have first choice in location of certificates within said purchase, and the State Board of Colonization shall determine from what points the measurement of said lands shall commence, and issue to emigrants such certificates for location as shall secure to them their just rights, and that all colored persons that have heretofore been sent to Liberia from this state by our colonization society, shall each be entitled to a certificate entitling them to one hundred acres of land within the territory so purchased.

Section 3. The State Board of Colonization are authorized to give to each negro or mulatto that shall be entitled to the benefits of this act, who shall emigrate to Africa, when they shall need aid, for said purpose, the sum of fifty dollars out of the state colonization fund, and said board shall determine the right of applicants, giving the preference to whole families when they desire it.

Section 4. The county treasurers of the several counties of this state shall receive all donations in money to aid colonization that may be offered, and take charge of all bequests by will or otherwise, of real estate, or any assets whatever, and in cases of such bequests other than money, the board of county commissioners are hereby made a board of council in reference to such bequests, and shall instruct the said treasurer to take such steps as in their judgment will make the assets bring the most in money, and as converted to pay over to the state treasurer as heretofore provided, at the time required by law they shall pay in the state revenue.

Section 5. The governor, auditor and secretary of state, shall, ex officio, constitute the State Board of Colonization, and as such have full powers, by correspondence with the officers of the republic of Liberia, or other persons, to carry out the provisions contemplated by the second section of this act, in acquiring title to land in Africa, and to do all other things contemplated they should, to carry out the provisions of this act, and shall report their proceedings to each General Assembly of the state.

Section 6. It shall be the duty of the treasurer of state to receive from the county treasurers all colonization funds paid to him by them, and to pay out all such funds upon the order of the State Board of Colonization.

NUMBER 4

An act providing for the colonization of free Negroes, making appropriations thereof, and establishing a colonization agency. Approved March 3, 1853, Revised Statutes.

Section 1. Be it enacted by the General Assembly of the State of Indiana, That the sum of five thousand dollars per annum, for the years eighteen hundred and fifty-four, be appropriated out of the treasury, for the purpose of colonization; to be expended by the state board of colonization, according to the regulations of the law of 1852; and the proper officer of said board shall report their doings relative to the expenditure of said appropriation, to the next General Assembly.

Section 2. That the state board are authorized to commission an agent, or corresponding secretary, to aid said board in the general work of colonization, the salary of which officer shall not exceed six hundred dollars per annum, and said salary shall be paid out of the amount of appropriations made for colonization purposes.

Section 3. Whereas, the whole enterprise is at a stand, an emergency is hereby declared to exist for the enactment hereby made; wherefore, the same shall be in force from and after its passage.

NUMBER 5

An act to give additional power to the State Board of Colonization. Approved March 1, 1855, Revised Statutes.

Section 1. Be it enacted by the General Assembly of the State of Indiana, That the colonization funds heretofore appropriated for the purpose of aiding colored emigrants from this state to settle in Liberia, shall be expended according to the discretion of the State Board of Colonization: Provided, That not more than sixty-five dollars per emigrant be paid for the outfit and transportation of such: And provided, That such persons have been residents of Indiana since the adoption of the revised constitution: And provided, That not more than two hundred dollars per annum be expended as a contingent fund.

Section 2. Be it further enacted, That the officers of state constituting the State Board of Colonization, shall have the power to elect such officers as they may consider necessary to carry on the enterprise, and to fix their compensation, which shall be paid out of the annual appropriation made for colonization purposes: Provided, That not more than six hundred dollars of said annual appropriation be thus annually expended. This restriction, however, does not apply to funds coming into their hands from other sources, in the expenditure of which they must be governed by a wise discretion.

Section 3. That the State Board of Colonization shall have power to negotiate with the government of Liberia for land in Africa for use and benefit of colored persons emigrating to said country from this state, on the best terms possible; and so much of the law of 1852 as restricts the board in the mode of locating said land, is hereby repealed.

Section 4. Whereas an emergency exists for the immediate taking effect of this act, therefore this act shall be in force from and after its passage and publication in the Indian State Sentinel and Journal.

NUMBER 6

Colonization Board, Office of William W. Wick, Secretary. March 8, 1864. Indiana Documents, (1862-63).

To the Board of Colonization aforesaid, the undersigned, Secretary thereof, respectfully reports as follows:

It may well be doubted whether any law, now in force, makes it my duty to make any report, at this or any other time, to your honorable Board, or to the Legislative body, or other authority. Yet with a view to bring to the notice of both the Board and the Legislature, and also of the public, which will, ere long, exercise the privilege of choosing legislators, I think it my duty to submit to all a statement of the facts, the knowledge of which, from time to time the same came to me, has led my mind to the conclusion that the colonization cause, and the laws in support thereof, have resulted in almost a total failure, which failure will probably become the more conspicuous by further lapse of time.

This is now, and for several months past has been, so apparent to me that I would have resigned my petty office but for the consideration that the law requiring the appointment of Secretary or Agent of your Board would require the appointment of a successor, and I am unable to see why I may not as well occupy the sinecure as even a more eminent citizen.

The causes which have led to the defeat of the benign intention of the Legislatures of 1852, and subsequent years, are: First and principally, a growing aspiration of the African mind, having for its object equality with the white race, not so much politically as socially. The black man cares little for the privilege of holding office, or of voting, for the reason, that so long as he is denied social consociation with whites on equal terms, the legal privileges of holding office and of exercising the right of suffrage, are valueless in his estimation; for he can see no probability of the dominant race conceding to him any station yielding a sufficient amount of either dignity or emoluments to prove and establish his social equality. Social equality on the field, on the street, on the side-walk, in the house, at the table, and in the bed, (aye even in the bridal chamber,) as well as in the church, saloon, and ball-room, and at the theater, and other places of elegant amusement, is the dream of every African, (man or woman) and, without this, political rights and all other advantages are as apples of Sodom, full of ashes and bitterness.

Africans are by no means lacking in discretion. On the contrary they are recognized, not only by the common mind familiar with the race and their idiosyncracies, but also by the learned in the sciences of physiology, psychology and phrenology, as excelling the Caucasian race in that subtlety which enables a human being to carry on and carry out designs without betraying those designs by act or signs of demonstration, until an object is fully achieved; and even then an African, unless under the influence of violent excitement, is apt to be more reticent than will be his white neighbor. So much is this the case that it may well be believed that when the young African enlists in the army to aid in putting down the rebellion, such act cannot be attributed nearly so much to his ambition to vote at elections by the side of his white neighbor, or to achieve an election to an office which the white man, being the majority, might throw to him, as to other considerations and feelings. Picture to him the certainty of one day presiding at a public meeting, of being with the Governor and Judges, and being called out for a speech, or alluded to as the learned "citizen of African descent." Or get him into a dream of pulling the gloves of his white neighbor, who is standing up to be married. Or yet better tell him that a great poet has said: "None but the brave deserve the fair."

His logic and imagination will tell him that if "None but the brave deserve the fair," it must follow that the brave do deserve the fair; and visions of Caucasian complexions, auburn and flaxen hair, and azure eyes will come before him and point him to the battle-field, where the brave may, as he thinks, win the entire vision, and away he goes, inspired by his natural feelings and ambitions very different from the ideas which ordinarily prompts the white man to seek distinction and usefulness in the field of war.

Unfortunately, the minds of the African race have been led to think much of these things, for many years past, by white men professing to be their exclusive friends, who, from a variety of positions, have made them, and kindred ideas, the theme of many an eloquent period or paragraph. These efforts of white men having increased much since the formation of the Constitution, the African mind has become obtuse to conceptions of equality with the colored race who are successfully establishing a commonwealth in Liberia, and is wide awake only to the hope of social equality with the white races of the United States. Is it, then, any wonder that since 1856 not a single application for aid in emigrating to Liberia has been made, and at most but two or three from 1852 to 1856?

The number of colored people in Indiana has greatly increased within the last few years by the advent of immigrants from the Southern States engaged.

in the rebellion. I am aware that the fact of this increase is possibly denied. In the absence of statistics, the Honorable member of the Legislature can approximate truth by comparing notes. I have stated my convictions, derived from observation and the common understanding of the masses, laying no claim to infallibility, and owing to the temporary absence in the army of the United States of a host of laborers, these immigrants obtain employment, at good wages, very readily. The facility of obtaining employment may have tended somewhat to prevent applications for the benefits of the colonization laws; but it is certain that the desire for social equality with the white race has been the principal barrier, that desire being much more rampant in the minds of those recently escaped from slavery than in the minds of those who, having been born free or emancipated when young, have learned to moderate, in some degree, their aspiration for social equality. The great bulk of the immigration of the last two years and upwards, are of those who were slaves before their immigration.

When the soldiers in the field shall return to the common walks of life--i.e., to industrial pursuits--the call for the services of those commonly called contrabands will be quite or nearly at an end. Then, or soon thereafter, there may, and probably will be, applications for the transmission to the freedom and equality of Liberia, unless it should turn out that the present war, with its events and denouement, are found sufficient to usher in that social equality which, as stated above, is the summum bonum, the heart's longing of the African race. And, in that event, all colonization effort will be a stink in the African nostril.

Whether it will be best, under the circumstances which I have stated, and which are patent to all, to finally abandon colonization effort now, or to let the laws remain till the doubtful results above stated, become certain one way or the other--that is to say, until the African race either realize or abandon the dream of social equality, which for years has been and now is its "joy all the day, and its song in the night," and which it will in secret hug to its bosom as its hope, its dream, its very life, till the course of events shall bring the same to a finality of either realization or abandonment, will be for legislative consideration.

It has been suggested by eminent white citizens, advocates of the social equality of the white and colored races above named, and by others decidedly prejudiced against the same, that whenever such social equality and the intermarriage of the two races shall become not only legal but also fashionable, instead of the way being open for carrying on further colonization effort, those colored people in Liberia, who are there by the efforts of various colonization boards and societies, will hasten to return the to United States to enjoy the privileges conferred by the new ideas above named. I see no reason for expressing a contrary opinion. Indeed I concur therein.

In the course of the last few months I have received two or three letters from gentlemen of high character, residents of this State, making inquiries touching applicants for colonization of whom they professed to have a knowledge. In responding to these inquires I inadvertently committed an error in stating the amount of aid which could be rendered to an emigrant as only fifty dollars. But a very short time afterwards I addressed other letters to the same gentlemen explaining the error, and stating the Board had authority to appropriate sixty-five dollars to each emigrant, thus placing in their hands a correction of the matter in ample time for the applicants, in the serious desire of emigrating, (if any there were) to avail themselves of the next vessel of the Colonization Society which does not sail before some time in the coming season, or of any other vessel which might set sail for Liberia in the proper season.

I never heard any more of the matter, from which the inference is natural that no one had any serious thought of emigration. The applicants may yet be heard from, and so I hope, but scarce believe.

I have been more specific in setting forth the main causes of failure, of late years, of Colonization effort, because I have seen, in the course of a half century's observation of the American people, that they are seldom at leisure to foresee any coming evil or danger, but, especially if the same be of great magnitude, it is their way to await, and deride all warnings and predictions till the coming evil smites them in the face, and then (when it is too late) they will make spasmodic or herculean efforts to ward off the evil or danger, pretty uniformly attributing the evil to any but the true cause.

NUMBER 7

An act repealing the second section of an Act, Approved March 3, 1863, entitled "An act providing for the colonization of free Negroes, making appropriations thereof, and establishing a colonization agency." Approved March 6, 1865, Laws of Indiana.

Section 1. Be it enacted by the General Assembly of the State of Indiana, That section second of an act, approved March 3, 1863, entitled "An Act providing for the colonization of Free Negroes, making appropriations therefor, and establishing a colonization agency," be, and the same is hereby, repealed.

Section 2. Whereas the Colonization Agent, appointed under the provisions of the above recited act, is drawing an annual salary without rendering any adequate service to the State, it is therefore declared that an emergency exists for the immediate taking effect of this act, and the same shall be in force and take effect from and after its passage.

X

Kidnapping

Chattel slavery was a horrific practice in the United States; it was indeed a "peculiar institution," even to slave holders. Chattel slavery denied a large segment of an entire race of people their freedom. To the others who did not become slaves, the peculiar institution robbed them of their dignity and humanity. Laws which sanctioned slavery licensed white men to literally beat black men and women. Sometimes, slave owners punished enslaved Africans at public whipping posts. What a humiliating experience this must have been for grown-up Africans. Slavery also produced the office of the professional slave catcher. Most among their rank were unscrupulous, and they frequently seized free blacks and sold them into slavery. Legislators in most free states, including Indiana, considered manstealing a violation of state law. Hence, Indiana adopted laws to protect its free black population. Beginning in 1816, Indiana lawmakers stiffened requirements that enabled slave owners, their agents, slave catchers and free-lancers to remove alleged slaves from the state. The law required them to prove ownership before a judicial officer who could approve the rendition. Without a certificate from such an official, anyone caught removing an alleged slave violated state law and could be fined or imprisoned. Indiana was not reformist on the matter of race, however. The anti-kidnapping law says more about the state's unwillingness to allow residents from another state to trample upon the laws of Indiana. The following statutes illustrate Indiana's response to the kidnapping problem.

NUMBER 1

Proclamation on kidnapping indentured and colored servants. April 6, 1804. Indiana Historical Collections, (1922).

The Governor having received information that some evil disposed persons are about to transport from the Territory, certain indented servants of Color without their Consent first had and obtained, with a design as is supposed of selling them for slaves contrary to the law and dignity of the United States, he Issued a proclamation, forbidding and strictly enjoining the persons aforesaid from carrying into Execution their nefarious and inhuman design as they shall answer the same at their peril, and at the same time requiring and Commanding all magistrates and other civil officers to exert themselves in their several capacities in giving proper and necessary relief to all persons illegally confined for the purpose above-mentioned and to secure and Bring to Justice the perpetrators for the Violation of Law and Humanity.

NUMBER 2

An act to prevent manstealing. Approved Dec. 30, 1816, Laws of Indiana.

Section 1. Be it enacted by the General Assembly of the State of Indiana, That any person or persons hereafter, who shall forcibly take or arrest, or aid or abet in forcibly taking or arresting any person or persons with a design to take him, her or them out of the state, under any pretence whatsoever, without establishing his, her or their claim, according to the laws of this state or of the United States, shall be guilty of manstealing.

Section 2. Any person or persons being duly convicted of the crime of manstealing as is described in the preceding section of this act, shall for every such offence forfeit and pay sum of not more than one thousand nor less than five hundred dollars with costs of suit, recoverable by indictment or presentment in any court of record having competent jurisdiction, for every person so taken or attempted to be taken out of this state; and shall moreover be rendered ineligible to hold any office of honor, profit or benefit within this state hereafter.

Section 3. Any person or persons of any state or territory, having any claim to the service of any person or persons within this state, shall first go to some justice of the peace within the county, or judge of the supreme circuit courts and obtain a warrant, naming and describing the person or persons, directed to any sheriff or constable of such county, when such person or persons may be found, who shall forthwith, bring such person or persons before said judge or justice of the peace, who shall hear and examine all testimony, adduced both by plaintiff and defendant: and if in the opinion of said judge or justice of the peace the plaintiff's claim be well founded, he shall recognize such person or persons so claimed to appear at the next term of the circuit court, in and for said county; where he, she or they, shall have a fair and impartial trial by a jury of said county, and if on trial as aforesaid, the verdict and judgment shall go against such person or persons, the court shall grant the person claiming, him, her or them, a certificate authorizing such claimant to carry him, her or them out of the state, and should such person or persons fail to give security, for his, her or their appearance at said court, he, she or they shall be committed to the prison of the county, until such trial be had: Provided however, no person claiming, any such person or persons, shall be entitled to a certificate, authorizing him to take away such person or persons, until he has first paid all costs attending the trial of claim or claims.

Section 4. Any person in this state, who may hereafter give any person (owing service in any state or territory) a certificate or other testimonial of emancipation, shall for every such offence, forfeit and pay any sum not exceeding one thousand dollars, recoverable by indictment or presentment, in any court in this state having competent jurisdiction, and shall, moreover, be liable to an action for damage by the party injured.

Section 5. If any person or persons in this state, shall knowingly harbor or employ any person or persons held as a slave or slaves, in any other state or territory, who have without the consent of his, her or their owner or owners come into this state, or shall encourage any such person or persons to desert his, her or their master or mistress, or proper owner or owners, or shall after such owner or owners has established his, her or their claim or claims to such person or persons, and obtain a certificate according to law, to take him, her or them out of this state, use or attempt to use any violence, or in any way encourage such person or persons not to go with his, her or their owner or owners; every person or persons so offending, shall pay for every offence, any sum not exceeding five hundred dollars, to be recovered by indictment or presentment, before any court having competent jurisdiction.

NUMBER 3

The requisition of Robert Stephens, James Thompson, and Jesse Young as fugitives from the justice from the State of Kentucky. Gabriel Slaughter, Executive Office, State of Kentucky, December 11, 1819. Indiana Historical Documents, (1922).

With your excellency, I deeply regret the existence of cases requiring the exercise of this branch of our mutual duty.

The conflicting policy of different states renders it in some instances a matter of difficult and delicate interference, and demand in all cases a compliance with the requisites of law before a citizen of one state should be deprived of his liberty, and unheard sent to another for trial.

The demand which your excellency has made, not being brought within the provisions of the constitution and laws which point out my duty in such applications, I must decline interfering. Had the case been one within the provisions of the law, I should without hesitation have complied with your request.

***

His Excellency Jonathan Jennings, Governor of Indiana. Enclosure 2, December 24th, 1819.

I have had the honor to receive your Excellency's letter of the 11th inst., acknowledging the demand on my part of Robert Stephens, Jas. Thompson, and Jesse Young, as fugitives from the justice of this state.

It is for me to repeat the regret that such instances should occur to render such demands unavoidable on my part. It has been the policy of this state, and certainly has been mine, to provide as far as the principles of the constitution and laws of the United States, to facilitate the reclamation of fugitives from labor who may have fled to this state to avoid the service which may be due from them to persons claiming their labor. Our statutes prescribe punishment for those who shall harbor or prevent any person from reclaiming under the authority of law, fugitives from labor escaping for refuge within the limits of the state.

Believing that it has been an object with this state to discharge its duty to other and older members of the Union, with more confidence therefore shall we expect their constituted authorities to interpose and assist in bringing to public trial those charged with having violated our penal laws, and who may have fled after insulting the sovereignty of our state. Unfortunately this is not the first instance, and my expectations were that a similar demand would have previously been made.

It can only be a secondary object with the people of this state to bring to punishment the citizens of any other, but it has become necessary to put a final stop to those outrages by inflicting punishment, as an example to others, or by giving impulse to public opinion that such attempts are not only criminal but highly derogatory from the duties mutually due from citizens of the United States to the sovereignty and laws of every state in the Union.

Whether the documents upon which the late demand has been made were sufficient or otherwise, they were such as were certified to me by the order of the circuit court for the county of Harrison, under whose jurisdiction the indictments were found, with the expectation that in relation thereto I should discharge my duty. If, however, there shall have been clerical or other mistakes upon this subject, they would have been grounds of defence when the individuals charged should have been put on their trial. The act of congress, in such cases made and provided, renders an ex parte affidavit made charging the person or persons so demanded with having committed treason, felony, or other crime, sufficient to support such demand; and it is difficult to conclude that the documents accompanying the demand alluded to are not more substantial in good faith than that of an affidavit.

The first object of this government will be to ensure the execution of its laws, with which its sovereignty is inseparably connected; and it will be for the government of Kentucky to explain to the citizens of this state the principles and reasons upon which your Excellency declines an interference.

Permit me to solicit an early reply, accompanied with the indictments forwarded by General Tipton, the late agent for the state, and accept the assurance of my high respect as well for yourself, as the state over which you preside.

***

Kentucky kidnappers of Indiana Negroes, January 17, 1820, Senate Journal.

Since my message of the 15th inst., I have received another communication relative to the fugitives from the justice of this state, from the governor of the state of Kentucky, accompanied by the copies of the indictments, certified to me from the Harrison circuit court, upon which the demand was made. Copies of this letter, together with copies of the indictments, are herewith laid before the General Assembly.

***

Gabriel Slaughter, Executive Office, State of Kentucky.

I have had the honor of receiving your Excellency's letter of the 24th ult., in answer to mine of the 11th of said month, in which I informed your Excellency that as the demand made on me by your letter of the 30th of November, and the documents forwarded therewith, of certain persons as fugitives from justice, I must decline interfering, as the case was not brought within the constitution and laws in such cases provided.

It has always been the object of the government of this state to promptly discharge its duty as a member of the Federal Union, as well to the national Government, as to that of the coordinate states.

Our federal constitution has wisely intrusted to the general government the enacting of laws which shall point out the mode and manner of making application for fugitives from justice, and the consequent duty of the executive of the state applied to in such a case.

Looking then to the provisions of the laws of congress on this subject, and to the letter of your excellency and the documents accompanying the same, I could entertain no doubt but that they did not meet the requisitions of the law. In this opinion I was fortified by the opinion of several gentlemen of the first respectability who were consulted by me, and in whose knowledge of the constitution and laws of the country great confidence ought to be placed; and upon a review of that opinion I have no cause to doubt its correctness.

I will take this occasion to remark that the decision which I formed arose not from any alleged circumstance of the case, but would have governed on a similar application from any other state, and for any other alleged crime.

I therefore forbear making any remarks on the particular case, or upon the particular time chosen for making this application, considering the period which has elapsed since the transaction is alleged to have taken place.

It would be gratifying to me in the discharge of my official duty to meet the approbation of any section of our common country that may be affected by any of my official acts. A careful regard to what the best dictates of my judgment point out as my duty to all concerned must, however, be the means used to attain that end.

I have been thus explicit with your Excellency, as from the tenor of your letter it would seem you had taken up the idea that in the course I had taken on this subject there was not a proper respect paid to the constituted authorities of your state,--than which nothing could have been further from my intentions.

I inclose, in pursuance of your request, the documents sent with your former letter. You will discover, amongst other things in relation to them, that there is no evidence that they were found by the grand jury.

And it must always be a matter of my duty in the executive of the state applied to, to judge of the sufficiency of the documents on which he is called upon to cause a citizen to be arrested.

***

State of Indiana, Harrison County, Circuit Court, November Term, 1818.

The grand jurors impanelled and sworn to inquire for the body of the county of Harrions, on their oath, present that Robert Stephens, yeoman, and James Thompson, yeoman, and Jesse Young, yeoman, all of the State of Kentucky, on the twenty-second day of November, in the year of our Lord one thousand eight hundred and eighteen, at Corydon, in said county of Harrison, with force and arms, did feloniously and forcibly steal and take Susan, a woman of color, and carry her from this State, to the State of Kentucky, against the form of the statute in such case made and provided, and against the peace and dignity of the state of Indiana.

And the jurors aforesaid, on their oath aforesaid, do further present, that the said Robert Stephens, the said James Thompson, and the said Jesse Young, on the same twenty-second day of November aforesaid, at Corydon aforesaid, in said county of Harrison, and with force and arms, forcibly arrested the body of Susan, a woman of color, with the design to take her, the said Susan, out of this state, without establishing the claim of them, the said Robert Stephens, James Thompson, and Jesse Young, or either of them, or the claim of any other person, to the said Susan, according to the laws of this state or of the

United States, contrary to the form of the statute in such case made and provided, and against the peace and dignity of the state of Indiana.

***

Henry Hurst, Prosecuting Attorney, State of Indiana.

I, Henry W. Heth, Clerk of the Circuit court of said county, do certify the above to be a true copy of the original indictment filed in my office.

In testimony whereof, I have hereto, subscribed my name, and affixed the seal of our said court, at Corydon, this -- day of -- in the year 1819, the third year of the State, and of the independence of the United States, the forty-fourth.
(Seal)

***

The jurors for the state of Indiana, and the body of the county of Harrison, upon their oath, present, that Robert Stephens, late of the county aforesaid, yeoman, on the fifth day of June, in the year one thousand eight hundred and eighteen, with force and arms in the county aforesaid, did forcibly take and carry out of the state of Indiana aforesaid, a certain negro woman named Susan, without establishing his claim according to the laws of the state, or of the United States, contrary to the statute in such case made and provided, and against the peace and dignity of the United States.

***

I, Henry W. Heth, Clerk of the Circuit Court of said county, do certify the within to be a true copy of the original indictment filed in my office.

In testimony whereof, I have hereto subscribed my name, and affixed the seal of our said Court, at Corydon, this -- day of --in the year 1819, the third year of the state, and of the independence of the United States, the forty-fourth.
(Seal)

***

I, Robert A. New, Secretary of State for the state of Indiana, certify that Henry W. Heth, whose certificate appears to the two preceding indictments, is Clerk of the Circuit Court, in and for the county of Harrison and state aforesaid, and that full faith and credit should be given to his official acts as such.

Given under my hand, and state seal, of the state, this 27th day of November, 1819.
(Seal)

***

Special message on the recovery of fugitives from justice, January 21, 1820. Senate Journal, 1819.

Herewith I lay before the General Assembly copies of a letter addressed to the Governor of Kentucky renewing my demand of Robert Stephens, James Thompson, and Jesse Young, as fugitives from the justice of this state; which concludes, on my part, the correspondence with his Excellency on this subject.

***

To His Excellency Gabriel Slaughter, Governor of Kentucky. From Jonathan Jennings, Governor of Indiana.

Herewith I have the honor to renew my demand of Robert Stephens, James Thompson, and Jesse Young, as fugitives from the justice of this state; and have intrusted such demand, on its behalf, together with the accompanying documents, to a person in whom I have thought proper to place that confidence.

Since I addressed you my last letter, I have personally examined the original indictments on file, in the office of the clerk of the circuit court of this county, under the immediate jurisdiction of which the indictments were found, and discover that the originals shew that every requisite of the law had been complied with, to evince that there was "evidence that they were found by the grand jury."

In your Excellency's letter of the 11th ultimo, it is intimated that the conflicting policy of different states renders it, in some instances, a matter of difficult and delicate interference, and demands, in all cases, a compliance with the requisites of the law, before a citizen of one state should be deprived of his liberty, and unheard sent to another for trial. How this clashing policy can render it a matter of difficult and delicate interference to comply with the Constitution and laws of the United States, which do not seem to require technical nicety in the evidence of a criminal charge to support the demand of fugitives from justice, is not easy to be comprehended. Although the documents which accompanied my former application were considered insufficient by your Excellency to support that demand, I persuade myself that no objections will be made to the present; especially when reference is had to the assurance given in the latter clause of your first letter on this subject.

In your last communication, you state that the decision which you had formed on the demand arose not from any alleged circumstance of the case, but would have governed on a similar application from any other state, or for any other alleged crime. This assurance was entirely unnecessary, as my respect for your Excellency's character precludes the idea that, in the discharge of the duties of your exalted station, you would suffer the circumstances of any case, or the source of any demand of this nature, to divert you from that line of conduct which is marked out by the paramount authorities of the United States; or for a moment to permit partial distinctions to render you forgetful of the rights which the state of Indiana can never consent to relinquish. From a review of the correspondence emanating on my part, I can discover no portion of it which will bear a construction so degrading to the government over which I have the honor to preside.

With your Excellency, likewise, I shall forbear making any particular remarks on the circumstances marking the transaction which gave rise to the request, as they would not be otherwise than unpleasant to your feelings; and inasmuch as the Constitution and laws of the United States are entirely silent as to the time when a demand shall be made: in relation to time, therefore, connected with this subject, upon which your Excellency has thought proper to criticize, allow me to take this occasion to inform you that I shall hold myself accountable only to the government and citizens whom in this instance I represent.

While the duties of my station compel me to urge the present application for the fugitives in question, permit me to assure your Excellency that I shall on all occasions cultivate the friendly intercourse and urbanity of feeling between the sister states, on which the welfare of the Union so essentially depends. An object no less than the punishment and prevention of crimes seems to have given rise to the provisions of the Federal Constitution, and the laws to enforce them, on the subject of bringing to trial persons charged with offenses in one state and having fled to another. Yet their well meant provisions will not only fall short of their object, but will themselves prove sources of discord and dissension, unless they are observed in good faith by the respective parties concerned in their execution. It is not denied that the executive applied to is, in some measure, to judge of the sufficiency of the document on which the demand of the arrest of a citizen is founded; but it is contended that his right ceases whenever it is ascertained that such document is a copy of an indictment found, or an affidavit made, before the proper authorities, charging the person or persons demanded with having committed treason, felony, or other crime, certified as authentic by the proper authority of the state or territory from which the person or persons so charged shall have fled. Such document attends this application; and it is confidently believed that your Excellency will render the persons charged, to take their trial under the laws of this state, leaving it to them and to their counsel to avail themselves of technical informalities, if any exist, in the instrument on which they shall be arraigned.

It would seem that fugitives from the justice of either of the states should, by the constitution and laws of the United States, be delivered up, and unheard sent for trial to the state or territory from whence such person or persons shall have fled, whether the indictment be defective or otherwise, with as much propriety as that any person, upon a defective indictment, should, unheard, be apprehended and brought to trial, if found within the proper bailiwick of a sheriff.

***

Special message of Governor Jonathan Jennings on the refusal of Kentucky to return fugitives, December 4, 1820. House Journal, 1820.

It will be recollected that during the last session of the General Assembly copies of a correspondence between the acting Governor of Kentucky and myself were submitted to your consideration, relating to a demand upon his Excellency for certain fugitives from the justice of this state. At the close of the last session the demand was renewed, but the delivery of the fugitives was ultimately refused notwithstanding the assurances previously given.

***

Report of the Judiciary Committee of the House for the State of Indiana on the Governor of Indiana and the Acting Governor of Kentucky, respective fugitives from justice from the State of Indiana.

The Judiciary Committee have, according to order, had the communication of his Excellency the Governor respecting the demand made by him on the acting Governor of Kentucky, of certain fugitives from justice, and have agreed to report as follows:

From the papers before your committee, it appears that Robert Stephens, a member of the Kentucky legislature, and others, have been indicted at the November term of the Harrison circuit court for manstealing, were demanded of the acting governor of Kentucky as fugitives from justice, and that the legislature of Kentucky, on being informed of the demand made, did by resolution refuse the surrender of Stephens, and the same was also refused by the acting governor of Kentucky. The point principally relied on by the legislature in their refusal to deliver up Mr. Stephens, is that the law of Indiana, for the violation of which he had been indicted, is inconsistent with the constitution of the United States. The indictment, among other things, charges Stephens and others with having feloniously and forcibly arrested Susan, a woman of color, with a design to take her, the said Susan, out of this state (to wit, Indiana) without establishing the claim of the, the said Stephens and others, according to the laws of this state and of the United States.

To prove the unconstitutionality of the law under which this indictment was founded, a clause of the second section of the fourth article of the constitution of the United States is referred to, which is as follows.

"No person held to service or labor in one state under the laws thereof, escaping into another, shall, in consequence of any law or regulation therein, be discharged from such service or labor, but shall be delivered up on the claim of the party to which such service or labor may be due."

From this clause a conclusion is drawn that Congress has the sole power to regulate the mode of claiming persons owing service and labor in one state and escaping to another, and of punishing all abuses that may accrue from improper claims. But your committee can not admit the justness of the above conclusions. They would infer that, as states are only prohibited from discharging the obligations to serve, this single prohibition implies that any other regulation of the subject might be made at the discretion of the several states; and a further proof that no more was intended than to prohibit one state from emancipating the slaves of another may be found in the tenth article amendatory of the constitution, which provides that the powers not delegated to the United States by the constitution nor prohibited by it to the states are reserved to the states respectively or to the people.

The law of the United States respecting persons escaping from their masters fixes no penalty for abuses that arise under it; and though it is said that the courts of Kentucky will remunerate him who may illegally be seized and brought thither without just cause, yet those courts cannot punish criminal offenses committed in another state, nor can be admitted for a moment that those states alone where slavery is tolerated are to try the right to freedom, where it is disputed, and to prohibit and punish manstealing. Though the law of Congress provides that judges, magistrates of counties, and so forth, in certain cases, may give a certificate by which a fugitive owing service or labor may be recovered, yet this law, so far as it imposes duties on state officers, is not binding,--for if such were the case they might, in time, be altogether perverted from what our constitution intended. If, therefore, the constitution of the United States, requiring the person owing service or labor to be delivered up on the claim of the party to whom the service or labor is due, is to affect state officers, state laws then ought to be made. No claim can be recognized nor delivery made unless by a competent court. If no state law on the subject be made, our courts have nothing to guide them in aiding a claim guaranteed by the constitution of the United States. As, therefore, Congress have not provided that abuses under this law should be punished, and from the small number of the United States judges who are authorized to act much inconvenience would arise, it became both the right and the duty of our state to pass some law on the subject. And though our statute may not please the unfortunate slave holder in every respect; yet, so far as it from discharging from service and labor, that it provides that state officers shall aid the restoration of fugitives from labor to the claimant; that as speedy a decision should be had as in questions of far less consequence than freedom; and that a penalty should be imposed upon those who, unauthorized either by the laws of the United States or this state, commit violence on others who, by our constitution, are presumed to be free.

Your committee cannot but view with regret the course that has been pursued by our sister state, and which, if persisted in, may be attended with the most fearful consequences. If the violators of our laws find protection in another state, and the wise provisions of the constitution that fugitives from justice shall be surrendered are disregarded, then, indeed, we may predict a speedy dissolution of those bonds, under which we have hitherto acted as members of one family--when our rights are again invaded force may be repelled with force.

That such expedients may not be adopted, is ardently to be desired; but they are to be feared when alleged crimes find mind to avoid judicial investigation. If any of the laws of Indiana are unconstitutional, and if any of the persons indicted in our courts are innocent, ought it not to appear from some other authority than the legislature of Kentucky, which, by its own constitution, is prohibited from exercising judiciary powers?

Your committee, considering that the constitutionality of the law which Mr. Stephens is accused of violating cannot be doubted, forbear me to remark on some other arguments brought forward by the Kentucky legislature, which relate to the policy of the law, for which we are not accountable to them.

Your committee beg leave to offer the following resolutions:

Resolved, that his excellency the governor be requested to communicate to the President of the United States, or to Congress, his proceedings on the demand made by him of the acting governor of Kentucky, of Robert Stephens and others, fugitives from justice, [and] enter into such negotiations on the subject as he may deem most for the honor of the state.

Resolved, That his excellency the governor is entitled to the thanks and confidence of this house for the attention he has bestowed on this subject, and the manner it has been conducted by him.

NUMBER 4

Governor Jonathan Jenning's message to the Senate of the State of Indiana regarding kidnapping of Negroes, December 11, 1819. January 15, 1820, Senate Journal.

I now submit, for the information of the General Assembly, copies of two letters, one of which received [from] and the other addressed to the governor of the commonwealth of Kentucky, on the subject of fugitives from the justice of this state.

During the year 1818, Col. John Weathers was appointed as the agent in behalf of this state to demand of the executive authority of Kentucky certain persons resident thereof, who had been indicted by the grand jurors of the county of Clark, for kidnapping. The agent, in this instance, has informed me that he forwarded the documents necessary in this case, but has not received any answer thereto.

At an after period, the grand jurors for the county of Harrison indicted certain other persons, resident of the same state, for kidnapping a certain person of color named Susan. This act was done during those hours which are requisite to constitute burglary; entering a house that was occupied as a mansion, and forcing her off without affording time to be invested with her usual apparel. The grand jurors, however, have indicted those persons for kidnapping only; though it is believed that some of them at least, were equally subject to be indicted of the crime of burglary.

Since the latter indictment, some time was suffered to elapse, with the hope that one or more of the persons indicted might again be found within the bailiwick of the sheriff in whose hands process was resting for their apprehension. This expectation being disappointed, General John Tipton [of Corydon] was duly authorized as agent in behalf of the state in this instance, upon whose prudence and promptitude every reliance was placed. Upon his appointment, he proceeded to the seat of government of Kentucky and made a formal demand; which was answered by the former of the letters, copies of which are herewith presented. The indefinite terms of this letter, with regard to the alleged defect in the indictments upon which the demand was made, render it difficult to ascertain those defects with precision, at least until a further communication shall be received from the governor of Kentucky, which was hoped for prior to this date.

Since my last letter on this subject, I have examined the original bills of indictment, to one of which there seems to be an objection, as much as it concludes "against the peace and dignity of the United States," instead of concluding "against the peace and dignity of the state of Indiana." And it may be possible that a variance may exist between the copies certified to me and the originals.

Such violations of our penal laws, with impunity, while they are qualified to detract from the dignity, are equally calculated to impair the rights of the sovereignty of the state; and so long as a portion of our citizens shall countenance or encourage such infractions upon claims to protection under the constitutional laws of the state, so long may we expect the deleterious effects of their influence.

To discharge our duty with promptitude towards every member of the union shall be a high object as a government connected with and bounded by the ties which give force to that union; and as promptly to require a like discharge of duty from others, whenever constitutionally we are permitted and our rights authorize such demand.

Expense have accrued, and may accrue on this subject, which will be provided for by the General Assembly as far as necessity may require.

NUMBER 5

Crimes and punishment: Kidnapping. Laws of Indiana, (1843).

Section 11. Every person who shall forcibly steal and take, or forcibly and unlawfully arrest any man, woman, or child and carry or convey such man, woman, or child to parts without the state of Indiana, or aid or abet therein, or who shall forcibly and unlawfully take or arrest, or aid or abet in forcibly and unlawfully taking or arresting any person or persons whatever, with intent to take such person or persons to parts without the state, as aforesaid, without having first established a claim upon the services of such person or persons, according to the laws of this state or of the United States, shall be deemed guilty of kidnapping, and upon conviction thereof shall be fined in any sum not less than one hundred dollars nor more than five thousand dollars, and be imprisoned at hard labor in the state prison for any term of not less than two years nor more than fourteen years.

XI

Fugitive Slaves

In a state where race prejudice abounded, it is not surprising that Indiana whites enforced the federal Fugitive Slave Act of 1793, and its own fugitive slave law to the letter. These laws authorized slave holders to track down runaway slaves believed to be in Indiana and forcibly remove them from the state. The law required only a summary process to prove the validity of a slave owner's claim. Indiana law and the federal fugitive slave law also restrained white citizens who sometimes challenged the claim of slave holders. Abolitionists who participated in rescues were no doubt sincere. Others, however, did not want visiting slave holders trampling upon their free laws. Some whites thought keeping black refugees out of the state would solve the problem of visiting slave catchers working in Indiana. They stood along the Indiana-Kentucky border hoping to intercept any black refugee fleeing across the border. Neither this strategy, federal law, or state law were an effective deterrent to black refugees storming across the Indiana border into a state with at least a prohibition against slavery. In spite of the efforts of whites to discourage runaways, Indiana became a haven for many Africans seeking refuge from captivity.

NUMBER 1

An act relative to fugitives from labor. Approved, January 22, 1824, Laws of Indiana.

Section 1. Be it enacted by the General Assembly of the state of Indiana, That any person or persons of any state or territory, having any claim to the service of any person or persons within this state, may in person or by attorney, go before the clerk of any circuit court within this state, and make affidavit, that he, she or they, are the persons for whom he, she or they are agents or attorneys, have or has a just claim to the service of such fugitive person or persons, agreeably to the laws of the state from which such fugitive or fugitives from labor, hath or have fled, is also the name or names of the owner or owners; (when affidavit is made by attorney;) which affidavit shall be taken by such clerk and filed in his office; whereupon it shall be the duty of such clerk to issue his warrant, directed to the owner or owners of such fugitive from labor, or to his, her or their agent or attorney, commanding him or them forthwith to carry such fugitive before some justice of the peace or judge of the circuit court, or supreme court within this state; and it shall be the duty of the clerk to affix the county seal thereto, and the warrant so sealed as aforesaid, shall be sufficient authority for the person in whom possession the same may be, to authorize him to arrest such fugitive from labor, wherever he may be found in this state, and him to convey before some justice of the peace, judge of the circuit or supreme courts, that may reside in the county or district where such fugitive shall be found.

Section 2. It shall be the duty of such justice of the peace or judge, (as the case may be,) to cause such fugitive from labor to be taken into custody, and the same to commit to let to bail until the parties shall be ready for trial, which time shall not exceed sixty days, and shall be at the discretion of the justice or judge, upon the circumstances of the case made known by affidavit; and it shall be the duty of such justice of the peace or judge, as the case may be, to hear and determine the case in a summary way; and if such justice or judge shall be of opinion, that such fugitive did owe service according to the claim sworn to, he shall give such owner or agent a certificate of that fact, which shall be sufficient authority for such agent or owner, to remove such fugitive from the state; Provided however, That either party may appeal by paying the costs of such trial, and giving security for the costs that may accrue on such appeal; and in all cases where an appeal may be taken, it shall be the duty of the justice or judge to require of such fugitive from labor, to give security for his appearance, and abiding the event of such trial, and on failure thereof, to commit such fugitive to the jail of the county, there to be kept at the expense of the appellant until the time of such trial: Provided also, That no such appeal shall be granted to such fugitive from labor, until he or she shall make out and file affidavit, that he or she does not owe service.

Section 3. In all cases where an appeal may be granted under the provisions of this act, it shall be the duty of the justice of the peace, or the judge, as the case may be, granting such appeal, to issue his warrant to the sheriff of the county, directing him forthwith to notify the associate judges thereof, or any circuit judge having jurisdiction in such county; whose duty it shall be, when so notified, to attend at the court house of the county, in which such arrest shall have been made, on the day named in the warrant of the judge or justice as aforesaid, which day shall not be more than five days after the arrest; and it shall be the duty of such sheriff, to summon a good and lawful jury of the county, who shall attend at the time and place appointed for trial, and for failure so to do, shall be subject to like penalties as jurymen are in other cases.

Section 4. That on the appearance of the parties before such special court, if either of the parties shall make it appear to the satisfaction of such court, that they cannot safely go into trial at that time, such court may continue such cause, until the ensuing term of the circuit court for said county, and shall send up a transcript of their proceedings to said court, together with the proceedings had before the judge or justice, before whom the first proceedings were had; on which the clerk of said circuit court shall docket such suit, where the same shall stand for trial, subject to the same rules of law and proceedings generally, as other civil actions are; any thing herein to the contrary notwithstanding.

NUMBER 2

An act relative to crime and punishment in dealing with runaway slaves. Approved February 10, 1831, Laws of Indiana.

Section 37. That if any person, without proper authority, shall give to any one owing service in any state or territory within the United States, a certificate or other testimonial of emancipation, or shall knowingly harbor or employ any such one owing service as aforesaid, or held as a slave, who may have come to this state without the consent of his or her owner, or shall encourage or assist any such one to desert or not go with his or her owner, or shall use any violence, or other means to prevent, let or hinder any person, in lawfully recovering any fugitive, slave or person owing service, such person so offending, shall upon the conviction thereof, be fined in any sum not exceeding five hundred dollars, and be liable for damages to any person or persons injured by any of the said acts.

NUMBER 3

Giving free papers or assisting slaves to escape. Laws of Indiana, (1843).

Section 115. If any person, without proper authority, shall give to any one owing service in any state or territory within the United States, a certificate or other testimonial of emancipation, or shall knowingly harbor or employ any such one, owing service as aforesaid, or held as a slave, who may have come into this state without the consent of his or her owner or shall encourage or assist any such one to desert or not go with his or her owner, or shall use any violence or other means to prevent, let, or hinder any person in lawfully recovering any fugitive slave or person owing service, such person so offending, shall, upon conviction thereof, be fined in any sum not exceeding five hundred dollars, and be liable for damages to any person or persons injured by any of the said acts.

Section 116. Every person who shall obstruct the execution of any legal process, or who shall forcibly free any person from legal arrest, knowing such person to be under arrest, shall, upon conviction thereof, be fined in any sum not exceeding ten thousand dollars, or be imprisoned for any term of time not exceeding six months.

XII

Testimony and Witness

Indiana law did not allow people of color to testify against a white. State law defined blacks, mulattoes and Indians as ineligible witnesses. A person of color could not protect himself or herself from a white in court unless another white testified against the assailant. Thus, a white could murder, assault, or rob a person of color, and, without a white witness, or a sympathetic judge, the victim would be powerless in court. Indiana statute deprived people of color legal protection from whites. The Civil War brought a few changes, as it did in most states. Indiana repealed its testimony law; yet, people of color could rarely testify against whites. The following documents illustrate Indiana's policy during the nineteenth century on its witness and testimony law.

NUMBER 1

An act regulating the practice in the General Court, and Court of Common Pleas, and for other purposes. Laws of Indiana, (1807).

Section 24. No Negro, Mulatto or Indian shall be a witness except in pleas of the United States against Negroes, Mulattoes or Indians, or in civil pleas, where Negroes, Mulattoes or Indians alone shall be parties.

Section 25. Every person other than a Negro, of whole grand fathers or grand mothers, any one is, or shall have been a Negro, although all his other progenitors, except that descending from a Negro, shall have been White persons, shall be deemed a Mulatto, and so every person who shall have one fourth part or more of Negro blood, shall in like manner be deemed a Mulatto.

NUMBER 2

An act to regulate the practice in suits at law. Approved January 29, 1831, Laws of Indiana.

Section 251. No negro, mulatto or Indian, shall be a witness, except in pleas of the state against negroes, mulattoes, or Indians, and in civil causes where negroes, mulattoes, or Indians alone are parties: every person other than a negro having one-fourth part of negro blood or more, or any one of whose grandfathers or grandmothers shall have been a negro, shall be deemed an incompetent witness, within the provisions of this article.

NUMBER 3

An act to prohibit the evidence of Indians and persons having one-eighth or more of Negro blood in all cases where white persons are parties in interest. Approved February 14, 1853, Revised Statutes.

Section 1. Be it enacted by the General Assembly of the State of Indiana: No Indian, or person having one-eighth or more of negro blood, shall be permitted to testify as a witness in any cause in which any white person is a party in interest.

NUMBER 4

Competent Witness. Filed in the office of W. A. Peelle, Secretary of State. Approved March 17, 1861, Revised Statutes.

Section 1. Be it enacted by the General Assembly of the State of Indiana, That sec. 238, in article 13, of an act, entitled "An act to revise, simplify, and abridge the rules, practice, pleadings, and forms in civil cases in the courts of this state, to abolish distinct forms of action at law, and to provide for the administration of justice in a uniform mode of pleading and practice, without distinction between law and equity," approved June 18, 1852, be, and the same is hereby repealed.

Section 2. Every free white person of competent age shall be a competent witness in any civil cause or proceeding, and no person shall be disqualified as a witness by reason of interest in the event of that or any other suit, or because such person is a party in said action or proceeding. Any person a party in the action may testify in his own behalf, or in behalf of any other party or parties therein, and any one person or party in a suit may compel any other person or party therein to testify under the same regulations as other witnesses may be compelled, and the interest in the suit of any witness shall be regarded only as to his or her credibility, and shall not affect his or her competency.

Section 3. Persons insane at the time of examination; children under ten years of age, and incapable of properly understanding the facts about which they are examined; husband and wife as to matters for or against each other, or as to communications made to each other during marriage; attorneys at law as to confidential communication from a client, or advice given to such clients' physicians as to any matters confided to them in the course of the duties of their profession; clergymen concerning any confessions made to them in the course of discipline enjoined by the church, shall not, in either case, be included in the second section of this act, or be competent witnesses, unless with the consent of the party making such confidential communications: Provided, that where a negro, Indian, or person excluded on account of mixed blood is a party to a cause, his opponent shall also be excluded: And provided further, that in all suits where an executor, administrator, or guardian is a party in a case where a judgment may be rendered either for or against the estate represented by such executor, administrator, or guardian, neither party shall be allowed to testify as a witness, unless required by the opposite party, or by the court trying the cause, except in cases arising upon contracts made with the executor, administrator, or guardian of such estate.

NUMBER 5

An act to amend "An act in relation to witnesses," and to repeal Section 238 of Article 13, of an act entitled An act to revise, simplify, and abridge the rules in cases in the courts of this State. Approved December 21, 1865, Laws of Indiana.

Section 1. Be it enacted by the General Assembly of the State of Indiana, That section three of an amended act of the above entitled act, which section reads as follows, to-wit:

"Section 3. Persons insane at the time of examination; children under ten years of age and incapable of properly understanding the facts about which they are examined; husband and wife, as to matters for or against each other, or as to communications made to each other during marriage; attorneys at law, as to confidential communications from a client, or advice given to such clients; physicians, as to any matters confided to them in the course of profession; clergymen, concerning any confessions made to them in the course of discipline enjoined by the church, shall not, in either case, be included in the second section of the act to which this is an amendment, or be competent witnesses, unless with the consent of the party making such confidential communications: Provided, That where a negro, Indian, or person excluded on account of mixed blood, is a party to a cause, his opponent shall be excluded; and provided further, that in all suits where an executor, administrator, or guardian is a party in a case where a judgment may be rendered either for or against the estate, represented by such executor, administrator, or guardian, neither party shall be allowed to testify as a witness, unless required by the opposite party, or by the court trying the cause, except in cases arising upon contracts made with the executor, administrator, or guardian of such estate, and in cases where a party to a suit, pending in any court in this State, whose deposition has been taken in such suit, and is on file in such court, dies, and such suit is prosecuted by or against the executor or administrator of such deceased party, the opposite party shall be allowed to testify on the trial of the cause, and such deposition may be read in evidence by and on behalf of the representative of such deceased party; and provided further, that in all suits against heirs, founded on a contract with, or demand against, the ancestor, the object of which is to obtain title to, or possession of, land or other property of such ancestor, or to reach or affect the same in any way, neither party shall be allowed to testify as a witness, as to any matter which occurred prior to the death of such ancestor, unless required by the opposite party; and the assignor of the plaintiff in any such suit, where there has been an assignment of the cause of action, shall be deemed and held to be a party within this provision," be and the same is hereby amended so as to read as follows, to-wit:

Section 3. Persons insane at the time of examination; children under ten years of age, and incapable of properly understanding the facts about which they are examined; husband and wife as to matters for or against each other, or as to communications made to each other during marriage; attorneys at law, as to confidential communications from a client, or advice given to such clients, physicians as to any matters confided to them in the course of their profession; clergymen, concerning any confessions made to them in the course of discipline enjoined by the church, shall not, in either case, be included in the section of the act to which this is an amendment, or be competent witnesses unless with the consent of the party making such confidential communication; Provided, That were a negro, Indian or person excluded on account of mixed blood is a party to a cause, his opponent shall be excluded; And provided further, That in all suits where an executor, administrator or guardian is a party in a case where a judgment may be rendered either for or against the estate represented by such executor, administrator or guardian, neither party shall be allowed to testify as a witness unless required by the opposite party, or by the court trying the cause, except in cases arising upon contracts made with the executor, administrator or guardian of such estate, and in case where a party to a suit pending in any court in this State, whose deposition has been taken in such suit, and is on file in such court, dies, and such suit is prosecuted by or against the executor, or administrator of such deceased party, the opposite party shall be allowed to testify on the trial of the cause, and such deposition may be read in evidence by, and on behalf of the representative of such deceased party: And provided further, That in all suits by or against heirs, founded on a contract with or demand against the ancestor, the object of which is to obtain title to, or possession of land or other property of such ancestor, as to reach or affect the same in any way, neither party shall be allowed to testify as a witness as to any matters which occurred prior to the death of such ancestor, unless required by the opposite party; and the assignor of the plaintiff in any such suit where there has been an assignment of the cause of action shall be deemed and held to be a party within this provision.

Section 4. It is declared that an emergency exists for the immediate taking effect of this act; it is therefore declared to be in force from and after its passage.

NUMBER 6

An act defining who shall be competent witnesses in any court or judicial proceeding in this state, and to repeal all laws and parts of laws in conflict with the provisions of this act. Approved December 20, 1865, Laws of Indiana.

Section 1. Be it enacted by the General Assembly of the State of Indiana, That all persons of competent age, without distinction as to color or blood and not otherwise by law rendered incompetent, shall be competent witnesses to testify in any proceeding or suit, civil or criminal, in any Court in this State: Provided, That no negro or mulatto who has come, or who shall hereafter, come into this State in violation of the Thirteenth Article of the Constitution of the State, shall, while said Article continues in force, be competent to testify as a witness in any case in which a white person shall be a party in interest.

Section 2. All laws and parts of laws now in force and in conflict with the provisions of this act, are hereby repealed.

Section 3. It is hereby declared that an emergency exists for the immediate taking effect of this act; it is therefore declared that this act shall take effect and be in force from and after its passage and publication in the Indianapolis Journal and Herald.

NUMBER 7

An act defining who shall be competent witnesses in any court or judicial proceeding in this state, and to repeal all laws and parts of laws in conflict with the provisions of this act. Approved March 11, 1867, Laws of Indiana.

Section 1. Be it enacted by the General Assembly of the State of Indiana, That every person of competent age may be a witness in any civil or criminal cause or proceeding, and no person shall be disqualified as a witness by reason of interest in the event of that or any other action, or because such person is a party in said action or proceeding other than criminal. Any person, party in a civil action, may testify in his own behalf, or in behalf of any other party or parties therein, and any one person or party in a suit may compel any other person or party therein to testify under the same regulations as other witnesses may be compelled, and the interest in the suit of any witness shall be regarded only as to his or her credibility, and shall not affect his or her competency.

Section 2. Persons insane at the time of examination, children under ten years of age, and incapable of properly understanding the facts about which they are examined, husband and wife as to matters for or against each other, or as to communications made to each other during marriage, except that the wife shall be a competent witness in cases of prosecutions against the husband for assault and battery upon the person of his wife, and except also that in suits by the husband and wife jointly for an assault and battery upon the wife, such wife shall be a competent witness to prove the assault and battery. Attorneys at law, as to confidential communications from a client, or advice given to such clients; physicians, as to matters confided to them in course of their profession; clergymen, concerning any confessions made to them in course of discipline enjoined by the church, shall not in any case be competent witness, unless with the consent of the party making such confidential communication: Provided, That in all suits where an executor, administrator, or guardian, is a party in a case where a judgment may render either for or against the estate represented by such executor, administrator or guardian, neither party shall be allowed to testify as a witness unless required by the opposite party, or by the court trying the cause, except in cases arising upon contracts made with the executor, administrator or guardian of such estate, and in cases where a party to a suit pending in any court in this State, whose deposition has been taken in such suit, and is on file in such court, dies and such suit is prosecuted by or against the executor or administrator of such deceased party, the opposite party shall be allowed to testify, on trial of the cause, on all material points and matters of fact embraced in the deposition, and on no other facts, and such deposition may be read in evidence by and on behalf of the representatives of such deceased party: And provided further, That in all suits by or against heirs, founded on a contract with, or demand against, the ancestor, the object of which is to obtain title to, or possession of, land or other property of such ancestor, or to reach or affect the same in any way, neither party shall be allowed to testify as a witness as to any matter which occurred prior to the death of such ancestor, unless required by the opposite party or by the court trying the cause, and the assignor of the plaintiff in any such suit, where there has been an assignment of the cause of action, shall be deemed and held to be a party within this provision.

Section 3. All laws and parts of laws now in force and in conflict with the provisions of this act are hereby repealed.

Section 4. It is hereby declared that an emergency exists for the immediate taking effect of this act; therefore the same shall take effect and be in force from and after its passage.

XIII

Public Education

Indiana law barred African-American children from its common schools until 1865. Philanthropists and civic organizations formed by black residents were the only source of funding for schools before the Civil War. The state legislature created a separate school system for black children in 1865, funded by assessments on property owned by black residents. There was one exception to the separate-school-rule. For example, the legislature mandated that in districts where to few black people lived to fund a school for their children, the youths of both races would attend the same school. This exception was rare and applied to a small section of the state. Segregation in Indiana continued unabated until after Brown v. Board of Education (1954), which declared segregated schools inherently unequal.

NUMBER 1

An act to provide for a general system of common schools, the officers thereof, and their respective powers and duties, and matters properly connected therewith, and to establish township libraries, and for the regulation thereof. Approved March 5, 1855, Revised Statutes.

Section I. Be it enacted by the General Assembly of the State of Indiana, That there shall be annually assessed and collected, as the state and county revenues are assessed and collected, on the list of property taxable for state purposes, the sum of ten cents on each one hundred dollars worth of property, and fifty cents on each poll: Provided, however, that the taxes aforesaid shall not be levied and collected from negroes nor mulattoes, nor shall their children be included in any enumeration required by this act, nor entitled to the benefits thereof.

NUMBER 2

An act to render taxation for common school purposes uniform and to provide for the education of the colored children of the state. Approved May 13, 1865, Laws of Indiana.

Section 1. Be it enacted by the General Assembly of the State of Indiana, That in assessing and collecting taxes for school purposes under existing laws all property, real and personal, subject to taxation for State and county purposes, shall be taxed for the support of common schools without regard to the race of color of the owner of the property.

Section 2. All children of the proper age, without regard to the race or color, shall hereafter be included in the enumeration of the children of the respective school districts, townships, towns and cities of this State for school purposes; but in making such enumeration the officers charged by law with that duty shall enumerate the colored children of proper age, who may reside in any school district, in a separate and distinct list from that in which the other school children of such school district shall be enumerated.

Section 3. The Trustee or Trustees of each township, town or city, shall organize the colored children into separate schools, having all the rights and privileges of other schools of the township: Provided, if there are not a sufficient number within attending distance, the several districts may be consolidated and form one district. But if there are not a sufficient number within reasonable distance to be thus consolidated, the Trustee or Trustees shall provide such other means of education for said children as shall use their proportion, according to numbers, of school revenue to the best advantage.

Section 4. All laws relative to school matters, not inconsistent with this act, shall be deemed applicable to colored schools.

Section 5. Whereas, an emergency exists for the immediate taking effect of this act, the same shall be in force from and after its passage.

NUMBER 3

Education in the common schools. Approved March 6, 1865, Revised Statutes.

Section 1. The school trustees of the several townships, towns and cities, shall take, or cause to be taken, between the tenth (10th) day of April and the thirtieth day of the same month, each year, an enumeration of all unmarried persons between the ages of six and twenty-one years, resident within the respective townships, towns or cities. Each person required or employed to take such enumeration shall take an oath or affirmation to take the same accurately and truly to the best of his skill and ability. Such oath or affirmation shall be made a matter of record and kept on file in the office of the school trustees. In making said enumeration, the trustee, or person so employed shall distinguish between the white and colored children, enumerating them in separate lists, and shall list the names of parents, guardians, heads of families, or persons having charge of such child or children, male or female, shall list the full name and give the sex and age of each child so enumerated, shall secure the signature of either parent, guardian, head of family, or person having charge of such child or children, certifying to the correctness of the same, or if this is impossible, shall secure the signature of some responsible person who can certify to the correctness of said list; and he shall give the number of the school district to which such parent, guardian, head of family or person having charge of such child or children, is attached for school purposes, and the number and initials which designate the congressional township in which such parent, guardian, head of family or person having charge of such child or children resides.

***

Approved March 8, 1873.

Section 2. The Trustee or Trustees of such township, town, or city may organize the colored children into separate schools of the township, town, or city, having all the rights, privileges, and advantages of all other schools of the township, town, or city: Provided, That in case there may not be provided separate schools for the colored children, then such colored children shall be allowed to attend the public schools with white children; Provided, further, That when any child attending such colored school shall, on examination and certificate of his or her teacher, show to the Trustee or Trustees of any township, town, or city that he or she has made a sufficient advancement to be placed in a higher grade than that afforded by such colored school, he or she shall be entitled to enter the school provided for white children of a like grade, and no distinction shall therein be made on account of race or color of such colored child.

NUMBER 4

An act to amend section three of an act entitled "An act to render taxation for common school purposes uniform, and to provide for the education of the colored children of the state, Approved May 13, 1869." Approved March 5, 1877, Laws of Indiana.

Section 1. Be it enacted by the General Assembly of the State of Indiana, That section three of said act be and the same is hereby amended to read as follows, to-wit: Sec. 3. The Trustee or Trustees of such township, town or city, may organize the colored children into separate schools of the township, town or city, having all the rights, privileges and advantages of all other schools of the township, town or city: Provided, That in case there may not be provided separate schools for the colored children, then such colored children shall be allowed to attend the public schools with white children: And provided further, That when any child attending such colored school shall, on examination and certificate of his or her teacher, show to the Trustee or Trustees of any township, town or city, that they have made sufficient advancement to be placed in a higher grade than that afforded by such colored school, he or she shall be entitled to enter the school provided for white children of a like grade, and no distinction shall therein be made on account of race or color of such colored child.

Section 2. Whereas, there are a large number of colored children in this State that have not now equal educational advantages with white children, there is an emergency for the immediate taking effect of this act, therefore it shall take effect and be in force from and after its passage.

XIV

Civil and Legal Rights

The civil rights laws of Congress brought temporary relief to Americans of African ancestry after the Civil War. Some states, including those in the Old Northwest, accepted Congress's reform laws only because they assumed that they applied to Rebel states only. When the civil rights act of 1866 and 1875 mandated equal access to public facilities such as inns, theaters, and parks, northern states reluctantly followed along. Indiana also complied with the new federal policy, and the state legislature adopted statutes to protect the civil rights of black citizens. State compliance with federal law did not mean that Indiana, or any other northern state, was ready to fully desegregate public places. The Supreme Court wasn't ready either. In a series of cases culminating in the Civil Rights Cases (1883), the court struck down civil rights statutes. Indiana also softened its laws. By the turn of the century, the state resorted to de facto segregation. The following documents show the effort to achieve civil rights reform in Indiana, but the legal prescriptions rarely came close to reality in the Hoosier State.

NUMBER 1

Conveyance of land. Approved March 11, 1861, Revised Statutes.

Section 1. No person except a citizen of the United States, or an alien who shall be at the time a bona fide resident of the United States, an Indian, a negro, or a mulatto or other person of mixed blood, shall take, hold, convey, devise, or pass by descent, lands, except in such cases of descent or devise as are provided for by law: And Provided further, That the marriage of a woman with an alien, and her residence with her husband in a foreign State or country, shall not bar her right to hold, convey, devise, and pass by descent, lands which may have come to her by descent or purchase.

Section 2. All bona fide sales, conveyances, purchases, and devises heretofore made by an Indian, negro, or a mulatto or other person of mixed blood, and all estates heretofore acquired by any Indian, negro, or a mulatto or any person of mixed blood, by conveyance, devise, or descent, are hereby legalized, and such tenants are hereby declared to hold the same as fully and to the same extent as though there was no disability to the contrary: Provided, That nothing herein contained shall affect any suit or proceeding now pending in any of the Courts of this State.

NUMBER 2

An act to protect all persons in their civil and legal rights, prescribing penalties for their violation to be recovered in a civil action, defining certain misdemeanors and fixing their penalties and declaring an emergency. Approved March 9, 1885, Revised Statutes.

Section 1. Be it enacted by the General Assembly of the State of Indiana that all persons within the jurisdiction of said State shall be entitled to the full and equal enjoyments of the accommodations, advantages, facilities and privileges of inns, restaurants, eating-houses, barber shops, public conveyances on land and water, theaters, and all other places of public accommodations and amusement, subject only to the conditions and limitations established by law and applicable alike to all citizens.

Section 2. That any person who shall violate any of the provisions of the foregoing section by denying to any citizen, except for reasons applicable alike to all citizens of every race and color, and regardless of color or race, the full enjoyment of any of the accommodations, advantages, facilities, or privileges in said section enumerated, or by aiding or inciting such denial, shall for every such offense, forfeit and pay a sum not to exceed one hundred dollars to person aggrieved thereby, to be recovered in any court of competent jurisdiction in the county where said offense was committed, and shall also, for every such offense, be deemed guilty of a misdemeanor, and upon conviction thereof shall be fined not to exceed one hundred dollars, or shall be imprisoned not more than thirty days, or both: And provided further, That a judgment in favor of the party aggrieved, or punishment, or a committal upon an indictment, affidavit, or information, shall be a bar to further or other prosecution or suit.

Section 3. That no citizen of the State of Indiana possessing all other qualifications which are or may be prescribed by law, shall be disqualified, to serve as grand or petit juror in any Court of said State on account of race or color, and any officer or other person charged with any duty in the selection or summoning of jurors who shall exclude or fail to summon any citizen for the cause aforesaid, shall, on conviction thereof, be deemed guilty of a misdemeanor, and be fined not more than one hundred dollars, or imprisoned not more than thirty days, or both.

Section 4. This act shall take effect and be in force from and after its passage.

NUMBER 3

Equal accommodations for all persons. Approved March 9, 1885, Revised Statutes.

Section 1. Equal accommodations for all persons. All persons within the jurisdiction of said State shall be entitled to the full and equal enjoyments of the accommodations, advantages, facilities and privileges of inns, restaurants, eating-houses, barber shops, public conveyances on land and water, theaters, and all other places of public accommodations and amusement, subject only to the conditions and limitations established by law and applicable alike to all citizens.

Section 2. Suit for penalty. Any person who shall violate any of the provisions of the foregoing section by denying to any citizen, except for reasons applicable alike to all citizens of every race and color, and regardless of color or race, the full enjoyment of any of the accommodations, advantages, facilities, or privileges in said section enumerated, or by aiding or inciting such denial, shall, for every such offense, forfeit and pay a sum not to exceed one hundred dollars to the person aggrieved thereby, to be recovered in any court of competent jurisdiction in the county where said offense was committed, and shall also, for every such offense, be deemed guilty of a misdemeanor, and upon conviction thereof shall be fined not to exceed one hundred dollars, or shall be imprisoned not more than thirty days, or both. And provided, further, that a judgment in favor of the party aggrieved, or punishment, or a committal upon an indictment, affidavit, or information, shall be a bar to further or other prosecution or suit.

Section 3. No citizen of the State of Indiana possessing all other qualifications which are or may be prescribed by law, shall be disqualified to serve as a grand or petit juror in any Court of said State on account of race or color, and any officer or other person charged with any duty in the selection or summoning of jurors who shall exclude or fail to summon any citizen for the cause aforesaid, shall, on conviction thereof, be deemed guilty of a misdemeanor, and be fined not more than one hundred dollars, or imprisoned not more than thirty days, or both.

Summary of Cases

Although the Ordinance of 1787 bound Indiana to prohibit slavery, its leaders early on found creative ways to circumvent the ordinance. The agricultural potential of Indiana and the interest of immigrating whites to preserve slavery produced successive petitions to Congress to rescind or modify the ordinance. Congress denied their requests. However, by the time Indiana entered the Union as a free state, it had made slavery possible under the guise of indentured servitude. The state supreme court found ways to uphold the prohibition against slavery, approve indentured servitude, and validate the state's racial code as prescribed by the legislature.

Territorial leaders succeeded in rationalizing slavery by arguing that the prohibition in the ordinance applied only to slaves brought into the territory after 1787. According to this interpretation, slaves already in the region, and their children, were unaffected by the Ordinance of 1787. The supreme court rejected this thesis in State v. Lasalle (1820). Lasalle, a slave holder, entered Indiana allegedly before adoption of the ordinance. He held Polly, a black woman, as a slave. Abolitionists disputed his claim and carried the case to the supreme court. The court rejected Lasalle's claim, declaring Polly a free woman. Later in Vaughan v. Williams (1845), a federal court affirmed the automatic emancipation rule, declaring that slaves were automatically freed when brought into Indiana with the knowledge and consent of their owner. State and federal courts upheld the fugitive slave law, however. As Ray v. Donnell (1845) shows, slaves who escaped from a slave jurisdiction were returnable under state and federal fugitive slave laws.

The black laws of Indiana also barred black children from common schools. Occasionally, school masters sympathetic to civil rights admitted black youths to private schools. Invariably, white parents objected, and the dispute ended up in court. Lewis v. Henley (1850) addressed this question.

The supreme court ruled that the state education policy did not extend to a black who paid tuition to a private school. By this decision the court acknowledged that the education law did not mean that black children were not entitled to an education. Hence, the *Lewis* case laid the foundation for a segregated educational system. The court affirmed this opinion in the *Polke* case (1854).

The judiciary in Indiana upheld the black laws. The courts preserved the state's racial policy regarding miscegenation and immigration. In Beebe v. State (1855) and State v. Gibson, (1871) the supreme court concluded that natural law "forbids" mixed marriages. In the *Barkshire* case (1856), the court annulled the marriage of a black couple because one party had entered the state in violation of the immigration law. On the other hand, the supreme court sometimes rejected the testimony law which prohibited the testimony of a black against a white. State and local courts, however, should not be considered antislavery or pro-civil rights. It was neither. As the following cases show, the judiciary in Indiana simply upheld the racial policy of the state.

Select Annotated Cases

In Re Susan, 23 Federal Cases 444 (2 Wheeler Cr. Cas 594) (1818)
A federal district court upheld the federal Fugitive Slave Act of 1793, which provided for the return of runaway slaves. The court considered the act superior to any remedy provided by state law.

State v. Lasalle, 1 Indiana 60 (1820)
A slave holder named Lasalle claimed Polly, a "woman of color," whom he brought into Indiana. State law, however, prohibited slavery, and when Polly asserted her freedom, a lower court ruled in the master's favor. Polly then carried the dispute to the state supreme court. Lasalle claimed that he had purchased Polly prior to adoption of the Northwest Ordinance of 1787, which had abolished slavery, but the court rejected his argument and freed Polly under the laws of Indiana, which had prohibited slavery.

Vaughan v. Williams, 28 Federal Cases 1115 (3 McLean 530) (1845)
By 1840, most Northern states had adopted the automatic emancipation rule, the notion that a slave became free the moment he entered a free jurisdiction. The Vaughan case involved this question, and a dispute arose when alleged slaves entered Indiana with the consent of their master. Abolitionists encouraged them to sue for freedom, and the litigants focused on whether the slaves had been taken into the state. The supreme court ruled that there "can be no doubt that the slaves were, thereby entitled to their freedom." Once free, they could not be forced back into slavery.

Ray v. Donnell, 20 Federal Cases 325 (4 McLean 504) (1849)
An enslaved woman named Caroline escaped from Kentucky with four children. They reached Indiana in 1847. Woodson Clark, an Indiana resident,

captured the family and held them for the slave holder. A sympathetic white named "Donnell" challenged the slave catcher's claim and lured away the runaways. The claimant sued, and the court awarded him damages under the fugitive slave law, holding that the slaves had escaped from a jurisdiction which recognized slavery.

Norris v. Newton, 18 Federal Cases 322 (5 McLean 92), (1850)
Four blacks escaped from the plantation of John Norris, a Kentucky slave holder. They remained in hiding for two years. When Norris captured the blacks, whites attempted a rescue, and the dispute ended up in court. The judge concluded that the enslaved persons had escaped from a jurisdiction which recognized slavery; hence, they were returnable under the Fugitive Slave Act of 1793. The plaintiff thereby successfully sued the obstructors for violating federal law.

Lewis v. Henley, 2 Indiana Report 332 (1850)
James Lewis petitioned the state supreme court for a writ of mandamus to compel a school district to dismiss black children. The trustees explained that the children had paid their own tuitions, so they were not chargeable to the state. The court accepted this reasoning, explaining that the statute that barred blacks from the common schools did so to achieve social segregation and not to deny that black children did not need an education. To require that blacks finance their own education satisfied the aim of the statute.

Norris v. Crocker, 13 Howard 429 (1851)
A slave holder sought damages against a white for harboring an alleged runaway slave. The plaintiff asked the court for $500 in damages. The suit was pending in 1850 when Congress approved the revised fugitive slave law. The court held that the new statute had repealed that section of the 1793 law which related to the damages requested; hence, "the repeal does bar this action."

Polke v. Harper, 5 Indiana Report 241 (1854)
A black child had been enrolled in a common school organized to educate white children. A white parent objected and sued the board of trustees. A school administrator explained that the school was private and therefore was exempt from the state's segregation law. The court agreed, concluding that the petitioner had "no right to interfere" with a private school.

Woodward v. State, 6 Indiana Report 492 (1855)
A grand jury indicted Woodward, a black man, "for an assault . . . upon a white man." At the trial, a black man came forth as a witness for the defense. A lower court refused him under the state testimony law, which prohibited a black to testify against a white. The supreme court reversed the judgment.

Beebe v. State, 6 Indiana Report 501 (1855)
A black and a white had married in violation of Indiana's miscegenation law. The court explained that if a mixed marriage was just a matter of taste, residents could possibly do as they pleased. But "the state deems the product of such marriages [e.g. mulatto children] . . . an undesirable class of persons." The court upheld the statute, although it recognized it had violated the person's "unalienable" rights. It offered the ruling for "the public good."

Freeman v. Robinson, 7 Indiana Report 321 (1855)
Freeman, an alleged slave, brought action against a U.S. marshall named Robinson. Robinson had assaulted him and exposed his naked body to Indiana residents. Freeman charged that Robinson had also extorted money from him and wrongly accosted him as a runaway slave. The court held for Freeman and defended his common law right to damages.

Barkshire v. State, 7 Indiana 389 (1856)
A lower court convicted Arthur Barkshire, a free black, who had brought his wife Elizabeth into Indiana in violation of the state's immigration law. "The policy of the state is . . . clearly evolved. It is to exclude any further ingress of negroes, and to remove those already among us as speedily as possible." According to the constitution all contracts signed by blacks were to be voided, including marital ones. Hence, the court did not recognize Barkshire's marriage and ordered his wife to leave the state.

Weaver v. State, 8 Indiana 410 (1856)
A lower court convicted Henry Weaver, a mulatto, "for disturbing a common school." The defense called two African Americans as witnesses. The "prosecuting attorney objected to their being sworn unless the defendant would admit that said witnesses were niggers." Weaver refused and was convicted. On appeal, the supreme court held for Weaver, concluding that witnesses could be admitted or refused according to law, independent of any special conditions set by the prosecutor.

Graham v. Crocket, 18 Indiana 119 (1862)
This dispute involved the sale of a horse under a state law called the Three Hundred Dollar Act. A lower court had ruled for Crocket, a person of color, but Graham appealed the finding and won. Crocket had called African Americans as witnesses, but the appellant court excluded them under the state testimony law, which denied blacks the ability to testify against a white person. The supreme court reversed the judgment.

Riley v. Watson, 18 Indiana 291 (1862)
Two Indiana whites captured some blacks and removed them from the state on suspicion that they had escaped from Kentucky. The alleged slaves had

marks on their bodies that matched those mentioned in an advertisement. The slave catchers received a $300 reward. Watson who had been with the two whites sued for one-third of the reward. The judge instructed the jury to determine whether the blacks were legally slaves. The defense objected and asked the court to put its instructions in writing, to which the court refused. The defense appealed. The supreme court reversed the lower court's decision because of this procedural error.

Hatwood v. State, 18 Indiana 492 (1862)
The state prosecuted Mahon Hatwood, a mulatto, for coming into Indiana in violation of its immigration law. The court rejected evidence that he had been tried earlier and discharged for the same allegation. The court upheld the immigration statute, but dismissed the case because the state had not provided for the removal of blacks convicted under the law.

Smith v. Moody, 26 Indiana 299 (1866)
Smith, an African American, sued Moody for failing to satisfy a promissory note. Smith, a native of Ohio, had settled in Indiana in 1851. A lower court ruled against Smith, holding that he had entered Indiana in violation of the state's immigration law. This statute voided all contracts made by blacks upon entering into the state. The state supreme court reversed the decision, holding that persons of African ancestry are citizens of the United States.

Turner v. Parry, 27 Indiana 163 (1866)
This case involved the admission of testimony by a mulatto against a white. The supreme court admitted the black as a witness under an 1865 state law that removed the color bar and the federal Civil Rights Act of 1866 which made blacks citizens.

Ex Parte Lindley, Executor, 32 Indiana 367 (1869)
John Williams, an African American, assigned Lindley executor of his estate. Lindley assigned the funds, which amounted to almost $6,000, to pay debts and to educate Williams' children. A lower court closed the trust against the wishes of Lindley. The supreme court reversed the decision and ordered the money restored to Lindley.

Grimes' Executors v. Harmon, 35 Indiana 198 (1871)
Samuel Grimes bequeathed in his will an estate of more than $36,000 to the "orthodox protestant clergymen of Delphi" and for the "education of colored children." A lower court voided the will because it did not specify each recipient by name. The supreme court sustained the ruling, concluding that "the devise and bequest are void for vagueness and uncertainty."

State v. Gibson, 36 Indiana 389 (1871)
The state indicted a mulatto male who had married a white woman named Jennie Williams. A lower court "quashed" the indictment. The state appealed under an Indiana law that prohibited interracial marriages. The supreme court considered the question as to whether the Fourteenth Amendment and the Civil Rights Act provided for the marriage of whites and blacks. The court did not think so, holding that natural law "forbids their marriage."

Shipman v. State, 38 Indiana 549 (1872)
A lower court convicted Shipman for the murder of John C. Kelly. Shipman, who explained that he had been attacked by Kelly, claimed that he had acted in self-defense, and petitioned the court for a new trial. He intended to present "Moore, a colored washerwoman," as a witness, but the court upheld his conviction, concluding that, "No good reason is shown why their affidavits were not or could not be procured" at the first trial.

Cary v. Carter, 48 Indiana 327 (1874)
Carter sued a school district for denying admission to his children on account of their African ancestry. A lower court ruled in his favor. On appeal, the supreme court reviewed the state policy of segregation, concluding that the history of the black laws of Indiana made it unreasonable to suppose that the framers of the Constitution . . . intended to provide for the education of the children of that race in our common schools with the white children of the state." The court thereby ignored federal civil rights law, concluding that education was a matter of state policy.

Suggested Readings

Ball, T. H. Northwest Indiana from 1800 to 1900; or A View of our Region Through the Nineteenth Century (1900).

Barnhardt, John D. Indiana to 1816: The Colonial Period (1971).

Dillion, John B. A History of Indiana from its Earliest Exploration by Europeans to the Close of Territorial Government in 1816 (1971).

Elbert, Elmer D. "Southern Indiana in the Nineteenth Century." Ph.D. diss., Indiana University, 1967.

Gahl, Daniel R. "Indiana and the Sectional Pattern, 1828-1842." Ph.D. diss., Northwestern University, 1963.

Hawkins, Herbert Indiana's Road to Statehood: A Documentary Record (1964).

Madison, James H. The Indiana Way: A State History (1986).

_______. "The Northwest Ordinance and Constitutional Development in Indiana," 2 International Journal of Social Education, 1987: 16-29.

Miller, Marion C. "The Anti-Slavery Movement in Indiana." Ph.D. diss., University of Michigan, 1938.

Pierce, Merrily. "Luke Decker and Slavery: His Cases With Bob and Anthony, 1817-1822," 3 Indiana Magazine of History, 1989: 31-49.

Robbins, Coy D. (comp.), Orange County, Indiana: African Americans Americans Enumerated in the 1850 Census Journal of the Afro or 3 American Historical and Genealogical Society 1987: 99-113.

Strassweg, Elga. "The Kidnapping of Horace Bell," 46 Indiana History Bulletin 1969: 105-108.

Walsh, Justin E. The Centennial History of the Indiana General Assembly, 1816-1978, (1987).

Wimberly, Ware W. "Missionary Reforms in Indiana, 1826-1860: Education, Temperance, Antislavery." Ph.D. diss., Indiana University, 1977.

Part Three

ILLINOIS,
December 3, 1818

Americans had long recognized the agricultural potential of the Northwest Territory. Since the 1740s, American colonists had formed land companies to facilitate settlement of the area. France and Britain had also recognized the opportunity to encourage trade in the region. The Ohio River which flowed southward into the Mississippi River could become a highway to transport goods from the interior to the harbor in New Orleans. The rich soil in the Old Northwest made it likely that farmers from the southern colonies could be lured to the Northwest and to Illinois. French traders had brought enslaved Africans into the area since the 1720s to work in salt and lead mines. English speculators recognized that slave holders could be enticed by the fertile soil and climate, and by the prospect of bringing slaves into Illinois. Land claims held by individual colonies delayed mass emigration until the Northwest Territory became the common land of the United States in 1781.

France introduced slavery in Illinois in 1719, and the practice continued unencumbered until 1781. For the next few years, Congress and its committee listened to proposals on whether the Northwest Territory should be free or slave. Proposals favoring freedom appeared in 1781 when Timothy Pickering recommended to Congress that it prohibit slavery in a parcel of land reserved for veterans of the Revolutionary War. Congress ignored his request and formed a committee in 1784 under Thomas Jefferson to organize the Northwest Territory. Jefferson proposed to his committee that slavery be allowed in the territory until 1800. He assumed that slave holders would approve of this sixteen-year sanction for slavery. Slave holders found Jefferson's proposal alarming. They wanted to practice slavery without any restrictions. The committee didn't approve of his proposal either. Jefferson left the committee when Congress assigned his a diplomatic post in France. Congress formed new committees to organize the Northwest Territory. None did more than propose temporary governments until 1787.

A new committee drafted a plan acceptable to most politicians in 1787. Before sending the document on to Congress Nathan Dane attached Article 6 to the proposal, which prohibited slavery. Hurrying to go home, Congress adopted the Ordinance and its prohibition against slavery without debate.

Slave-holding Illinoisans condemned Article 6. They interpreted the article to mean that slavery could not exist in Illinois. Some slave holders complained that the government could not deprive them of their property without just compensation. Others packed their bags and left the territory. Still others remained in the territory to work for rescission or modification of the article. Slave holders in Illinois, therefore, joined their colleagues in Indiana who petitioned Congress to rescind Article Six.

Unable to achieve rescission, whites devised a scheme to circumvent the provision. There were many models from which whites could choose. Neighboring Indiana had found a solution in indentured servitude, which created de facto slavery. The zeal with which white settlers pursued slavery demonstrates influences far beyond Indiana, however. Both Indiana and Illinois inherited settlers from the South, where slavery and a color-charged culture had developed since the seventeenth century. It is not surprising, therefore, that white Illinoisans wanted to enslave African Americans. Restrained by the Ordinance of 1787, they, like whites in Indiana, and to a lesser extent, Ohio, blended the race and legal culture of the South with their region, which prohibited slavery. Illinois became a free state mainly in name; its African-American population lived on the fringe of slavery. State policy and laws came as close to recognizing slavery as possible, without directly violating Article 6 in the Ordinance. The state also oppressed free blacks in ways not unlike their Southern kinsmen.

Illinois and Indiana whites began their scheme of circumventing the Ordinance in 1803 when they inaugurated the indentured servitude system. The law permitted immigrating slave holders to bring enslaved African Americans into the region as servants. To conceal their intentions, they signed labor contracts with black servants. It is ludicrous to assume that an enslaved person could negotiate an equitable contract with a slave owner. Nonetheless, these agreements were enforceable in court. Aside from token considerations about the care and needs of servants--such as adequate food, shelter, and clothing--the contract obligated male servants to work for their master until age thirty-five and females until age twenty-eight. The law also empowered masters to discipline, lease, or sell servants. Furthermore, state law subjected the offsprings of servants to age and gender grades regarding terms of service. Illinois law virtually approved slavery.

When Illinois applied for statehood, the territorial legislature had decided on the status of blacks brought into the province by whites from the South. Unlike in Ohio, the question of civil rights for African Americans was not a serious consideration at the Illinois Constitutional Convention. Illinois convention delegates struggled over whether they should sanction slavery outright or create so much ambiguity in the constitutional clause that de facto slavery would be disguised. Since Article 6 in the Ordinance of 1787 made de jure slavery unlikely, and whites had failed in their efforts to repeal the article, the delegates opted for the strategy of ambiguity. Article 6 of the Illinois Constitution, therefore, began with these words: "Neither slavery nor involuntary servitude shall *hereafter* [author's emphasis] be introduced into this state." The word hereafter indicates that convention delegates opposed only the *introduction* of slaves after 1818.

What followed in Article 6 of the Illinois Constitution was firm support for servitude. The constitution provided a basis for holding a person in a state of slavery until at least age twenty-one for males and eighteen for females, with the prospect of longer terms, providing the servant conceded to the arrangement. Obviously, in a culture which insisted on obedience, black servants had few choices, especially when dealing with planters who were skilled in exploiting laborers. That single clause in the state's constitution, therefore, reduced blacks to the status of slaves. Also, after statehood, Illinois law authorized slave owners to use corporal punishment when disciplining slaves, denied slaves the ability to ratify contracts, and prohibited the assembly of more than two African Americans at a time. Illinois law also required a slave to carry a pass when traveling in the state.

Illinois adopted its first comprehensive slave code--black laws--in 1819. Through the codes, Illinois discouraged the immigration of free blacks by compelling them to produce a certificate of freedom and to register with a county clerk. Refugees without a certificate would not have legal residence; consequently, they were ineligible for employment, subject to removal, or could be sold as runaway slaves. Illinois did not welcome blacks; it welcomed slave holders who brought along blacks as laborers.

Illinois also restrained masters who considered the free North the place to release worn-out slaves. Some people argued that the state's immigration law was necessary to prevent Illinois from becoming a dumping ground for slave holders. Stephen Douglas argued that Illinois would not become "an asylum for all the old and decrepit and broken-down Negroes that may emigrate or be sent to it."[1] Whites threatened to resort to violence if the legislature of Illinois did not restrict black immigration. One anti-black spokesman threatened that whites "would take the matter into their hands, and commence a war of extermination."[2]

A visiting master could legally free a slave in Illinois by paying a $1,000 bond for each person released in the state. This policy was mainly a prohibitive measure; Illinois, one of the most proslavery free states in the Union, did not want an extensive free black population. Illinois might have faced an immigration crisis had it granted refuge to southern blacks. Its denunciation of black people, however, did not emanate from its migration problem; rather, from strong racial prejudice among whites in the state against people of color.

The strategy of intimidation did not restrain black Illinoisans for long; a movement to repeal the black laws germinated in the state. African Americans formed a society called the Repeal Association, a group dedicated to condemning and rescinding the black laws. John Jones, a black emigrant to Illinois during the early nineteenth century, rose to become the most prominent black leader to denounce the black laws. Jones, who was born free in North Carolina, left the Tar Heel State because he anticipated greater freedom in the North. He was greeted in Illinois by state officials who insisted that he conform to the black laws. Jones registered his name in 1844, pursuant to the Illinois immigration and residency statute. A skilled tailor, he made a small fortune in that business. Unpleasant experiences as a freeman continually disturbed him, so he joined the repeal association to help do away with the black laws. Along the way Jones entered politics. Ultimately, he became a notary public and, after the Civil War, a county commissioner in Illinois.

Had it not been for the Civil War, reform probably would not have come to Illinois before the twentieth century. Unlike its Ohio counterpart, the Illinois legislature did not repeal any part of the black laws before the war. The war, therefore, transformed Illinois; it forced the legislature to repeal the black laws. Black Illinoisans also benefitted from civil rights reforms initiated by Congress in 1866. Illinois adopted a few civil rights laws of its own. Civil rights reform in Illinois was a half-hearted effort, however, and the state remained rigidly segregated into the twentieth century. This is the story chronicled in this segment of *The Black Laws*. It presents a history of the pattern of discrimination in Illinois from the territorial stage in the late 1700s to the end of the next century.

NOTES

1. Leon F. Liwack, North of Slavery: The Negro in the Free State, 1790-1860, (Chicago: University of Chicago Press, 1961) pp. 67-68; Eugene H. Berwanger, The Frontier Against Slavery; Wetern Anti-Negro Prejudice and the Slavery Extension Controversy, (Urban: University of Illinois Press) p. 37.

2. Litwack, North of Slavery, p.37.

I

Declaration of Rights

Illinois set forth a bill of rights in its constitution, enumerating legal rights that could not be abridged by the state or its citizens. Illinois also prohibited slavery in compliance with Article 6 of the Northwest Ordinance of 1787. It was possible for Illinois to extend civil rights to African Americans during its territorial phase and the early years after statehood. The state, however, made it easy for whites to bring in slaves under the guise of indentured servitude. Illinois required emigrating slave holders to only sign labor contracts with each servant brought into the state. This principle of freedom and bondage in Illinois may seem contradictory even though the majority of whites never pretended to be liberal towards blacks. Most whites wanted Illinois to be a state exclusively for persons of European ancestry. Also wanting cheap laborers the whites circumvented Article 6 in the Ordinance. Without cheap laborers, some planters reasoned, Illinois would face a tough time reaching its agricultural potential. Consequently, Illinois proclaimed Jeffersonian notions about freedom, while rejecting equality between blacks and whites. The state constitution approved this dual policy inaugurated by the territorial legislature in 1803, and later refined by the general assembly of Illinois.

NUMBER 1

Constitution of Illinois, Article 8, 1818.
That the general, great and essential principles of liberty and free government may be recognized and unalterably established, we declare,

Section 1. That all men are born equally free and independent, and have certain inherent and indefeasible rights; among which are those of enjoying and defending life and liberty, and of acquiring, possessing and protecting property and reputation, and of pursuing their own happiness.

Section 2. That all power is inherent in the people, and all free governments are founded on their authority and instituted for their peace, safety, and happiness.

Section 3. That all men have a natural and indefeasible right to worship Almighty God according to the dictates of their own consciences; that no man can of right be compelled to attend, erect or support any place of worship, or to maintain any ministry against his consent; that no human authority can in any case whatever control or interfere with the rights of conscience; and that no preference shall ever be given by law to any religious establishments or modes of worship.

Section 4. That no religious test shall ever be required as a qualification to any office or public trust under this state.

Section 5. That elections shall be free and equal.

Section 6. That the right of trial by jury shall remain inviolate.

Section 7. That the people shall be secure in their persons, houses, papers, and possessions from unreasonable searches and seizures; and that general warrants whereby an officer may be commanded to search suspected places without evidence of the fact committed, or to seize any person or persons not named, whose offenses are not particularly described and supported by evidence, are dangerous to liberty, and ought not to be granted.

Section 8. That no freeman shall be imprisoned or disseized of his freehold, liberties or privileges, or outlawed or exiled, or in any manner deprived of his life, liberty or property, but by the judgment of his peers or the law of the land. And all land which have been granted as common to the inhabitants of any town, hamlet, village or corporation, by any persons, body politic or corporation, or by any government having power to make such grant, shall forever remain common to the inhabitants of such town, hamlet, village or corporation: and the said commons shall not be leased, sold or divided under any pretence whatever: Provided, however, that nothing in this shall be so construed as to affect the commons of Cahokia or Prairie du Pont: Provided also, that the general assembly shall have power and authority to grant the same privileges to the inhabitants of the said villages of Cahokia and Prairie du Pont as are hereby granted to the inhabitants of other towns, hamlets, and villages.

Section 9. That in all criminal prosecutions, the accused hath a right to be heard by himself and counsel; to demand the nature and cause of the accusation against him; to meet the witnesses face to face; to have compulsory process to compel the attendance of witnesses in his favor. And in prosecutions by indictment or information, a speedy public trial by an impartial jury of the vicinage: and that he shall not be compelled to give evidence against himself.

Section 10. That no person shall, for any indictable offence, be proceeded against criminally by information, except in cases arising in the land or naval forces, or the militia when in actual service, in time of war or public danger, by leave of the courts, for oppression or misdemeanor in office.

Section 11. No person shall, for the same offence, be twice put in jeopardy of his life or limb; nor shall any man's property be taken or applied to public use, without the consent of his representatives in the general assembly, nor without just compensation being made to him.

Section 12. Every person within this state ought to find a certain remedy in the laws, for all injuries or wrongs which he may receive in his person, property or character; he ought to obtain right and justice freely, and without being obliged to purchase it, completely and without denial, promptly and without delay, conformably to the laws.

Section 13. That all persons shall be bailable by sufficient sureties, unless for capital offenses, where the proof is evident or the presumption great; and the privilege of the writ of habeas corpus shall not be suspended, unless when in cases of rebellion or invasion, the public safety may require it.

Section 14. All penalties shall be proportioned to the nature of the offence, the true design of all punishment being to reform, not to exterminate mankind.

Section 15. No person shall be imprisoned for debt, unless upon refusal to deliver up his estate for the benefit of his creditors, in such manner as shall be prescribed by law, or in cases where there is strong presumption of fraud.

Section 16. No ex post facto law, nor any law impairing the validity of contracts shall ever be made; and no conviction shall work corruption of blood or forfeiture of estate.

Section 17. That no person shall be liable to be transported out of this state for any offence committed within the same.

Section 18. That a frequent recurrence of the fundamental principles of civil government is absolutely necessary to preserve the blessings of liberty.

Section 19. That the people have a right to assemble together in a peaceable manner to consult for their common good, to instruct their representatives, and to apply to the general assembly for redress of grievances.

Section 20. That the mode of levying a tax shall be by valuation, so that every person shall pay a tax in proportion to the value of property he or she has in his or her possession.

Section 21. That there shall be no other banks or monied institutions in this state but those already provided by law, except a state bank and its branches, which may be established and regulated by the general assembly of the state as they may think proper.

Section 22. The printing presses shall be free to every person who undertakes to examine the proceedings of the general assembly or of any branch of government; and no law shall ever be made to restrain the right thereof. The free communication of thoughts and opinions is one of the invaluable rights of man, and every citizen may freely speak, write, and print on any subject, being responsible for the abuse of that liberty.

Section 23. In prosecutions for the publication of papers investigating the official conduct of officers, or of men acting in a public capacity, or where the matter published is proper for public information, the truth thereof may be given in evidence. And in all indictments for libels the jury shall have the right of determining both the law and the fact, under the direction of the court as in other cases.

NUMBER 2

Constitution of Illinois, Article 6, 1818.

Section 1. Neither slavery nor involuntary servitude shall hereafter be introduced into this state, otherwise than for the punishment of crimes, whereof the party shall have been duly convicted; nor shall any male person, arrived at the age of twenty-one years, nor female person, arrived at the age of eighteen years, be held to serve any person as a servant, under any indenture hereafter made, unless such person shall enter into such indenture while in a state of perfect freedom, and on condition of a bona fide consideration received or to be received for their service. Nor shall any indenture of any negro or mulatto hereafter made and executed out of this state, or if made in this state, where the term of service exceeds one year, be of the least validity, except those given in cases of apprenticeship.

II

Militia Policy

Illinois barred African Americans from its militia primarily because of racial prejudice. Illinois lawmakers, as other whites in the Old Northwest, were aware of the exemplary military service rendered by African Americans in colonial wars. Yet, through constitutional and legislative means the state ignored their service record and reserved the militia for "free white male inhabitants." This policy was consistent with the rest of the state's racial code.

NUMBER 1

Constitution of Illinois, Article 5, 1818.

Section 1. The militia of the state of Illinois shall consist of all free male able bodied persons, (negroes, mulattoes and Indians excepted,) resident of the state, between the ages of eighteen and forty-five years, (except such persons as now are, or hereafter may be exempted by the laws of the United States or of this State,) and shall be armed, equipped, and trained as the general assembly may provide by law.

NUMBER 2

Constitution of Illinois, Article 8, 1848.

Section 1. The militia of the state of Illinois shall consist of all free male able-bodied persons, (negroes, mulattoes and Indians excepted,) resident of the state, between the ages of 18 and 45 years, except such persons as now are or hereafter may be exempted by the laws of the United States or of this state, and shall be armed, equipped and trained as the general assembly may provide by law.

NUMBER 3

Militia. Approved March 3, 1845, Revised Statutes.

Section 1. All free white male inhabitants, resident in this State, who are or shall be of the age of eighteen, and under the age of forty-five years, except as hereinafter excepted, shall severally and respectively be enrolled in the militia by the captain or commanding officer of the company within whose bounds such citizen shall reside, within ten days after he shall be informed of such residence; and also, those who may from time to time arrive at the age of eighteen, who shall reside in the bounds of his company; and shall without delay notify such person by an officer or non-commissioned officer of the company; and every such person so notified shall, within six months thereafter, provide himself with a good musket, fuzee or rifle, with proper accoutrements. The field officers, ranking as commissioned officers, shall be armed with a sword and pair of pistols, and the company officers with a sword; and every person so enrolled, and providing himself with arms and accoutrements required as aforesaid, shall hold the same exempt from execution, distress, or for tax: Provided, No private shall be compelled to appear on parade with arms unless he actually has them.

III

Suffrage and Elections

Only white males were eligible to vote in Illinois. Unable to choose representatives or hold political office themselves, blacks were left at the mercy of whites. Like in other states of the Old Northwest, race prejudice influenced lawmakers who wanted not only to discourage the emigration of free blacks or runaway slaves, but also to oppress African Americans already in Illinois. The state legislature did not want to offer any illusion of freedom to African Americans; slave or free. The state's suffrage and election laws, therefore, were an important feature of the racial policy of Illinois.

NUMBER 1

Census. March 3, 1845, Revised Statutes.

Section 5. Each commissioner shall commence taking such enumeration on the first day of July in each year in which such enumeration is required to be taken, and shall ascertain and set down in a book to be kept for that purpose, in a convenient tabular form, the following facts: The number each, of white males and females of ten years of age and under; over ten and not over twenty; over twenty and not over thirty; over thirty and not over forty; over forty and not over fifty; over fifty and not over sixty; over sixty and not over seventy; over seventy and not over eighty; over eighty and not over ninety; over ninety and not over one hundred; over one hundred: Also, the number of white male persons between the ages of eighteen and forty-five years, subject to military duty: Also, each, of free male and female persons of color, of all ages; of indentured or registered servants and their children; of French negroes and mulattoes held in bondage: Also, the number of manufactories of every kind, and the annual product of each kind; the number and annual product of coal mines; the value of live stock; value of grains produced; value of all other agricultural products; the number of pounds of wool; number of mills and distilleries; the number of universities or colleges; academies and grammar schools, and common schools, with the number of pupils in each.

Section 10. Each free person, over the age of sixteen years, whether heads of families or not, belonging to any family within any county, made or established in this state, shall be and hereby is obliged to render to the commissioner appointed in said county, if required, a true account, to the best of his or her knowledge, of every person belonging to such family, respectively, according to the several descriptions aforesaid, on pain of forfeiting twenty dollars, to be sued for and recovered by action of debt, by such commissioner, for the use of the proper county: Provided, That in all cases where any such fine shall be assessed against any minor or minors, the same shall be paid by his, her or their parent or guardian; and in case of his or her refusal to pay the same, an attachment may be issued to enforce the payment thereof.

NUMBER 2

Constitution of Illinois, Article 6, 1848.

Section 1. In all elections every white male citizen above the age of 21 years, having resided in the state one year next preceding any election, shall be entitled to vote at such election; and every white male inhabitant of the age aforesaid, who may be a resident of the state at the time of the adoption of this constitution, shall have the right of voting as aforesaid; but no such citizen or inhabitant shall be entitled to vote, except in the district or county in which he shall actually reside at the time of such election.

Section 2. All votes shall be given by ballot.

Section 3. Electors shall, in all cases, except treason, felony or breach of the peace, be privileged from arrest during their attendance at elections, and in going to and returning from the same.

Section 4. No elector shall be obliged to do militia duty on the days of election, except in time of war or public danger.

Section 5. No elector shall be deemed to have lost his residence in this state by reason of his absence on the business of the United States, or of this state.

Section 6. No soldier, seaman or marine in the army or navy of the United States, shall be deemed a resident of this state in consequence of being stationed at any military or naval place within the state.

Section 7. No person shall be elected or appointed to any office in this state, civil or military, who is not a citizen of the United States, and who shall not have resided in this state one year next before the election or appointment.

Section 8. The general assembly shall have full power to pass laws excluding from the right to suffrage persons convicted of infamous crimes.

Section 9. The general elections shall be held on the Tuesday next after the first Monday of November, biennially, until otherwise provided by law.

IV

Servants and Slaves

Illinois sanctioned a form of slavery during its territorial period, whereby emigrating whites could bring slaves into the territory and maintain control over them. Imitating the slave codes of the South, Illinois authorized masters to punish slothful servants. Black residents could also employ servants in Illinois, just as they could own slaves in the Southern states. They could not, however, own a white servant. The state set free any white servant purchased by a black. Illinois law also approved the employment of hired-out slaves, a practice that extended legal slavery far beyond the South.

NUMBER 1

An act concerning Negroes and Mulattoes. Approved December 22, 1814, Illinois Acts.

Whereas the erection of mills and other valuable improvements are greatly retarded in this Territory, from the want of Laborers, and whereas also experience has proved that the manufacture of salt in particular, at the United States Saline cannot be successfully carried on by white laborers, and it being the interest of every description of inhabitants to afford every facility to the most extensive manufacture of that article, so necessary to them all, that the most natural means of obtaining a certainty of the necessary supplies thereof at the lowest price.

Section 1. Be it enacted by the Legislative Council and house of Representatives of the Illinois Territory, and it is hereby enacted by the authority of the same that if any slave whatsoever, shall voluntarily hire himself or herself, within the Territory, by the consent of his or her master, for any term not exceeding twelve months, his or her continuance in the Territory according to such hiring shall not operate in any way whatever to injure the right of property in the master, in and to the services of such slave or slaves, Provided however that in all such cases such slave or slaves shall be examined privately, separate and apart from his or her owner by a Justice of the peace or any clerk of a court, as to his or her voluntary consent, and a certificate of such Justice or clerk shall be conclusive evidence of such Voluntary consent, and may be admitted to record, and provided that said slave or slaves, shall for the time being, be considered and treated as indented servants. This act shall commence and be in force from the passage thereof.

NUMBER 2

Constitution of Illinois, Article 6, 1818.

Section 2. No person bound to labor in any other state shall be hired to labor in this State, except within the tract reserved for the salt-works near Shawneetown; nor even at that place for a longer period than one year at any one time; nor shall it be allowed there after the year 1825. Any violation of this article shall effect the emancipation of such person from his obligation to service.

Section 3. Each and every person who has been bound to service by contract or indenture in virtue of the laws of Illinois Territory heretofore existing, and in conformity to the provisions of the same, without fraud or collusion, shall be held to a specific performance of their contracts or indentures; and such negroes and mulattoes as have been registered in conformity with the aforesaid laws shall serve out the time appointed by said laws: Provided, however, That the children hereafter born of such person, negroes or mulattoes, shall become free, the males at the age of twenty-one years, the females at the age of eighteen years. Each and every child born of indentured parents shall be entered with the clerk of the county in which they reside, by their owners, within six months after the birth of said child.

NUMBER 3

An act to license and regulate taverns. Approved February 27, 1819, Revised Laws.

Section 8. And be it further enacted, That no person shall, by any means, presume to furnish, supply, or sell to any bond servant or slave, any rum, brandy, spirits, or any other strong liquors, or strong water, mixed or unmixed, either within or without doors, nor shall receive, harbor, or entertain any slave or servant in or about his, her, or their houses, without special license had and obtained under the hand of such master or mistress of such slave or bond servant respectively, under the penalty, for the first offence, of three dollars, and for every succeeding offence, four dollars, to be recovered before any one of the justices of the peace of the county where the offence is committed, on the proof of one or more credible witnesses, or upon the view of any justice within the respective counties where the act shall be committed.

NUMBER 4

An act to amend an act entitled "An act respecting free Negroes, mulattoes, servants, and slaves." Approved January 3, 1825. Laws of Illinois.

Section 1. Be it enacted by the people of the state of Illinois represented in the General Assembly, That any person who may have failed or neglected to comply with the provisions of the third section of the act above recited, and to which this is an amendment, shall be, and they are hereby released and entirely discharged from any penalty incurred under the provisions of the said act, or from any verdict or judgment rendered against them in any of the counties of this state: Provided always, That such person or persons shall, within sixty days after the passage of this act, enter into bond, agreeably to the provisions of the said act, to the county commissioners of the county wherein such penalty may have been incurred, or verdict or judgment rendered, to indemnify the said county from any charge or liability, of any description whatsoever, heretofore incurred, or that may hereafter be incurred, on account of the emancipation of any person or persons of the description in the said act named, and on the further condition of the payment of all costs of suit accumulated by or under any prosecution instituted against such person for an infringement of the said third section of the act to which this is an amendment.

NUMBER 5

An Act to amend an act, entitled "An act respecting free Negroes, mulattoes, servants and slaves." Approved February 1, 1831, Laws of Illinois.

Section 1. Be it enacted by the people of the State of Illinois, represented in the General Assembly, That no black or mulatto person shall hereafter be permitted to come and reside in this State, until such person shall have given bond and security, as is required in the first section of the act to which this is an amendment. Any person who shall hereafter bring into this State, any black or mulatto person, in order to free him or her from slavery, or shall directly, or indirectly, bring into the State, or aid or assist any person in bringing any such black or mulatto person to settle or reside therein, shall be fined one hundred dollars, on conviction, or indictment, or before any justice of the peace in the county where such offense shall be committed.

NUMBER 6

Tavern keepers selling to slaves. Revised Statutes, (1833).

Section 130. Every tavern keeper, or other retailer of spirituous liquors, who shall barter, sell, or exchange, any wine, rum, gin, brandy, whiskey, or other spirituous liquors, to any black or mulatto servant or slave, without the consent of the master or mistress of such servant or slave, and every person, whether a tavern keeper or not, who shall sell, barter, or exchange any wine, rum, gin, brandy, whiskey, or other spirituous or mixed liquors, to any Indian or Indians in this State, shall, on conviction, be fined in the sum of ten dollars for each offence.

NUMBER 7

Apprentices. Approved March 3, 1845, Revised Statutes.

Section 10. The age and time of service of every apprentice or servant shall be inserted in his or her indentures; but if such age shall be unknown, then it shall be inserted according to the best information, which age shall, in relation to the term of service, be deemed and taken as the true age of such minor.

Section 11. In all indentures it shall be provided that the master or mistress shall cause such clerk, apprentice or servant, to be taught to read and write, and the ground rules of arithmetic; and shall also, at the expiration of such term of service, give to such apprentice a new Bible, and two complete suits of new wearing apparel, suitable to his or her condition in life: Provided, That if such minor be a negro or mulatto, it shall not be necessary to require that he or she taught to write or the knowledge of arithmetic.

NUMBER 8

Attachments in circuit courts. Approved March 3, 1845, Revised Statutes.

Section 24. When any sheriff or other officer shall serve an attachment on slaves, or indentured or registered colored servants, or horses, cattle or live stock, and the same shall not be immediately replevied or restored to the debtor, it shall and may be lawful for such officer to provide sufficient sustenance for the support of such slaves indentured, or registered colored servants, and live stock, until the same shall be sold, or otherwise legally disposed of, or discharged from such attachment. He shall receive therefor a reasonable compensation, to be ascertained and determined by the court out of which the attachment issued, and the same shall be charged in the fee bill of such officers, and shall be collectable as part of the costs in the attachment.

NUMBER 9

Embezzlement by servants. Approved March 3, 1845, Revised Statutes.

Section 70. If any clerk, apprentice or servant, whether bound or hired, to whom any money, bank bill or note, or goods or chattels, shall be entrusted or delivered by his or her master or mistress, shall withdraw himself or herself from his or her master or mistress, and go away with the said money, bank bill or note, or goods or chattels, or any part thereof, with intent to steal the same, and defraud his or her master or mistress thereof, contrary to the trust and confidence in him or her reposed by his or her said master or mistress, or being in the service of his or her said master and mistress, shall embezzle the said money, bank bill or note, goods or chattels, or any part thereof, or otherwise shall convert the same to his or her own use, with like purpose to steal the same, every such person so offending shall be deemed guilty of larceny, and be punished accordingly.

NUMBER 10

Offenses relative to slaves, indentured servants, and apprentice, Approved March 3, 1845, Revised Statutes.

Section 151. If any keeper of a public house or retailer of spirituous liquors, shall receive, harbor, entertain or trust any minor or apprentice within the age of twenty-one years, or any servant or slave, knowing them to be such, after having been cautioned or warned to the contrary by the parent, guardian, master or mistress of such minor, apprentice, servant or slave, in the presence of one or more credible witnesses; every such keeper of a public house, or retailer of spirituous liquors as aforesaid, so offending, shall, upon conviction thereof, be fined in the sum of twelve dollars, and shall, moreover, forfeit his or her license.

NUMBER 11

Day laborers. Approved February 17, 1857, Session Laws.

Section 1. That the county commissioners' courts of the several counties in this state, at the March term annually, shall fix and cause to be entered upon the records of their courts, a certain number of days, not exceeding five nor less than two, that each and every able bodied man, between the ages of twenty-one and fifty years (men of color not excepted), shall labor on some public road within the county during the year; and it shall be the duty of the clerk of said court to certify the number of days fixed as aforesaid in the notice to each supervisor appointed in said county.

V

Immigration and Residency

Lawmakers in Illinois had placed limits on black emigration since the territorial period. An 1813 statute also discouraged free blacks from entering Illinois. Penalties for violating immigration and residency laws included corporal punishment. To obtain legal residence, a black emigrant had to produce a certificate of freedom and post a bond for his welfare and behavior. Before statehood, the law also required black residents to register with a county clerk, and forbade a slave holder from bringing an enslaved black to Illinois in order to emancipate the person. These statutes also denied free blacks and whites civil rights by outlawing interracial marriages or any sort of cohabitation between blacks and whites.

NUMBER 1

An act to prevent the migration of free Negroes and mulattoes into this Territory and for other purposes. Approved December 8, 1813, Laws of Illinois.

Section 1. Be it enacted by the Legislative Council and House of Representatives of the Illinois Territory That it shall not be lawful for any free negro or mulatto to migrate in this Territory, and every free negro or mulatto who shall come into this Territory contrary to this act shall and may be apprehended and carried by an citizen before some Justice of the peace of the county where he shall be taken; which Justice is hereby authorized to examine, and order to leave the Territory every such free negro or Mulatto, which said free negro or Mulatto shall be allowed from the time of his examination before the Justice of the peace fifteen days to depart from the Territory, and if after the expiration of the said fifteen days he or she shall be found in the Territory he or she shall be carried before a Justice of the peace who shall order him or her to be whipped on his or her bare back not exceeding thirty-nine stripes nor less than twenty-five stripes and if he or she shall thereafter remain in the Territory fifteen days he or she may be punished in the same manner as aforesaid and so on as long as he or she shall refuse or fail to depart from the Territory.

Section 2. Be it further enacted that all free negroes and Mulattoes now residing in the Territory shall within six months after the passage of this act apply to the clerk of the court of Common Pleas of the County in which such negro or mulatto may reside to be registered and numbered by the clerk, which register shall specify the name, age, color, and stature of said free negro or mulatto, a copy of which register signed by the clerk shall be delivered to the said free negro or mulatto for which the clerk shall demand of him or her the sum of fifty cents--Provided however that no negro or mulatto as aforesaid, shall claim the benefit of this section until he, she, or they produce to such clerk satisfactory evidence that he, she, or they is, or are entitled to freedom--Provided also that no negro or mulatto who is claimed as a servant or slave by any person or persons shall be entitled to the benefit of this section.

Section 3. Be it further enacted that if any such Free negro or mulatto being of the age of twenty-one years shall neglect to procure such certificate it shall be the duty of any Justice of the Peace of the county wherein he or she may be found to order him or her to leave the Territory as in the first section of this act, and the said free negro or mulatto shall be subject to the same penalties for refusing to leave the Territory as is provided in the first section of this act.

Section 4. Be it further enacted that if any such free negro or mulatto shall hereafter be convicted before any Justice of the peace of the county where the offence was committed, of stealing, or harboring runaway negroes or mulattoes or slaves belonging to persons either in this Territory or elsewhere. The said Justice of the peace whose duty it shall be to take cognizance of such offenses, shall order him or her to receive on his or her bare back not less than thirty-nine nor more than fifty lashes and the Justice shall order him or her to depart from Territory in thirty days, and if such free negro or mulatto shall neglect to depart accordingly, he or she shall be dealt with in the same manner as is provided in the first section of this act.

Section 5. Be it further enacted that any such free negro or mulatto who is required by this act to register with the said clerk in the same manner all such free negroes or mulattoes residing with him or her as may be under the age of twenty-one years. And on failure thereof such free negroes and mulattoes being under the age of twenty-one years may be carried before the court of common pleas of the county, whose duty it shall be to bind them out until they attain the age of twenty-five years. This act to commence and be in force from and after the passage thereof.

NUMBER 2

An act to amend an act entitled "An act respecting free Negroes, mulattoes, servants and slaves." Approved January 17, 1829, Laws of Illinois.

Section 1. Be it enacted by the People of the State of Illinois, represented in the General Assembly, That no black or mulatto person shall hereafter be permitted to come and reside in this State, until such person shall have given bond and security, as is required in the first section of the act to which this is an amendment. Any person who shall hereafter bring into this State, any black or mulatto person, in order to free him or her from slavery, or shall directly, or indirectly, bring into the State, or aid or assist any person in bringing any such black or mulatto person to settle or reside therein, shall be fined one hundred dollars, on conviction, or indictment, or before any justice of the peace in the county where such offence shall be committed.

NUMBER 3

An act in relation to free Negroes and Mulattoes. Approved February 19, 1841, Laws of Illinois.

Section 1. Be it enacted by the People of the State of Illinois, represented in the General Assembly, That every black or mulatto person, being a native of this State, and residing within the same, may at any time enter his or her names, together with the names of his or her family, with the clerk of the circuit court of the county in which he or she may reside, together with the evidence of his or her freedom, which shall be entered on record by said clerk, together with a description of all such persons; and thereafter the clerks' certificate of such record shall be prima facia evidence of his or her freedom and offer them the same protection, and have the same effect in law, as is given to certificates granted in the pursuance of the fourth section of the act entitled "An act respecting free negroes, mulattoes, servants and slaves," approved, March thirtieth, one thousand eight hundred and nineteen: Provided, nevertheless, That nothing herein contained shall be construed to bar the lawful claim of any person or persons to any such negro or mulatto.

NUMBER 4

Negroes and mulattoes. Approved March 3, 1845, Revised Statutes.

Section 1. No black or mulatto person, shall be permitted to reside in this State, until such person shall produce to the county commissioners' court where he or she is desirous of settling, a certificate of his or her freedom; which certificate shall be duly authenticated in the same manner that is required to be done, in cases arising under the acts and judicial proceedings of other States. And until such person shall have given bond, with sufficient security, to the people of this State for the use of the proper county, in the penal sum of one thousand dollars, conditioned that such person will not, at any time, become a charge to said county, or any other county of this State, as a poor person, and that such person shall, at all times, demean himself or herself, in strict conformity with the laws of this State that now are or hereafter may be enacted; the solvency of said security shall be approved by said clerk. The clerk shall file said bond, and if said bond shall in any condition thereof be broken, the whole penalty shall become forfeited, and the clerk, on being informed thereof, shall cause the said bond to be prosecuted to effect. And it shall be the duty of such clerk to make an entry of the certificate so produced and indorse a certificate on the original certificate, stating the time the said bond was approved and filed; and the name and description of the person producing the same; after which it shall be lawful for such free negro or mulatto to reside in this State.

Section 2. If any person shall harbor such negro or mulatto as aforesaid, not having such certificate, and given bond, and taken a certificate thereof, or shall hire, or in anywise give sustenance to such negro or mulatto, not having such certificate of freedom, and of having given bond, shall be fined in the sum of five hundred dollars, one-half thereof to the use of the county, and the other half to the party giving information thereof: Provided, This section shall not affect any negro or mulatto who is now a resident of this State.

Section 3. It shall be the duty of all free negroes and mulattoes who shall come to reside in this State, having a family of his or her own, and having a certification of freedom mentioned in the first section of this chapter, to give to the clerk of the county commissioners' court, at the time of making an entry of his certificate, a description with the name and ages of his, her, or their family, which shall be stated by the clerk in the entry made by him of such certificate; and the clerk shall also state the same on the original certificate: Provided, however, That nothing contained in this or the preceding section of this chapter, shall be construed to prevent the overseers of the poor in any township from causing any such free negro or mulatto to be removed, who shall come into this State contrary to the provisions of the statute concerning the poor.

Section 4. Every black or mulatto person (slaves and persons held to service excepted) residing in this State, shall enter his or her name, (unless they have heretofore entered the same,) together with the name or names of his or her family, with the clerk of the county commissioners' court of the county in which they reside, together with the evidence of his or her freedom; which shall be entered into the record by the said clerk, together with a description of all such persons; and thereafter the clerk's certificate of such record shall be sufficient evidence of his or her freedom: Provided, That nothing in this chapter contained, shall be construed to bar the lawful claim of any person or persons to any such negro or mulatto.

Section 5. Every black or mulatto person who shall be found in this State, and not having such a certificate as is required by this chapter, shall be deemed a runaway slave or servant, and it shall be lawful for any inhabitant of this State, to take such black or mulatto person not produce such certificate as aforesaid, it shall be the duty of such justice to cause such black or mulatto person to be committed to the custody of the sheriff of the county, who shall keep such black or mulatto person, and in three days after receiving him, shall advertise him, at the court house door, and shall transmit a notice, and cause the same to be advertised for six weeks in some public newspaper printed nearest to the place of apprehending such black person or mulatto, stating a description of the most remarkable features of the supposed runaway, and if such person so committed shall not produce a certificate or other evidence of his freedom, within the time aforesaid, it shall be the duty of the sheriff to hire him out for the best price he can get, after having given five days previous notice thereof, from month to month, for the space of one year; and if no owner shall appear and substantiate his claim before the expiration of the year, the sheriff shall give a certificate to such black or mulatto person, who, on producing the same to the next circuit court of the county, may obtain a certificate from the court stating the facts and the person shall be deemed a free person, unless he shall be lawfully claimed by his proper owner or owners thereafter. And as a reward to the taker up of such negro, there shall be paid by the owner, if any, before he shall receive him from the sheriff, ten dollars, and the owner shall pay to the sheriff for the justice, two dollars, and reasonable costs for taking such runaway, as other prisoners. Provided, however, That the proper owner, if any there be, shall be entitled to hire any such runaway from the sheriff, after deducting the expenses of the same: And, provided also, That the taker up shall have a right to claim any reward which the owner shall have offered for the apprehension of such runaway; Should any taker up claim any such offered reward, he shall not be entitled to the allowance made by this section.

Section 6. If any negro or mulatto, being the property of a citizen of the United States, residing without this State, shall hereafter come into this State for the purpose of hiring himself or herself to labor in this State, and shall afterwards institute, or procure to be instituted, any suit or proceedings, for the purpose of procuring his or her freedom, it shall be the duty of the court before which such suit or proceeding shall be instituted and pending, upon being satisfied that such negro or mulatto had come into this State for the purpose aforesaid, to dismiss such suit or proceeding, and cause the same to be certified to the sheriff of the county, who shall immediately take possession of such negro or mulatto, whose duty shall be to confine such negro or mulatto in the jail of his county, and notify the owner of such slave of the commitment aforesaid, and that said owner make immediate application for said slave; and it shall be the duty of the sheriff, on such application being made, after all reasonable costs and charge being paid, to deliver to said owner such negro or mulatto slave.

Section 7. Every servant, upon the expiration of his or her time, and proof thereof made before the circuit court of the county where he or she last served, shall have his or her freedom recorded, and a certificate thereof, under the hand of the clerk, which shall be sufficient to indemnify any person for entertaining or hiring such servant; and if such certificate should happen to be torn or lost, the clerk, upon request, shall issue another, reciting therein the loss of the former.

Section 8. Any person who shall hereafter bring into this State any black or mulatto person, in order to free him or her from slavery, or shall directly or indirectly bring into this State, or aid or assist any person in bringing any such black and mulatto person to settle or reside therein, shall be fined one hundred dollars, on conviction or indictment, or before any justice of the peace in the county where such offence shall be committed.

Section 9. If any slave or servant shall be found at a distance of ten miles from the tenement of his or her master, or the person with whom he or she lives, without a pass, or some letter or token, whereby it may appear that he or she is not in possessing of any authorization from his or her master, employer or overseer, it shall and may be lawful for any person to apprehend and carry him or her before a justice of the peace, to be by his order punished with stripes, not exceeding thirty-five at his discretion.

Section 10. If any slave or servant shall presume to come and be upon the plantation, or at the dwelling of any person whatsoever, without leave from his or her owner, not being sent upon lawful business, it shall be lawful for the owner of such plantation, or dwelling house, to give or order such slave or servant ten lashes on his or her bare back.

Section 11. Riots, routs, unlawful assemblies, trespasses and seditious speeches, by any slave or slaves, servant or servants, shall be punished with stripes, at the discretion of a justice of the peace, not exceeding thirty-nine and he who will, may apprehend and carry him, her or them before such justice.

Section 12. If any person or persons shall permit or suffer any slave or slaves, servant or servants of color, to the number of three or more, to assemble in his or their out-house, yard or shed, for the purpose of dancing or revelling, either by night or by day, the person or persons so offending shall forfeit and pay the sum of twenty dollars with costs, to any person or persons who will sue for and recover the same by action of debt or by indictment, in any court of record, proper to try the same.

Section 13. It shall be the duty of all coroners, sheriffs, judges and justices of the peace, who shall see or know of, or be informed of any such assemblage of slaves or servants, immediately to commit such slaves or servants to the jail of the county, and on view or proof thereof, order each and every such slave or servant to be whipped, not exceeding thirty-nine stripes, on his or her bare back, on the day next succeeding such assemblage, unless it shall happen on a Sunday, then on the Monday following; which said stripes shall be inflicted by any constable of the township, if there should be one therein, or otherwise by any person or persons whom the said justices shall appoint, and who shall be willing so to inflict the same: Provided, however, That the provisions hereof shall not apply to any persons of color who may assemble for the purpose of amusement, by permission of their masters, first had in writing, on condition that no disorderly conduct is made use of by them in such assemblage.

Section 14. In all cases of penal laws, where free persons are punishable by fine servants shall be punished by whipping, after the rate of twenty lashes for every eight dollars, so that no servant shall receive more than forty lashes at any one time unless such offender can procure some person to pay the fine.

Section 15. No person shall buy, sell, or receive of, to or from any servant or slave, any coin or commodity, without leave or consent of the master or owner of such slave or servant, and any person so offending shall forfeit and pay to the master or owner of such slave or servant four times the value of the thing so bought, sold or received, to be recovered with costs of suit, before any court having cognizance of the same.

Section 16. Any such servant being lazy, disorderly, guilty of misbehavior to his master or master's family, shall be corrected by stripes, on order from a justice of the county wherein he resides; or refusing to work, shall be compelled thereto in like manner, and moreover shall serve two days for every one he shall have so refused to save, or shall otherwise have lost, without sufficient justification. All necessary expenses incurred by any master for apprehending and bringing home any absconding servant, shall be repaid by repaid by further services, after such rates as the circuit court of the county shall direct, unless such servant shall give security, to be approved by the court, for the payment in money within six months after he shall be free from service, and shall accordingly pay the same.

Section 17. All contracts between masters and servants, during the time of service, shall be void.

Section 18. The benefit of any contract of service shall be assignable by the master to any person being a citizen of this State, to whom the servant shall, in the presence of a justice of the peace, freely consent that it shall be assigned, the said justice attesting such free consent in writing; and shall also pass to the executors, administrators and legatees of the master.

Section 19. No negro, mulatto or Indian, shall at any time purchase any servant, other than of his own complexion; and if any of the persons aforesaid shall nevertheless, presume to purchase a white servant, such servant shall immediately become free, and shall be so held, deemed and taken.

Section 20. Servants shall be provided by the master with wholesome and sufficient food, clothing and lodging, and at the end of their service, if they shall not have contracted for any reward, food, clothing and lodging, shall receive from him one new and complete suit of clothing, suited to the season of the year, to-wit: a coat, waistcoat, pair of breeches and shoes, two pair of stockings, two shirts, a hat and blanket.

Section 21. If any servants shall at any time bring in goods or money during the time of their service, shall by gift or other lawful means, acquire goods or money, they shall have the property and benefit thereof to their own use; and if any servant shall be sick or lame, and so become useless or chargeable, his or her master or owner shall maintain such servant until his or her time of service shall be expired; and if any master or owner shall put away any lame or sick servant, under pretence of freedom, and such servant becomes chargeable to the county, such master or owner shall forfeit and pay thirty dollars to the overseers of the poor of the county wherein such offence shall be committed, to the use of the poor of the county, recoverable with costs, by action of debt, in any circuit court; and moreover, shall be liable to the action of the said overseers of the poor at the common law for damages.

Section 22. The circuit court of every county shall, at all times, receive the complaints of servants, being citizens of any of the United States of America, who reside within the jurisdiction of such court, against their masters or mistresses, alleging undeserved or immoderate correction, insufficient allowances of food, raiment or lodging or any failure in the duties of such master or mistress as prescribed in this chapter, and the said circuit court shall hear and determine complaints of masters and mistresses against their servants, for desertion without good cause, and may oblige the latter, for loss thereby occasioned, to make restitution by further services after the expiration of the time for which they had been bound.

Section 23. Any black, colored or mulatto man and white woman, and any white man and black, colored or mulatto woman, who shall live together in an open state of adultery or fornication, or adultery and fornication, shall be indicted, and on conviction, severally fined, in any sum not exceeding five hundred dollars, and confined in the penitentiary for a term not exceeding one year. For the second offence, the punishment shall be double; for the third, trebled, and in the same ratio for each succeeding offence.

NUMBER 5

Senate report of the judiciary committee relative to Negroes. Approved March 1, 1847, Illinois Documents.

That the prayer of the petition cannot be granted, because the grant of it would be to disregard the best interests of the citizens of this State, and in conflict with the Constitution of this State. 1st. To repeal all laws making a distinction between the negro and the white man, would be to invite an emigration of emancipated negroes to become residents of this State, by thousands, and thereby increase an evil already felt in this State, for the

Legislature will soon, without the aid of laws, such as asked for in the petition, be called on for remedy by the removal of the African from our State. A result which will be effected, whether by peaceful means, or by violence, time alone will determine. The committee believe that no acts of legislation will or can ever raise the African in this country above the level in which the petitions find him. And that if he is not content with the provisions of our laws, Africa, the land of his fathers, a climate congenial with his nature, lies open before him, where he may test the powers of his mind for self-government. Here he never can aspire to such privileges while there remains one of the Anglo-Saxon race. 2d. It would be a violation of our State Constitution, for it provides in section 27th of the second article, that in all elections, all white male inhabitants above the age of twenty-one years, having resided in this State six months next preceding the election, shall enjoy the right of an elector. This section of the constitution prescribes the limits of the governing power in this State, and in that limit the African is not to be found; hence he is excluded, and ever will be in this State, from the elective franchise.

A very able report was made to the House of Representatives on this subject, at the last session of the Legislature, which it was then believed would set this question forever at rest; and to unanswerable arguments of that report the committee would refer the petitioners, with this suggestion, that if the petitioners are free white inhabitants of this state, that the prayer of this petition asks not to redress any grievance of which they should complain; and should they be negroes, the committee would remark that this State cannot be regarded by them as their permanent haven, and that their request can never be granted.

NUMBER 6

An act to prevent the immigration of free Negroes into this state. Approved February 12, 1853, Laws of Illinois.

Section 1. Be it enacted by the people of the state of Illinois, represented in the General Assembly, That if any person or persons shall bring, or cause to be brought into this state, any negro or mulatto slave, whether said slave is set free or not, shall be liable to an indictment, and, upon conviction thereof, be fined for every such negro or mulatto, a sum not less than one hundred dollars, nor more than five hundred dollars, and imprisoned in the county jail not more than one year, and shall stand committed until said fine and costs are paid.

Section 2. When an indictment shall be found against any person, or persons, who are not residents of this state, it shall be the duty of the court before whom said indictment is pending, upon affidavit being made and filed in said court by the prosecuting attorney, or any other credible witness, setting forth the non-residence of said defendant, to notify the governor of this state, by causing the clerk of said court to transmit to the office of the secretary of state a certified copy of said indictment and affidavit, and it shall be the duty of the governor, upon the receipt of said copies, to appoint some suitable person to arrest said defendant or defendants, in whatever state or county he or they may be found, and to commit him or them to the jail of the county in which said indictment is pending, there to remain and answer said indictment, and be otherwise dealt with in accordance with this act. And it shall be the duty of the governor to issue all necessary requisitions, writs, and papers to the governor or other executive officer of the state, territory, or province where such defendant or defendants may be found: Provided, that this section shall not be construed so as to affect persons, or slaves, bona fide traveling through this state from and to any other state in the United States.

Section 3. If any negro, or mulatto, bond or free, shall hereafter come into this state and remain ten days, with the evident intention of residing in the same, every such negro or mulatto shall be deemed guilty of a high misdemeanor, and for the first offence shall be fined the sum of fifty dollars, to be recovered before any justice of the peace in the county where said negro or mulatto may be found. Said proceedings shall be in the name of the people of the state of Illinois, and shall be tried by a jury of twelve men. The person making the information or complaint shall be a competent witness upon said trial.

Section 4. If said negro or mulatto shall be found guilty, and the fine assessed be not paid forthwith to the justice of the peace before whom said proceedings were had, it shall be the duty of said justice to commit said negro or mulatto to the custody of the sheriff of said county, or otherwise keep him, her or them in custody; and said justice shall forthwith advertise said negro or mulatto, by posting up notices thereof in at least three of the most public places in his district, which said notices shall be posted up for ten days, and on the day and at the time and place mentioned in said advertisement, the said justice shall, at public auction, proceed to sell said negro or mulatto to any person or persons who will pay said fine and costs for the shortest time; and said purchaser shall have the right to compel said negro or mulatto to work for and serve out said time, and he shall furnish said negro or mulatto with comfortable food, clothing and lodging during said servitude.

Section 5. If said negro or mulatto shall not within ten days after the expiration of his or her, or their time of service as aforesaid, leave the state, he, she or they shall be liable to a second prosecution, in which the penalty to be inflicted shall be one hundred dollars, and so on for every subsequent offence the penalty shall be increased fifty dollars over and above the last penalty inflicted, and the same proceedings shall be had in each case as is provided for in the preceding sections for the first offence.

Section 6. Said negro or mulatto shall have a right to take an appeal to the circuit court of the county in which said proceedings shall have been had, within five days after the rendition of the judgment, before the justice of the peace, by giving bond and security, to be approved by the clerk of said court to the people of the state of Illinois, and to be filed in the office of said clerk within said five days, in double the amount of said fine and costs, conditioned that the party appealed will personally be and appear before said circuit court, at the next term thereof, and not depart said court without leave, and will pay said fine and all costs, if the same shall be so adjudged by said court; and said security shall have the right to take said negro or mulatto into custody, and retain the same until the order of said court is complied with. And if the judgment of the justice of the peace be affirmed in whole or in part, and said negro or mulatto be found guilty, the said circuit court shall thereupon render judgment against and negro or mulatto and the security or securities on said appeal bond, for the amount of fine so found by the court, and all costs of suit, and the clerk of said court shall forthwith issue an execution against said defendant and security as in other cases, and the sheriff or other officer to whom said execution is directed shall proceed to collect the same by sale or otherwise: Provided, that this section shall not be so construed as to give the right to retain the custody of said negro or mulatto for a longer time than ten days after the rendition of said judgment by said circuit court.

Section 7. In all cases arising under the provisions of this act, the prosecuting witness, or person making the complaint and prosecuting the same, shall be entitled to one half of the fine so imposed and collected, and the residue of said fine shall be paid into the county treasury of the county in which said proceedings were had; and said fines, when so collected, shall be received by said county treasurer and kept by him as a distinct and separate fund, to be called the "charity fund," and said fund shall be used for the express and only purpose of relieving the poor of said county, and shall be paid out by said treasurer upon the order of the county court of said county, drawn upon him for that purpose.

Section 8. If after any negro or mulatto shall have been arrested under the provisions of this act, any person or persons shall claim any such negro or mulatto as a slave, the owner, by himself, or agent, shall have a right, by giving reasonable notice to the officer or person having the custody of said negro or mulatto, to appear before the justice of the peace and prove his or their right to the custody of said negro or mulatto as a slave, and if said justice of the peace shall, after hearing the evidence, be satisfied that the person or persons claiming said negro or mulatto, is the owner of and entitled to the custody of said negro or mulatto, in accordance with the laws of the United States passed upon this subject, he shall, upon the owner or agent paying all costs up to the time of claiming said negro or mulatto, and the costs of providing the same, and also the balance of the fine remaining unpaid, give to said owner a certificate of said facts, and said owner or agent so claiming shall have a right to take and remove said slave out of this state.

Section 9. If any justice of the peace shall refuse to issue any writ of process necessary for the arrest and prosecution of any negro or mulatto, under the provisions of this act, upon complaint being made before said justice by any resident of his county, and his fees for said service being tendered him, shall be deemed guilty of nonfeasance in office, and upon conviction thereof punished accordingly; and in all cases where the jury find for the negro or mulatto, or that he, she or they are not guilty under the provisions of this act, the said justice of the peace shall proceed to render judgment against the prosecuting witness, or person making the complaint, and shall collect the same as other judgments: Provided, that said prosecuting witness, or person making said complaint, in case judgment is rendered against him, shall have a right to take an appeal to the circuit court, as is provided for in this act in case said negro or mulatto is found guilty.

Section 10. Every person who shall have one-fourth negro blood shall be deemed a mulatto.

Section 11. This act shall take effect and be in force from and after its passage.

NUMBER 7

Report of the minority of the select committee in opposition to the repeal of the laws in relation to the emigration of colored persons in the state of Illinois, and granting them certain rights. Illinois Documents, 1857.

The select committee, to which was referred sundry petitions of "free white citizens of Illinois," and of certain colored inhabitants thereof, asking that the colored people of the state may be admitted to an equal and common participation in the free schools of the state; to the right of testifying in all cases in courts of justice; to all the rights of citizenship and of suffrage; and for the repeal of all laws now in force preventing the emigration of free negroes into the state, and discriminating between the white and black races, have had the same under consideration, and the minority of your committee would beg leave to report:

That, touching the praying of the petitioners in reference to the common school law, the minority of your committee cannot perceive that the present school law works any wrong or oppression to the colored people of the state. The tax collected from that class of inhabitants is, upon application, refunded to them, so that while the colored children may not be admitted to the same schools with the white children, it is yet true that the blacks are not taxed to educate the whites.

If the object of the petitioners be, as it clearly is, to admit the negro children to the same schools and classes with the whites, and upon entire quality, the minority of your committee would have no objection to such a state of things for those whose tastes, habits, feelings and affections would fit them for such communion, the minority of your committee have grave objections to the enactment of any law requiring the children of Anglo-Saxon blood and the descendants of the Norman conqueror to be placed in the same schools and classes with a race long degraded, and between which and the white race there exist prejudices and antipathies which, as they seem to be founded in the very constitution of the races, will perhaps never be effaced.

The minority of your committee cannot assent to the prayer of the petitioners for the repeal of certain laws to prevent the immigration of free negroes into this state. Upon the adoption of our present constitution, article fourteenth was separately submitted to a vote of people, to be approved by them before it should constitute a part of the constitution. That article was approved by a large majority of the voters of the state of Illinois, and was consequently incorporated into that instrument. That article declares "the general assembly shall, at its first session under the amended constitution, pass such laws as will effectually prohibit free persons of color from immigrating to and settling in this state, and to effectually prevent the owners of slaves from bringing them into this state for the purpose of setting them free." That provision of the constitution is explicit and mandatory, and in the enactment of the laws, the repeal of which is prayed for by the petitioners, the legislature of the state has only discharged a clear constitutional duty; nor do the laws now in force appear any too severe to accomplish the purpose of that provision of the constitution. Apart from the constitution, however, and upon grounds of public policy, the minority of your committee are of the opinion that the highest interests of state would require the enactment and execution of laws similar to those now on the statute book. It must be conceded by all that the free negro population of the state add but little to the education, the wealth, the religion, the morals and the civilization of the state, and the highest economic and moral considerations would require our cities to be filled and our prairies tilled by the white man rather than the black man.

In regard to the prayer of the petitioners for the admission of the colored people to the rights of suffrage, and of testifying in all cases in courts of justice, the minority of your committee beg leave to say, that this is a government of the white man, and established for the white man, and while the black man is alike with the white man protected by law in the enjoyment of his property, his liberty and his life, the minority of your committee can see no good reason for complaint on the part of the colored race or their peculiar friends, because the colored people may not be admitted into a full participation of all the rights of a government established for the white race.

On the shores of Ethiopia is being tested the capability of the negro race for self-government, and your committee would recommend to the colored people of this state who may desire to exercise the rights of suffrage, to emigrate to that republic, where they may enjoy the privileges prayed for in their petition.

The minority of your committee recognize in the prayer of the petitioners a purpose to abolish all distinctions between the white and black races, and to place them, in every respect, both politically and socially, upon terms of perfect equality. To such a proposition the minority of your committee can never assent. The Creator has established the greatest diversity in all His works of earth, of sky, and of man; and if His wisdom has created diversities and antipathies between the white and black races, the minority of your committee are not disposed to question the wisdom or distrust the arrangements of Providence. It is a fact indisputable that there exist great antipathies between the white and black races, and whether they be constitutional or whether they be prejudices of habit and education, the existence of such antipathies is a fact which no legislator is at liberty to disregard.

The diversities and antipathies between these races are deep-seated and apparently constitutional, and such as no legislation can eradicate; and the minority of your committee are disposed to recognize them as a part of the economy and dispensation of Providence; and while in the opinion of some, perhaps, the arrangements of Providence might be improved, the minority of your committee are of the opinion that the wisdom of this legislature is not equal to Providence; and the minority of your committee are the more strongly of this belief, inasmuch as the members of the present general assembly were elected in a time of high party excitement, and may be presumed to have been selected for their partisan zeal rather than for their wisdom and learning.

In view of the facts set out in this report, the minority of your committee would recommend that the prayer of the petitioners be not granted, and ask to be discharged from the further consideration of the same.

NUMBER 8

An act to repeal section sixteen of the Revised Statutes, entitled "An act to prevent the immigration of free negroes into this state," commonly known as the "Black Laws." Approved February 7, 1865, Laws of Illinois.

Section 1. Be it enacted by the People of the State of Illinois, represented in the General Assembly, That section sixteen (16,) division III, chapter XXX, of the Revised Statutes of this state, entitled "Criminal Jurisprudence," and chapter LXXIV of said Revised Statutes, entitled "Negroes and Mulattoes," and an act of the general assembly of this state, approved February 12, 1853, entitled "An act to prevent the immigration of free negroes into this state," be and the same are hereby repealed; also section 23, chapter XL, Revised Statutes, entitled "Evidence and Depositions."

Section 2. This act to be in force from and after its passage.

NUMBER 9

Message from the governor on the black laws. January 3, 1865, House Journal.

Of the black laws I have but little to say, except to recommend that you sweep them from the statute books with a swift, relentless hand. My opinion of them cannot be better expressed than in the language of a resolution, which, as a member of the General Assembly, in February, 1849, I had the honor in a feeble minority to advocate, "declaring the laws of the State, applicable to negroes and mulattoes, tyrannical, iniquitous and oppressive upon this weak, harmless and unfortunate class, and unbecoming the statutes of a free, magnanimous, enlightened and christian nation." They were originally enacted to gratify an unjustifiable public prejudice against the friends of liberty, and an inhuman feeling towards a poor, unfortunate class of our fellow-citizens. They assumed a fact, which, to the honor of the Jeffersonian Ordinance of 1787, never existed: that slavery did or could exist in the free State of Illinois. Section nine of these laws provides that "if any slave or servant shall be found ten miles from the tenement of his or her master without a pass, he may be punished with stripes, not exceeding thirty-five"--thus, by the phraseology of the law, recognizing the existence of the institution of slavery within our borders, and prescribing an infamous punishment. It is unconstitutional, as decided by the Supreme Court in this State, "in attempting to legislate upon the subject of the rendition of fugitive slaves to their masters, over which subject the court decides that Congress has supreme and exclusive power." It authorizes a system of slavery, by providing that every colored man who shall be found in this State, "without having a certificate of freedom," shall be deemed a runaway slave or servant--"to be committed to the custody of the sheriff of the county, who shall advertise him at the court house door," and "to hire him out for the best price he can get," "from month to month," "for the space of one year." Any law, thus placing any man, white or black, in the power of a purchaser, for money, is utterly inconsistent with the humanity of the age of the spirit of our free constitution. These laws are unconstitutional, because by the laws of many of our states free colored persons are citizens, and the constitution of the United States expressly provides that "the citizens of each state shall be entitled to all the privileges of citizens in the several states."

An examination of the various provisions of these laws will satisfy this General Assembly of their inhumanity, and the humane and philanthropic will everywhere hail their repeal with joyful acclamations.

In reply to those who say that if these laws are repealed we shall have a large influx of free negroes into this State, I have to answer that the laws are now almost a dead letter. Negroes are not kept out of the State by them, for it is only now and then, indeed a rare case, that a man can be found who is barbarian enough to insist upon the application of the penalties imposed by these laws. And upon the subject I cannot present my views better than by the following extract from my message of January 5th, 1863. Referring to the emancipation policy of the administration, I say:

"I am sure of two things: First, that when slavery is removed, this rebellion will die out, and not before. Second--I believe and predict, and commit the prediction in this state paper to meet the verdict of my successors in office and of posterity, that the change brought about by the policy of emancipation will pass off in a way so quietly and so easily, that the world will stand amazed that we should have entertained such fears of its evils. During the war, there will be necessarily some suffering among so many slaves thrown out of employment, and many, perhaps large numbers of them, will seek a temporary refuge in the free states, and every man who has a human heart within him will treat them kindly; but with the return of peace, the demand for labor in the South will be greatly increased, and there will be an exodus not only of these fugitives, but of the free colored population, to the south. The demand for labor in the South will be greatly increased by the subdivision of large farms into numerous small ones, in the hands of a much larger number of owners; also by the reclamation of immense regions of fertile country in all our southern states, waiting for only the touch of free labor, the settlement of which has been retarded by the existence of slavery, tending, as it always has, and necessarily always will, to discourage the immigration of free white citizens. No reasonable fears of competition with the free labor of the northern states need be entertained, because the emancipated slave will have protection and employment upon the soil which he has heretofore cultivated in bondage. Emancipation does not increase the number of negroes by an additional one. There will not be a single acre of land less for cultivation, but a great deal more will probably be cultivated; there will be the same and an increasing demand for the culture of cotton, tobacco, sugar and rice, for which the negro is peculiarly adapted; the southern climate will remain unchanged, congenial to his constitution; and it is in the highest degree improbable that the negro will leave the state of his nativity, where his labor is in demand, where he understands, better than any one else, the business to be done, and where the climate is adapted to him, to seek the cold climates of the North, to face the strong competition of northern, skilled free labor, to encounter the prejudice against his color, and the pauperism and neglect which would meet him on every hand."

I will not say that legislation will not be necessary upon this subject of the residence of free negroes in our midst; but I will say, that whatever is necessary should be free from political prejudice, having regard to the welfare of our own, free, white citizens, and, at the same time, marked with humanity and a due regard to that unfortunate class of our fellow beings whom Providence, in its wise and inscrutable plans, has placed in our care.

NUMBER 10

The black laws. February 7, 1865, Illinois State Journal.

A large number of the colored people of this city assembled on North 4th street yesterday, and fired 62 guns in honor of the senators and representatives who voted for the repeal of the odious black laws. After the firing the company proceeded to the Methodist Colored Church where they were addressed by several colored gentlemen among whom was Mr. John Jones of Chicago, who made a most interesting and able speech, well worthy of a report if we had room. Rev. Mr. Caven read the black laws; he was listened to with the most marked attention. The meeting was orderly, and everything was conducted in a manner honorable to those who had the supervision of the affair.

NUMBER 11

An act to repeal section sixteen of the Revised Statutes, commonly known as the black laws. House Journal, (1865).

Mr. Wike moved the following as an amendment to said bill, viz: "The provisions of this bill shall not take effect or be in force until the same shall first have been submitted to the people of the State of Illinois for their ratification or rejection at the next general election to be held in said State, and unless the same shall have received a majority of the legal votes cast at said election for or against said provisions.

Mr. Smith moved that the said amendment be laid upon the table. It was decided in the affirmative, Yeas--45, Nays--34.

Ordered that the title be as aforesaid, and that the Clerk inform the Senate thereof, and ask their concurrence therein.

VI

Kidnapping

Federal and state support for slavery empowered slave owners in their efforts to capture and forcibly remove runaway slaves. Some Northern states, including Massachusetts and Pennsylvania, adopted personal liberty laws in order to shield free blacks from unscrupulous slave catchers. The states in the Old Northwest did not adopt personal liberty laws; nevertheless, most of them adopted modest laws against kidnapping. Illinois also adopted laws to prevent the kidnapping of free blacks. But anti-kidnapping laws were rarely an effective deterrent to violence against free blacks.

NUMBER 1

An act to more effectively prevent kidnapping and for other purposes. Approved January 17, 1825, Laws of Illinois.

Section 1. Be it enacted by the people of the state of Illinois represented in the General Assembly, That if any person or persons shall kidnap, steal, seize, take, and carry away, from and out of this state or from and out of any one county in this state, into any other county, or shall make an attempt to do the same, any negro, mulatto, or person of color, with intent to subject such negro, mulatto, or person of color to involuntary slavery or servitude, to which he or she is not liable, or shall cause or procure it to be done, or shall aid, abet, or assist any other person in doing it, the person or persons so offending, upon conviction thereof, shall be deemed guilty of felony, and shall be punished with stripes, not less than twenty-five, nor more than one hundred, and shall stand in the pillory not less than two nor more than four hours, and shall also be fined in the sum of one thousand dollars, and pay the costs of prosecution.

Section 2. Be it further enacted, That if any person or persons shall hire, persuade, entice, decoy or seduce by false pretenses, misrepresentations, or other means, any negro, mulatto, or person of color, not being a slave, to go out of this state, or be taken or removed therefrom, for the purpose, and with the intent, to sell such negro, mulatto, or person of color, and thereby subject him or her to slavery or servitude, or otherwise dispose of him or her, against his or her will, the person or persons so offending, and being thereof duly convicted, shall, in like manner, be deemed guilty of felony, and punished in the same manner as prescribed in the first section.

Section 3. Be it further enacted That, if any person or persons shall be accessory to the commission of either of the aforementioned offenses, such person or persons may be charged and indicted as principal, and punished accordingly.

Section 4. Be it further enacted, That no person entitled to the labor or service of any negro, mulatto, or person of color, by indenture, or other contract, made under the laws of the late territories of Indiana and Illinois, having a right to hold such person of color in temporary servitude by virtue of those laws, shall hire out or send such person of color to live or reside in any other state, territory, or foreign country, or shall suffer it to be done; nor shall any such person sell or otherwise dispose of any person of color, aforesaid to any citizen or resident of any other state, territory, or foreign country, or suffer such person of color to be removed, or reside in any other state, territory, or foreign country, before the expiration of his or her term of service, and every person so offending, and violating the provisions of this section, shall forfeit and lose all claim, right, and title to the service of such person of color; and shall, moreover, under a penalty of seven hundred dollars, for each and every person so sold, or otherwise, one half to the person so hired out, as aforesaid, the other half to the county treasury, where such prosecution may be commenced, together with costs, to be recovered by action of debt or indictment, in the name of the people of the state of Illinois, for the uses and purposes aforesaid, This act to take effect and be in force from and after the passage thereof.

NUMBER 2

Offenses relative to slaves, indentured servants, and apprentices. Approved March 3, 1845. Revised Statutes.

Section 159. If any person shall harbor or secrete any negro, mulatto or person of color, the same being a slave or servant, owing service or labor to any other persons, whether they reside in this State, or any other State or territory, or district within the limits and under the jurisdiction of the United States, or shall in anywise hinder or prevent the lawful owner or owners of such slaves or servants from retaking them in a lawful manner, every such person so offending, shall be deemed guilty of a misdemeanor, and fined, not exceeding five hundred dollars, or imprisoned, not exceeding six months.

Section 160. If any person or persons, entitled to the service or labor of any negro, mulatto or colored person, by indenture or other contract or registry made, or entered into under the laws of the late territory of Indiana or of Illinois, having a right to hold such person of color in temporary servitude, by virtue of those laws and the constitution of this State, shall hire out, or send any such negro, mulatto or colored person, or any of his or her children, to live or reside in any other State, territory or country, or shall cause, procure, or suffer it to be done, or shall sell or otherwise dispose of any such person of color, or the children of such, for the purposes aforesaid, to any citizen or resident of another State, territory or country, before the expiration of his or her term of service, every person so offending, and all purchasers of such colored persons so sold or removed, shall forfeit and lose all right and title or claim to the service of such person of color, and shall, on conviction, for each offence, be fined, not exceeding five hundred dollars, one-half to be applied to the use of the person injured, and the other half to the use of the county.

Section 161. If any keeper of a public house or retailer of spirituous liquors, shall receive, harbor, entertain or trust any minor or apprentice within the age of twenty-one years, or any servant or slave, knowing them to be such, after having been cautioned or warned to the contrary by the parent, guardian, master or mistress of such minor, apprentice, servant or slave, in the presence of one or more credible witnesses; every such keeper of a public house, or retailer of spirituous liquors as aforesaid, so offending, shall, upon conviction thereof, be fined in the sum of twelve dollars, and shall, moreover, forfeit his or her license.

NUMBER 3

An act to amend an act entitled, "An act relative to criminal jurisprudence," Approved January 6, 1827, and to provide for the regulation and government of the penitentiary. Approved February 9, 1831, Laws of Illinois.

Section 27. Any person convicted of the crime of kidnapping, as defined in the fifty-fifth, fifty-sixth, and fifty-seventh sections of the act to which this is an amendment, shall be punished by confinement in the penitentiary, for a term not less than one year nor exceeding seven years.

NUMBER 4

Offenses against persons or individuals. Approved March 3, 1845. Revised Statutes.

Section 54. False imprisonment is an unlawful violation of the personal liberty of another, and consists of confinement or detention without sufficient legal authority. Any person convicted of false imprisonment shall be fined in any sum not exceeding five hundred dollars, or imprisoned not exceeding one year in the county jail.

Section 55. Kidnapping is the forcible abduction or stealing away of a man, woman, or child, from his or her own country and sending or taking him or her into another.

Section 56. Every person who shall forcibly steal, take or arrest any man, woman, or child, whether white, black or colored, in this State, and carry him or her into another country, State or territory, or who shall forcibly take or arrest any person or persons whatsoever, with a design to take him or her out of this State, without having established a claim according to the laws of the United States, shall, upon conviction, be deemed guilty of kidnapping. Every person found guilty of kidnapping, shall be confined in the penitentiary for a term not less than one year, and not more than seven years, for each person kidnapped or attempted to be kidnapped.

Section 57. Every person who shall hire, persuade, entice, decoy or seduce, by false promises, misrepresentations and the like, any negro, mulatto or colored person, not being a slave, to go out of this State, or to be taken or removed therefrom, for the purpose and with the intent to sell such negro, mulatto or colored person into slavery or involuntary servitude, or otherwise to employ him or her for his or her own use, or to the use of another, without the free will and consent of such negro, mulatto or colored person, any person so offending, shall be deemed to have committed the crime of kidnapping, and upon conviction thereof, shall be punished as in the preceding section.

NUMBER 5

Kidnapping. February 15, 1855, Session Laws.

Section 1. That whenever the governor of this state shall receive information satisfactory to him, that any inhabitant of this state has been decoyed, kidnapped, or transported away from this state, into any other state or territory of the United States, for the purpose of restraining such person in his or her liberty, or reducing such person to slavery, or any other unlawful purpose, or that such person is wrongfully seized, imprisoned, or held in slavery in any of the states or territories of the United States, on the allegation or pretence that such person is a slave, or by color of any usage or rule of law prevailing in said state or territory is deemed or taken to be a slave, or not entitled of right to the personal liberty of an inhabitant of this state, it shall be the duty of said governor to take such measures as he shall be the duty of said governor to take such measures as he shall deem necessary to procure such person to be restored to his or her liberty, and returned to this state. The governor is hereby authorized to appoint such agent or agents as he shall deem necessary to effect the restoration and return of such person, and shall furnish said agent with such credentials and instructions to accomplish the object of his appointment. The governor may determine the compensation to be allowed such agent for his services and necessary expenses.

Section 2. Such agent shall proceed to collect the proper proof to establish the right of such person to his or her freedom, and shall perform such journeys, take such measures, institute and procure to be prosecuted such legal proceedings, under the direction of the governor, as shall be necessary to procure such person to be restored to his or her liberty, and returned to this state.

Section 3. The accounts for all services and expenses incurred in carrying this act into effect, shall be audited by the auditor of public accounts, and paid by the treasurer, on his warrant, out of any moneys in the treasury of this state not otherwise appropriated. The treasurer may advance, on the warrant of the auditor, to such agent, such sum or sums as the governor shall certify to be reasonable, to enable him to accomplish the purposes of his appointment, for which advance such agent shall account for on the first audit of his account.

NUMBER 6

Offenses relative to servants and slaves, indentured servants and apprentices. Approved February 18, 1857, Session Laws.

Section 159. If any person shall harbor or secrete any negro, mulatto or person of color, the same being a slave or servant, owing service or labor to any other persons, whether they reside in this state or any other state or territory or district within the limits hinder or prevent the lawful owner or owners of such slaves or servants from retaking them in a lawful manner, every such person, so offending, shall be deemed guilty of a misdemeanor, and be fined, not exceeding five hundred dollars, or imprisoned, not exceeding six months.

Section 160. If any person or persons, entitled to the service or labor of any negro, mulatto or colored person, by indenture, or other contract or registry made, or entered into under the laws of the late territory of Indiana or of Illinois, having a right to hold such person of color in temporary servitude, by virtue of those laws and the constitution of this state, shall hire out, or send any such negro, mulatto or colored person, or any of his or her children, to live or reside in any other state, territory or country, or shall cause, or suffer it to be done, or shall sell or otherwise dispose of any such person of color, or the children of such, for the purposes aforesaid, to any citizen or resident of another state, territory or country, before the expiration of his or her term of service, every person so offending, and all purchasers of such colored persons so sold or removed, shall forfeit and lose all right and title or claim to the service of such person of color, and shall, on conviction for such offense, be fined, not exceeding five hundred dollars, one-half to be applied to the use of the person injured, and the other half to the use of the county.

Section 161. If any keeper of a public house, or retailer of spirituous liquors, shall receive, harbor, or entertain any minor or apprentice, within the age of twenty-one years, or any servant or slave, knowing them to be such, after having been cautioned or warned to the contrary by the parent, guardian, master or mistress of such minor, apprentice, servant or slave, in the presence of one or more credible witnesses; every such keeper of a public house or retailer of spirituous liquors as aforesaid, so offending, shall upon conviction thereof, be fined in the sum of twelve dollars, and shall, moreover, forfeit his or her license.

VII

Testimony and Witness

Illinois law first prohibited the testimony of a black or mulatto against a white in 1803. The legislature designated as mulatto any person having one-fourth "Negro blood" or any person having at least one-half "Indian blood." In a state where they were denied testimony against a white, blacks had little chance of defending themselves in a dispute involving a white. The law left African Americans powerless; such, to be sure, was one aim of the black laws. Illinois lawmakers assumed that if they deprived African-American residents of their legal and civil rights, they would leave the state. Moreover, the legislators assumed that their oppressive laws would discourage runaway slaves from seeking refuge in Illinois.

NUMBER 1

Who may be witnesses in criminal cases. Approved March 3, 1845, Revised Statutes.

Section 16. No black or mulatto person or Indian shall be permitted to give evidence in favor or against any white person whatsoever. Every person who shall have one-fourth part or more of negro blood shall be deemed a mulatto; and every person who shall have one-half Indian blood shall be deemed an Indian.

NUMBER 2

Evidence and Depositories. Approved March 3, 1845. Revised Statutes.

Section 23. A negro, mulatto, or Indian shall not be a witness in any court, or in any case, against a white person. A person having one-fourth part negro blood shall be adjudged a mulatto.

NUMBER 3

Perpetuation of testimony. Approved March 3, 1845, Revised Statutes.

Section 19. In all cases hereafter, where any person or persons shall desire to perpetuate the remembrance of any fact, matter or thing, which may relate to the boundaries or improvements of name of any portion or district of country; regarding the ancient customs, laws or usages of the inhabitants of this country, as far as the same may relate to the future settlement of the land claims; or touching the marriage or pedigree of any person or persons, or in relation to the title to slaves or servants; or any other matter or thing necessary to the security of any estate, real or personal, or mixed, or any private right whatever, it shall be lawful for such person or persons, upon filing a petition supported by affidavit, in the circuit court of the proper county, setting forth particularly the fact or facts intended to be established, a dedimus potestatem or commission, directed to any two justices of the peace, or to any clerk of the circuit or county commissioners' court of the county wherein such testimony is to be taken, and may, thereupon, proceed to take such deposition or depositions as shall be pray for in said petition.

NUMBER 4

Competency of witnesses. Approved March 3, 1845, Revised Statutes.

A negro, mulatto or Indian shall not be a witness in any court, or in any case, against a white person. A person having one-fourth part negro blood shall be adjudged a mulatto.

Criminal cases.

Section 15. The party or parties injured shall, in all cases, be competent witnesses, unless he, she or they shall be rendered incompetent by reason of his, her or their infamy, or other legal incompetency other than that of interest. The credibility of all such witnesses shall be left to the jury, as in other cases.

Section 16. No black or mulatto person shall be permitted to give evidence in favor or against any white person whatsoever. Every person who shall have one-fourth part or more of negro blood shall be deemed a mulatto;

and every person who shall have one-half Indian blood shall be deemed an Indian.

Section 17. Approvers shall not be allowed to give testimony.

Section 18. The solemn affirmation of witnesses shall be deemed sufficient. A false and corrupt affirmation shall subject the witness to all the penalties and punishment provided for those who commit willful and corrupt perjury.

VIII

Runaway Slaves and Servants

Whites in Illinois embraced a strong proslavery bias. A newspaper correspondent in Ohio considered Illinois the most proslavery free state in the Union. This label was appropriate. As we have seen, Illinois approved slave labor under the guise of indentured servitude and approved an assortment of policies to subordinate its black residents. The State also protected slave holders by adopting a fugitive slave law, mandating that runaways be delivered to a bona fide claimant. Furthermore, the legislature prescribed punishment for anyone who harbored or aided the escape of a runaway slave or servant. The following documents also demonstrate that the legislature abridged the civil rights of Indians. State law denied Indians the opportunity to purchase whiskey and required black and white merchants to obtain a special license in order to sell "legal" quantities to Indians.

NUMBER 1

An act concerning the Kaskaskia Indians. Approved December 22, 1814, Laws of Illinois.

Whereas a former law of this Legislature has been found insufficient to prevent evil disposed persons from selling and giving intoxicating drinks to the Kaskaskia Indians or from cheating and defrauding the said Indians out of their property by pretended or real purchases and whereas the former practice is productive of disorder and other pernicious consequences and the latter a violation of moral Justice and good policy. For remedy thereof,

Section 1. Be it enacted by the legislative council and house of Representatives and it is hereby enacted by the authority of the same, That if any white person or free person of color either male or female shall hereafter without license from the Governor as superintendent of Indian affairs within this Territory or from some sub-agent appointed by him either sell or give to any Kaskaskia Indian or any other Indian residing with them any quantity of whiskey, gin, brandy, rum, cider or other intoxicating drink such person so offending shall forfeit and pay twenty dollars to be recovered upon warrant before any Justice of the peace who shall upon conviction of such offence issue execution returnable in thirty days against either the body or goods of such offender as may be required of the said Justice of the peace, and upon such execution there shall be no security whatever taken.

Section 2. If either of the offenses stated in the above section, shall be committed by any negro or mulatto being the slave or servant of any person whatever, It shall be the duty of a Justice of the peace upon application to him made according to law to issue his warrant against such negro, or mulatto and upon proof of the offenses above mentioned or either of them having been committed by said negro or mulatto, the Justices of the peace before whom such proof may be made shall order him or her so offending to receive on his or her bare back if for the first offence fifteen lashes and for every subsequent offence of like kind double that number. Provided however that the said corporal punishment shall be inflicted if the owner of any other person will in behalf of said negro or mulatto pay the sum of twenty dollars for each offence respectively.

Section 3. That it shall not be lawful for any person whatever without license from the Governor or some sub-agent appointed by him to purchase or receive by gift or otherwise of any of the before mentioned Indians, any horse mare gun Tomahawk, knife, Blanket Strouding, calico, saddle bridle, or any goods, wares, or merchandize whatever, that all such sales and purchases, or gifts shall be considered as fraudulent on the part of the buyer or receiver, and that any white person or free person of color whatever so buying or receiving any such articles of any one of those Indians shall be liable to pay a fine of twenty dollars to be recovered before a Justice of the peace who shall upon conviction of any such offender issue execution in like manner as is directed in the first section of this act, and the said offender shall restore the article or articles so bought or received & shall moreover be liable to a suit in the supreme court for the fraud of buying or receiving any such article as aforesaid whatever the amount or value thereof may be and in all cases of Judgment against him or her, he or she shall pay the costs.

Section 4. If either of the offenses stated in the last preceding section of this act shall be committed by any negro or mulatto being the slave or servant of any other person, the said negro or mulatto so offending shall be subject to the same proceedings and punishment under the same conditions as are prescribed the second section of this act, and the owner shall either cause said negro or mulatto to restore any article or articles so purchased, or received by him or her or said owner shall be liable in default thereof to the same proceedings as if such owner had actually himself or herself bought or received in the said article or articles contrary to the intention of this law.

Section 5. In all the above cases and in all other cases of injuries done to the said Indians it shall be lawful for the Governor of the Territory or any sub-agent appointed by him, to sue or warrant as the case may require in behalf of any such injured Indian.

Section 6. All fines imposed by this law after deducting thereout all necessary expenses, shall be paid by the Governor or a subagent, to the injured Indian or Indians.

Section 7. It shall be the duty of all Justices of the peace, sheriffs and constables to aid and assist in the execution of this law according to their respective offices.

NUMBER 2

Offenses relative to slaves, indentured servants, and apprentices. Approved March 3, 1833, Revised Laws.

Section 149. If any person shall harbor or secrete any negro, mulatto or person of color, the same being a slave or servant, owing service or labor to any other persons, whether they reside in this State, or any other State or territory, or district within the limits and under the jurisdiction of the United States, or shall in anywise hinder or prevent the lawful owner or owners of such slaves or servants from retaking them in a lawful manner, every such person so offending, shall be deemed guilty of a misdemeanor, and fined, not exceeding five hundred dollars, or imprisoned, not exceeding six months.

Section 150. If any person or persons, entitled to the service or labor of any negro, mulatto or colored person, by indenture or other contract or registry made, or entered into under the laws of the late territory of Indiana or of Illinois, having a right to hold such person of color in temporary servitude, by virtue of those laws and the constitution of this State, shall hire out, or send any such negro, mulatto or colored person, or any of his or her children, to live or reside in any other State, territory or country, or shall cause, procure, or suffer it to be done, or shall sell or otherwise dispose of any such person of color, or the children of such, for the purposes aforesaid, to any citizen or resident of another State, territory or country, before the expiration of his or her term of service, every person so offending, and all purchasers of such colored persons so sold or removed, shall forfeit and lose all right and title or claim to the service of such person of color, and shall, on conviction, for each offence, be fined, not exceeding five hundred dollars, one-half to be applied to the use of the person injured, and the other half to the use of the county.

IX

Miscegenation of the Races

Whites embraced a strong bias against interracial marriages or social intercourse of any kind where blacks and whites were concerned. Driven by Negrophobia, they claimed that black immigration would foster miscegenation, and they used their paranoia to justify a variety of laws regulating social contact between blacks and whites. It is not surprising, therefore, that Illinois lawmakers prohibited interracial marriages, prescribed penalties for offenders and nullified all marriages contrary to state law. State law also penalized persons who performed illegal marriages. For decades, lawmakers had assumed that the black laws were so overwhelming that it was unlikely that an interracial marriage would take place in Illinois. By the 1840s, however, it became apparent that both genders sometimes crossed racial lines in intimate relationships. Among the reforms brought by the Civil War was legal recognition of interracial marriages. Doubtless, public opinion continued to frown on such relationships.

NUMBER 1

White and colored persons committing adultery and fornication together. Approved December 3, 1844, Session Laws.

That any black, colored or mulatto man and white woman, and any white man and black, colored or mulatto woman, who shall live together in an open state of adultery or fornication, shall be indicted, and on conviction, shall be severally fined in any sum not exceeding five hundred dollars, and confined in the penitentiary for any term not exceeding one year: Provided, That nothing in this act shall be construed to extend to any case in which the man and woman living together as aforesaid shall both be white persons: And provided, further, That the offense herein provided for, shall be sufficiently proved by circumstances which raise the presumption of cohabitation and unlawful intimacy; and for a second offense, such man or woman shall be severally punished twice as much as for the first offense, and for the third offense trebling, and thus increasing the punishment for each succeeding offense.

NUMBER 2

Marriages. Approved March 3, 1845, Revised Statutes.

Section 1. All male persons over the age of seventeen years, and females over the age of fourteen years, may contract and be joined in marriage: Provided, in all cases where either party is a minor, the consent of parents or guardians be first had, as is hereinafter required.

Section 2. No person of color, negro or mulatto, of either sex, shall be joined in marriage with any white person, male or female, in this State; and all marriages or marriage contracts, entered into between such colored person and white person, shall be null and void in law; and any person so marrying or contracting to marry, shall be liable to pay a fine, be whipped in not exceeding thirty-nine lashes, and be imprisoned, not less than one year; and shall be held to answer in no other than a criminal prosecution, by information or indictment. And any clerk who shall knowingly issue a license to any such colored person, negro or mulatto, or to any white person to be joined to a negro or mulatto, in manner aforesaid, or if any officer or person authorized to solemnize marriages in this State, shall join any such colored person, negro or mulatto in marriage with a white person, such magistrate or other person so offending as aforesaid, on conviction thereof, shall be fined, in a sum not less than two hundred dollars, to be sued for and recovered in any court of record in this State, the one-half for the use of the county in which said suit is brought, and the other half to the person suing for the same; and thereafter be ineligible to any office in this State.

Section 3. All persons belonging to any religious society, church or denomination, may celebrate their marriage according to the rules and principles of such religious society, church or denomination; and a certificate of such marriage, signed by the regular minister, or if there be no minister, then by the clerk of such religious society, church or denomination, registered as hereinafter directed, shall be evidence of such marriage.

Section 4. Any persons wishing to marry, or be joined in marriage, may go before any regular minister of the gospel, authorized to marry, by the custom of the church or society to which he belongs, any justice of the supreme court, judge of any inferior court, or justice of the peace, and celebrate or declare their marriage in such manner and form as shall be most agreeable.

NUMBER 3

Who may contract marriages. Revised Statutes, (1845).

Section 1. All male persons over the age of seventeen years, and females over the age of fourteen years, may contract and be joined in marriage: Provided, In all cases where either party is a minor, the consent of parents or guardians be first had, as is hereinafter required.

Section 2. No person of color, negro or mulatto, of either sex, shall be joined in marriage with any white person, male or female, in this state; and all marriages or marriage contracts, entered into between such colored person and white person, shall be null and void in law; and any person so marrying, or contracting to marry, shall be liable to pay a fine, be whipped, in not exceeding thirty-nine lashes, and be imprisoned not less than one year, and shall be held to answer in no other than a criminal prosecution, by information or indictment. And any clerk who shall knowingly issue a license to any such colored person, negro or mulatto, or to any white person to be joined to a negro or mulatto, in manner aforesaid, or if any officer or person authorized to solemnize marriages in this state, shall join any such colored person, negro or mulatto in marriage with a white person, such magistrate or other person, so offending as aforesaid, on conviction thereof, shall be fined, in a sum not less than two hundred dollars, to be sued for and recovered in any court of record in this state, the one-half for the use of the county in which said suit is brought, and the other half to the person suing for the same, and thereafter be ineligible to any office in this state.

Section 3. All persons belonging to any religious society, church or denomination, may celebrate their marriage according to the rules and principles of such religious society, church or denomination; and a certificate of such marriage, signed by the regular minister, or if there be no minister, then by the clerk of such religious society, church or denomination, registered as hereinafter directed, shall be evidence of such marriage.

Section 4. Any persons wishing to marry, or be joined in marriage, may go before any regular minister of the gospel, authorized to marry, by the custom of the church or society to which he belongs, any justice of the supreme court, judge, of any inferior court, or justice of the peace, and celebrate or declare their marriage, in such manner and form as shall be most agreeable.

Section 5. Any minister of the gospel, justice of the supreme court, judge or justice of the peace, who shall celebrate any marriage, shall make a certificate of such marriage, and return the same, with the license, to the clerk of the county commissioners' court, who issued such license, within thirty days after solemnizing such marriage.

Section 6. The clerk of the county commissioners' court, after receiving such certificate, shall make a registry thereof, in a book to be kept by him for that purpose only; which registry shall contain the christian and surnames of both the parties, the time of their marriage, and the name of the person certifying the same; and said clerk shall, at the same time, indorse on such certificate, that the same is registered, and the time when; which certificate shall be carefully filed and preserved and the same, or a certified copy of the registry thereof, shall be evidence of the marriage of the parties.

Section 7. If any clerk shall, for more than one month, refuse or neglect to register any marriage certificate, which has been, or may hereafter be, delivered to him for that purpose (his fee therefor being paid), he shall be liable to be removed from office, and shall moreover pay the sum of one hundred dollars, to the use of the party injured, to be recovered by action of debt in any court having cognizance of the same.

Section 8. If any minister, justice of the supreme court, judge or justice of the peace, having solemnized a marriage, or clerk of any religious society, as the case may be, shall not make return of a certificate of the same, as required, within the time limited, to the clerk of the commissioners' court of the county in which such marriage was solemnized, he shall forfeit and pay one hundred dollars for each case so neglected, to go to the use of the county, to be recovered by indictment. And if any minister of the gospel, justice of the supreme court, judge or any other officer or person, except as hereinbefore excepted, shall solemnize and join in marriage any couple without a license as aforesaid, he shall, for every such offense, forfeit and pay one hundred dollars, to the use of the county, to be recovered by indictment.

Section 9. No person shall be joined in marriage as aforesaid, unless their intention to marry shall have been published at least two weeks previous to such marriage, in the church or congregation to which the parties, or one of them, belong; or unless such persons have obtained a license, as herein provided.

Section 10. In all cases when publication of such intention to marry has not been made, as before described, the parties wishing to marry shall obtain a license from the clerk of the county commissioners' court of the county where such marriage is to take place; which license shall authorize any regular minister of the gospel authorized to marry by the church or society to which he belongs; any justice of the supreme court, judge or justice of the peace, to celebrate and certify such marriage; but no such license shall be granted for the marriage of any male under twenty-one years of age, or female under the age of eighteen years, without the consent of his or her father, or if he be dead or incapable, of his or her mother or guardian to be noted in such license. And if any one marries them without consent as aforesaid, he shall forfeit and pay the sum of three hundred dollars, to the use of such father, mother or guardian, to be sued for and recovered in any court having cognizance thereof; and for the purpose of ascertaining the age of the parties, such clerk is hereby authorized to examine either party, or other witness on oath.

NUMBER 4

An act to establish the validity of marriages contracted, wherein one or both of the parties were slaves at the time, and to establish the legitimacy of their offspring, as to the right to inherit property. Approved May 5, 1891, Laws of Illinois.

Section 1. Be it enacted by the People of the State of Illinois, represented in the General Assembly: That all marriages that have been contracted wherein one or both of the parties were slaves at the time, shall be considered equally valid and binding as though the parties thereunto were free and the child or children of such marriages shall be deemed legitimate and placed upon exactly the same footing (as to the right to inherit property as well from their brothers, sisters and other relations as from their parents) as any child or children born of parents who were lawfully wedded and not slaves.

The provisions of this act shall extend to all marriages entered into between such slaves, whether contracted and entered into within or without this State, so far as the right to inherit property within this State is concerned.

X

Civil and Legal Rights

Congress adopted legislation to protect the legal rights of African Americans after the Civil War. Most northern states, including Illinois, also adopted civil rights laws. In most cases, Illinois made only token gestures of its commitment to racial equality. For example, Illinois law provided equal access to public accommodations, including restaurants, theaters, and inns. The state also prescribed penalties for residents who violated the legal rights of anyone solely on account of race, ancestry, or previous condition of servitude. Citizens convicted of such an act could be fined up to $500 or imprisoned. Illinois made these declarations so long as they were in vogue at the federal level. When federal protections for civil rights receded during the late nineteenth century, Illinois lawmakers retreated as well. Illinois, therefore, entered the twentieth century as a rigidly segregated state.

NUMBER 1

Educating persons of color. Approved February 18, 1857, Session Laws.

Section 80. In townships in which there shall be persons of color, the board of trustees shall allow such persons a portion of the school fund equal to the amount of taxes collected for school purposes from such persons of color in their respective townships.

NUMBER 2

An act to protect all citizens in their civil and legal rights and fixing a penalty for violation of the same. Approved June 10, 1885, Laws of Illinois.

Section 1. Be it enacted by the People of the State of Illinois, represented in the General Assembly: That all persons within the jurisdiction of said State shall be entitled to the full and equal enjoyment of the accommodations, advantages, facilities and privileges of inns, restaurants, eating houses, barber shops, public conveyances on land, or water, theaters, and all other places of public accommodation and amusement, subject only to the conditions and limitations established by law, and applicable alike to all citizens.

Section 2. That any person who shall violate any of the provisions of the foregoing section by denying to any citizen, except for reasons applicable alike to all citizens of every race and color, and regardless of color or race, the full enjoyment of any of the accommodations, advantages, facilities, or privileges in said section enumerated, or by encouraging such denial, shall, for every such offense, forfeit and pay a sum not less than twenty-five (25) dollars nor more than five hundred (500) dollars to the person aggrieved thereby, to be recovered in any court of competent jurisdiction, in the county where said offense was committed: and shall also for every such offense, be deemed guilty of a misdemeanor, and upon conviction thereof, shall be fined not to exceed five hundred (500) dollars, or shall be imprisoned no more than one year, or both: And, provided, further, that a judgment in favor of the party aggrieved, or punishment upon an indictment, shall be a bar to either prosecution respectively.

NUMBER 3

An act to amend an act entitled "an act to protect all citizens in their civil and legal rights and fixing a penalty for violation of the same," approved June 10, 1885, by adding additional sections. Approved June 3, 1891, Laws of Illinois.

Section 1. Be it enacted by the People of the State of Illinois represented in the General Assembly: That "An act to protect all citizens in their civil and legal rights and fixing a penalty for violation of the same," approved June 10, 1885, be amended by adding additional sections to be known as sections three (3) and four (4).

Section 3. Justices of the peace in the county where the offense is committed shall have jurisdiction in all civil actions brought under this act to recover damages, to the extent of the jurisdiction of justices of the peace to recover a money demanding other actions as fixed by law, and either party shall have the right to have the cause tried by jury and to appeal from the judgment of the justice in the same manner as in other civil suits.

Section 4. When such action shall be brought originally before a justice of the peace and an appeal taken from the judgment of the justice to the circuit, superior or county court, such court to which the appeal is taken shall upon the trial de novo of such appeal, have jurisdiction to render a judgment for a sum exceeding the jurisdiction of the justice in the same manner as though such suit had originally been begun in such circuit, superior or county court: Provided, that the plaintiff shall within thirty days after the transcript is filed in the court to which the appeal [is] taken, file his declaration in such cause in the same manner as in original suits, and there upon process shall issue, against the defendant and the cause shall proceed in all respects the same as in original actions brought in such court. Where a declaration is filed the appeal shall not be dismissed without the consent of the plaintiff.

NUMBER 4

An act to amend an act entitled "An act to protect all citizens in their civil and legal rights and fixing a penalty for violation of the same. Approved June 10, 1897, Laws of Illinois.

Section 1. That all persons within the jurisdiction of said State shall be entitled to the full and equal enjoyment of the accommodations, advantages, facilities and privileges of inns, restaurants, eating houses, hotels, soda fountains, saloons, barber shops, bath rooms, theaters, skating rinks, concerts, cafes, bicycle rinks, elevators, ice cream parlors or rooms, railroads, omnibuses, stages, street cars, boats, public conveyances on land and water and all other places of public accommodation and amusement, subject only to the conditions and limitations established by law, and applicable alike to all citizens.

Summary of Cases

Joined to the Indiana Territory until 1809, Illinois inherited the policy of that territory regarding slavery. An 1803 statute, approved by Indiana lawmakers, made slavery legal. Illinois lawmakers hurriedly protected slavery in the constitution adopted in 1818. In addition to indentured servitude, and limited terms for slaves brought into Illinois by an immigrating master, the state also accommodated its laws to include admittance of hired-out slaves, and preserved for the master the children born to servants and slaves. In *Nance v. Howard* (1828), the state supreme court considered black servants as merely chattels. Under these policies, Illinois acquired an extensive slave population, more than any other free state in the Union.

The courts in Illinois also approved comity for traveling masters. In Willard v. the People (1843), the court recognized transit as a legal right of slave holders. Julius Willard, who allegedly secreted a slave while in transit, was convicted for violating the federal fugitive slave law. With this decision, the court revised the opinion of circuit court Judge John D. Caton who, in another case, had ruled that "a master [who] voluntarily bought his slave within the state, the slave becomes from that moment free, and if he escapes from his master while in this State, it is not an escape from slavery."[1] This automatic emancipation rule, adopted in most Northern states by 1843, had not been approved by the courts in Illinois. Transit was at issue in this case, and the supreme court rejected the notion that state law emancipated a slave who merely entered Illinois.

The supreme court, however, did render decisions that benefitted African Americans. In Cornelius v. Cohen, for example, the supreme court rejected the claim of a master for the services of the offspring of his servant. The court reached its decision on a procedural error, not because of sympathy for blacks. The court rendered a similar opinion in Boon v. Juliet (1836). The court held that offsprings of a servant were not controlled by the indentured servitude law, adopted after the birth of the children. In the *Kinney* case, decided in 1840, the court awarded damages to Thomas Cook, a worker who had been defrauded by his employer. African-American litigants, therefore, sometimes benefitted from favorable court decisions.

On the other hand, the judicial system in Illinois supported the racial policy of the state. It upheld federal and state fugitive slave laws. It convicted residents who harbored runaways or in any way interfered with the capture of a fugitive slave. In Hays v. Borders, for example, the supreme court convicted the defendant for violating the federal fugitive slave law. The following cases illustrate the adjudication of race and slavery in Illinois.

NOTE

1. N. Dwight Harris, The History of Negro Servitude in Illinois, (A. C. McClure and Company, 1904) pp. 11-12, Paul Finkelman, An Imperfect Union: Slavery, Federalism, and Comity, (Chapel Hill: University of North Carolina Press, 1981), p. 97.

Select Annotated Cases

Cornelius v. Wash, Breese 63, (1825)
George, a black man, brought action against Robert Whiteside and F. Bradshaw to recover his freedom. Joseph Cornelius hired R. Wash to litigate the case on George's behalf. A lower court held for George and awarded him $400 in damages. Whiteside appealed but the decision was sustained.

Cornelius v. Cohen, Breese 92, (1825)
In 1804, Rachael, a "free negro woman," signed an indentured servant contract with Cornelius. During the term of service she gave birth to a girl. Cornelius claimed her service under Illinois law. The court ruled for Rachael because of a procedural error committed by the plaintiff.

Coles v. County of Madison, Breese 115 (1826)
County commissioners brought action against Edward Coles for bringing slaves into an Illinois county without paying. Illinois law required masters to pay $1, 000 for each enslaved African American brought into the state by a visiting slave holder in order to emancipate his slaves. An 1825 law freed masters from the state statute adopted in 1819 prescribing this penalty. The court upheld this law, concluding that the "legislature have the constitutional power to pass the act of 1825, releasing Coles."

Mears v. Morrison, Breese 172 (1827)
This case involved the transfer of an African-American indentured servant under Illinois law, which provided for a system of indentured servitude.

Nance, a girl of color v. Howard, Breese 182 (1828)
Nance entered Illinois as a servant with a contract to serve until the age of 32. A dispute arose as to whether such a servant could be seized and sold as property. Illinois law recognized registered servants as property. Consequently, they could be seized and sold to satisfy the obligation of their master.

Fanny, a woman of color v. Montgomery, Breese 188 (1828)
After Fanny escaped from slavery in Kentucky, her owner hired slave catcher John Housten to apprehend her. Housten, after capturing the woman, forcibly restrained her. Abolitionists complained about his treatment of the woman and sued the slave catcher for using excessive force. A lower court concluded "that no more force was used than necessary." On appeal the supreme court reversed the opinion but allowed the defendants to amend their plea. The warrant did not specify that Fanny had escaped from Kentucky nor that she owed service in Kentucky. Consequently, the court released Fanny from slavery.

Phoebe, a woman of color v. Jay, Breese 207 (1828)
Phoebe had agreed to serve Joseph Jay as an indentured servant for forty years. After Jay's death his son inherited his estate, including the slaves. Phoebe refused to cooperate. The young Jay, who was also administrator of his father's estate, used force to compel her. Phoebe brought suit against him. The court ruled that "he had no power to compel the plaintiff to attend to the ordinary business."

Littleton v. Moses, a man of color, Breese 9 (1831)
Moses complained that he had been enslaved against his will. The court advised the jury that employment did not constitute restraint. In order to recover damages, evidence of suppression of liberty was required.

Boon v. Juliet, a woman of color, I Scammon 258 (1836)
Juliet and her children were indentured servants. Under Illinois law, the children would be released at age eighteen if female and twenty-one if male. The children were born before adoption of the indentured servitude policy and were not controlled by it. It "is not pretended that any law of the Territory rendered them in any manner, whatever, liable to serve the owner of their mother."

Choisser v. Hargrave, I Scammon 317 (1836)
Barney Hargrave brought action against Choisser for false imprisonment and assault. Choisser brought Hargrave into Illinois in 1816 and registered him as an indentured servant in 1818. The court ruled for Hargrave because Choisser exceeded the thirty day requirement to register servants brought into the state.

<u>Nixon v. The People</u>, 2 Scammon 267 (1840)
A grand jury indicted Nixon for assaulting with intent to kill a man of color. A jury later convicted Nixon. On appeal, the supreme court sustained the judgment.

<u>Kinney v. Cook</u>, 3 Scammon 232 (1840)
Thomas Cook, a man of color, sued William Kinney for wages earned during employment. Evidence showed that Cook had been held as a slave, though he was a freeman. A lower court awarded him wages. The supreme court affirmed the decision, declaring that "with us the presumption is in favor of liberty."

<u>Bailey v. Cromwell</u>, 3 Scammon 71 (1841)
The administrators of Cromwell brought action against Bailey, upon a promissory note, to purchase a black woman. Cromwell did not own her, however, so the court ruled for the plaintiff. On appeal the supreme court reversed the judgment, declaring that in Illinois the presumption favored freedom. "The sale of a free person is illegal."

<u>Sarah, alias Sarah Borders, a woman of color v. Andrew Borders</u>,
4 Scammon 341 (1843)
Andrew Borders purchased Sarah from a Kentucky slave holder. He brought her into Illinois and registered her as an indentured servant. Borders used force to compel Sarah to perform her duties. The court agreed that he might have been unjust but it upheld Illinois law providing for legally registered indentured servants.

<u>Chambers v. The People</u>, 4 Scammon 351 (1843)
A lower court convicted Chambers for harboring a runaway servant. The supreme court reversed the verdict, dissatisfied that the defendant knew that the persons involved were fugitives from labor.

<u>Willard v. The People</u>, 4 Scammon 461 (1843)
A circuit court indicted Williard for "secreting" Julia, a runaway slave. A lower court convicted him under federal law. The supreme court affirmed the opinion.

<u>Eells v. The People</u>, 4 Scammon 498 (1843)
Durkee brought action against Eells for harboring slaves who escaped from his Missouri farm. The court convicted Eells and fined him $400. Later, Eells appealed the case to the U.S. Supreme Court, which upheld his conviction.

Williams v. Jarrot, I Gilman 120 (1843)
The plaintiff, a man of color, was the slave of a Tennessee master who sold him as an indentured servant in Illinois. He escaped. Once captured, the claimant battered him. A lower court held for defendants. On appeal the supreme court reversed the judgment on rule of evidence.

Hays v. Borders, I Gilman 46 (1844)
An action brought by Mr. Montiff, charging the defendant with aiding indentured servants. A jury found the defendant guilty and awarded the plaintiff $300 in damages.

Joseph v. Jarrot, 2 Gilman I (1845)
Joseph and his family sued the defendant to recover wages and to achieve their emancipation. The defendant claimed that he had inherited the family. A lower court concluded that Joseph was a slave under the law, but the state's supreme court reversed the opinion. "The record does not show when the plaintiff was born, whether before or after the adoption of the State Constitution."

Patterson v. Edwards, 2 Gilman 720, (1845)
Mrs. Edwards brought suit against Maria Patterson, accusing her of slander. Patterson had said that "Mrs. Edwards has had children by a Negro, and all her children are Negroes." The jury for a lower court agreed and awarded her $220. The Supreme Court reversed the verdict.

Thornton's Case, II Illinois 332, (1849)
Hempstead Thornton, an African American, charged that Jones, a county constable, deprived him of his liberty. Jones had mistaken him as a runaway slave. The court discharged Thornton because Prigg v. Pennsylvania (1842) had nullified state legislation intending to impede or facilitate the apprehension of runaway slaves.

Owens v. The People, 13 Illinois 59 (1851)
Thomas Hobbs, a man of color, executed a bond with a Mr. Owens when Hobbs entered Illinois. The state alleged that Hobbs had not produced a certificate of freedom. A lower court ruled for the state, mandating that Owens pay the bond. The supreme court reversed the opinion, concluding that the county had wrongly applied the law. Only free blacks were eligible to post bond.

Ingalls v. Bulkley, 13 Illinois 315 (1851)
Bulkley sent two boys, one white, the other black, after a horse. The defendant "would not let either of the boys have the horse"; they were minors. A lower

court ruled for Bulkley. On appeal the supreme court reversed the opinion, concluding that the age of the boys was a consideration in the case.

Hone v. Ammons, 14 Illinois 29 (1852)
Hone, a slave catcher, apprehended a free black American and sold him into slavery. Hone received a promissory note from Mr. Ammons, who purchased the free African-American for consideration, but the defendant refused to honor the note when due. A circuit court ruled for the defendant. The supreme court upheld the verdict, holding that the alleged black was a free man the moment he entered Illinois. Without proof of slavery, the presumption favored freedom in Illinois.

Moore, Executor of Eells v. The People, 14 Howard 13 (1852)
This case originated in Illinois and was appealed to the U.S. Supreme Court. Plaintiff charged that Eells violated the state's fugitive slave law. Counsel for Eells argued that the Supreme Court had voided state fugitive slave legislation in 1842. The Court affirmed Eells' conviction, holding that "we are of the opinion that the act of Illinois, upon which this indictment is founded, is constitutional."

Campbell v. The People, 16 Illinois 17 (1854)
A circuit court indicted Campbell, an African American, for murder. The evidence showed that he had defended himself against assault from the deceased. The supreme court reversed the judgment, explaining that "In this [case] the [lower] court unquestionably erred."

Glenn v. The People, 17 Illinois 105 (1855)
The authorities arrested William Glenn under the state's black immigration policy. A justice of the peace convicted him and fined him $50. The circuit court affirmed the opinion, but the supreme court reversed the judgment. "The affidavit does not allege that the negro came into this state, and for ought that appears, he may have resided in this State at the time of the passage of the act of 1853, or have been born in this state."

Rodney v. Illinois Central Railroad Co., 19 Illinois 42 (1857)
The plaintiff charged the Illinois Central Railroad Company with aiding a runaway slave by allowing him to board the train while in Missouri. The court ruled that Illinois did not recognize slavery. Consequently, the slave was automatically free when he entered the state. According to the state court's interpretation of Prigg v. Pennsylvania (1842) only federal courts could approve the capture and return of runaway slaves.

Bennett v. Waller, 23 Illinois 97 (1859)
Timothy Webster, a policeman, was brought to trial for allegedly stealing the cane of a black abolitionist lecturer. Webster claimed he had found the cane in a bar.

Nelson (a mulatto) v. The People, 33 Illinois 390 (1864)
State officers arrested Nelson under the black immigration law of 1853. The court convicted him and fined him $50. The circuit court affirmed the verdict. The supreme court upheld the ruling.

Roundtree v. Baker, 52 Illinois 241 (1869)
This case involved the sale of a slave girl named Eliza. An Illinois resident delivered and sold the woman in Kentucky. The supreme court would not enforce the contract for the sale.

Suggested Readings

Alvord, Clarence W. The Illinois Country, 1673-1818, 1920.

Angle, Paul. "The Illinois Black Laws," Chicago History, 8, 1967.

Angle, Paul M. ed. Prairie State: Impressions of Illinois, 1673-1967, 1968.

Barnhart, John D. "The Southern Influence on the Formation of Illinois," Illinois State Historical Society Journal, 32, 1939.

Boggess, Arthur Clinton. The Settlement of Illinois, 1778-1830, 1908.

Fishback, Mason M. "Illinois Legislation on Slavery and Free Negroes," Illinois State Historical Society Journal, 9, 1904.

Gertz, Elmer. "The Black Laws of Illinois," Journal of the Illinois State Historical Society, 56, 1963.

Gliozzo, Charles A. "John Jones and the Illinois Black Laws," Social Sciences Research Publication. Pamphlet, published by University of Minnesota, 1975.

Gridley, J. N. "A Case Under an Illinois Black Law," 4 Illinois State Historical Society Journal, 1912.

Harris, N. Dwight. The History of Negro Servitude in Illinois, and the Slavery Agitation in that State, 1906.

Jones, John. The Black Laws of Illinois, and a Few Reasons Why They Should be Repealed, 1864.

Litwack, Leon F. North of Slavery: The Negro in the Free States, 1790-1860, 1961.

Woodson, Carter G. A Century of Negro Migration, 1918.

Part Four

MICHIGAN, January 26, 1837

The African-American population in Michigan was rather small during most of the eighteenth and nineteenth centuries. If the black laws adopted in the Old Northwest were in response to a refractory population of Africans, it is reasonable to assume that in Michigan, with few blacks, color-based legislation would not have been necessary. But Michigan adopted the black laws and subjugated African Americans as effectively as any of its neighbors. The experience of blacks in Michigan demonstrates how racial prejudice can be learned and transferred from one generation to another. White Americans in Michigan inherited and embraced the racism of American culture and law. Consequently, the state's lawmakers adopted the black laws although the number of African-Americans in Michigan was negligible.

Africans had made contact with the Michigan Territory when westerners initially penetrated North America. African pioneers joined Europeans as explorers and city builders. Jean Baptiste Point DuSable, for example, is Michigan's best known black pioneer. Although we know little about DuSable, some scholars credit him with founding Chicago, the first city in Illinois. To his contemporaries, he was an imposing figure, standing more than six feet tall with a firm athletic build. Later, DuSable moved into the Michigan Country where he settled among the Ottawa Indians, married an Ottawa woman and, as legend has it, became the blood brother of Chief Pontiac, who led the Ottawa and other native American communities in an uprising against the colonies in 1763.

Most African Americans in Michigan were not city builders like DuSable, however. The majority were slaves who labored as dockworkers, lumberjacks, carriage drivers, and farmhands. Unwilling to adjust to servitude anywhere in America, enslaved blacks often escaped to gain their freedom. Sometimes they fled into the mountains where they formed maroon communities, or sometimes they fled as far away as Canada. The most dramatic incident in

Michigan involved a black woman named Ann Wiley who, along with Jean Contencineau, a Frenchman, conspired to flee their master's farm. They planned their daring escape in 1774. Wiley and Contencineau could feign the master-slave relationship easily enough, but the two lacked money to finance their escape. They agreed to break into their owner's home and steal the cash and clothing they needed before embarking on their journey. For reasons that are not clear, they decided to conceal the burglary by setting the house on fire. Their conspiracy delayed them long enough for the slave holder who claimed them to capture them. The planter made an example of Wiley and Contencineau by hanging them within view of his other servants.

Slave holders in Michigan obviously considered their "chattels" valuable, both because of the labor value and the high cost of purchasing slaves. Slavery, however, never became extensive in Michigan. Whites there did not struggle to circumvent the Ordinance of 1787 as did their counterparts in Indiana and Illinois. When Michigan applied for statehood in 1835, its Constitution prohibited slavery. The ease whereby Whites did away with slavery cannot be attributable to their benevolence, however. Experience elsewhere in the Territory had proven that any effort to keep slaves in the Northwest was futile. For Michigan planters the decision not to employ slaves was because they did not believe it was vital to their prosperity. Although whites in Michigan did not disguise slavery in the form of indentured servitude, lawmakers there still developed and enforced the black laws.

The black laws of Michigan repeated principles adopted by neighboring states. The legislature closed the militia to blacks, and, until after the Civil War, enforced a system of segregation in public education. Michigan lawmakers discouraged emigration of blacks by compelling them to produce "free papers" before they could obtain legal residence or employment. State officials also required black emigrants to post a bond to assure that should he or she become destitute, the person would not receive relief from the state. The bond could also be seized by county officials should an African American destroy property or in any way misbehaved. State law also required each emigrating African American to sign the registry kept in the clerk's office in each county. Finally, legislators made it a crime for anyone who harbored or secreted a runaway slave, or interfered with a slave holder who exercised his legal right to capture and remove a runaway slave.

The racial policy of Michigan emboldened professional slave catchers who sometimes tracked runaway slaves to the state. Few ethical men became professional slave catchers and unscrupulous hunters were little concerned about the status of a black when they removed them as slaves. They were motivated by the cash they could receive for returning a legal slave or selling a free black as a slave. Surprisingly, whites in Michigan were less incensed by kidnapping than whites in more conservative states, including Ohio and Indiana. Consequently, lawmakers in Michigan made only modest efforts to protect free blacks.

Whites in Michigan were certain that they could not practice slavery, and they vehemently opposed its extension into the Old Northwest. Their opposition to slavery was also a conservative attitude. Firstly, slave laborers competed with wage-earning white workers. Secondly, Michigan lawmakers, like most politically conscious northerner and midwesterners, became increasingly alarmed by the rapacious demands of the "slave power." When Congress approved the Kansas-Nebraska Act of 1854, potentially extending slavery, whites in Michigan condemned the law as a ploy to extend slavery.

Whites in Michigan certainly had a "two-ness" about themselves on matters concerning race. On the one hand, they opposed slavery's extension. On the other hand, they created the state's black laws. The following documents describe this pattern of racial discrimination in the state and legal culture of Michigan. Although the State produced fewer racial codes than its neighbors, its lawmakers maintained the tradition of the Old Northwest by closing its doors to black refugees and subjugating free black residents.

I

Declaration of Rights

The bill of rights in Michigan's constitution gave little indication that it protected the civil rights of whites only. The State's declaration of rights reads as if delegates to the Constitutional Convention desired to protect the legal rights of all residents of the State, including African Americans. The Constitution protected freedom to assemble, trial by jury, and freedom of the press. Free African-American residents of the state were, theoretically, recipients of these rights. The State also protected free blacks from kidnapping. Following the law in the Territory, Michigan prohibited slavery. Furthermore, the constitution included none of the loopholes found in the constitutions of other states in the Old Northwest. Michigan's declaration of rights reads as if the State was an egalitarian community.

NUMBER 1

Constitution of Michigan, 1835, Article 1.

Section 1. All political power is inherent in the people.

Section 2. Government is instituted for the protection, security, and benefit of the people; and they have the right at all times to alter or reform the same, and to abolish one form of government and establish another, whenever the public good requires it.

Section 3. No man or set of men are entitled to exclusive or separate privileges.

Section 4. Every person has a right to worship Almighty God according to the dictates of his own conscience; and no person can of right be compelled to attend, erect, or support, against his will, any place of religious worship, or pay any tithes, taxes, or other rates, for the support of any minister of the gospel or teacher of religion.

Section 5. No money shall be drawn from the treasury for the benefit of religious societies, or theological or religious seminaries.

Section 6. The civil and religious rights, privileges, and capacities of no individual shall be diminished or enlarged on account of his opinions or belief concerning matters of religion.

Section 7. Every person may freely speak, write, and publish his sentiments on all subjects, being responsible for the abuse of that right; and no laws shall be passed to restrain or abridge the liberty of speech or of the press. In all prosecutions or indictments for libels, the truth may be given in evidence to the jury; and if it shall appear to the jury, that the matter charged as libellous, is true, and was published with good motives and for justifiable ends, the party shall be acquitted; and the jury shall have the right to determine the law and the fact.

Section 8. The person, houses, papers and possessions of every individual, shall be secure from unreasonable searches and seizures; and no warrant to search any place, or to seize any person or things, shall be issued without describing them, nor without probable cause, supported by oath or affirmation.

Section 9. The right of trial by jury shall remain inviolate.

Section 10. In all criminal prosecutions, the accused shall have the right to a speedy and public trial by an impartial jury of the vicinage; to be confronted with the witnesses against him; to have compulsory process for obtaining witnesses in his favor; to have the assistance of counsel for his defence; and in all civil cases, in which personal liberty may be involved, the trial by jury shall not be refused.

Section 11. No person shall be held to answer for a criminal offence, unless on the presentment or indictment of a grand jury, except in cases of impeachment, or in cases cognizable by justices of the peace, or arising in the army or militia when in actual service in time of war or public danger.

Section 12. No person for the same offence shall be twice put in jeopardy of punishment; all persons shall, before conviction, be bailable by sufficient sureties, except for capital offenses, when the proof is evident or the presumption great; and the privilege of the writ of habeas corpus shall not be suspended, unless when, in case of rebellion or invasion, the public safety may require it.

Section 13. Every person has a right to bear arms for the defence of himself and the state.

Section 14. The military shall, in all cases, and at all times, be in strict subordination to the civil power.

Section 15. No soldier shall, in time of peace, be quartered in any house without the consent of the owner, nor in time of war, but in a manner prescribed by law.

Section 16. Treason against the state shall consist only in levying war against it, or in adhering to its enemies, giving them aid and comfort; no person shall be convicted of treason, unless on the testimony of two witnesses to the same overt act, or on confession in open court.

Section 17. No bill of attainder, ex post facto law, or law impairing the obligation of contracts, shall be passed.

Section 18. Excessive bail shall not be required; excessive fines shall not be imposed; and cruel and unjust punishments shall not be inflicted.

Section 19. The property of no person shall be taken for public use, without just compensation therefor.

Section 20. The people shall have the right freely to assemble together, to consult for the common good, to instruct their representatives, and to petition the legislature for redress of grievances.

Section 21. All acts of the legislature, contrary to this or any other article of this constitution, shall be void.

NUMBER 2

Constitution of Michigan, Article 11, 1835.

Section 1. Neither slavery nor involuntary servitude shall ever be introduced into this state, except for the punishment of crimes of which the party shall have been duly convicted.

II

Kidnapping

Michigan's declaration of rights deteriorated, at least for African-American residents soon after the State's first legislature assembled. For example, professional slave catchers, and other freelancing whites, made kidnapping free blacks a regular routine throughout the North. The legislature in Michigan, however, made modest efforts to protect its free black citizens. The State's lawmakers considered kidnapping an infringement of state law. They were less offended when slave catchers trampled upon the legal rights of their African-American residents. Michigan's official code on race, therefore, was barely egalitarian in comparison to other states in the Northwest Territory.

NUMBER 1

An act to regulate blacks and mulattoes, and to punish the kidnapping of such persons. Approved April 13, 1827, Laws of Michigan.

Section 1. Be it enacted by the Legislative Council of the Territory of Michigan, that from and after the first day of May next, no black or mulatto person shall be permitted to settle or reside in this Territory, unless he or she shall produce a fair certificate, from some court within the United States, of his or her actual freedom, which certificate shall be attested by the clerk of said court, and the seal thereof annexed thereto by the said court.

Section 2. That every black or mulatto person, now residing in this Territory, shall, on or before the first day of January next, enter his or her name, together with the name or names of his or her children, in the office of the clerk of the county court, in the county in which he, she, or they reside which shall be entered of said record by said clerk, and there after the clerk's certificate of said record shall be sufficient evidence of his or her freedom: Provided, that such black or mulatto, at the time of making such registry, shall have been born into this Territory, or produce a fair certificate as aforesaid, of such freedom, which shall be deposited in the clerk's office; and for entry and certificate, the person obtaining the same shall pay to the clerk twelve and a half cents: Provided, nevertheless, that nothing in this act contained, shall bar the lawful claim to any black or mulatto person.

Section 3. That if any person or persons shall harbor or secrete any black or mulatto person, the property of any person whatever, or shall in anywise hinder or prevent the lawful owner or owners, from retaking and possessing his or her black or mulatto servant or servants, such person shall, upon conviction thereof before any justice of the peace in the county, be fined in a sum not less than ten, nor more than fifty dollars, at the discretion of the court, one half thereof for the use of the informer, and the other half for the use of the township where the offense shall have been committed, excepting in the county of Wayne, where the same shall be appropriated as is provided for in the fifth [eighth] section of this act.

Section 4. That every black or mulatto person who shall come to reside in this Territory, with such certificate as is required in the first section of this act, shall, within one year, have the same recorded in the clerk's office in the county in which he or she means to reside, for which he or she shall pay to the clerk twelve and a half cents, and the clerk shall give him or her a certificate of such record.

Section 5. That in case any person or persons, his or their agent or agents, claiming any black or mulatto person that now is, or hereafter may be, in this Territory, may apply to any justice of the county court, or justice of the peace, and shall make satisfactory proof that such black or mulatto person or persons is or are the property of him or her who applies or for whom application is made, the said judge or justice is hereby empowered and required by his precept, to direct the sheriff or constable to arrest such black or mulatto person or persons, and deliver the same to the claimant or claimants, his or their agent or agents, for which service the sheriff or constable shall receive such compensation as they are entitled to receive in other cases for similar services.

Section 6. That no black or mulatto person shall be permitted to emigrate into and settle within this Territory, unless such black or mulatto person shall, within twenty days thereafter, enter into bond, with one or more freehold sureties, in the penal sum of five hundred dollars, before the clerk of the county court, in which such black or mulatto person may wish to reside to be approved of by the clerk, conditioned for the good behavior of such person, in case he or she thereafter be found within any township in this Territory, unable to support him, her or themselves; and if any black or mulatto person shall migrate to this Territory, and not comply with the provisions of this act, it shall be the duty of the overseers of the poor of the township where such black or mulatto person may be found, to remove immediately such black or mulatto person, in the same manner as is required in the case of paupers; and if such black or mulatto person should return, such black or mulatto person shall be proceeded against as is provided for in the "Act for the punishment of idle and disorderly persons."

Section 7. That it shall be the duty of the clerk before whom such bond may be given, as aforesaid, to file the same in his office, and give a certificate thereof to such black or mulatto person; and the said clerk shall be entitled to receive the sum of one dollar for the bond and certificate aforesaid, on the delivery of the certificate.

Section 8. That if any person, being a resident of this Territory, shall employ or counsel any such black or mulatto person, as aforesaid, contrary to the provisions of this act, any person so offending shall forfeit and pay, for every such offense, any sum not exceeding one hundred dollars, the one half to the informer, if he shall prosecute for the same and the other half for the use of the poor of the township in which such person may reside (excepting in the county of Wayne, where the same shall be paid into the county treasury, and be appropriated for the purchase of lands, and the erection of poor-houses on the same), to be recovered by action of debt, before any court having competent jurisdiction: And moreover, be liable for the maintenance and support of such black or mulatto, provided he or she shall become unable to support themselves.

Section 9. That if any person or persons, under any pretense whatsoever, shall, by violence, fraud, or deception, seize upon any free black or mulatto person, within this Territory, and keep or detain such free black or mulatto person in any kind of restraint or confinement, with intent to transport such free black or mulatto person out of this Territory, contrary to law, or shall, in any manner, attempt to carry out of the Territory any black or mulatto person, without having first taken such black or mulatto person before some judge of the circuit or county court, or a justice of the peace of the county wherein such black or mulatto person was taken agreeably to the provisions the Act of Congress made and provided, and there prove his right to such black or mulatto person, every such person so offending shall be deemed guilty of a misdemeanor, and on conviction thereof, before any court having competent authority to try the same, shall be sentenced to hard labor in the penitentiary, for any space of time not less than one, nor more than ten years, at the discretion of the court.

Section 10. That it shall be the duty of the district attorneys of the respective counties to prosecute all violations of this act, when thereunto required, and to be entitled to the same compensation, in the manner provided for in the act to prevent gaming.

NUMBER 2

An act to amend an act entitled "An act to regulate blacks and mulattoes, and to punish the kidnapping of such persons." Approved June 23, 1828, Laws of Michigan.

Section 1. Be it enacted by the Legislative Council of the Territory, that all sheriffs and constables in this Territory, in their respective counties, are vested with the same powers, and are required upon the overseer of the poor in the act to which this act is amendable, in removing certain Negroes and mulattoes in said act specified.

Section 2. That the presiding judge, when holding the circuit or county court in any of the counties in this Territory, shall constantly give this act in his charge to the grand jury at the sessions of such court, who shall diligently inquire if the said act is duly executed, and to present any violation of the same that may come to their knowledge.

NUMBER 3

Offenses against lives: Kidnapping and selling as slaves. Approved July 15, 1838, Revised Statutes.

Section 17. Every person who, without lawful authority, shall forcibly or secretly confine or imprison any other person, within this State, against his will, or shall forcibly carry or send such person out of this State, or shall forcibly seize and confine, or shall inveigle or kidnap any other person, with intent either to cause such person to be secretly confined or imprisoned in this state, against his will, or to cause such person to be sent out of this state against his will, or to be sold as a slave, or in any way held to service against his will; and every person who shall sell, or in any manner transfer for any term the service or labor of any negro, mulatto, or other person of color who shall have been unlawfully seized, taken, inveigled or kidnapped from this state to any other state, place or country, shall be punished by imprisonment in the state prison not more than ten years, or by fine not exceeding one thousand dollars, or both, at the discretion of the court.

Section 18. Every offence mentioned in the preceding section, may be tried either in the county in which the same may have been committed, or in any county in or to which the person so seized, taken, inveigled, kidnapped or sold, or whose services shall be so sold or transferred shall have been taken, confined, held, carried or brought; and upon the trial of any such offence, the consent thereto of the person so taken inveigled, kidnapped or confined, shall not be a defence, unless it shall be made satisfactorily to appear to the jury, that such consent was obtained by fraud, nor extorted by duress or by threats.

NUMBER 4

An act to amend section twenty-five of the revised statutes: Kidnapping with intent to sell. Approved February 15, 1859, Laws of Michigan.

Section 1. The People of the State of Michigan enact, That section twenty-five, of said chapter one hundred and fifty-three, be amended so as to read as follows:

Section 25. Every person who willfully, and without lawful authority, shall forcibly or secretly confine or imprison any other person within this State against his will, or shall forcibly carry or send such person out of this State, or shall forcibly seize and confine, or shall inveigle or kidnap any other person, with intent either to cause such person to be secretly confined or imprisoned in this State against his will, or to be sold as a slave, or in any way held to serve against his will, and every person who shall sell, or in any manner transfer for any time, the service or labor of any negro, mulatto, or other person of color, who shall have been unlawfully seized, taken, inveigled or kidnapped from this State, to any other State, place or country, or who shall bring any negro, mulatto, or other person of color, into the State, claiming him or her as a slave, shall be punished by the imprisonment in the State Prison not more than ten years, or by fine not exceeding one thousand dollars.

III

The Slavery Controversy

Michigan produced a small but vigorous cadre of antislavery leaders who condemned the federal Fugitive Slave Act of 1850. The minority status of such leaders was typical during the abolitionist movement. They were not humanitarians; most were concerned mainly with the growth of "the slave power." To curb the political clout of slave holders, antislavery reformers asked Congress to curtail the admission of slave states to the Union. Consequently, legislative resolutions condemning slavery were designed mainly to slow its expansion to the West.

NUMBER 1

Joint resolution respecting slavery in the territories. Approved February 4, 1857, Laws of Michigan.

Whereas, The people of this State did, at the late Presidential and State election, unequivocally condemn the fugitive slave law of 1850, and the principles and practical workings of the Kansas-Nebraska act of 1854; repudiating by a most distinct and emphatic utterance the repeal of the Missouri restriction, and the doctrine of Squatter Sovereignty;

And Whereas, The people have thus, by an overwhelming and unprecedented majority, endorsed the resolutions of instruction passed at the last session of this body;

And whereas, These instructions were utterly disregarded, notwithstanding the previous and oft-repeated avowal, on the part of our Senators of the doctrine of instructions;

And whereas, The experience of the last two years has but deepened our conviction of the imperative necessity of checking the encroachments of the slave power: Therefore,

Be it resolved by the Senate and House of Representatives, That in the name and by the authority of the people of the State of Michigan, we respectfully demand of our Senators, and earnestly ask of our Representatives, in Congress, to resist to the utmost the admission of any more slave states into the Union; and to use their best exertions to secure the immediate admission of Kansas as a free State, the repeal of the fugitive slave law of 1850, and the prohibition by law of slavery in all the territories and in the District of Columbia.

Resolved, That the Governor be requested to forward copies of the foregoing preamble and resolution to our Senators and Representatives in Congress.

This joint resolution is ordered to take immediate effect.

NUMBER 2

Joint resolutions instructing our senators and representatives in Congress in relation to the affairs of Kansas. Approved February 10, 1857, Laws of Michigan.

Whereas, It appears by the report of the special committee of the House of Representatives of the United States, sent to the territory of Kansas in the summer of 1856, under a resolution of the House, that the first legislature of said territory were, in open violation of the Kansas-Nebraska Act, chosen by the votes of bodies of men from Missouri and other slave-holding States, who, by fraud and violence, succeeded in imposing upon the people of the territory a body of men claiming to possess legislative authority, but whose acts of pretended legislation are, by reason of such fraud and violence, void and of no effect; and

Whereas, Many of said acts are tyrannical, and a gross infringement of the constitutional rights of the people of the United States, and, as they have been justly characterized a disgrace to the civilization of the age; therefore,

Resolved by the Senate and House of Representatives of the State of Michigan, That our Senators in Congress be instructed, and our Representatives requested, to use their best exertions to procure the passage of an act of Congress declaring the Kansas code (so called) null and void, and particularly those provisions thereof which violate the freedom of speech and the press; which require of all territorial officers, counselors and attorneys test oaths in support of slavery; which require of the voter a base and degrading oath to support the fugitive slave law, as a condition of exercising the elective franchise; which disqualify jurors for their opinions against slavery, or which inflict cruel and unusual punishments (such as the wearing of the ball and chain) on persons convicted under said fraudulent and unconstitutional acts.

Resolved, That the Governor transmit a copy of the above preamble and resolutions to each of our Senators and Representatives in Congress.

The joint resolutions shall take immediate effect.

NUMBER 3

Joint resolution relative to the extension of slavery. Approved February 3, 1858, Laws of Michigan.

Whereas, The people of the State of Michigan have shown an unyielding hostility to the further extension of slavery, by a large majority, at every election since eighteen hundred and fifty-four, (1854,) when their will could be expressed in reference to that subject;

And whereas, The Legislature of the State of Michigan have on two several occasions instructed their Senators and requested their Representatives to act in accordance with the above expressed sentiment, in Congress, which instructions have been by some of those thus instructed, wholly disregarded; therefore,

Resolved by the Senate and House of Representatives of the State of Michigan, That our Senators be instructed and our Representatives requested to use all proper means to prevent the further extension of slavery in the territories of the United States, or the admission of any more slave States into the Union; to oppose the admission of Kansas into the Union under the Lecompton constitution, or any constitution maintaining slavery therein;

Resolved, That the Governor be requested to forward copies of the foregoing preamble and resolution to our Senators and Representatives in Congress.

IV

The Militia

When delegates assembled in 1835 to write Michigan's first Constitution, they said nothing about the "color" of men eligible for militia service. In peace time, whites considered militia service a badge of honor. Ostensibly, constitutional law extended this privilege to all residents including black Americans. There is no evidence that African-American men attempted to enlist; yet, it is a plausible theory. Convention delegates closed this loophole in 1850, making militia service an honor reserved for whites only.

NUMBER 1

Constitution of Michigan, Article 17, 1850.

Section 1. The militia shall be composed of all able-bodied white male citizens between the ages of eighteen and forty-five years, except such as are exempted by the laws of the United States or of this State; but all such citizens of any religious denomination whatever, who, from scruples of conscience, may be averse to bearing arms, shall be excused therefrom, upon such conditions as shall be prescribed by law.

V

Public Education

Michigan law provided for desegregation in public education soon after the Civil War. The civil rights reforms initiated by Congress made desegregation possible in Michigan. It's statutes, however, left a loophole enabling the department of education to circumvent the official policy concerning desegregation. For example, educators promoted children by their current performance. While white children are not smarter than black youths, the previous experiences of black children under a system of oppression in Michigan and the nation, made it unlikely that black youths had the same educational preparation as the whites.

NUMBER 1

All residents may attend common school. Approved March 7, 1871, Laws of Michigan.

Section 28. All persons, residents of any school district, and five years of age, shall have an equal right to attend any school therein; and no separate school or department shall be kept for any persons on account of race or color: Provided, That this shall not be construed to prevent the grading of schools according to the intellectual progress of the pupil, to be taught in separate places as may be deemed expedient.

VI

Miscegenation of the Races

Michigan lawmakers outlined several criteria regulating marriages. State law prohibited such unions as the basis of polygamy, insanity, and race. Although, whites had strong opinions against interracial marriages, the legislature affirmed the validity of black and white families after the Civil War.

NUMBER 1

An act to amend section one and to repeal section thirty-two of chapter one hundred and seventy, of the compiled laws of eighteen hundred and seventy-one, being compiler's sections forty-seven hundred and thirty-three, amended, and forty-seven hundred and sixty-four, repealed, relative to divorce. Approved April 11, 1883, Laws of Michigan.

Section 1. The People of the State of Michigan enact, That section one of chapter one hundred and seventy, of the compiled laws of eighteen hundred and seventy-one, being compiler's section four thousand seven hundred and thirty-three, relative to divorce, be and the same is hereby amended so as to read as follows:

Section 1. All marriages which are prohibited by law on account of consanguinity or affinity between the parties, or on account of either of them having a former wife or husband then living, and all marriages solemnized when either of the parties was insane or an idiot, shall, if solemnized within this State, be absolutely void, without any decree of divorce or other legal process: Provided, That the issue of such marriage, except that contracted while either of the parties thereto had a former husband or wife living, shall be deemed legitimate.

Section 2. Section thirty-two of chapter one hundred and seventy of the compiled laws of eighteen hundred and seventy-one, being compiler's section four thousand seven hundred and sixty-four, is hereby repealed.

NUMBER 2

An act to amend section six of chapter one hundred and sixty nine, of the compiled laws of eighteen hundred and seventy-one, being compiler's section four thousand seven hundred and twenty-four, relative to marriage. Approved June 15, 1899, Laws of Michigan.

Section 1. The People of the State of Michigan enact, That section six of chapter one hundred and sixty-nine, of the compiled laws of eighteen hundred and seventy-one, being compiler's section four thousand seven hundred and twenty-four, relative to marriage, be and the same is hereby amended so as to read as follows:

Section 6. No insane person or idiot shall be capable of contracting marriage. All marriages heretofore contracted between white persons and whose wholly or in part of African descent are hereby declared valid and effectual in law for all purposes, and the issue of such marriages shall be deemed and taken legitimate as to such issue and as to both of the parents.

NUMBER 3

Marriages declared valid. Approved April 11, 1883, Revised Statutes.

Section 6. No insane person or idiot shall be capable of contracting marriage. All marriages heretofore contracted between white persons and those wholly or in part of African descent are hereby declared valid and effectual in law for all purposes, and the issue of such marriages shall be deemed and taken legitimate as to such issue and as to both of the parents.

VII

Civil and Legal Rights

Civil rights laws in Michigan provided for equal access to public places including inns, theaters, and restaurants. These statutes prescribed penalties for violators. The laws also extended to blacks the ability to participate fully in court proceedings, such as grand jury service. In addition, state law required that insurance companies make no distinction on account of race when collecting premiums.

NUMBER 1

An act to protect all citizens in their civil rights. Approved May 28, 1885, Laws of Michigan.

Section 1. The People of the State of Michigan enact, That all persons within the jurisdiction of said State shall be entitled to the full and equal accommodations, advantages, facilities, and privileges of inns, restaurants, eating-houses, barbershops, public conveyances on land and water, theaters, and all other places of public accommodation and amusement, subject only to the conditions and limitations established by law and applicable alike to all citizens.

Section 2. That any person who shall violate any of the provisions, of the foregoing section, by denying to any citizen, except for reasons applicable alike to all citizens of every race and color, and regardless of color or race, the full accommodations, advantages, facilities, or privileges in said section enumerated or by aiding or inciting such denial, shall for every such offense be deemed guilty of a misdemeanor, and upon conviction thereof, shall be fined not to exceed one hundred dollars, or shall be fined not to exceed one hundred dollars, or shall be imprisoned not more than thirty days, or both.

Section 3. That no citizen of the State of Michigan, possessing all other qualifications which are or may be prescribed by law, shall be disqualified to serve as grand or petit juror in any court of said State on account of race or color, and any office or other person charged with any duty in the selection or summoning of jurors; who shall exclude or fail to summon any citizen for the cause aforesaid, shall, on conviction thereof, be deemed guilty of a misdemeanor, and be fined not more than one hundred dollars, or imprisoned not more than thirty days, or both.

NUMBER 2

An act to amend an act entitled "An act in relation to life insurance companies transacting business within this State." Approved May 4, 1893, Laws of Michigan.

Section 1. The People of the State of Michigan enact, that chapter one hundred and thirty-one of Howell's Annotated Statutes of the State of Michigan, being an act entitled "An act in relation to life insurance companies transacting business within this State," is hereby amended by adding one new section thereto to stand and be known as section thirty-two, and to read as follows:

Section 32. That no life insurance company doing business in this State shall make any distinction or discrimination between white persons and colored persons, wholly or partially of African descent, as to the premiums or rates charged for policies upon the lives of such persons, or in any other manner whatever; nor shall [any] such company demand or require a greater premium from such colored persons than is at that time required by such company from white persons of the same, age, sex, general condition of health and prospect of longevity; nor make or require any rebate, diminution or discount upon the amount to be paid on such policy in case of death of such colored person insured; nor insert in the policy any condition, nor make any stipulation whereby such person insured shall bind himself or his heirs, executors, administrators and assigns to accept any sum less than the full value or amount of such policy in case of a claim accruing thereon by reason of the death of such person insured, other than such as are imposed on white persons in similar cases; and any such stipulations or conditions so made or inserted shall be void. Any company which shall violate any of the provisions of this section shall forfeit to the State the sum of five hundred dollars for each violation, to be recovered by Attorney General by appropriate action in any court of competent jurisdiction, and any judgment therefor may be collected in the same manner as is herein provided for collecting judgments rendered in favor of policy holders. And any officer or agent who shall violate any of the provisions of this section shall be deemed guilty of a misdemeanor, upon conviction thereof shall violate any of the provisions of this section shall be punished by imprisonment in the county jail not exceeding one year, or by a fine of not less than fifty dollars, and not exceeding five hundred dollars, or by both such fine and imprisonment, in the discretion of the court.

Summary of Cases

Looking back over nineteenth century Michigan history, it is not surprising that slavery was never debated or litigated extensively. From the territorial period, white emigrants had gone to Michigan seeking greater opportunities than they had in the East, or to escape competition with slave labor in the South. Moreover, Michigan's soil, climate, and economy made the use of large-scale agricultural laborers unlikely. Indentured servitude or hired-out slaves never became an industry in Michigan. The African-American population remained comparatively small throughout the antebellum era. There were only two themes in Michigan's early judicial history that involved black residents: runaway slaves and enfranchising African Americans.

Like most states, except Wisconsin, the courts in Michigan joined federal courts to uphold federal fugitive slave laws. The courts supported the idea that a slave holder should be able to capture a runaway slave and that persons who obstructed the process were punishable under federal laws. Obstruction could have meant aiding a runaway slave, participating in a rescue, or denying knowledge of the whereabouts of an alleged refugee.

For example, when a district court reviewed the case of Gitler v. Graham (1848), the court supported Gitler's claim that his slaves escaped to Michigan in 1843, where they stayed unmolested until 1848. The whites who knew them considered them free; and if they had been slaves, it did not seem to matter to the whites. Gitler, the slave holder from Kentucky, produced an affidavit for their arrest. He and his men caused a scene when apprehending the refugees. Whites who knew the refugees believed they were free. During the fracas, the alleged slaves escaped. Gitler, unable to immediately pursue them, sued the men who interfered under federal law. A federal district court ruled in Gitler's favor.

Suffrage was another controversial topic for state courts. Michigan followed the policy of Ohio on this question. Both states devised a visible admixture test to determine voting eligibility for persons with a mixture of Caucasian, African, or Indian blood. If the features of the person in question appeared more white than black, that person was considered white under the racial code of the state. Sometimes the people making these judgments disagreed, and the matter ended up in court.

Other cases portray this theme in the annotated cases which follow. In Douglas v. Farrar (1847), the court reviewed a dispute whether a registrar disqualified an elector because he did not appear white. The justices on the bench ruled that the plantiff's Caucasian features predominated. Thus, he had been illegally barred from the voting booth. The court also held this opinion in People v. Dean (1866): "whenever white blood predominates--[amounting to] less than one-fourth of African blood," such persons are white under the law.

Select Annotated Cases

Denison v. Tucker, 1 Blume 385 (1807)
The territorial court of Michigan considered the status of enslaved blacks held in the territory before adoption of the Ordinance of 1787. Justice Augustus B. Woodward ruled that the ordinance applied only to slaves taken into the Territory after 1787. Others in the territory prior to that year were not affected by the antislavery clause in the ordinance.

Pattinson v. Whitaker, 1 Blume 414 (1807)
Justice Woodard also reviewed the fugitive slave clause in the Northwest ordinance and the U.S. Constitution, restricting constitutional law and slavery to the United States and its territories only. Therefore, slaves who escaped from a foreign country such as Canada would automatically become free when they entered the United States.

Douglass v. Farrar, 2 Gordon 411 (1847)
Douglass, a person of mixed ancestry, sued Farrar, an election inspector, for refusing his vote. The jury ruled for the plaintiff and assessed damages, pending the court's ruling on the ratio of his white and black ancestry. The judged in the case ruled that his European ancestry predominated and ordered his registration.

Gitler v. Graham, 10 Federal Cases 424 (4 McLean 402) (1848)
A Kentucky slave holder named Gitler brought action against Graham to recover runaway slaves. The enslaved persons had absconded from Kentucky in 1843. Once located in Michigan, black and white residents interfered with their removal. During the fracas, the alleged slaves escaped. The plaintiff sued and the court upheld the fugitive slave law.

Day v. Ownes, 5 Michigan 520 (1858)
This case involved a passenger vessel in intrastate commerce. The owner had agreed to provide a black man passage on the boat but refused him a cabin pass. The passenger sued the steamboat owner. A lower court ruled that special accommodation, such as a cabin pass, is subject to regulation. The U.S. Supreme Court affirmed this ruling.

People v. Dean, 14 Michigan 406 (1866)
The state prosecuted the defendant, a man of color, "for illegal voting." The court evaluated a ratio under the visible admixture test which would have made a person of mixed blood white under the law. The state constitution had enfranchised whites only, the state court explained: "it has never occurred to anyone that different shades of color could afford . . . ground[s] of compromise." The court concluded that whenever white blood "predominates [so] that they have less than one-fourth of African blood," such person's are white under the law.

Hedgeman v. Board of Registration, 26 Michigan 51 (1872)
The Board of Registration in Michigan refused to register a black resident. The victim applied for a unit of mandamus from the state supreme court "to compel the respondents to register" him. The plaintiff claimed that he had become a citizen under the Fourteenth Amendment of the United States Constitution, that , although he had been born in Canada, his parents had escaped from slavery in Virginia and fled across the border before the war. The Court concluded that the refugees had not been citizens of Virginia. Their son, therefore, was not a citizen either but that he could become a naturalized citizen.

Suggested Readings

Bemis, Edward W. Local Government in Michigan and the Northwest. Read before the American Social Science Association, 1883.

Berwanger, Eugene. The Frontier Against Slavery: Western Anti-Negro Prejudice and the Slavery Extension Controversy, 1967.

Dancy, John C. "The Negro People in Michigan," 24 Michigan Historical Magazine, 1940.

Fahrenbacher, Don. The Dred Scott Decision: Its Significance in American Law and Politics, 1978.

Fields, Harold. "Free Negroes in Cass County," Michigan History, 1960.

Finkelman, Paul. An Imperfect Union: Slavery, Federalism, and Comity, 1970.

Glazier, Sidney. Negroes in Michigan Before the Civil War.

Lanman, James H. History of Michigan, From its Earliest Colonization to the Present Time, 1855.

Morris, Thomas. Free Men All: The Personal Liberty Laws of the North, 1780-1861, 1974.

Utley, Henry M., and Byron M. Cutcheon. Michigan as a Province, Territory, and State. 4 vols., 1906.

Voegeli, Jacque. Free but Not Equal: The Midwest and the Negro During the Civil War, 1967.

Part Five

WISCONSIN, May 29, 1848

The statutes in this volume demonstrate what happened to the natural rights of African Americans in states where legislatures did not adopt color-based laws. As this volume shows, the states in the Old Northwest trampled upon civil rights, particularly the legal rights of blacks. Interference with citizenship rights did not stop with African Americans, however. The law advised whites on employment, philanthropy, and compelled them to participate in the capture and removal of alleged runaways even when their conscience dictated otherwise. Wisconsin, the last state formed from the Old Northwest, did not develop black laws. Thus, it offers scholars an opportunity to review the racial policy of a free state that did not adopt "slave codes." Could it be that Wisconsin provided leadership for the older states in the Old Northwest when they dismantled the black laws? Or, did Wisconsin embrace racism in its legal culture such as the racial policy already entrenched when Wisconsin became a state? The following summary considers these questions.

Settlers in the Old Northwest had managed to bring slaves into the territory in violation of the Ordinance of 1787. Wisconsin was no exception. Southern whites, along with army officers, brought slaves into Wisconsin to work in lead mines and on farms. A few free African Americans also emigrated to Wisconsin voluntarily, hoping to enjoy a better life than they had in the South. So did runaway slaves, who sought refuge from bondage in the South. Nevertheless, the African-American population in Wisconsin grew slowly and remained negligible for decades. In 1840, for example, there were 185 free and eleven enslaved African-Americans in Wisconsin. The free population grew to only 635 in 1850, far below the average for blacks in other states in the Old Northwest. Consequently, whites in Wisconsin did not feel overwhelmed by the presence of African Americans. Had the state been inundated with refugees from the South, it is certain that Wisconsin would have adopted statutes to curb their emigration and produce laws to regulate their mobility, residence, and employment. While this assessment is only speculation, the actually assertions of whites fall far below the conduct of an egalitarian community.

Wisconsin's racial policy suggests that the absence of a statutory policy of discrimination means little in a community guided by its racist beliefs. The legislature in Wisconsin did not produce black laws, at least technically. Yet Caucasians there shared the racial beliefs of whites in other states in the Old Northwest. Moreover, the racial phobia embraced by whites in Wisconsin were extreme and irrational. They were especially paranoid about interracial sex, especially relationships white women shared with black men. Whites called this conduct miscegenation.

The outlook of whites about miscegenation influenced their political policy. For example, whites believed that should the state grant African Americans the legal rights to which they were entitled, it would have been tantamount to approving interracial relationships. Most whites, especially the men, vigorously opposed enfranchising black Americans or protecting their civil rights. As one spokesman put it, to grant citizenship rights to black Americans would encourage them to "marry our sisters and daughters, and smutty wenches or brothers and sons."[1] These sentiments notwithstanding, the legislature placed no further restrictions on its black residents.

The subject of African-American suffrage became heated by the 1840s. As in the antislavery movement, a minority of whites supported enfranchising blacks. The legislature defeated bills proposing black suffrage in 1844 and 1846 respectively. A referendum vote in 1846, with about 50 percent of the whites voting in the negative, defeated the black suffrage bill by a vote of 14,615 to 7,664. Suffrage reformers achieved success in 1849 on another referendum vote. Black males finally won their legal right to vote in Wisconsin. The black suffrage question remained unsettled, however. Then in 1866 the supreme court reviewed the suffrage referendum in a dispute involving Gillespie v. Palmer. The court finally held valid the 1849 statute, holding the black suffrage law valid.

The legal system in Wisconsin provided leadership for the Old Northwest on federal fugitive slave legislation. Antislavery leaders throughout the Old Northwest objected to federal fugitive slave legislation, and most states considered the runaway slave problem a matter for sovereign states to resolve. Wisconsin led the opposition, and its leaders deemed the Fugitive Slave Act of 1850 a violation of state law. The 1850 statute authorized marshals and commissioners to operate in the states with authority to capture and remove alleged slaves, and it compelled citizens to enforce the measure by joining a posse when summoned by a marshall. The supreme court of Wisconsin was the only state tribunal to declare the fugitive slave law unconstitutional. It was a futile effort, however; federal judges revised the state's decrees.

The following documents provide a history of Wisconsin's racial policy. They demonstrate that the suffrage issue concerned whites in Wisconsin more than any other question. They also describe a transformation of the state's racial code during the Civil War, and by the end of the century, the legislature had adopted modest civil rights laws. Nonetheless, Wisconsin rarely marched far ahead of its neighbors in its social customs regarding race relations, and lawmakers there made African Americans second-class citizens.

NOTE

1.Eugene H. Berwanger, The Frontier Against Slavery, p. 36.

I

Declaration of Rights

Wisconsin, the last state formed from the Old Northwest, adopted a bill of rights that included a prohibition against slavery. Unlike her sister states, Wisconsin never adopted a comprehensive list of black laws. The state was not neutral on race, however. Negrophobia pervaded the region and miscegenation and other social issues made most whites paranoid. They harbored strong feelings against African Americans and the prospect of racial mixing. For instance, whites believed that enfranchising blacks would foster interracial marriages. Although an unusual idea it helps to explain why whites in Wisconsin disfranchised blacks.

NUMBER 1

Constitution of Wisconsin, Article 1, 1848.

Section 1. All men are born equally free and independent, and have certain inherent rights: among these are life, liberty and the pursuit of happiness. To secure these rights, governments are instituted among men, deriving their just powers from the consent of the governed.

Section 2. There shall be neither slavery nor involuntary servitude in this state, otherwise than for the punishment of crime, whereof the party shall have been duly convicted.

Section 3. Every person may freely speak, write, and publish his sentiments on all subjects, being responsible for the abuse of that right, and no laws shall be passed to restrain or abridge the liberty of speech or of the press. In all criminal prosecutions or indictments for libel, the truth may be given in evidence; and if it shall appear to the jury that the matter charged as libelous be true, and was published with good motives and for justifiable ends, the party shall be acquitted; and the jury shall have the right to determine the law and the fact.

Section 4. The right of the people peaceably to assemble to consult for the common good, and to petition the government or any department thereof, shall never be abridged.

II

Suffrage and Elections

Wisconsin did not disfranchise blacks in the state's first constitution. On the other hand, the constitution did not enfranchise them either. The constitution recognized only white males and Indians who had become citizens of the United States as eligible voters. In 1866, the supreme court ruled in Gillespie v. Palmer that the right of suffrage extended to African Americans.

NUMBER 1

Constitution of Wisconsin, Article 3, 1848.

Section 1. Every male person, of the age of twenty-one years or upward, belonging to either of the following classes, who shall have resided in the state for one year next preceding any election, shall be deemed a qualified elector at such election:

1. White citizens of the United States.
2. White persons of foreign birth, who shall have declared their intention to become citizens, conformably to the laws of the United States on the subject of naturalization.
3. Persons of Indian blood, who have once been declared by law of congress to be citizens of the United States, any subsequent law of congress to the contrary notwithstanding.
4. Civilized persons of Indian descent, not members of any tribe. Provided, That the legislature may, at any time, extend by law the right of suffrage to persons not herein enumerated; but no such law shall be in force until the same shall have been submitted to a vote

of the people at a general election, and approved by a majority of all the votes cast at such election.

Section 2. No person under guardianship, non compos mentis, or insane, shall be qualified to vote at any election: nor shall any person convicted of treason or felony be qualified to vote at any election unless restored to civil rights.

NUMBER 2

An act submitting the question of the extension of the right of suffrage to a vote of the People. Approved March 22, 1849, Laws of Wisconsin.

The People of the State Wisconsin, represented in Senate and Assembly, do enact as follows:

Section 1. A separate ballot may be given at the ensuing general election by every person having a right to vote, to be deposited in a separate box, upon the question of the adoption of a law of section two of this bill. Upon the ballots given for the adoption of section two of this bill, shall be written or printed, or partly written and partly printed, the words "Equal suffrage to colored persons, Yes," and upon ballots given against the adoption of section two, in like manner, the words "Equal suffrage to colored persons, No," and said ballots shall be so folded that the words "equal suffrage" shall appear on the outside. If at the said election a majority of all the votes cast at such election shall be given in favor of equal suffrage to colored person[s], then said section two of this bill shall be a law.

Section 2. Every male colored inhabitant of the age of twenty-one years or upwards, who shall have resided in this state for one year next preceding any election, shall be deemed a qualified elector at such election, and eligible to hold any office in the state, subjected however to the regulations contained in sections two, three, four, five and six of the constitution of this state.

NUMBER 3

An act to extend the right to suffrage, 1865. Approved April 10, 1865, Laws of Wisconsin.

The people of the state of Wisconsin, represented in senate and assembly, do enact as follows:

Section 1. The right of voting is hereby extended to male persons of African blood, who shall have attained the age of twenty-one years or upwards, with the same qualifications and restrictions now imposed upon other voters in section one of article on suffrage in the constitution.

Section 2. The act, before it takes effect, shall be submitted to the people at a general election to be held on the Tuesday next succeeding the first Monday of November 1865, when, if such majority of votes as is required by the constitution, be cast for it, it shall be of force and effect under the requirements hereinafter prescribed; but if such majority be not cast for it, it shall have no force or effect.

Section 3. The form of the ballot to be used on this occasion, shall be for the affirmative, "for extension of suffrage," for the negative, "for the extension of suffrage, no," which shall be on the general ballot used at the said election, and deposited in the same box, and all persons qualified by law to vote at any election in this state, shall be deemed voters on this question.

Section 4. These votes shall be counted and returned by the inspectors of the election, in all respects as votes for state officers are counted and returned.

Section 5. The officers now designated by law to canvass the returns of votes for state officers, shall canvass the returns on this question, at the same place and under the same regulations and restrictions now provided by law for canvassing and declaring the returns of elections for state officers.

Section 6. Within three days after the determination of such canvass, it shall be the duty of the canvassers to certify the result of the said canvass to the governor, who shall, thereupon, without delay, make proclamation of the result, and publish the same, daily and weekly, for two weeks, in all newspapers printed in the state; when, if the result shall be in favor of the extension of suffrage, this act shall immediately after such publication be of force and effect, but if not in favor of it, then this act shall have not force or effect.

Section 7. This act immediately after its passage, shall be published, and at least three months previously to said general election, the secretary of state shall send or cause to be sent a correct copy of it to every newspaper in the state, which newspaper upon publication of the same, shall be entitled to pay for the same out of the state treasury, at the rates paid for other legal advertising.

III

Runaway Slaves

Inevitably, the fugitive slave debate reached Wisconsin, and its lawmakers rejected the 1850 Fugitive Slave Act. They argued that comity did not require a free state to participate in the capture and removal of runaway slaves. In a series of legislative reports the assembly issued a strong condemnation against the fugitive slave law. The state supreme court joined the debate, ruling that the federal Fugitive Slave Act was unconstitutional. The supreme court of Wisconsin was the only court to take this action. The supreme court of the United States reversed this opinion in Ableman v. Booth (1858).

NUMBER 1

REPORT: The judiciary committee have had under consideration a resolution instructing your committee to enquire into the expediency of passing a law to prohibit the use of jails and prisons in this state for the imprisonment of persons convicted under a law of the United States, known as "the fugitive slave act," and a majority of your committee instruct me to report a bill for that purpose. March 14, 1855, House Journal.

Your committee render the following reasons for the conclusion to which they have arrived:

The privilege granted by this state to the government of the United States, to use the prisons and jails of this state for the purpose of confining or imprisoning persons convicted under the laws of the United States, is a mere act of comity, and the right to exercise that privilege is dependant altogether upon the laws of this state. The United States government has no power or authority whatever to use any jail or prison within this state, for any purpose whatever in time of peace, except such as may be expressly given by the laws of this state. Your committee do not believe that the right to use our prisons by the United States government had anything to do with the admission of Wisconsin into the Union, or has not anything to do with her right to stay in, and therefore the repeal of the statutes of this state so far as they authorize the imprisonment of persons committed or confined under or by virtue of the acts of congress known as the fugitive slave acts, will not, in the judgment of your committee, be an act of treason or nullification, or lead to a dissolution of the Union.

The supreme court of this state has declared the fugitive slave act of 1850 to be unconstitutional, and the majority of your committee cannot see the propriety of allowing the use of our jails and prisons for confining persons arrested or ordered to be imprisoned under said act. There is no rule of comity which can warrant us in permitting the use of our prisons to confine persons under an act which is declared, judicially, to be void, and the enforcement of which, under a republican form of government, is so repugnant to that common law which is declared in the books to be the "absolute perfection of reasons."

"The law favors liberty, and the freedom of a man from imprisonment; and therefore kind interpretations shall be made on its behalf. If a man is unlawfully imprisoned he may have an action of trespass for false imprisonment, and recover damages; or he may have the writ of habeas corpus, and upon return of this writ by the gaoler, setting forth by whom he was committed, and for what cause, he ought to be discharged if it appears to be against law."

In the opinion of your committee it needs only a careful consideration of correct principles, and an occasional review of our duties and obligations as men, to clearly point out the way we should go upon a subject like this. Your committee cannot see that it is a crime to do an act which involves no degree of moral turpitude, and so long as it is no crime for any human being to seek that freedom to which he is entitled, it should not be counted a crime in any to assist his neighbor in doing that which it is right should be done. The only way in which we can divest ourselves from responsibility or accountability, for the evils or curses of an institution, abhorrent to every moral sense, is to withdraw all countenance from its supporters, and all assistance from those who would make men chattels for gain. We believe the bill herewith reported, exempting our prisons for any use under the provisions of the fugitive slave law, humane and just toward those sought to be protected by the act, and we believe it also to be a great public necessity whereby we may protect our own citizens in their personal rights and privileges, rights as old as man, and as enduring as his race.

NUMBER 2

Minority report of the judiciary committee, to whom was referred a bill for an act to repeal chapter 8 of the public acts of the session of 1857. Senate Journal, 1858.

"The people of the United States, in order to form a more perfect Union, establish justice, insure domestic tranquility, provide for the common defence, promote the general welfare and secure the blessings of liberty to themselves and their posterity, ordained and established the Constitution for the United States of America." "That Constitution contemplated a division and distribution of the powers incident to a sovereign state, between the general government of the United States, and the government of each particular state; a distribution not depending on local limits, but by selecting certain subjects of common interest, and placing them under the entire and exclusive jurisdiction of the United States." And by the admission of this state into the Union on an equality with the original states, the people of the State of Wisconsin voluntarily pledged their loyalty to the Constitution of the United States.

Article 4, section 2 of the Constitution, contains these provisions:

1. The citizens of each state shall be entitled to all privileges and immunities of citizens of the several states.
2. A person charged in any state with treason, felony, or other crime, who shall flee from justice, and be found in another state, shall, on demand of the executive authority of the state from which he fled, be delivered up to be removed to the state having jurisdiction of the crime.

No person held to service or labor in one State under the laws thereof, escaping into another, shall, on consequence of any law or regulation therein, be discharged from such service or labor; but shall be delivered up upon claim of the party to whom such service or labor may be due.

As there was no general principal in the law of nations, or in the comity of independent states, requiring the equality of rights of their respective citizens, or the extradition of fugitives from justice or labor; these provisions were deemed essential in the formation of the Union. The Constitution was formed in the year 1787, and went into operation in the year 1789. The mode of delivering up fugitives from justice, or labor, was not prescribed until the passage of the act by Congress, on the 12th of February 1793. That act was passed in the House of Representatives, with but seven negative votes; and by the Senate without a division; and was signed by Jonathan Trumbull of Connecticut, as Speaker of the House of Representatives, by John Adams, Vice President; and was approved by George Washington, President of the United States. The Constitution and the act of congress contemplate the extradition of apprentices under indenture, without indenture, without regard to color, as well as of slaves. At the adoption of the Constitution, almost every state was a slave state. The law authorizing the claimant to have the hearing of the alleged facts, that the person arrested was a fugitive from his state and that he owed him service or labor in that state, before the State magistrates. The magistrates continued to act under that law, as they have always acted under acts of Congress, authorizing them to issue warrants and bind over persons charged with violating the criminal laws of the Untied States, until they are either prohibited from discharging their duty, by statutes of the Northern States, or were inducted to withhold their official aid to their brothers of other States, by abolition societies and profligate politicians. That kind of local legislature and influence engendered a spirit of rebellion and mobocracy, which rendered it both uncertain and unsafe, for a man to claim a fugitive from labor in any of the Northern States.

This state of things rendered the supplement act of 1850 a necessary measure for the perpetuity of this Union. This supplement confines the power of examination and extradition of the fugitive, to the judges of the United States, and to commissioners appointed by these judges. And, it also authorizes a warrant of arrest of the fugitive, and imposes the same responsibility upon the Marshal, as in all other cases, to receive and execute the warrant, and to pay the claimant the value of the property in case of a rescue. That this law and its supplement, are constitutional was never doubted by any judicial tribunal, or by any jurist laying claim to respectability, until the Supreme Court of this young State, made a contrary decision. All the courts of the United States, and of the several States sanctioned, approved and enforced the law; and they continue to do so, notwithstanding the decision of our Supreme Court.

The Supreme Court of this State pronounced the law unconstitutional, because there was no trial by jury provided for; and commissioners not clothed with judicial power under the constitution of the United States, were authorized to act. The constitution does not contemplate a trial by jury in the State wherein apprehended, of a fugitive from either justice or labor; but the expressive constitutional demand is, that the fugitive shall be delivered up on claim. The trial by jury of the legal rights and duties and penalties of the fugitive, is to be had in the State from which he had fled. The fugitive from justice is to be delivered up for trial by jury in the State from which he had fled, upon proof that he is the person charged with the offense. And the fugitive from labor, whether slave or apprentice, is to be delivered up for trial in the same State upon proof of identity, and that he there owes service or labor. And hearing the claim is merely the discharge of a judicial act. It is not part of the judicial power conferred upon the United State's Court by the Constitution--no more than binding over a person to answer to an indictment. The binding over, or order of extradition, is a judicial act, preliminary to the exercise of judicial power. Judicial power is the power or authority to adjudicate upon, determine and enforce by execution the legal rights of the parties. The power conferred on the Commissioners cannot affect the law, for the Judges can act.

The act of this State contemplates the issuing of writ of habeas corpus against an officer or person having a fugitive in custody, under the authority of the United States. And it creates heavy penalties for the resistance of the writ so issued. And it also declares judgments for any violation of the act of Congress void; and it authorizes a writ of replevin against the Marshall or officer for property seized under execution in satisfaction of such judgments.

That this act is a nullity, will appear from the following principles and authority: The power surrendered by the several states and conferred on the United States by the Constitution, are exclusive in the United States. And in article 6 of the Constitution it is declared that--"This Constitution, and the laws of the United States which shall be made in pursuance thereof, and all treaties made or which shall be made under the authority of the United States, shall be the supreme law of the land; and the judges in every state shall be bound thereby, anything in the constitution or laws of any state to the contrary notwithstanding." This provision determines the fate of the state law, and binds the judges in this State to declare it utterly void. The acts of Congress are the supreme law of the land, and the judges in every state are bound to enforce them in spite of a state law to the contrary. The judges of the state are sworn to support the Constitution of the United States; and must submit to it and to the laws passed under it, equally with the judges of the United States.

***

At a very early day after the adoption of the Constitution of the Untied States, the Legislature of Pennsylvania passed an act affecting, and in resistance of the admiralty jurisdiction of the District Court of the United States, under that act, the power of the state was called into requisition. In the case of United States v. Peters 5 Cranch reports 115, the validity of that act was passed upon by the Supreme Court of the U. S., and the State submitted. The District Judge was then compelled by mandamus to issue his process and maintain his jurisdiction. Chief Justice Marshall remarked in his opinion--"If the legislature of the several states may, at will, annul the judgments of the Courts of the United States, and destroy the rights required under these judgments, the Constitution itself becomes a solemn mockery, and the nation is deprived of the means of enforcing its laws by instrumentality of it own tribunals. So fatal a result must be deprecated by all; and the people of Pennsylvania, not less than the citizens of every other State, must feel a deep interest in resisting principles so destructive of the Union, and in averting consequences so fatal to themselves. The act in question assigns as a motive for its interposition in this particular case, that the sentence, the execution of which it prohibits, was rendered in a cause over which the federal courts have no jurisdiction. If the ultimate right to determine the jurisdiction of the Courts of the Union, is placed by the Constitution, in the several state Legislatures, then this act concludes the subject; but if that power necessarily resides in the supreme judicial tribunal of the nation, then the jurisdiction of the District Court of Pennsylvania, over the case in which that jurisdiction was exercised ought to be most deliberately examined; and that act of Pennsylvania with whatever respect it may be considered cannot be permitted to prejudice the question."

And it was determined, that the state had no constitutional right to resist the legal process, which may directed in the case.

In this state, judgments rendered in the courts of the State are, by law, liens in the counties in which they are rendered, or in which transcripts are filed. In other states the law runs that, no judgments shall be liens except in the counties in which they are rendered or transcripts filed. The difference is merely in phraseology, not in effect. In all such states, judgments in the courts of the United States are liens throughout their jurisdiction, and as such are recognized in the courts of the sates and of the United States. The limits of the state, in the exercise of the jurisdiction of the federal courts, is as the limits of the county to the local courts. The principles of the state law are adopted, but the instruments which give effect to those principles are necessarily different, and they are made to operate throughout a more extended jurisdiction.

In this case the court says: "In those states where the judgment in the execution of a state court creates a lien only within the county in which the judgment is entered, it has not been doubted that a similar proceeding in the court of the United States would create a lien to the extent of its jurisdiction. This has been the practical construction of the powers of the courts of the United States, whether the lien was held to be created by the issuing of process or by express statute. Any other construction would materially affect, and in some degree subvert the judicial power of the union." And the court further declares that--"The lien if not an effect of the judgment, is inseparably connected with it. And this is the case, whether the lien was created by the judgment and execution, or by statute. And in either case, where the right has attached in the courts of the United States, a state has no power by legislation or otherwise to modify or impair it. Retrospective laws of a remedial character may be passed; but no legislative act can change the right and liabilities of parties, which have been established by a solemn judgment." "The plaintiff acquired a right under the authority of the United States, and that right may be protected from any judgment of the state court which shall impair it, under the twenty-fifth section of the judiciary act"; by writ of error to the state court from the supreme court of the United States. No state statute can operate proprio vigore, to affect directly or indirectly the jurisdiction, process, proceedings or judgments of the federal courts. That part of the law allowing the writ of replevin is equally null and void, and entirely imperative. The general replevin law does not authorize a writ of replevin against the Marshal. One jurisdiction cannot send its officers to take persons or property out of the custody of another, and a co-ordinate jurisdiction. The attachment of property by an officer, pre-supposes a right to take possession and custody, and to make such possession and custody conclusive. If the other officer attaches upon the same process, he has a right to hold possession, or answer the exigency of the process. If he levies upon an execution he is bound to sell, according to the command of the writ. . . . In Peck v. Jenness 7 Howard 612, an attachment was issued from the State Court and served by seizing property. The defendants in the attachment were discharged, under the bankrupt law of the United States, whose assignee claimed the property. The lien of the attachment was preserved. The Court say--"It is a doctrine of law too long established, to require a citation of authorities, that, where a court has jurisdiction, it has a right to decide every question which occurs in the cause, and whether its decision be correct, or otherwise, its judgment, till reversed, is regarded as binding in every other court; and that, where the jurisdiction of a court, and the right of a plaintiff to prosecute his suit in it, and once attached, that right cannot be arrested or taken away by proceedings in another court. These rules have their foundation, not merely in comity, but on necessity. For if one may enjoin, the other may retort by injunction, and thus the parties be without remedy; being liable to a process for contempt, if they dare to proceed in the other. Neither can one take property from the custody of the other by replevin or any other process, for this would produce a conflict extremely embarrassing to the administration of justice.

In all cases of concurrent jurisdiction, the court which first has possession of the subject must determine it exclusively, Smith v. McIver, 9 Wheaton 532. The party, at whose suit property is attached, has a constitutional and legal right to the law of the court issuing the process. The officer legally claims the same; and, also, the protection of the court in serving his process. A court of another government and different jurisdiction cannot interpose between that plaintiff and the property attached, and transfer the legal possession to, or vest the legal title in, a third person; or assume the exclusive custody or disposition of the property. When goods are seized, they are in the custody of the law, and they cannot be transferred into the custody of a court of another jurisdiction, at the instance of any person, on the plea that he has a demand against them, or that they had been wrongfully taken and detained from him. He must submit his case to the consideration of the court having the custody of the goods; or wait until a final disposition be made of them, as in the case of conflicting executions. He can at any time bring trover or trespass against the officer; but he cannot take from the officer by replevin.

State courts have no authority to enjoin a judgment or execution, or restrain a party in a court of the United States; neither can the United States courts interfere with proceedings or suits in the State courts.

The government of the United States and of the several States are sovereign and independent, within their respective limits as prescribed in their several constitutions. Equally so, are the courts, which are component parts of the respective governments, independent of each other. One court has no power to supervise, or enjoin, or interfere with proceedings and judgments in the other; excepting where expressly authorized by the Constitution of the United States in cases of decisions of the State courts against the constitution, or a treaty, or a law, or authority, or an officer, of the United States; as for instance, if the courts of this State should enforce this law against an officer of the United States, it would be a decision against the constitution and law and authority of the United States, and a writ of error would lie from the supreme court of the United States to the supreme court of this State. It is well known by those practicing in the United States court for this State, that the marshal is not allowed to serve a replevin or other process to take property from the custody of a sheriff.

What has been said in regard of the judgments and writ of replevin, will apply to the writ of habeas corpus authorized by the act in question.

In Prigg v. Pennsylvania, 16 Peters 539, the Supreme Court of the United States, in the opinion delivered by Justice Story, says--"It cannot be doubted that the constitution requires the delivery of the fugitives on the claims of the master; and the natural inference certainly is, that the national government is clothed with appropriate authority and functions to enforce it. A claim of a fugitive slave is a controversy in a case arising under the constitution of the United States, under the express delegation of judicial authority given by that instrument. The constitutionality of the act of Congress relating to fugitives from labor has been affirmed by the adjudication of the State tribunals, and by those of the courts of the United States. If the question of the constitutionality of the law was one of doubtful construction, such long acquiescence in it, and such extensive and uniform recognition of it would in the judgment of the court entitle the subject to be at rest." In that case the court decided that an act of the legislature of Pennsylvania, creating penalties against persons reclaiming fugitive slaves under the constitution was unconstitutional and void. No State law or regulation can be permitted to interfere with, or obstruct the just rights of the owner to claim his slave, derived from the constitution of the United States, or with the remedies prescribed by Congress to aid and enforce the same.

The constitution and laws of the United States provide for the writ of habeas corpus, from the federal courts and magistrates; hence there was neither necessity for, nor propriety in the enactment of the act in question. If any person is wrongfully imprisoned under United States process, the federal courts are competent to discharge him. The remedy is as prompt and summary as when administered by state courts or judges; and by conceding to each government the free and unobstructed execution of its own laws, and exercise of its own authority, harmony is maintained and perpetuated in the workings of our complex system of government. In the states blessed with a well regulated judiciary, all that is necessary to show is, that the commitment or detainer is under the constitution, or a law of the Untied States, or a treaty, and is issued by judicial authority of the Untied States, and the power of the state court is at an end. Any further proceeding under the writ of habeas corpus from a stare magistrate is considered coram non judice and void. In such a case that is, when the prisoner is in fact, held under process issued from a federal tribunal, under the constitution, or law of the Untied States or treaty, the officer has not alternative but to refuse to deliver him up, or to allow him to pass from his hands, in any state of the proceedings. He must stand upon his process and authority, and if resisted, maintain them with all the powers conferred on him for that purpose. An interference by a writ of habeas corpus, allowed under the act of the state would be a direct infraction of the constitution and laws of the Untied States, and would render the person suing out of serving such writ, amenable to the criminal laws of the Untied States for resisting their process. Russell on crimes, 410.

In addition to this, it would bring the officers of the two governments into disgraceful, if not deadly conflict. And the person suing out of serving such writ on the Marshall, is liable to the claimant of the slave for his value.

The defendant sued out the attachment at his peril. It was a fraud on the master's right. The fact being established, that the negro was a fugitive slave, the attachment was no justification to the party, who caused it to be issued. The entering into a contract with the slave, and the endeavor to hold him under the contract, contravened the law of the Untied States, which protects the master, or owner of fugitive slaves, in all his rights, as such owner. The interference of any individual, by suing out process, or otherwise, under the pretence of a debt contracted by the negro, was an act illegal and void.

And in States whose judiciary entertain proper respect for their own institutions as well as for those of the United States, their highest courts refuse to entertain jurisdiction of the habeas corpus, for the purpose of inspecting judicial process issued under authority of the United States, or of reviewing judgments or decrees of the federal courts, or of other courts.

The cases are numerous which decide that the judgments of a court of record, having general jurisdiction of the subject, although erroneous, are binding until reversed. It is universally understood that the judgments of the Courts of the United States, although their jurisdiction be not shown in the pleadings, are yet binding on all the world; and that this apparent want of jurisdiction can avail the party only on writ of error. The judgment of the Circuit Court in a criminal case, is of itself evidence of its own legality, and requires for its support no inspection of the indictment on which it is founded. The law trusts the court with the whole subject, and has not confided to this court the power of reversing its decisions. We cannot usurp that power by the instrumentality of the writ of habeas corpus. It is very evident that the writ of habeas corpus, issued by a State magistrate against a United States officer, to take a prisoner from his custody, is an illegal writ, of no validity whatever, upon principal and authority. And it is also void under the act of this State, for being in direct violation of the constitution of the United States, which expressly declares that "No person held to service or labor in one State under the laws thereof, escaping into another, shall in consequence of any law or regulation therein, be discharged from such service or labor; but shall be delivered up on claim of the party to whom such labor or service may be due." The whole scope of the State law is to divest the authorities of the United States of the only constitutional jurisdiction of the subject and to vest it in the State courts, without constitutional power, by usurpation gross and rebellious, in the form of law, and by an abuse of the great writ of habeas corpus.

NUMBER 3

An act to repeal an act entitled "Of the writ of habeas corpus, relative to fugitive slaves." Approved March 12, 1860, Senate Journal.

Have considered the same, and a majority report a substitute, repealing so much of said act as presents even a question of constitutionality. Your committee do not deem it necessary to enter into the discussion of the grave question involved, of the finality of an act of Congress, endorsed by the Federal Judiciary, or of that other equally important one, of the power of the States to judge of the infraction of their rights, when necessity requires it, nor yet to point out the obvious distinction between the protection of rights in the Union, under the Constitution, and the assumption of rights not claimed through, and the defiance of powers conceded to that Constitution. It is certain that if the Fugitive Slave Law is unconstitutional the sovereign writ of habeas corpus is as available to thwart its operations without our Personal Liberty Law as with it. If it is constitutional, it follows that our statute is inoperative. Whatever opinion may be entertained of the constitutionality of the act of Congress, which we do not intend to discuss, it is certain that our statute is either unnecessary or unconstitutional. We are neither required to adopt the extreme view of complete submission, that the general government is the final judge of the extent of delegated powers, which might result in despotism, or that other conclusion of the power of the State to interpose their judgments when in their opinion the line which divides the two jurisdictions has been encroached upon, and the exercise of which may lead to anarchy. Is not rather this very diversity of construction a part of that system of mutual checks and balances, where the enlightened consciences of a free people sit in judgment, to restrain intemperate zeal or quicken flagging patriotism and declare in unmistakable language that neither despotism nor anarchy shall undermine our institutions. Either view carried to its ultimate absurdity would lead to a disruption of the government, or the destruction of the liberties it was designed to perpetuate. An acquiescence in the right of the people to mould the government as to them shall seem best, with time for calm reflection, is the universal solvent for all evils and dangers. From every tribunal an appeal lies to the people themselves; and by the quiet but omnipotent power of public opinion, working revolutions more wonderful than the sword has ever known, laws destructive of the rights of the people or judicial decisions by which such laws are sustained, are rendered obsolete or their repeal enforced.

In proposing this modification we have not failed to note the fact that whatever necessity may have called for the enactment of this statute, that necessity has passed away, and whatever just indignation devised it for protection against the most cruel and barbarous law known to civilized governments, no single instance has ever arisen for its application. If then its continuance is of no practical service to ourselves, and furnishes even the slightest pretext for impeaching our loyalty to the Federal Constitution, can we not afford to remove it, even though we may believe it does not conflict with that instrument?

It was never supposed or desired that this law should free us from the obligation to deliver up fugitives from labor, however much the moral sentiments of the people may recoil from its fulfillment. The inhuman manner in which that obligation was sought to be enforced, was the cause of its enactment. A part of your committee has failed to find in the Constitution a warrant for any Congressional law for that purpose; but it is admitted that its contemporaneous exercise by the framers of the Constitution itself, or their immediate presence, the many judicial sanctions which this power has received and only one dissenting judgment may be fairly urged as determinative of its existence, and the States absolved from any legislation to this end. And practically, it is of little importance, in its application to this subject, so that it be exercised with reason and humanity, and not so perverted as to be as likely to ensure the capture of the freeman as the return of the fugitive.

The proposed amendment retains so much of this law, as makes it the duty of the District Attorneys to protect and defend the party arrested, from unlawful seizure; to see to it that neither conspiracy, fraud, nor force shall remove him from the State, and in paying the pound of flesh, that not one drop of christian blood be spilt. Ample authority and power is vested in him by general laws for this purpose, and the general statute against kidnapping, imposes penalties and safeguards as severe as legislation can devise. In submitting this recommendation, we have no fear of being supposed to yield to the threats of traitors, with arms in their hands. While by treason in high places, the means of executing those threats were in their hands, we could well afford to bide the time; but with the removal of duress, we are willing to be both just and generous. Though its continuance furnished no real ground of complaint, it has been used by designing men at home and abroad to inflame passion and prejudice, and drive still further asunder the already clashing elements. We may thus remove straws from the paths of stumbling brethren, and disarm misguided or determined foes; charity may still declare "if meat make my brother to offend I will eat no flesh while the world standeth."

We but reflect the united sentiment of our people, while offering to remove from our statute everything that may give offense, in demanding that other States shall fulfill their obligations and prevent the imprisonment and lynching of citizens, without a charge of crime. The obligation to enforce in behalf of humanity and justice, the full letter of the bond ought at least to be regarded as imperative as on the side of oppression, and when in conflict with the natural instincts of humanity. The paltry excuse of a want of alacrity in returning an occasional runaway slave, enlists all the vigor of government, too feeble to satisfy the exactions made upon us; while the equally solemn covenant, that "citizens of each State shall be entitled to all privileges and immunities of citizens in the several States," commands not even a passing notice; and outrages so flagrant as would have brought us to a war with the whole universe, find no notice with a National Congress, or the special defenders of the peculiar institution. The forcible rescue of a negro from slavery sets the elements in motion; imprisonment, lynching, scouring of a white man, is a mere peccadillo. If the General Government needs additional power in any direction, it is respectfully suggested that this is a most wholesome point for its application.

We have also the right to demand from a government claiming to be guided by the principles of equity and justice, such modifications in the Fugitive Slave Law as shall remove the more repulsive features, and not compel citizens, on pain of fine and imprisonment to forget their manhood, their God, and the mothers that bore them, may be expected to prefer the penalty to obedience.

In the urgent necessity which we now recognize for a vigorous government, care should be taken that a principle should not be surrendered which would make it destructive in time of peace, or place it in irresponsible power, beyond control, and able to subvert the States, while in their legitimate spheres. The need is not for additional power, but the prompt exercise of that already vested. And in placing herself, beyond all cavil, in the right, Wisconsin is entitled to demand the just, the wise, the humane administration of the government as to secure a "perfect union, establish justice, insure domestic tranquility, provide for the common defense, promote the general welfare, and secure the blessings of liberty."

IV

Personal Liberty and Legal Rights

Wisconsin adopted a modest policy to protect free blacks. It provided punishment for persons convicted of kidnapping. It also encouraged protection of liberty rights. By the end of the decade the legislators adopted a statute to protect blacks in the enjoyment of civil rights. Its civil rights laws were never extensive, however. The last state formed from the Old Northwest embraced a cold policy toward African Americans.

NUMBER 1

Kidnapping: offenses against life and person. Statutes of Wisconsin, 1858.

Section 42. Every person who, without lawful authority, shall forcibly or secretly confine or imprison any other person within this state against his will, or shall forcibly carry or send such person out of this state against his will, or shall forcibly seize and confine, or shall inveigle or kidnap, any other person, with intent either to cause such person to be secretly confined or imprisoned in this state against his will, or to be sold, the person who shall sell, or in any manner transfer for any term, the service or labor of any negro, mulatto, or other person of color, who shall have been unlawfully seized, taken, inveigled, or kidnapped from this state to any state, place, or country, shall be punished by imprisonment in the state prison, not more than two years nor less than one year, or by fine, not exceeding one thousand dollars nor less than five hundred dollars.

Section 43. Every offense mentioned in the text of the preceding section may be tried either in the county in which the same may have been committed, or in any county in or to which the person so seized, taken, inveigled, kidnapped, or sold, or whose services shall be so sold or transferred, shall have been taken, confined, held, carried, or brought; and upon the trial of any such offense, the consent thereto of the person so taken, inveigled, kidnapped, or confined, shall not be a defense unless it shall be made satisfactorily to appear to the jury that such consent was not obtained by fraud, nor extorted by duress or by threats.

NUMBER 2

On repeal of (so called) personal liberty bill. Approved February 11, 1862, Senate Journal.

A bill to repeal certain sections in chapter 158 of the Revised Statues, while concurring with the majority of the committee in recommending the passage of the bill, except as to sections 52, 54 and 57, feels constrained to dissent in the main from the report of the majority of said committee; and in order to repel any possible inference that concurrence in such recommendation is predicated upon the basis of such report, the undersigned respectfully submits the following minority report:

The section of the Revised Statutes embraced within the bill under consideration are similar in their character and purport to laws enacted about the same time by several of the free States, and the question very naturally arises why were these laws passed?

A brief examination of this question seems to be necessary not only for the purpose of correctly understanding and appreciating the law sought to be repealed, but for the reason that the majority report seems to indicate that its passage was due to a state of excitement in the pubic mind for which there existed no adequate cause.

On the 18th day of September, one thousand eight hundred and fifty, after a protracted discussion of various measures connected with the subject of slavery, Congress enacted a new Fugitive Slave Law which had been prepared by Mr. Mason, then a Senator from the State of Virginia, and now notorious as a traitor and a rebel, with the avowed object of facilitating the arrest of fugitives from labor, and intended to supply alleged defects in the law of 1793. The provisions of this law were such as to virtually deny the right of trial by jury to any person alleged to be a fugitive from labor, no matter by whom such allegation might be made, or whether true or false, provided certain prescribed forms had been complied with. The law moreover conferred upon commissioners extraordinary judicial powers, and made the vital question of the right of a man to his liberty dependent on a mere summary examination, controlled mainly by affidavits which might or might not be true. In addition, the law imposed vindictive penalties upon all persons harboring or in any manner aiding and assisting such fugitives, knowing them to be such, as offered a bribe of five dollars for a decision by the commissioners adverse to the liberty of the accused.

Under this law, which was and is a disgrace to the country and the age, and which has been admitted by prominent southern statesmen to be justly offensive to the North, it were easy to show, as has been repeatedly shown, that free men might be accused or claimed unjustly and in violation of every right sacred among civilized communities, and reduced to the status of slaves. Indeed, as a matter of fact, of the first eight persons claimed as fugitives from labor, under this law, four were afterwards found to have been free men.

When we consider the sacredness of the right thus flagrantly invaded under the color and authority of law, we can hardly be surprised that the spirit of a brave and free people should have been thoroughly moved, nor can their avowed hostility to the odious provisions of the law be properly regarded or characterized as an "excess," resulting from "passion and prejudice."

The impression which largely prevailed, that this law was intended as an offence and a humiliation to the anti-slavery sentiment of the county, coupled with the facts that it was deemed by many jurists to be unconstitutional, and had been made instrumental in depriving free men of their birth-right, furnished the occasion, and as many believed the necessity for the passage of acts by the States as such to protect the liberty of their citizens. Hence the passage by the Legislature of this State of the bill under consideration.

It is true that many of the leading anti-slavery men of the country doubted the policy of such legislation, and that in a majority of the Northern States, it was not favored; but by no one except such as spoke in the interest of the slave power, was the Fugitive Slave Law regarded as otherwise than odious and disgraceful. And so it must continue to be regarded by those, with whom reverence for the rights of manhood rests upon principle and not upon chance or accident.

And while it is therefore true that the enactment of this character of legislation was not necessarily the measure of hostility to slavery, it is most emphatically true that its repeal or modification can in no sense be regarded as evidence of abatement of that hostility. The State of Vermont has just repealed a similar law without division, and yet it is unquestionably true that slavery and the Fugitive Slave Law never had so few apologists in that sturdy, freedom-lowing State as at the present hour.

The repeal is simply due to a change of circumstances, and to the fact that there is no longer any necessity for the existence of the law. And it may be remarked in this connection that our personal liberty bill, at least a portion of it, was not intended to be incorporated into and made a part of the permanent polity of the State. This may be inferred as well from the fact that we have another stringent provision on the subject of kidnapping, as from the specific features of the bill itself. It was aimed at a particular law of Congress and derived its essential importance from the fact of such law having been enacted, and the danger of outrages being committed under it within the State of Wisconsin.

We might rest here, and place our vote in favor of repealing or modifying the bill upon the change of circumstances already adverted to, and which renders it morally certain that no farther necessity exists for its continuance; but as the majority of your committee have chosen to give a much wider range to the discussion, the undersigned does not feel at liberty to dismiss the subject without referring to some of the propositions and inferences of the majority report.

The idea, which is more than hinted at, that the present effort to disrupt the Government is due to the existence of personal liberty laws on the part of the Free States, or some of them, is so superficial and narrow as to naturally excite suspicion of the sincerity of its authors. It is not only at variance with the philosophy but with the history of the case, as will be attempted to be shown. Nor is it believed that those who have been the allies of the slave power during the whole history of its aggression, and encourages its ambitions by a prompt acquiescence in its demands, can now fairly change the burden of responsibility for the issue of that aggression upon those who have opposed that power. In others words, it does not lie with the allies of that power to charge its folly and guilt upon the opponents of that power. It may be alleged, without fear of contradiction, that had the interested plans and purposes of the Southern States found no encouragement at the North; had these plans and purposes received the same opposition from all that they received from a part, the overthrow of this Government would not have been contemplated, much less attempted.

But the folly of this pretense is apparent when we remember that the States most interested in this subject resisted the efforts of the Cotton States to precipitate them out of the Union, and that the States leading off in the rebel cause were those which had never suffered and could not have suffered from personal liberty bills. South Carolina which has not lost a fugitive from service for years-except the one who followed the redoubtable Caleb Cushing off, from the Charleston Convention--more than any other State incited and brought about the present rebellion; while Kentucky, and Maryland, and Delaware, all border States, decided by unprecedented majorities to remain in the Union; and to these States we might also add Tennessee and Western Virginia-both of which indicate the same purpose by the votes of their people. This is a sufficient answer to the intimation put forth by the majority of your committee. But aside from this it is believed that in no single instance have these laws been operative in defeating an authorized claim. Mr. Buchanan boasted, in his last annual message, that in every contested case during his administration the fugitive had been returned to bondage. This certainly does not afford much plausibility to the idea that personal liberty laws have furnished slave holders any just cause of complaint.

If, however, it is meant to say that it was the opposition of the Free States to the policy and purposes of the slave power, evidenced by such acts as the passage of the bill under consideration, which offended the South, the undersigned will have little difficulty in concurring in the proposition. It cannot be doubted that the cotton States would have remained in the Union till the crack of doom, had there been no objection to their using it for their own purposes; and it would seem that they were willing to remain on this condition only. If it is a misfortune that the condition was not complied with, it is one which must be charged to the majority of the American people, by whom the question was dared to be decided!

But it must not be understood that opposition to the policy of the Slave States was other than defensive. At no time has it been proposed to interfere with any of the domestic institutions of the States. On the contrary, the party succeeding to the government at the close of Mr. Buchanan's administration, have uniformly disclaimed any authority or desire to do so. They opposed the aggressions of slavery only. They desired to restrict the evil to present limits, and to restore the Government to the principles of its founders. Indeed, the whole controversy on this subject, has grown out of the purpose to force slavery upon free territory, and not to force freedom upon slave territory; this is all that need be known upon the point.

That all the constitutional rights of the slave States were secure under the administration of Mr. Lincoln has never been seriously questioned.

Upon this point the following testimony is cited, being among the last public words uttered by the late Senator Douglas:

"What is the alleged cause for this invasion of the rights and authority of the government of the United States? The cause alleged is that the institutions of the Southern States are not safe under the Federal Government. What evidence has been presented that they are insecure? I appeal to every man within the sound of my voice to tell me at what period, from the time that Washington was inaugurated down to this hour, have the rights of the Southern States been more secure than they are at this moment? When in the whole history of this government have they stood on so firm a basis? For the first time in the history of this Republic there is no restriction by act of Congress upon the institution of slavery anywhere within the limits of the United States. Then it cannot be the Territorial question which has given them a cause for rebellion. Can any man tell me of any one act of aggression that has been committed or attempted since the last Presidential election that justifies this violent disruption of the Federal Union?"

The undersigned submits to the candor of this body, that those words are a sufficient answer to that part of the majority report which undertakes to insinuate that the party in power has been disposed to "violate the dearest constitutional" of the slave-holder. The violation of constitutional right, it is believed, consists in presuming to think that slavery is not the "divine institution" its champions allege it to be, and in withholding assent to the convenient doctrine, that minorities have the right to rule! This is, however, by no means the first time the constitution has been employed perversely. It is the work of craft and built in all ages to assume the guise of virtue and to attempt to cast upon the opposition the brand which itself should wear.

"The Son of Man" was crucified by those who claimed special reverence for the "Laws and the Prophets." The martyrs of the Middle Ages were brought to the stake by those who assumed to be the conservators of holiness and christian charity. The liberalists of France, in the stormy revolution of '92, were guillotined in the name of liberty. The hapless citizens of soil once dedicated to freedom, were in our own day subjected to every conceivable wrong and outrage, aye, to death itself, under the persistent cry of "law and order" and it has been in the name of the constitution that it has been sought to nationalize, and foster, and protect "the sum of all villains," and to make a great and noble instrument, framed to conserve the "blessings of liberty," the shield and cover for chattel slavery.

The action of the Southern States, while it was without causes and in direct and palpable violation of the duties and obligations of "good citizens," was not the result of any sudden and spasmodic influence. The election of Mr. Lincoln was the pretext but not the true reason for such action. The revolution set on foot by the champions of the slave power was the growth of time--the fruit of gradual development. The public mind is not educated to the point of treason in a day nor a year. Its existence in organized form presupposes an anterior struggle of opposing forces. And such has been the fact. The system of chattel slavery prevailing at the south is but one of the many forms of despotism. It is a perpetual war upon human rights, and necessarily antagonistic in spirit to the principles of our government. Our fathers tolerated it and suffered it to have a place for the time being, upon the belief and expectation that it must at no distant day cease to exist. With this view they placed limits and restrictions upon it which they deemed sufficient to accomplish such object. But instead of disappearing, it has grown more and more powerful, and for the last thirty years has been perpetually struggling for the control of the government, until at length, having been hurled from power by an aroused and indignant people, it has made war upon and attempted to overthrow that government. In a recent powerful speech of John Bright, made at Rochdale, the following language was used: "For thirty years it (slavery) has been constantly coming to the surface, disturbing social life and overthrowing almost all political harmony in the working of the United States. In the north there is no secession, there is no collision but this disturbance, and this insurrection was formed wholly in the south and in the slave states. The object of the south is this: to escape from the majority which wishes to limit the area of slavery."

In the South Carolina Convention, called for the purpose of taking that state out of the Union, Mr. Packer said "secession is no spasmodic effort that has come suddenly upon us. It has been gradually culminating for a long series of years."

Said Mr. Ingliss: "Most of us have had this subject under consideration for the last twenty years."

Said Mr. Keitt: "I have been engaged in this movement ever since I entered political life."

Said Mr. Rhett: "It is nothing produced by Mr. Lincoln's election, or the non-execution of the Fugitive Slave law. It is a matter which has been gathering head for thirty years."

In a recent discussion in the United States Senate, Mr. McDougall, a democratic Senator from California, used the following expressive words:

"There has been a systematic, organized war against the institutions established by our fathers since 1832. This is known to all men who have read carefully the history of our country. If I had the leisure or had consulted the authorities, I would give it year by year, and date by date, from that time until the present; how men adverse to our republican institutions have been organizing war against us because they did not approve of our republican institutions."

Senator Lathan, of the same State, in alluding to the conduct of Southern leaders, in a speech made at the last session of Congress, said: "I believe, Mr. President, that these gentlemen were acting in pursuance of a settled and fixed plan to break up and destroy the government."

We might multiply authorities on this head; they are to be found in the speeches of Southern statesmen and in the columns of Southern newspapers; but we do not deem it necessary.

We have said, and now repeat, that revolutions are not the result of spasmodic effort. It is "first the blade and then the ear, and then the corn in the ear." That the South, petted and humored to the very verge of forbearance, should have become like a spoiled child, and rebelled against rightful authority, because it could not have its own way, is not surprising; but that any one acquainted with the history of the country should find the occasion of the present rebellion in the action of the Northern States, is passing strange.

But it is to be remembered--and to those who are content to calmly await the verdict of time, there is satisfaction in the assurance--that the historian has a work to perform in this as in other cases. When heated expression and partisan phrases shall have passed away and been forgotten as the ephemeral productions of the hours, and the iron pen of history shall come to gather up the data from which an unbiased and final conclusion shall be drawn, the long line of "abuses," "oppressions," and "outrages" which at length results in open rebellion, will have their due consideration. Nothing will be extenuated, nor aught set down in malice.

It will then be determined whether those who have courage will sustain and defend the slave power up to the verge--the very point of secession, or those who have resisted that power are responsible for the great evils which it has precipitated upon the country.

In anticipation of the historians office we beg to be indulged for a moment in adverting to some of the numerous facts and circumstances which will challenge attention:

Of the fourteen Presidents who have been elected, seven were citizens of slave states, and of the remaining seven, three received the votes of the Southern people, enjoyed their confidence and administered the government to their entire satisfaction; nor has one of the whole number ever exercised or thought of exercising the functions of the office in hostility to their interests. And from the fact that every Southern President, but one, has been re-elected, while no Northern President has been thus fortunate, it happens that out of the seventy-three years or thereabouts since the organization of the present government Southern men and slave holders have occupied the Presidential chair forty-eight years and three months, or a little more than two-thirds of the time.

Of our foreign missions, including consulships, it will be found that no period for many years, have the citizens of Northern States enjoyed their proportionate share, while the Senate, controlled by the slave interest, has kept perpetual "watch and ward" to see that no foreign minister went abroad, who had not come from the South, or was not acceptable to the South.

Of the nine Judges of the Supreme Court of the United States the eight millions of people of the Southern States had at, and previous to the rebellion, five, while the eighteen millions of the North, had but four.

In the Senate of the United States, there has hardly been a Standing Committee organized for years, of any importance, which has not been composed of a majority of southern men; while the Speakership of the house of Representatives, one of the most important positions in the Government, has been held by southern men and slave holders, nearly two-thirds of the time since the origin of the Government.

An examination of the army and navy rolls, at any period prior to the rebellion, would reveal the same propensity for monopolizing places of honor and profit. Indeed, Mr. Holmes, of South Carolina, once said in his place in Congress, when rallied upon this very fact, that "it was proper that the South should furnish the army and naval officers, and the North, the soldiers and marines!"

In the matter of the mail service, too, we find another item of "oppression." The reports of the Post Office Department, show that the Federal Government has furnished the mails to the seven cotton States at an annual expense of five millions while receiving but a million and a half.

Take up the Constitution and examine carefully all the constitutional guarantees of the citizen, and tell me what one has been violated to the damage of the complaining States or the people thereof.

Nor is this all. While Northern men and women have been mobbed and visited with every conceivable outrage and indignity in the land of boasted chivalry, is it not a matter of public notoriety that the citizens of Southern

States have been uniformly received and treated with distinguished consideration among us of the North--our halls and lecture rooms, our courtesies and hospitalities placed freely at their disposal.

But more than this, our history reveals the fact that in every considerable controversy between the North and the South on questions of policy, the latter has been successful, and the former has been compelled to yield. Take every important question which has hinged upon the antagonistic systems of the two sections, and which has assumed, in any sense, a sectional aspect, and you may witness this truth. I need only mention the admission of Missouri; the Tariff of 1832; including the Fugitive Slave Law; and finally the repeal of the Missouri Compromise.

But why pursue this branch of the subject further? There is no feature more indelibly stamped upon our history than the fact that the slave oligarchy, so far from being "wronged," "oppressed" and "outraged," has been the power nearest the throne, and has, almost without exception, dictated the policy, and directed the energies of the government; and the extraordinary effort of the majority of your committee to ingeniously pervert the facts of history is the only apology to be offered for consuming so much time upon this point.

The undersigned cannot indulge the expectation, which seems to have been entertained by the majority, that our action upon this bill is calculated to have a favorable influence upon southern rebels. They refused all overtures long since, and publicly announced upon the election of a President not satisfactory to themselves, that they would not remain in the government if they could not dictate their own terms, nor can it have escaped their attention that no proposition has at any time been made by a single rebel State of the condition upon which it would remain in the Union, if that condition could be complied with. It has moreover been shown that these laws furnished no just cause of complaint and no apology for treason and rebellion.

We cannot solace ourselves with the belief that their repeal will make even a ripple in the tide of treacherous sea. There is an argument more potent and effectual and better suited to the case--the only argument by which the dignity of the government can be sustained and rebellion subdued, and is the argument wielded by loyal battalions. If rebellion is ever to be put down, it is to be done, not by concession, not by coaxing, but by the vigorous employment of the necessary military force.

The amendments proposed by the undersigned, retain the features of the law deemed practically valuable, and the reasons for repealing the balance are to be found in the facts that all necessity has passed, and that the retention of the same can do no good, while it must continue to be a subject of irritation which ought to be avoided. The Federal Government has passed from the grasp of the slave power, never, it is firmly believed to be restored to its possession. With this change new duties and new responsibilities are imposed upon, and must be assumed by that government.

The true interests of freedom are to be developed in our nation, not primarily by States acting in their individual spheres and according to their own peculiar and perhaps diverse inclinations, but by the whole body of the people operating through a national organization, in a common direction and for a common purpose. From this theory there would have been no departure had the Federal Government held firm to the original landmarks upon which its beneficent mission was conceived, by which its early career was guided.

The part of the majority report which refers to the resolutions of 1859, will not be noticed here, as another report has been submitted at the present session upon that subject.

It is a pleasure to be able to concur in so much of that report as refers to the general willingness and desire of all parties to support the Government in this hour of peril. It may be that there are a few who, wedded to old alliances and old theories, still worship at deserted shrines, refusing to turn their faces to the sun. These, however, are the extreme partisans and small politicians. But the masses of the people are patriotic, and brave and true and here is the nation's hope. They know the Government is the people's Government, and they are determined to save it at whatever cost. Nor are they unmindful of the fact that notwithstanding the trials and sacrifices and privations which are required to be endured, it is amid such stormy struggles, amid the thunders of revolution, and at the cost of courage and blood, that the foundations of justice are more broadly laid and humanity receives new impetus and new inspiration in its onward and upward march.

And what is party, what are Presidents and cabinet when compared with the interests at stake in such a crisis as this? Parties may dissolve, administrations may change, but the principles for which we struggle--the glorious fabric of a Free Government shall endure.

Gathering new strength and new vitality from a new baptism of blood, planting its foundations deeper down in the imperishable elements of truth, it shall stand towering victorious over every assault, and like some proud monument rising from the sea, look down with serene composure from its shining altitude upon the harmless waves which now sparkle in the sun light and now lash its rock-bound base. There let it stand amid the conflicts of the ages.

NUMBER 3

An act to protect all citizens in their civil and legal rights. Approved April 13, 1895, Laws of Wisconsin.

The people of the state of Wisconsin, represented in senate and assembly, do enact as follows:

Section 1. That all persons within this state shall be entitled to the full and equal enjoyment of the accommodations, advantages, facilities and privileges of inns, restaurants, saloons, barber shops, eating houses, public conveyances on land and water, theaters, and all other places of public accommodation or amusement, subject only to the conditions and limitations established by law and applicable alike to all persons of every race and color.

Section 2. That any person who shall violate the foregoing section or any part thereof, by denying to any person, except for reasons by law applicable alike to all persons, the full enjoyment of any of the accommodations, advantages, facilities or privileges enumerated in said section, or by aiding or inciting such denial, or by requiring any person to pay a larger sum than the regular rate charged by such person for such or any of such advantages, facilities, accommodations or privileges, shall for every such offense, be liable to the person aggrieved thereby, in a sum not less than five dollars, as damages, with costs, to be recovered in any court of competent jurisdiction in the county where said offense was committed, and shall also, for every such offense be deemed guilty of a misdemeanor and shall be fined not more than one hundred dollars, with costs, or shall be imprisoned in the county jail for not more than six months, or by both such fine and imprisonment; provided, however, that a judgment in favor of the party aggrieved or punishment upon an information filed, shall be a bar to either prosecution respectively.

Section 3. This act shall take effect and be in force from and after its passage and publication.

Summary of Cases

Litigation involving race in Wisconsin trailed the adjudication of this subject in the Northwest Territory. The black population in Wisconsin remained small, so whites rarely felt they had to come into direct contact with them. Unlike Ohio where the visible admixture test arose, the courts in Wisconsin rarely came into contact with that issue. And unlike Indiana, where slavery arose under the pretext of indentured servitude, Wisconsin escaped such a practice. In contrast to Ohio where antislavery lawyers made the runaway slave issue controversial, jurists in Wisconsin went farther than the lawyers and courts in any of the other states, even those that became the center of the antislavery movement.

The supreme court in Wisconsin was the only court to render unconstitutional any federal Fugitive Slave Law. The supreme court ruled that the federal statute of 1850 "attempts to confer judicial power; [and] it is a denial of the fugitive to have those questions decided by a jury." This achievement was short lived, however. The U.S. Supreme Court reversed the ruling.

The following cases demonstrate that the runaway slave issue was the most controversial in Wisconsin. Barring a few exceptions, the rights of refugees from the South and the authority of a state court to void federal law, the courts in Wisconsin was obsessed with this crisis of the 1850s.

Select Annotated Cases

U.S. ex re. Garland v. Morris, 26 Federal Cases 1318 (2 American Law Register 348) (1854)
A Missouri citizen obtained a warrant for the capture of Joshua Glover, an alleged slave. A federal marshall arrested Glover and jailed him in Milwaukee. City officials brought charges against the claimant for assault and battery. Meanwhile, a mob rescued Glover. The court condemned the rescue and ordered the release of the man who participated in the capture of Glover.

U.S. v. Rycraft, 27 Federal cases 918 (1854)
A federal district court convicted John Rycraft for rescuing a slave in violation of federal law. A slave catcher had apprehended a runaway slave, observed guidelines in the 1850 fugitive slave law, and, after receiving a certificate attempted to carry the slave out of town. Rycraft and his abolitionist colleagues rescued the alleged slave.

In re Booth, 3 Wisconsin 1, (1854)
Booth, who had allegedly harbored a runaway slave, brought action against Ableman, a U.S. Marshall, who illegally detained him. Booth also questioned the power of a justice of the peace to act in cases involving runaway slaves, and his attorneys argued that the 1850 fugitive slave law was unconstitutional. The state court declared the act of Congress void. "First, because it attempts to confer judicial power; and second, because it is a denial of the right of the fugitive to have those questions decided by a jury."

Ex parte Booth, 3 Wisconsin 145 (1854)
This case also involved Ableman who had continued to detain Booth under a warrant issued by a federal judge. The court reasoned that the case was

pending in a federal court, which had exclusive jurisdiction. No state court, therefore, could interfere. It denied the application to review the case.

In re Booth and Rycraft, 3 Wisconsin 157 (1854)
Booth and Rycraft, who aided Joshua Glover, an alleged runaway slave, appealed to the state supreme court for remedy after their conviction. The court agreed that it had authority to release the prisoners. It declared that the men should be discharged.

Ableman v. Booth and U.S. v Booth, 21 Howard 506 (1858)
The authorities charged Booth with violating federal law when he helped a runaway slave escape in 1854. The U.S. Supreme Court denied the ability of a state court to interfere with a federal case. It reversed the decision of the Wisconsin court in the case of Ableman, Both, and Rycraft.

Arnold v. Booth, 14 Wisconsin (1861)
The defendant brought action to recover a printing press and a steam engine that had been taken by the plaintiff. The plaintiff alleged that he had acquired the merchandise after it had been confiscated by the authorities and sold. (This dispute involved the slave case in which Booth was a party.) A lower court held for the plaintiff. The supreme court reversed the opinion and ordered a new trial.

Suggested Readings

Baker, Florence E. "A Brief History of the Elective Franchise in Wisconsin," State Historical Society of Wisconsin Proceedings, 1893: 116-112, 120-121.

Berthrong, Donald J. "Social Legislation in Wisconsin, 1836-1900," PhD dissertation, University of Wisconsin, 1952.

Davidson, John N. "Negro Slavery in Wisconsin," 40 Wisconsin State Historical Society Publications, 1892.

Fishel, Leaslie H. "Negro Suffrage in Wisconsin," 46 Wisconsin Magazine of History, 1963.

Foner, Eric. Free Soil, Free Labor, Free Men: The Ideology of the Republican Party before the Civil War, 1970.

________. "Politics and Prejudice: The Free Soil Party and the Negro," 50 Journal of Negro History, 1965.

Gregory, John G. "Negro Suffrage in Wisconsin," 11 Transactions of the Wisconsin Academy of Sciences, Arts, and Letters, 1898.

Hurst, James W. The Growth of American Law: The Lawmakers, 1950.

Smith, Guy-Harold. "The Settlement and the Distribution of the Population in Wisconsin," 24 Transactions of the Wisconsin Academy of Science, Arts and Letters, 1929.

Srebecker, Robert G. "The Supreme Court of Wisconsin Territory," State Historical Society of Wisconsin Proceedings, 1912.

Thompson, William F., ed. The History of Wisconsin, 4 vols., 1973.

Index

Page numbers in boldface indicate the main discussion--including the states where legislatures adopted the black laws--of the subjects listed.

About the Author

STEPHEN MIDDLETON is Assistant Professor of History at North Carolina State University. He received his Ph.D. from Miami University, Ohio. He is the author of *Ohio and the Antislavery Activities of Salmon P. Chase* (1990), and of several articles on pre-Civil War Ohio.

www.ingramcontent.com/pod-product-compliance
Lightning Source LLC
LaVergne TN
LVHW011902200926
848484LV00002B/505
9780313280160